Fifth Edition

Multicultural Education of Children and Adolescents

M. Lee Manning
Old Dominion University

Leroy G. Baruth
Appalachian State University

Boston ◆ New York ◆ San Francisco
Mexico City ◆ Montreal ◆ Toronto ◆ London ◆ Madrid ◆ Munich ◆ Paris
Hong Kong ◆ Singapore ◆ Tokyo ◆ Cape Town ◆ Sydney

Senior Series Editor: Kelly Villella Canton
Series Editorial Assistant: Annalea Manalili
Marketing Manager: Darcy Betts Prybella
Editorial Production Service: Omegatype Typography, Inc.
Composition Buyer: Linda Cox
Manufacturing Manager: Megan Cochran
Electronic Composition: Omegatype Typography, Inc.
Cover Administrator: Jenny Hart

For related titles and support materials, visit our online catalog at www.pearsonhighered.com.

Between the time website information is gathered and then published, it is not unusual for some sites to have closed. Also, the transcription of URLs can result in typographical errors. The publisher would appreciate notification where these errors occur so that they may be corrected in subsequent editions.

Library of Congress Cataloging-in-Publication Data

Manning, M. Lee.
   Multicultural education of children and adolescents / M. Lee Manning, Leroy G. Baruth.—
5th ed.
         p.   cm.
   Includes bibliographical references and index.
   ISBN-13: 978-0-205-59256-2 (pbk.)
   ISBN-10: 0-205-59256-2 (pbk.)
   1. Multicultural education—United States.   2. Indians of North America—Education.
3. African American children—Education.   4. Asian American children—Education.
5. Hispanic American children—Education.   I. Baruth, Leroy G.   II. Title.
   LC1099.3.M36 2009
   370.117—dc22

                                                                                              2008011418

Printed in the United States of America

10 9 8 7 6 5 4 3   12 11 10

Allyn & Bacon
is an imprint of

www.pearsonhighered.com

ISBN 10: 0-205-59256-2
ISBN 13: 978-0-205-59256-2

To my family: My wife, Marianne;
and my children, Jennifer and Michael

MLM

To my brother, Carroll, who has devoted
most of his professional career to the
education of children and adolescents

LGB

About the Authors

M. Lee Manning

Dr. Manning is a professor and eminent scholar in the Department of Educational Curriculum and Instruction at Old Dominion University. He taught fifth-, sixth-, and seventh-grade language arts for five years in the public schools of South Carolina. His professional interests and expertise include middle school education, multicultural education, and classroom management.

Dr. Manning has authored or coauthored twenty-four books and over 200 journal articles. Selected books include *Multicultural Counseling and Psychotherapy: A Lifespan Approach* (Pearson Education, with Leroy G. Baruth), *Teaching in the Middle School* (Pearson Education, with Dr. Katherine Bucher), and *Classroom Management: Models, Applications, and Cases* (Pearson Education, with Dr. Katherine T. Bucher). In addition, he has made approximately thirty national presentations, mostly on some aspect of middle school education and multicultural education.

Leroy G. Baruth

Dr. Leroy "Lee" Baruth is professor and chair of the Department of Human Development and Psychological Counseling at Appalachian State University in Boone, North Carolina. Dr. Baruth is celebrating his fortieth year in the education field. He has authored/edited more than thirty-five books and numerous articles. Lee received his doctorate at the University of Arizona and has a bachelor's of science degree and master's of science degree from Minnesota State University–Mankato. Prior teaching and counseling experience includes the University of South Carolina, the Minnesota Department of Manpower Services, and the Byron (Minnesota) Public Schools. He is very grateful to his students who have taught him so much during his more than four decades in the education field.

Brief Contents

Contents

4 Understanding American Indian Children and Adolescents   78

5 Understanding Arab American Children and Adolescents   100

6 Understanding Asian American Children and Adolescents   120

7 Understanding European American Children and Adolescents   142

8 Understanding Hispanic American Children and Adolescents   162

11 Individual and Cultural Differences   236

Preface

Our Nation's Increasing Cultural Diversity

Multicultural Education of Children and Adolescents is based on the premise that people from culturally different backgrounds enrich the United States and that a better understanding of people and their differences leads to higher levels of acceptance and respect for all people. This fifth edition is being published at a time when all demographic projections indicate that the number of people of differing cultures in the United States will increase.

The Hispanic American population outnumbers the African American population, and people of European ancestry will soon be in the minority. At this time, the Asian American population is increasing dramatically. Without doubt, the high birthrates among some cultural groups, increasing numbers of Spanish-speaking people, and the recent influx of immigrants from Southeast Asia will increase the cultural diversity of the United States and challenge its citizens to accept and respect all people whatever their cultural background, ethnicity, race, sexual orientation, socioeconomic status, gender, or religion.

At one time during the nation's history, the "melting pot" theory proposed to erase differences and to acculturate, or "melt," cultural differences. In essence, the person of a different cultural background was supposed to forsake cherished and traditional cultural values and adopt "American values," probably those of the middle-class European American population. This concept viewed differences as wrong or inferior and promoted wholesale abandonment of cultural heritage.

Realistically, the melting pot is not an accurate model—people have difficulty giving up cultural characteristics or they live in enclaves in which assimilation with the mainstream society is unnecessary. Likewise, some people have chosen to maintain their culture as well as to adopt American values. Regardless of the reasons, the melting pot has not accounted for all the citizenry as some proposed; the nation is a heterogeneous mixture of different peoples.

Serious questions continue to plague educators and other concerned people: Why is there an increase in racism? More than fifty years after the landmark *Brown* decision, why are schools still segregated? Why do elementary and secondary schools address primarily the needs of some learners and allow others to fall behind? Why do people fear diversity? Why are victims often blamed for their problems? These questions defy easy answers and evince many people's belief that differences are negative manifestations in need of eradication.

Rather than provoking anger or causing fear, differences in values, customs, and traditions should be celebrated and considered a means of enriching the United States. We do not claim that the people who perceive differences as enriching will eliminate racism and acts of violence. Celebrating differences, though, is a first step, especially if efforts focus on today's children and adolescents, who will lead the nation during the twenty-first century. Considering differences to be positive and enriching, however, is only a beginning. Significant change will require more comprehensive and deliberate efforts.

Elementary and secondary schools can play a major role in teaching acceptance and respect for all forms of diversity. The schools, in fact, are logical places to begin instilling feelings of acceptance for all people. Schools, however, must do more than pay lip service; effective curriculum reflects diversity, and appropriate learning materials represent all people in positive and meaningful roles. We believe wholeheartedly that multicultural education should be a total-school approach, rather than simply a unit or Multicultural Education Week approach. Although teaching about multiculturalism is an admirable concept, schools should also model acceptance and respect for cultural diversity. Schools that teach about cultural differences and celebrate diversity but whose actions indicate racism or a lack of respect fail in their multicultural efforts.

Our Reasons for Writing This Book

We wrote this fifth edition of *Multicultural Education of Children and Adolescents* to provide pre-service and in-service educators with a knowledge of the six prevalent cultural groups and to show the components of responsive multicultural education programs. The text staunchly maintains that multicultural education programs require a total-school effort—that is, that administrators, teachers, librarians/media specialists, special-education teachers, counselors, and communications disorders specialists have vital roles in the multicultural education program. Similarly, we believe that multicultural efforts should be comprehensive. The curriculum, instructional strategies, materials, environment, and school practices should reflect multiculturalism and should show a genuine respect for all forms of diversity.

Our Selection of Cultural Groups

After careful consideration of and reflection on the increasing cultural diversity of the United States, we decided to focus on six broad groups of people (listed alphabetically): African, American Indian, Arab, Asian, European, and Hispanic American. These groups are, and in all likelihood will continue to be, the most populous groups in elementary and secondary schools. Choosing only these groups does not negate the importance of other cultures. We hope and expect that learning about diversity in these cultures will motivate readers to explore the values, customs, and traditions of other cultures.

A Word of Caution

Any discussion focusing on characteristics of children and adolescents and their cultural backgrounds risks stereotyping and an overdependence on generalizations. The many differences resulting from cultural, intracultural, socioeconomic, geographic, generational, gender, sexual orientation, and individuality factors among people contribute to their diversity and to the difficulty of describing individuals of various cultures. Although we based this text on current and objective information, it remains crucial for educators to understand individual children and adolescents within a culture through conscientious study and first-hand contact. Failing to understand individuals and failing to consider crucial differences may result in assuming too much cultural homogeneity—for example, that all Hispanic cultural groups share identical values, problems, and cultural expectations or that all Asian Americans fit the "model minority" label.

 # The Organization of the Book

Multicultural Education of Children and Adolescents is divided into three parts and fourteen chapters. Part I introduces multicultural education as a concept and documents the increasing cultural diversity of the United States. Part II provides a cultural portrait of children and adolescents in the African, American Indian, Arab, Asian, European, and Hispanic cultures. Part III focuses on topics that educators should consider when planning and implementing programs that teach acceptance and respect for cultural diversity and also examines issues that will continue to challenge educators in the twenty-first century.

New to This Edition

Content and features new to the fifth edition include the following:

◆ Opening scenarios, which provide introductions to all chapters
◆ Chapter 2 (a new chapter), which elaborates on various types of diversity
◆ Gender Perspectives features, located in all chapters, that highlight gender as an integral aspect of multicultural education
◆ An expanded section on socioeconomic status and conditions in Chapter 2 and specific coverage in culture chapters (Chapters 3–8)
◆ Case Studies with accompanying Questions for Discussion in all chapters
◆ Expanding Your Horizons features that recommend current journal articles, books, and Internet sites
◆ Points to Ponder features, located in all chapters, that guide readers to pause and reflect on the topic just discussed
◆ An entirely new appendix filled with rich children's and adolescents' literature for all cultures

Supplements

Instructor's Manual and Test Bank

Prepared by the authors, this manual is available for download by logging into the Instructor Resource Center (IRC) at www.pearsonhighered.com/educator.

Acknowledgments

An author's only chance and hope for making a valuable contribution lies in the willingness of others to offer advice and to share their expertise. We want to thank Katherine T. Bucher and Kasey Garrison for their valuable contributions. We also want to thank reviewers Leah Alviar, Our Lady of the Lake University; Nyaradzo Mvududu, Seattle Pacific University; Edward M. Olivos, California State University–Dominguez Hills; and Barbara Tyler, Sul Ross State University–Rio Grand College, for their helpful comments. Our appreciation is also extended to people of all cultures who have contributed to the richness of our lives and the nation.

MLM
LGB

Multicultural Education and Its Response to Our Nation's Increasing Diversity

Part I introduces multicultural education as a concept and documents the increasing cultural diversity of the United States. Chapter 1 examines the multicultural education movement and its role in elementary and secondary schools. Chapter 2 looks at our nation's increasing diversity and the ways that people's differences enrich our schools. These chapters reflect a belief that educators have a professional responsibility to teach respect for diversity as well as to teach all students the concepts of social justice, equality, and democracy.

Multicultural Education

**Understanding the material and activities
in this chapter will help the reader to:**

◆ Define multicultural education and explain its fundamental purposes.

◆ List several goals, assumptions, concepts, and principles of multicultural education.

◆ List several myths and misconceptions about multicultural education.

◆ Explain briefly the historical milestones and legal precedents of multicultural education.

◆ Explain interdisciplinary approaches and how multiculturalism can be integrated through curricular experiences.

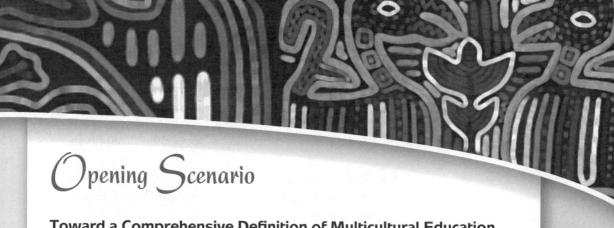

Opening Scenario

Toward a Comprehensive Definition of Multicultural Education

Led by Mr. Taylor, the administrators and staff at Public School (PS) 105 met to plan and implement their multicultural education program. Two goals emerged from their deliberations: (1) They want a comprehensive, all-encompassing program and (2) they want an interdisciplinary program.

Rather than addressing only cultural backgrounds, this group agreed that their program should direct attention to a broad range of differences: ethnicity, race, gender, social class, sexual orientation, and individual. They wanted a program that recognized the vast differences among children and adolescents, such as the many different cultures that make up the Hispanic American population, the vast differences among Asian Americans, and the diversity among African Americans.

Goal 1—A program that addresses as many differences as possible. The decision was made to examine each difference, including its influence on learning and other school-related activities, and then to look at the curriculum, instructional approaches, print and nonprint media, school policies, extracurricular activities, and the cultural composition of the administration, faculty, and staff. Although this constituted a task of some magnitude, the group recognized the advantages of having a multicultural education program that genuinely addresses diversity in its broadest definition.

Goal 2—A program that demonstrates a total commitment to an interdisciplinary effort, one in which multiculturalism permeates the school day. Although the committee recognized the legitimacy of unit approaches and that multicultural education was one subject, it also recognized that an interdisciplinary approach would be most effective for several reasons. Specifically, the interdisciplinary approach could achieve the following:

1. Provide a means of including multicultural education experiences in all subject areas, for example, showing the contributions of all cultural groups in the various disciplines.

2. Ensure broad involvement of all educators responsible for the various discipline areas.
3. Show students from culturally different backgrounds as well as majority-culture learners that the school is committed to serious multicultural education efforts.
4. Provide a wide variety of instructional approaches and learning experiences.
5. Make all school personnel feel that they are a part of the multicultural education program and responsible for its success.

The educators at PS 105 felt good about their multicultural education efforts: Everybody was involved. Teachers and administrators examined curricular and instructional practices and reconsidered school policies, and their efforts crossed disciplinary lines. ◆

Overview

The tremendous cultural, ethnic, religious, and socioeconomic diversity in schools today calls for multicultural education programs that reflect understanding and respect for children's and adolescents' differences. The multicultural education movement has particular relevance for the new century because of the continuing influx of people into the United States and because of the enlightened and more humane perspective that diversity enriches, rather than weakens, a nation. This chapter examines the fundamentals and principles of multicultural education and considers the various aspects that make programs successful.

Multicultural Education for Culturally Pluralistic Schools

In this section, we describe our (the authors') preferred definition of multicultural education and examine principles, concepts, goals, and assumptions that form the basis for responsive multicultural education programs. We then look at several myths and provide an overview of historical events and court decisions that have contributed to multicultural education.

Definition

Various groups and individuals define multicultural education in numerous ways. Some definitions address the perspectives of specific disciplines, such as education, anthropology, sociology, and psychology. Other definitions represent the views of accrediting agencies and professional organizations that are concerned with what teachers need to teach and what students need to learn.

We think the following definition most effectively meets the goals and purposes of multicultural education for children and adolescents. Multicultural education is both a concept and deliberate process designed to do the following:

◆ Teach learners to recognize, accept, and appreciate differences in culture, ethnicity, social class, sexual orientation, religion, special needs, and gender
◆ Instill in learners during their crucial developmental years a sense of responsibility and a commitment to work toward the democratic ideals of justice, equality, and democracy

Mulvihill (2000) maintained that multicultural education has always been a contested terrain because of tensions and debates over what the field includes and does not include. Although theories of multicultural education have been developed, they have not always taken into account the debates surrounding the terms *gender* and *sex* or the multiple feminist theories that focus on the more critical aspects of social justice. In fact, some believe multicultural education's influence as a change agent depends on the tensions it creates and on its success in working to resolve conflicts among various groups. In her article, Mulvihill (2000) looked at some of the tensions between gender studies and multicultural education, such as understanding gender as a category of analysis, theoretical constructions of feminism, and building an educational agenda for social justice.

Mulvihill (2000) focused attention on gender as well as feminist and critical education theories, especially as to how they relate to social justice. She proposed that multicultural education has an obligation to take advantage of the contributions of women and gender studies, especially because feminist pedagogy deals consistently with all the central issues inherent in multicultural education.

In Gender Perspectives 1.1, Asher (2007) discusses the challenges of educating teachers to engage, rather than deny or repress, differences that emerge as the dynamic context-specific intersections of race, culture, gender, and sexuality.

> **Points to Ponder   1.1**
>
> **Determining Differences to Include in Multicultural Education**
>
> Consider the differences and characteristics we included in our definition. Some might disagree with nontraditional views on sexual orientation, ability/disability, and gender. What do you think? Do people whose views are nontraditional have a culture of their own? For example, each person has his or her own cultural background, but wouldn't he or she also have a culture of sexual orientation, a culture associated with a disabling condition, or a culture associated with being either male or female? How inclusive do you think multicultural education should be?

Gender Perspectives 1.1

RACE, CULTURE, GENDER, AND SEXUALITY

Asher (2007) contends that multicultural discourse and practice are well established in the field of education. The effort has focused on the struggles of diverse students and communities, various theoretical perspectives, critical pedagogy, and cultural studies, feminism, critical race theory, race, identity, and representation. One may argue that multicultural education has generally focused on race and culture, with limited attention being focused on differences of sexuality, gender, and class.

In her article, Asher explains three vignettes: "Outing the Creole Self," "Family Values," and "The Wicca Closet." Then she offers insights into each as she further explains the intersections of race, culture, gender, and sexuality. In a study of diversity, one cannot just focus on one or more differences. She or he must focus on all types of differences and how one type affects another type.

Another excellent section in Asher's article is "Unpacking the Tensions: Implications for Curriculum and Pedagogy." In this section, Asher recommends a teacher education classroom "that serves as a safe place, where students can speak freely about their differences and how the differences affect lives." We recommend this article to all readers who want to know more about the intersections of race, culture, gender, and sexuality (as well as the tensions inherent to these differences).

Source: Asher, N. (2007). Made in the (multicultural) U.S.A.: Unpacking tensions of race, culture, gender, and sexuality in education. *Educational Researcher, 36*(2), 65–73.

Principles

Appropriate multicultural education requires more than simply providing cultural information about ethnic groups. Several fundamentals necessary to the promotion of effective multicultural education allow learners and teachers of various cultures to maintain integrity and dignity.

First, students need curricular materials appropriate to their cultural backgrounds. These materials should enhance students' self-concept, engage student interest in classroom learning, and provide examples, vocabulary, and models that relate to students' cultural backgrounds. Second, major curricular focuses should include skills in analysis and critical thinking. Third, materials, activities, and experiences should be authentic and multidimensional to help students understand ethnic differences and cultural diversity. They should include both cognitive and affective skills.

Concepts

It is especially important for teachers to understand three concepts of multicultural education, because it is the educator's concept of the term that determines his or her program's direction and issues.

First, multicultural education is a product in which there is emphasis on the study of ethnicity—for example, the contributions or characteristics of a group of people. This concept, which addresses teaching about different ethnic and cultural groups, may be best described as *ethnic studies*.

Second, multicultural education emphasizes the role of oppression of one group by another and the oppressors' atonement or compensation for past injustices. Dealing primarily with targeted oppressed groups (and possible solutions to their problems), this concept considers multicultural education a concern only of minorities.

The third concept views multicultural education as a teaching process that emphasizes the intrinsic aspects of culture and its influence on teaching and learning processes. Such a concept of multicultural education recognizes the belief that to obtain what one is entitled to requires a fair system and an equal chance to acquire social and academic skills. It incorporates that (1) certain historical facts and events must be taught and (2) an adequate understanding of present conditions, as well as general human behavior, comes about with knowledge of historical facts.

> **Points to Ponder** ◆ **1.2**
>
> **Surveying for Gender Bias**
>
> Visit several elementary or secondary schools to determine gender bias. Prepare a survey that examines (but is not limited to) such items as teacher-student interactions, instructional methods, grouping strategies, questioning strategies, and classroom environment. What evidence do you see that teachers recognize and address gender differences? Are boys and girls being treated equally and equitably? How might multicultural education address the bias in treatment of boys and girls (if, in fact you find evidence of bias)?

Goals

Effective multicultural education programs have well-defined goals—ones for which educators can plan and implement multicultural experiences. Readers will recall that educators at PS 105 in the Opening Scenario agreed to two major goals: a comprehensive program and interdisciplinary efforts. While goals vary with respective school environments, several goals should provide a foundation for all effective multicultural efforts.

First, a basic goal of all multicultural education should be development of the knowledge, skills, and attitudes necessary to function in a culturally diverse society and to promote social justice for all people. Sometimes called *cross-cultural* or *multicultural skills*, these three attributes (knowledge, attitudes, and skills) lead to an awareness, understanding, and acceptance of all types of diversity. Developing these skills also helps people better understand their own and others' differences.

Second, an important goal is to change the total educational environment so that it promotes a respect for a wide range of differences, enables all cultural groups to experience equal educational opportunities, and promotes social justice for all learners.

A third goal should be educators' enlightenment of the social, political, and economic realities encountered in a culturally diverse society. For example, students benefit when teachers respect differences and similarities; understand intracultural and individual differences; develop a better understanding of the impact of social injustices of students' motivation to learn and willingness to demonstrate positive behavior; and develop a positive attitude toward one's own cultural background.

Again, goals will vary with each respective school situation. For example, while one school might choose to adopt broad goals, another school might choose to have more specific goals, such as these: (1) Teach from multicultural perspectives to promote positive gender, racial, cultural, class, and individual identities as well as promote the recognition and acceptance of membership in many different groups. (2) Encourage social relationships to promote openness to and interest in others' differences and a willingness to include others in school and social activities. (3) Work to provide positive, healthy family–school relationships (which is a major focus of this text) and to promote the inclusion of immediate and extended families and caregivers.

Assumptions

Several assumptions underlie multicultural education and are, in fact, the philosophy on which this book, *Multicultural Education of Children and Adolescents*, is based.

Assumption 1

Cultural diversity is a positive, enriching element in a society because it provides individuals increased opportunities to experience other cultures as well as to understand their own. Rather than perceive it as a weakness to be remediated, educators should view cultural diversity as a strength with the potential for helping individuals better understand their own cultures. Similarly, as people reach higher levels of understanding and acceptance of other cultures, we hope that they will achieve similar heights of understanding and sensitivity in areas such as racism, sexism, and classism.

Assumption 2

Multicultural education is for all students. Some people believe that multicultural education is only for minority children and adolescents based on the odd notion that only minority youngsters need multicultural education. This notion completely fails to recognize that majority cultures can benefit from a better understanding of cultural differences and, eventually, of their own cultural backgrounds.

Assumption 3

Teaching is a cross-cultural encounter. All teachers and students have their own cultural "baggage"—their backgrounds, values, customs, perceptions, and, perhaps, prejudices. These cultural aspects play a significant role in teaching and learning situations and can have a substantial effect on behavior and learning. Socioeconomic status, ethnicity, gender, and language have a powerful and dynamic effect on one's outlook and attitude toward school and on one's actual school achievement.

Assumption 4

As demonstrated in the Opening Scenario about PS 105, multicultural education should permeate the total school curriculum, rather than be doled out in a one-course or a teaching-unit approach. Responsive multicultural education programs cannot accomplish lasting and worthwhile goals through "one shot" approaches. The school must be genuinely multicultural. Multiculturalism must embrace the curriculum, as defined in the broadest sense (every aspect of the school with which learners come in contact); the composition of the administration, faculty, and staff; expectations that reflect an understanding of different cultural groups, their attitudes toward school success, and their learning styles; and the recognition of all other aspects that may affect both minority- and majority-culture learners. A school that appears to address only majority needs and expectations will cause learners from culturally different backgrounds to feel like intruders or outsiders.

Assumption 5

Generally speaking, members of minority groups, students from low-income families, and students who are culturally different or speak a language other than English have not fared well in U.S. school systems. Any number of reasons may account for such students' lack of achievement: differing achievement orientations; problems resulting from language barriers; differing learning styles; curricula and school policies that are unresponsive to minority student needs; testing and assessment procedures that may be designed for middle-class white students; and a lack of understanding or acceptance of cultural differences. In any event, the high dropout rate among American Indians, African Americans, and Hispanic Americans substantiates the position that learners from culturally different backgrounds often do not succeed in U.S. schools.

Assumption 6

Schools will continue to experience and reflect increasing cultural diversity because of influxes of immigrants and refugees and the high birthrates of some cultural groups. To say that U.S. society continues to grow more diverse is an understatement. The arrival in this country of increasing numbers of people from culturally different backgrounds is one example. Increasing recognition of differences in gender, religion, socioeconomic group, sexual orientation, and geography are others. Multicultural education programs have the responsibility to reflect the rich diversity that characterizes U.S. society.

Assumption 7

Elementary and secondary schools have a responsibility to implement appropriate multicultural education programs. These programs must contribute to a better understanding of cultural differences, show the dangers of stereotyping, and reduce racism, sexism, and classism. Families are unquestionably children's first teachers of values, opinions, and attitudes. Ideally, families teach acceptance and respect for all people and their differences. Realistically speaking, however, children may learn that their culture, race, or ethnic backgrounds are "right" but that those of others are "wrong" or "inferior." Because considerable cultural diversity characterizes the U.S. educational system, the transmission of understanding and respect for cultural diversity is most feasible in elementary and secondary schools. Responsive programs must teach genuine respect and must work toward reducing racism, sexism, and classism. Admittedly, this is an undertaking of considerable magnitude; the teaching and modeling of respect for all people, however, may have the most dramatic impact during children's formative years.

Social Justice

One common definition of social justice focuses on human rights abuses and includes issues of minority groups, especially international justice, women's and children's issues, and war crimes and crimes against humanity. Another definition refers to the concept of a just society, where justice refers to more than just the administration of laws. It is based on the idea of a society that gives individuals and groups fair treatment and a just share of the benefits of society. While definitions vary, we feel that an emphasis on social justice should be a mainstay of any multicultural education programs.

Walker (2006) offers several characteristics of social justice:

◆ Educators employ democratic policies, nurture relationships with all the constituencies, and involve the larger community for a more democratic society.
◆ Educators emphasize inclusion and exercise ethical decision making at all levels of the system.
◆ Educators transform the school culture and the policies and practices that are part of the culture in an equitable society.
◆ Educators view social justice as a process and a goal, whereby the process leading to social justice is democratic, participatory, and inclusive and the goal is full and equal participation of all groups in a society, where resources are distributed equally, members are physically and psychologically safe, and members interact in a self-determining and interdependent manner.

Speaking primarily of principals and counselors, Walker (2006) maintains that despite our ideological dedication to equality and social justice, schools continue to be shaped by an educational system challenged by changing demographics and characterized by blatant inequality and failure. For well over a century, educators in the United States have confronted the issue of organizing the schools to support an increasingly diverse population and provide a socially just environment.

In summary, Howard and Solberg (2006) advocate for educators to become agents for social justice when creating, implementing, and supporting school-based interventions designed to promote school success, especially culturally relevant interventions that target youth from diverse and low-income backgrounds. Different advocates of social justice have developed different interpretations of what constitutes receiving fair treatment and a just share. It can also mean an equitable distribution of advantages and disadvantages within a society or community.

Myths and Misconceptions

At one time or another, most people have probably heard someone voice dire consequences about the results of multicultural education. Readers can probably make their own list of concerns, and in all likelihood, some educators at PS 105 in the Opening Scenario had doubts about multicultural education. This section will look at several myths and explain why multicultural education does not pose a threat.

Misconception 1—Multicultural Education Is for Others

Some people argue that multicultural education is an entitlement program and a curriculum movement for African Americans, Hispanic Americans, the poor, women, and other marginalized groups (e.g., gays, lesbians, and bisexuals). Our definition of multicultural education is broad and all encompassing, so it should be clear that we do not believe multicultural education is for only one group or type of diversity. In fact, our perceptions of multicultural education promote all groups and call for both learners and educators to acquire the knowledge, skills, and attitudes necessary to function effectively in a culturally diverse nation. Rather than focus only on specific gender and ethnic movements, multicultural education tries to empower all people to become knowledgeable, caring, and active citizens.

Misconception 2—Multicultural Education Is Opposed to Western Traditions Such as Individualism, Competition, and Goal Setting

In fact, multicultural education grew out of the civil rights movement of the 1960s, which was grounded in such democratic ideals as freedom, social justice, and equality.

Misconception 3—Schools Can Create Unity by Assimilating Students from Diverse Racial and Ethnic Groups into a Majority Culture

Unfortunately, in some cases, even when students from different backgrounds engage in cultural assimilation, they continue to experience exclusion (and racism, prejudice, and injustice) from others of culturally different backgrounds. Furthermore, the assimilation approach traditionally used by U.S. society and schools required a process of self-alienation.

Birkel (2000) maintains that *multicultural* (p. 22) has many meanings. To some, it means the acceptance and appreciation of diversity (an opinion emphasized throughout this book); to others, it means, an association with "political correctness" (p. 22). The term is also misunderstood as a program on race relations, as an affirmative action vehicle, and as a civil rights movement. It has also been charged as an attack on Western thought. Birkel sought to clarify the true meaning of multicultural education and to refute some of the fallacious ideas that have limited its success.

Birkel's (2000) major points include that multicultural education is neither political nor an attempt to establish blame or instill guilt. Such actions would negate the purpose of the movement, which is to promote unity rather than division among the American people. Another point is that rather than advocating the eradication of ethnicity and diversity, multicultural education advocates the teaching of factual and complete knowledge about the cultural groups that comprise the United States.

According to Birkel (2000), multicultural education is, first of all, education concerned with the teaching/learning processes and the acceptance and appreciation of diversity. Primarily, multicultural education is a way of teaching and learning. Elements include the skills of intercultural understanding and interaction, the integration of cultural content, and the building of positive attitudes.

Birkel (2000) thoughtfully explains what multicultural education is and what it is not. Some may argue with a few of the misconceptions (e.g., multicultural education promotes unity rather than division among the American people), but Birkel proposes a sound defense of multicultural education as a movement to promote the acceptance and appreciation of diversity.

A Brief Historical Overview

Before 1978, the Education Index did not include multicultural education in its listings; few pedagogical journals addressed the topic. During the 1970s and 1980s, however, increasing numbers of articles and books focused on multicultural education (Tiedt & Tiedt, 1999). Three forces contributed to the emergence of the multicultural education movement: (1) the civil rights movement came of age, (2) school textbooks came under critical analysis, and (3) assumptions underlying the deficiency orientation were changed to a more positive perspective.

The civil rights movement began as a passive, nonviolent means of changing laws that oppressed specific racial groups. By the late 1960s, the movement had matured into an energetic coalition uniting all Americans of color and directed toward self-determination and power. The movement severely criticized the U.S. school system because of curricula that focused attention only on Western culture. Similarly, few teachers knew about minority groups, their individual strengths and weaknesses, and their learning styles. In fact, schools considered cultural differences primarily weaknesses in need of remediation.

The 1970s saw the development of multicultural education into a more comprehensive approach. With cultural diversity and equal opportunity serving as an impetus, the multicultural education movement encouraged educators to examine and consider the relationships among culture, ethnicity, language, gender, disabling conditions, and social class in developing educational programs. Multicultural education that takes a social reconstructionist tack is a recent and controversial approach that represents an extension of multicultural education toward more definitive social action. This approach incorporates a curricular emphasis on (1) active student involvement in social issues such as sexism, racism, and classism; (2) the development of problem-solving ability and political action skills; and (3) the implementation of curricular adaptations, cooperative learning, and decision-making skills (Hernandez, 1989).

Banks (1988) described phases that place multicultural education in its proper historical perspective. During Phase I (monoethnic studies), the black civil rights movement began and African Americans demanded more African American teachers, more control of community schools, and the rewriting of textbooks to provide a more accurate portrayal of African Americans, their culture, and their contributions. Phase II (multiethnic studies) provided courses that focused on several minority groups and viewed experiences of ethnic groups from comparative perspectives. During Phase III (multiethnic education), an increasing number of educators recognized that the mere reforming of courses was insufficient to result in genuine educational reform.

In Phase IV (multicultural education), some educators became interested in an even broader development of pluralistic education that focused on reform of the total school environment. *Multicultural education* emerged as the preferred concept because it enabled educators to broaden their perspective to include a wider range of groups rather than maintain a limited focus on racial and ethnic minorities. Phase V is a slowly occurring process that includes strategies designed to increase the pace and scope of the institutionalization of multiethnic and multicultural education within schools (Banks, 1988).

The two world wars, mass immigrations to the United States, the intercultural movements, and racial disturbances all contributed to the emergence and development of multicultural education.

The Influence of Court Decisions

Ruling in favor of equal opportunity and human rights, several court decisions and laws also contributed to the present multicultural education movement. The U.S. Supreme Court, in *Brown v. Topeka Board of Education* (1954), ruled unconstitutional the segregation of black and white learners. In 1957, the U.S. Commission on Civil Rights was established to investigate complaints that alleged the denial of civil rights. In 1968, the federal Bilingual Education Act (BEA) was passed as part of Title VII of the Elementary and Secondary Education Act. The U.S. Commission on Civil Rights issued a report in 1975 called *A Better Chance to Learn: Bilingual–Bicultural Education,* designed for educators as a means of providing equal opportunity for language-minority students. This report provides only a brief listing of a few representative events that recognized cultural diversity and equal rights. These and other events, however, were the forerunners of the movement to recognize and teach respect for people from culturally different backgrounds.

Interdisciplinary Approaches

Multicultural education should be an integral aspect of all curricular areas, rather than just be administered through the social studies course. Likewise, a once-a-year Multicultural Week or unit focusing on African American history, tacos, and Asian dress and customs will not suffice. Such approaches have not worked and will not work, because diversity awareness does not necessarily result in acceptance of and respect for individuals within a cultural group. The curriculum, learning environments, and mindset of learners, faculty, and staff should become genuinely multicultural in nature and should reflect the cultural diversity of the school. Second, well-meaning multicultural education programs may serve only cosmetic purposes if students and school personnel harbor long-held cultural biases and stereotypes. In essence, to be effective, responsive multicultural education programs must recognize the need both to inform and to change negative attitudes and long-held prejudices.

The Effective Multicultural Educator

Competencies for effective multicultural educators fall into three categories—knowledge, skills, and attitudes—and each is necessary to the existence of the other. We briefly examine several examples here. Chapter 10 takes a more in-depth look at knowledge, attitudes, and skills and more specific teaching behaviors.

Knowledge includes an understanding of individual learners' cultures. American Indians, for example, place great importance on the concept of sharing. African Americans value the extended family and have a unique language usage. Asian Americans have a unique concept of generational and family relationships. *Machismo* is an integral part of Hispanic American culture, as is commitment to the Spanish language.

Points to Ponder 1.3

Planning Interdisciplinary Approaches

Talk with several teachers who are experienced with interdisciplinary curricular approaches. (In fact, several might be in the class.) Ask these teachers to offer suggestions for integrating multiculturalism throughout the curriculum. For example, specific questions should focus on culturally appropriate topics, materials that offer diverse perspectives and show respect for diversity, instructional methods that cater to diverse learning styles, and culturally appropriate assessment techniques.

Skills include recognizing and responding appropriately to learners' strengths and weaknesses and responding to the relationship between learning styles and culture. Skills-based teaching provides school experiences that embrace learners' orientations toward school and academic success. It requires teachers to select standardized tests and evaluation instruments with the least cultural bias and to use teaching methods that have proven especially appropriate for children and adolescents from culturally different backgrounds.

Attitudes include developing positive outlooks and values, creating culturally appropriate learning environments, and modeling for children respect and concern for all people. See Chapter 10 for a more detailed analysis of effective teaching behaviors in multicultural settings.

Case Study

Comprehensive Program Too Much?

In the Opening Scenario of this chapter, the teachers and administrators of PS 105 met to plan their multicultural education program. As you recall, their primary goal was to provide a program that addressed as many differences as possible. After eight months, they are now planning for the next school year and questioning some of their decisions. One of the questions being reconsidered is: Just what should multicultural education include?

Ms. Diaz says, "When multicultural education was first introduced, the focus was culture. Now, the definition has expanded to cover so many other topics. I am just not sure we can or should consider and plan a program for social class, social justice, and sexual orientation. I am just not sure our professional responsibilities include all this. We are content specialists, but we were not trained in multicultural education. Plus, we do not have the time to take on this extra responsibility. Again, I am just not sure we should be dealing with *all* types of diversity."

Mr. Taylor, the group leader, understands that other teachers and staff members feel the same way and has taken action with the hope that he can change the tone of the meeting. He perceives two problems: First, perhaps the group has taken on too much at one time. Possibly, he should have encouraged group members to take smaller steps. Second, he realizes that some genuine philosophical questions are being raised: Should multicultural education include sexual orientation and social class? Should its goals include social justice? Should the program be interdisciplinary?

At this point, Mr. Taylor suggests a 10 minute break (mainly so he can think and make some decisions!). Although he believes that the multicultural education program should be comprehensive, he also knows he has to have a group consensus on program directions. He asks himself some questions: How comprehensive should the program be? How can he convince the group that specific cultures accompany social class, social orientation, and other diversities? How can he show that an effective multicultural program must encompass more than just culture?

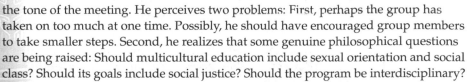

Questions for Discussion:

1. How comprehensive should a multicultural education program be? This is, in some ways, a personal question, because one's opinion will be based, at least in part, on her or his social class and sexual orientation or worldview. Still, we want you to decide what you think. How comprehensive should a multicultural education program be?

2. Respond to Ms. Diaz's statement: "I am just not sure our professional responsibilities include all this. We are content specialists, but we were not trained in multicultural education." We hear such statements all too often. In some cases, we have to admit the validity of the statement—some teachers are not trained in multicultural education. How can we, as educators, change such beliefs? Does Ms. Diaz really want to participate in the program? Remember that when Ms. Diaz spoke, others agreed but just did not want to express their opinions.

3. Did the group take on too many tasks when they designed the multicultural education program? Should they have planned a limited approach and then, after small steps, expanded to a more comprehensive program?

Summing Up

Educators planning and implementing multicultural education programs should remember to:

1. Address the wrongs of the past, such as racism, prejudice, and discrimination, but maintain the primary focus on the present understanding, respect, and acceptance of people of differing cultural backgrounds.

2. Consider multicultural education as an emerging concept that will continue to evolve as necessary to meet the needs of a society that is becoming increasingly diverse culturally.

3. Transmit facts and knowledge (including an awareness of cultural diversity) to help learners develop the skills necessary to interrelate positively with people of culturally diverse backgrounds.

4. Consider a total school curricular approach that integrates multicultural education in all teaching and learning situations.

5. Recognize multicultural education as an endeavor that has received considerable recognition and respect. Several areas of controversy and criticism continue to exist, however, and deserve attention.

6. Direct attention to issues such as sexism, agism, and classism, create more positive attitudes toward the disabled, and eliminate the racism, prejudice, and discrimination that plague U.S. society.

7. Address the ethnocentrism of learners and educators both.

8. Insist on multicultural education programs in all schools, rather than just in schools that have a culturally diverse student population.

Suggested Learning Activities

1. Outline a multicultural education program for a school that has a population 50 percent European American, 25 percent African American, 20 percent Hispanic American, and approximately 5 percent other culturally diverse groups. Respond specifically to such areas as the extent of emphasis on each culture; a determination of the content of the program and examination of attitudes; appropriate in-service sessions for administration, faculty, and staff; appropriate curriculum and instruction methods and materials; and methods of assessing the program.

2. Read several definitions of multicultural education, and then, on the basis of these definitions and your opinions, write your own definition of multicultural education. Should multicultural education include more than just culture, for example, and should the definition include diversity in religion, gender, social class, and sexual orientation?

3. Consider the following section, Implementing Research: Social Justice and Urban Schools, and then offer three specific ways educators can promote social justice in all schools.

Implementing Research

Social Justice and Urban Schools

Most people share the understanding that teaching social justice means providing students with a supportive learning environment that is fair, just, democratic, and compassionate. While many agree that social justice is a worthwhile goal, most do not view it as a perspective for educating students in urban school settings.

An article by J. Lalas (2007) examines different definitions and conceptualizations of teaching and learning for social justice and identifies the common principles that are applicable, relevant, and translate into classroom practice. The article also offers a glimpse of urban schooling, especially the social reality of isolation and poverty faced by its students.

After presenting several interesting definitions of social justice, Lalas (2007) focuses on how to achieve social justice in a classroom context. He calls for interaction, generation, and negotiation of meaningful experiences, which he defines as including the physical classroom arrangement, classroom discipline, key sources of authority, textbooks, assessment devices, assignments, and visual and supplementary materials. He then offers practical suggestions such as these:

- ◆ Understand oneself in relation to other individuals or group of individuals.
- ◆ Appreciate diversity and promote equity.
- ◆ Recognize inequities and determine how to diminish them.
- ◆ Create a culturally appropriate learning environment.
- ◆ Work together as a learning community.
- ◆ Engage in classroom activity.
- ◆ Think critically and reflectively.

Implementing the Research

1. First and probably most important, educators need to acquire an understanding of social justice and its importance in K–12 schools.
2. Educators need to start small to avoid trying to address *all* areas simultaneously. Such a plan will be too overwhelming. Instead, educators should have a deliberate and methodical plan that continues to have a high priority for implementation.
3. Educators should celebrate their progress toward social justice. Admittedly, social justice will be difficult to accomplish, but doing so is not impossible. Even small improvements and steps should be celebrated, and goals should always be refined.

Source: Lalas, J. (2007). Teaching for social justice in multicultural urban schools: Conceptualization and classroom implications. *Multicultural Education, 14*(3), 17–21.

Suggestions for Collaborative Efforts

Form groups of three or four that, if possible, represent our nation's cultural and gender diversity. Working collaboratively, focus your group's attention toward the following efforts.

1. In your group, discuss the following statement: "There are more differences in social class than there are differences in culture. For example, middle- or upper-class people of various cultures may be more alike (e.g., in terms of preferences in food, clothing, customs, traditions, and religion) than people of a given culture or race. In essence, social class may be the distinguishing factor among people." Have several members of your group interview people from different social classes and several people from different cultural backgrounds to compare and contrast differences and similarities.

2. Have one or two of your group members visit a school to examine and compare the multicultural education programs. How do schools differ in philosophy, commitment, approaches (unit or total curriculum integration), goals and objectives, treatment of holidays, and overall attempts to have a truly multicultural school?

3. Select a school known for its diverse student population. Have your group formulate an instrument (survey or checklist) to assess the school's efforts in multicultural education. Make sure it examines the cultural, racial, and ethnic composition of faculty, staff, and other professional personnel; whether organization and grouping methods segregate learners by race; and whether the curriculum and instruction materials reflect cultural diversity.

Expanding Your Horizons
Additional Journals, Books, and Internet Sites

Campano, G. (2007). *Immigrant students and literacy: Reading, writing, and remembering.* New York: Teachers College Press.

> Campano looks at challenges facing immigrant students as well as the various resources available to help them.

Carpenter, S., Zarate, M. A., & Garcia, A. A. (2007). Cultural pluralism and prejudice reduction. *Cultural Diversity and Ethnic Minority Psychology, 13*(2), 83–93.

> These authors tested models of cultural pluralism and demonstrated that highlighting differences among people reduces prejudice.

Chan, E. (2007). Student experiences of a culturally-sensitive curriculum: Ethnic identity development amid conflicting stories to live by. *Journal of Curriculum Studies, 39*(2) 177–194.

> Chan examines how students' experiences with a culturally sensitive curriculum can contribute to their sense of ethnic identity.

Mueller, M. P., & Bentley, M. L. (2007). Beyond the "Decorated Landscape" of educational reform: Toward landscapes of pluralism in science education. *Science Education, 91*(2), 321–338.

> Focusing on science education, these authors conclude that the main focuses of science education should be making informed choices and having opportunities to participate fully in society.

Muffoletto, R., & Horton, J. (2007). *Multicultural education, the Internet, and the new media.* Cressville, NJ: Hampton Press.

> As the title suggests, Muffoletto and Horton examine the role of the media and the Internet in promoting multicultural education.

National Association for Multicultural Education. www.nameorg.org

> This site provides information on the purposes, design, and implementation of effective multicultural education programs.

National Association for Bilingual Education. www.nabe.org

> This site promotes bilingual education, provides information, and sponsors an annual conference.

STANDARDS: The International Journal of Multicultural Studies. www.colorado.edu/journals/standards

> This site focuses on multiculturalism in education, including on-line syllabi, lesson plans, and book reviews.

Diversity

Understanding the material and activities in this chapter will help the reader to:

♦ Grasp the historical and contemporary perspectives toward cultural diversity—that is, the melting pot and salad bowl ideologies, respectively.

♦ Explain concepts such as culture, ethnicity, race, socioeconomic status, and gender, and explain why understanding these concepts is important when working with children and adolescents from various cultures.

♦ Explicate perspectives toward cultural diversity such as cultural deficit and cultural mismatch, and provide a rationale for adopting a positive and enriching perspective that appreciates cultural difference or cultural diversity.

♦ Explain how racism, discrimination, and stereotypes can hurt children and adolescents who are culturally different and how elementary and secondary schools can provide appropriate responses.

Opening Scenario

Toward a Salad Bowl Perspective

Mrs. Rowe detected relatively easily that the school expected all learners to assimilate to middle-class European American values and customs. Textbooks emphasized middle-class characters while downplaying members from other cultural groups; teaching styles and instructional strategies addressed the needs of middle-class learners; school rules and policies applied to all learners; school environments did little to celebrate cultural or gender diversity; and the administration, faculty, and staff provided little evidence that the school system had tried to employ professionals from various cultures. Learners with culturally different backgrounds who were unable or unwilling to adopt mainstream values suffered the consequences of lower achievement, poorer self-esteem, and a feeling of nonacceptance in the school.

Mrs. Rowe thought of ways to move the school toward a more "salad bowl" perspective, one in which learners from all cultures could retain their cultural values and traditions and in which the school could address the needs of all learners. Mrs. Rowe asked for the administration's advice and support. The administration then formed a committee consisting of Mrs. Rowe, a speech therapist, a special educator, a guidance counselor, several classroom teachers, and several parents representing different cultural groups. The committee decided to take deliberate action to make the entire school more responsive to learners with differing cultural backgrounds. They made plans to examine all phases of the school: textbooks and other curricular materials, the overall curriculum, instructional strategies, the efforts of special school personnel, the school environment, and efforts designed to celebrate diversity.

Mrs. Rowe and the committee realized they needed to be realistic. Changing the school would take time, commitment, and the efforts of all educators. They did achieve, however, two crucial steps: The school had realized the need for change and decided to take planned and deliberate action toward making all students feeling accepted. ◆

Overview

The increasing cultural diversity of the United States challenges elementary and secondary school educators to understand differing values, customs, and traditions and to provide responsive multicultural experiences for all learners. The melting pot theory, once thought to be a model of the assimilation of immigrants into the United States, obviously is not valid. People do not lose their differences when they immigrate to the United States. The melting pot theory is no longer considered a model, much less a means of achieving a just, equal, and accepting society. Educators need a sound understanding of cultural, ethnic, racial, socioeconomic, gender, and individual differences, especially in light of the wealth of cultural diversity of the nation that increases daily. This chapter examines cultural diversity in the United States and suggests that responsive multicultural education programs can address many challenges.

A Word of Caution

As we mentioned in the Preface, anyone writing and talking about the many kinds of diversity needs to use extreme caution. Mrs. Rowe realized the need to recognize diversity in the Opening Scenario.

As we look at diversity in this chapter, we cannot overemphasize the importance of recognizing individual differences. For instance, all Asian Americans are not alike. Differences exist due to differences in social class, acculturation, time in the United States, as well as a wealth of individual differences. Similarly, whenever possible, we need to specify a specific culture. That is, instead of using the term *Asian American,* we need to specify Japanese American, Chinese American, or whatever the Asian culture might be. When it is not feasible to name a specific culture, we should always remember that overgeneralizing can result in relying on stereotypes.

As you read this chapter, remember that many differences exist among cultures, social classes, and learners of differing sexual orientations. Also remember that *knowing* individuals requires conscientious study and first-hand contact.

Diversity

Culture

Culture can be defined in a number of ways, but recent definitions, while worded differently, basically connote similar meanings. We define *culture* as people's values, language, religion, ideals, artistic expressions, patterns of social and interpersonal relationships, and ways of perceiving, behaving, and thinking. People's basis for perceptions, as well as their actual perceptions, differ culturally. How we feel, think, respond, and behave reflects our cultural background.

It is important to say that all people have culture. Such a statement might appear strange, but a century or so ago, culture was thought to be the province of only some people. Educated people who were well read, literate, and knowledgeable in areas such as music, the arts, and drama had culture; those who did not were thought to lack culture. Today, we recognize that all people have culture.

People referred to as *bicultural* have competencies and can function effectively in two cultures. These people have mastered the knowledge of and are able to function effectively in two cultures. They feel comfortable in two cultures and have a strong desire to function effectively in them.

> **Points to Ponder 2.1**
>
> **Determining Culture**
>
> Consider your culture—how many do you have? You have a cultural background, but you also have a culture of region, sexual orientation, gender, socioeconomic status, and professional status: Are you a pre-service or an in-service teacher?

Race

Although the term *race* refers to biological differences among people, it has long been used to differentiate groups of people. Determining racial categories often proves difficult because of the wide variety of traits and characteristics people and groups share. Society has generally recognized differences between races (e.g., physical differences), but these differences satisfy only biological aspects and do not explain differences in social behavior.

There are several important points concerning race. First, despite the movements of large numbers of people from one geographic region to another and the influence of intermarriage across racial groups, the concept of race today still has a significant social meaning. Second, race contributes few insights to cultural understanding. There is seldom cultural correspondence between a person's nationality, geography, language, and religion and his or her racial category. Therefore, knowledge of a person's racial identity does not reveal much about his or her nationality, religion, and language.

Weiner (2006), in her review of Jane Bolgatz's book *Talking Race in the Classroom* (2005), maintains that teachers' efforts should extend beyond "heroes and holidays" to truly integrate race and racial experiences into the school experience. Bolgatz encourages teachers to challenge students to think about how race manifests in their daily lives and provides readers with concrete examples, such as personal experiences, different-size student groups, popular culture, current statistics, and hypothetical situations. Bolgatz (2005) also encourages teachers who discuss race to be self-reflective and critique their own attitudes and statements.

Difficulties the U.S. Bureau of the Census experienced in its documents show the confusion regarding race and ethnicity. For example, the census may ask people to define themselves in categories that are not mutually exclusive; that is, a person can have more than one racial or ethnic designation.

Ethnicity

The definition of *ethnicity* takes into consideration people's national origin, religion, race, and any combination thereof. Attributes associated with ethnicity include group image and sense of identity derived from contemporary cultural patterns; shared political and economic interests; and involuntary membership, although individual identification with the group may be optional. The extent to which individuals identify with a particular ethnic group varies considerably, and some may identify with more than one. Strong ethnic identification suggests a sharing and acceptance of ethnic group values, beliefs, behaviors, language, and ways of thinking.

The definition of ethnicity also includes a community of people within a larger society who are set apart by others or who set themselves apart primarily on the basis of racial identity and cultural characteristics such as religion, language, and tradition. The central factor is the notion of being set apart because of physical or cultural attributes or both.

Gender

The term *gender* describes masculinity and femininity—the thoughts, feelings, and behavior that identify one as either male or female. A multicultural education text would be remiss if it failed to address gender differences. Although many similarities exist between males and females, differences also exist, which educators should recognize and for which they should plan gender-appropriate educational experiences. Likewise, educators have a responsibility to clarify stereotypical beliefs about males and females.

We have included gender as a difference to be recognized in multicultural education because of the gender inequality that has long limited females' potential. While gender inequality is mostly considered during the adult years,

Baunach (2001) maintains that gender inequality actually begins during child-hood. Baunach's article provides a good argument for including gender in multicultural education efforts.

How might females differ from males? Research on gender and its effects has focused mainly on health concerns, social networks, self-esteem, achievement, self-image, and sex-role attitudes and behaviors:

1. Females and males report the same number of best friends; attributes they considered important in themselves and their same-sex friends differed according to sex. Males had larger social networks than females.
2. Females feel less positive about their bodies than males feel about theirs and assign different values than males do to different aspects of their bodies. Changes affecting the female body may make girls disappointed in their bodies. Boys, by contrast, may be less concerned with physical appearance and more interested in task mastery and effectiveness.
3. Females who have curricular choices often choose fewer mathematics courses than do males. The reason for this difference, however, is attributed to educators and counselors who steer females away from mathematics and science, not to actual weaknesses in females' native ability.
4. Females prove significantly more nontraditional in their sex-role behaviors. Both genders demonstrate more nontraditionalism in sex-role attitudes than in actual sex-role behaviors.
5. Females benefit more from group-oriented collaborative learning projects (e.g., cooperative learning), rather than individualistic and competitive projects, which many males prefer (Butler & Manning, 1998).

While significant changes to improve gender equity have been made, it would be unrealistic to say educators always treat boys and girls the same way. Gender inequities still exist. Schools sometimes promote exclusionary practices and exclude (perhaps not intentionally) girls from activities. While schools' tactics may be subtle, they sometimes discourage girls from participating in specific activities, clubs, and learning activities, and the same holds true for boys. Over the decades, some educational experiences have become gender specific. Educators will be wise to have nondiscrimination as a goal and to comply with all legal mandates of nondiscrimination by examining both curricular and extracurricular

Points to Ponder 2.2

School Practices and Gender

Make a list of school practices or education-related issues that might fail to address gender differences. Why do you think educators sometimes use school practices and harbor expectations that fail to address gender differences?

activities, reviewing policies that might unintentionally discriminate, and seeking changes in school policy and practice to reduce discrimination.

Sexual Orientation

We believe that multicultural education should include people of differing sexual orientation. We believe that gays and lesbians share specific cultural characteristics, experience injustices and discrimination the way racial and ethnic minorities do, and deserve educators capable of providing effective educational experiences. We also believe those with physical disabilities should be included in the definition because they have a culture of their own and often experience injustices in U.S. society. Such a position does not imply that these people do not share many similarities with others. It simply implies that, because of their differences and potential as targets of injustice, they should be included in the definition of multiculturalism and in multicultural education programs.

Gays, lesbians, and bisexuals have their own culture and experience many of the same problems as minorities. Educators teaching gay and lesbian students need to understand the special challenges (e.g., loneliness, isolation, ridicule) that gays and lesbians experience. We feel that sexual orientation should be perceived as a cultural difference, just as gender, race, ethnicity, and social class are considered differences. Teaching gay and lesbian students requires trying to understand these students' worldviews and perspectives on life.

About 10 to 13 percent of the population is gay or lesbian and this portion represents every race, creed, social class, and degree of disability. In fact, estimates suggest there are 2.9 million gay or lesbian adolescents in the United States. These students are from all cultural groups and from rural as well as urban schools. They have, for the most part, sat passively through the years of schooling where their identities as gay and lesbian people have been ignored or denied.

Students are becoming more visible each day through increased numbers of referrals to school counselors, school social workers, substance-abuse personnel, and various other support staff. Individual reasons for these referrals are diverse, but among the most common are efforts to clarify sexual orientation, anxiety, suicide attempts, substance abuse, low self-esteem, family conflict, and emotional isolation.

Educators should (1) provide factual information about youth sexuality, (2) abandon the myth that discussing homosexuality will cause young people to grow up to be gay or lesbian, (3) promote and protect the human and civil rights of all people in the classroom, and (4) encourage the hiring of and supporting gay and lesbian educators who can provide healthy role models.

MacGillivray and Kozik-Rosabal (2000) define GLBTQ as gay, lesbian, bisexual, transgendered, queer, and questioning. They suggest that the term GLBTQ supports the idea that no adolescent is being left out due to his or her sexual orientation. They also assert that GLBTQ is not just an urban issue—these students also attend schools in rural and suburban schools. Schools, in addition to meeting the needs of GLBTQ students, need to prepare heterosexual students for democratic citizenship in communities with significant populations of politically active and "out" GLBTQ people. MacGillivray and Kozik-Rosabal (2000) suggest that educators have an enormous task before them as they make schools safe for GLBTQ students.

Socioeconomic Conditions and Minorities

Socioeconomic disparities continue to plague people of color (African, Hispanic, Asian, Native Hawaiians/Pacific Islanders, and American Indians), including both differences with the majority culture as well as intergroup differences. For example, minority groups do not fare as well as the majority European American culture, and Hispanic and African American groups do not fare as well as Asian Americans. These disparities surface when one looks at disturbing statistics reflecting people living at the poverty line (or below), poorer health status, lack of health insurance, and numbers of children and adolescents participating in the school lunch program (American Psychological Association, 2007; Chong & Kim, 2006; Kaiser Family Foundation, 2007; Newman & Ralston, 2006). The population of the United States is racially and culturally diverse and is continuing to grow.

In 2005, nearly one-third of Americans identified themselves as belonging to an ethnic or racial-minority group. By 2050, this share is expected to increase by nearly half. The racial population varies by state, with states in the West and South having the highest shares of minority residents. People of color are more likely than non-Hispanic whites to have a low income, which may have implications for both their health and insurance status (Kaiser Family Foundation, 2007).

Socioeconomics/Poverty

The Kaiser Family Foundation (2007) has offered some disturbing statistics about minorities and living in lower economic conditions. For example, people of color are more likely to have a family income less than 200 percent of the federal poverty level than are whites. Over half of Hispanics, African Americans, and American Indians/Alaska Natives are poor or near poor, compared to 26 percent of whites and 33 percent of Asians and Pacific Islanders. The proportion of children who are poor or near poor is even higher. Figures 2.1 and 2.2 show the poverty status of the nonelderly and elderly U.S. population, respectively, by race and ethnicity in 2005.

Health Status

Health status is a function of several factors, including access to care and insurance coverage, socioeconomic conditions (education, occupation, income, and place of residence), genetics, and personal behavior. Racial and ethnic minority population groups (other than Asian Americans) rate their overall health worse than non-Hispanic whites.

While poor and low-income people of all races and ethnicities report worse health status than higher-income people, differences in overall health status by race/ethnicity persist even within income groups. Minority Americans frequently

figure **Poverty Status of Nonelderly Population by Race and Ethnicity, 2005**

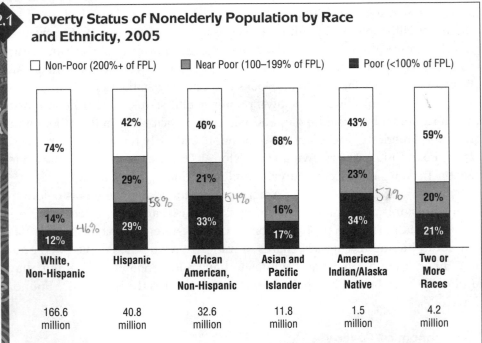

Notes: Individuals who reported more than one race group were categorized as "two or more races." Nonelderly includes individuals under age 65. FPL—Federal Poverty Level. The FPL for a family of four in 2005 was $19,971.

Source: *Key Facts: Race, Ethnicity & Medical Care, 2007 Update* (#6069-02), The Henry J. Kaiser Family Foundation, January 2007, p. 5. Reprinted with permission from The Henry J. Kaiser Family Foundation. The Kaiser Family Foundation, based in Menlo Park, California, is a nonprofit, private operating foundation focusing on the major health care issues facing the nation and is not associated with Kaiser Permanente or Kaiser Industries.

figure **2.2**

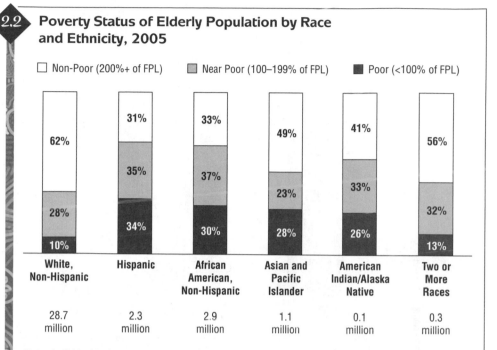

Poverty Status of Elderly Population by Race and Ethnicity, 2005

☐ Non-Poor (200%+ of FPL)   ☐ Near Poor (100–199% of FPL)   ■ Poor (<100% of FPL)

	White, Non-Hispanic	Hispanic	African American, Non-Hispanic	Asian and Pacific Islander	American Indian/Alaska Native	Two or More Races
Non-Poor	62%	31%	33%	49%	41%	56%
Near Poor	28%	35%	37%	23%	33%	32%
Poor	10%	34%	30%	28%	26%	13%
	28.7 million	2.3 million	2.9 million	1.1 million	0.1 million	0.3 million

Notes: Individuals who reported more than one race group were categorized as "two or more races." Elderly includes individuals age 65 and over. FPL—Federal Poverty Level. The FPL for a family of four in 2005 was $19,971.

Source: Key Facts: Race, Ethnicity & Medical Care, 2007 Update (#6069-02), The Henry J. Kaiser Family Foundation, January 2007, p. 6. Reprinted with permission from The Henry J. Kaiser Family Foundation. The Kaiser Family Foundation, based in Menlo Park, California, is a nonprofit, private operating foundation focusing on the major health care issues facing the nation and is not associated with Kaiser Permanente or Kaiser Industries.

report a higher prevalence of specific health problems, such as diabetes and obesity, which can have serious consequences for health and longevity. People with a family income 100 percent of the poverty level are more likely to rate their health as fair or poor compared to the near poor and nonpoor. When comparing racial/ethnic groups of similar incomes, the disparity in self-reported health is reduced but not eliminated (Kaiser Family Foundation, 2007).

Figures 2.3 and 2.4 show the percentages of people of fair or poor health status by race/ethnicity and race/ethnicity and income, respectively, in 2004.

Health Insurance Coverage

Health insurance coverage facilitates timely access to health care. People may receive health insurance coverage as a fringe benefit through their job, may be eligible for publicly financed coverage, or may purchase it on their own.

figure **People of Fair or Poor Health Status by Race/ Ethnicity, 2004**

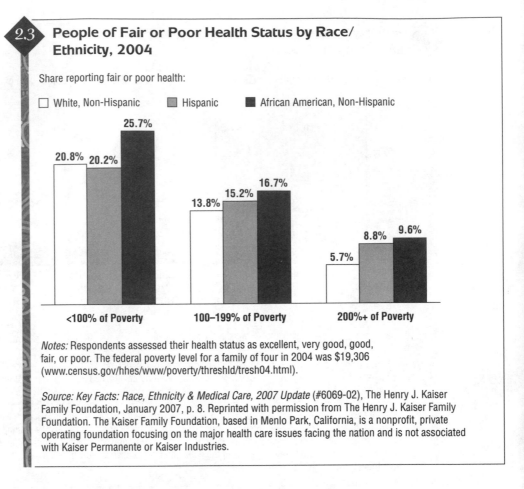

Share reporting fair or poor health:

☐ White, Non-Hispanic   ▨ Hispanic   ■ African American, Non-Hispanic

<100% of Poverty
- 20.8%
- 20.2%
- 25.7%

100–199% of Poverty
- 13.8%
- 15.2%
- 16.7%

200%+ of Poverty
- 5.7%
- 8.8%
- 9.6%

Notes: Respondents assessed their health status as excellent, very good, good, fair, or poor. The federal poverty level for a family of four in 2004 was $19,306 (www.census.gov/hhes/www/poverty/threshld/tresh04.html).

Source: Key Facts: Race, Ethnicity & Medical Care, 2007 Update (#6069-02), The Henry J. Kaiser Family Foundation, January 2007, p. 8. Reprinted with permission from The Henry J. Kaiser Family Foundation. The Kaiser Family Foundation, based in Menlo Park, California, is a nonprofit, private operating foundation focusing on the major health care issues facing the nation and is not associated with Kaiser Permanente or Kaiser Industries.

Approximately 46 million Americans—half of whom are racial/ethnic-minority Americans—have no health insurance at all. Racial and ethnic minorities are more likely than whites to be uninsured, even after accounting for work status (Kaiser Family Foundation, 2007).

Medicaid fills in the gaps for coverage for some racial and ethnic groups with lower incomes. Medicaid's role in providing coverage to racial- and ethnic-minority Americans is particularly important for children; the program's reach among adults is more limited due to program rules regarding categorical and financial eligibility.

Medicare is the federal program that provides coverage to people over 65 and to persons who are disabled under age 65, regardless of the financial means. Racial- and ethnic-minority Americans are a larger share of Medicare's under-65 disabled population than Medicare's elderly population.

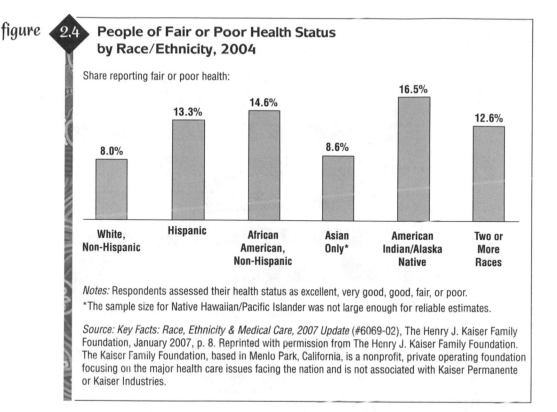

figure 2.4 **People of Fair or Poor Health Status by Race/Ethnicity, 2004**

Share reporting fair or poor health:

8.0%	13.3%	14.6%	8.6%	16.5%	12.6%
White, Non-Hispanic	Hispanic	African American, Non-Hispanic	Asian Only*	American Indian/Alaska Native	Two or More Races

Notes: Respondents assessed their health status as excellent, very good, good, fair, or poor.
*The sample size for Native Hawaiian/Pacific Islander was not large enough for reliable estimates.

Source: Key Facts: Race, Ethnicity & Medical Care, 2007 Update (#6069-02), The Henry J. Kaiser Family Foundation, January 2007, p. 8. Reprinted with permission from The Henry J. Kaiser Family Foundation. The Kaiser Family Foundation, based in Menlo Park, California, is a nonprofit, private operating foundation focusing on the major health care issues facing the nation and is not associated with Kaiser Permanente or Kaiser Industries.

Figure 2.5 shows the percentages of health insurance coverage of the nonelderly by age and race/ethnicity in 2005. Figure 2.6 shows the percentages of health insurance coverage of the nonelderly by race and ethnicity in 2005. Figure 2.7 (page 36) shows percentages of nonelderly Medicare beneficiaries by race and ethnicity in 2005.

National School Lunch Program

Another excellent indication of socioeconomic conditions among minorities is the National School Lunch Program (NSLP). Newman and Ralston (2006), writing in the U.S. Department of Agriculture bulletin, maintain that the NSLP serves more than 29 million children each day. Working with the Panel of the Survey of Income and Program Participation (SIPP), both the NSLP and SIPP suggest that the number of free-lunch recipients is about equally divided among white, African American, and Hispanic participants. The SIPP also concludes that two-thirds of participants from female-headed households receive free lunches.

figure 2.5

Health Insurance Coverage of the Nonelderly
by Age and Race/Ethnicity, 2005

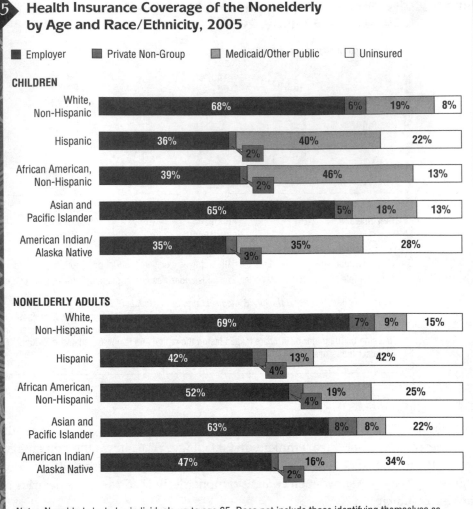

■ Employer ■ Private Non-Group ■ Medicaid/Other Public ☐ Uninsured

CHILDREN

White, Non-Hispanic: 68% | 6% | 19% | 8%

Hispanic: 36% | 2% | 40% | 22%

African American, Non-Hispanic: 39% | 2% | 46% | 13%

Asian and Pacific Islander: 65% | 5% | 18% | 13%

American Indian/ Alaska Native: 35% | 3% | 35% | 28%

NONELDERLY ADULTS

White, Non-Hispanic: 69% | 7% | 9% | 15%

Hispanic: 42% | 4% | 13% | 42%

African American, Non-Hispanic: 52% | 4% | 19% | 25%

Asian and Pacific Islander: 63% | 8% | 8% | 22%

American Indian/ Alaska Native: 47% | 2% | 16% | 34%

Notes: Nonelderly includes individuals up to age 65. Does not include those identifying themselves as "two or more races." "Other public" includes Medicare and military-related coverage; SCHIP is included in Medicaid.

Source: Key Facts: Race, Ethnicity & Medical Care, 2007 Update (#6069-02), The Henry J. Kaiser Family Foundation, January 2007, p. 15. Reprinted with permission from The Henry J. Kaiser Family Foundation. The Kaiser Family Foundation, based in Menlo Park, California, is a nonprofit, private operating foundation focusing on the major health care issues facing the nation and is not associated with Kaiser Permanente or Kaiser Industries.

figure **2.6** **Health Insurance Coverage of the Nonelderly by Race and Ethnicity, 2005**

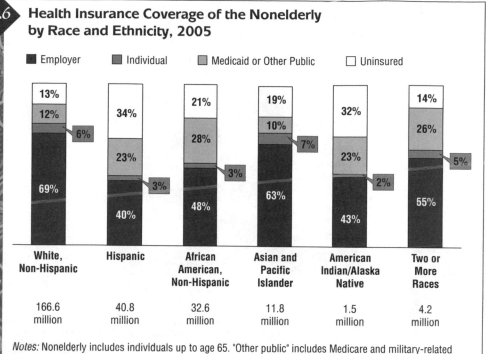

Notes: Nonelderly includes individuals up to age 65. "Other public" includes Medicare and military-related coverage; SCHIP is included in Medicaid.

Source: Key Facts: Race, Ethnicity & Medical Care, 2007 Update (#6069-02), The Henry J. Kaiser Family Foundation, January 2007, p. 14. Reprinted with permission from The Henry J. Kaiser Family Foundation. The Kaiser Family Foundation, based in Menlo Park, California, is a nonprofit, private operating foundation focusing on the major health care issues facing the nation and is not associated with Kaiser Permanente or Kaiser Industries.

Effects on Motivation, Identity, and School Achievement

What can we learn from the socioeconomic conditions of minorities? We should not blame them for having lower incomes, lower levels of health insurance, more medical problems, more numbers of free lunches, and, in some cases, lower academic achievement. Rather, we should look at the conditions that have led to these disparities and try to address each condition, whether racism, discrimination, or some other social ill. In addition, we need to look at the many Asians who have achieved tremendous success in the United States. Our conclusion is that we (individuals and the nation) should assist all people to raise their incomes, to increase their levels of health insurance, to reduce their medical problems, and to improve their educational aspirations and achievement.

Specifically, the educational difficulties of minorities result from a number of problems, but we believe many problems stem from socioeconomic problems.

figure **2.7** **Nonelderly Medicare Beneficiaries by Race and Ethnicity, 2005**

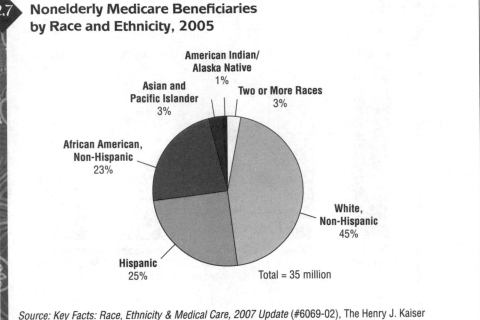

Source: Key Facts: Race, Ethnicity & Medical Care, 2007 Update (#6069-02), The Henry J. Kaiser Family Foundation, January 2007, p. 15. Reprinted with permission from The Henry J. Kaiser Family Foundation. The Kaiser Family Foundation, based in Menlo Park, California, is a nonprofit, private operating foundation focusing on the major health care issues facing the nation and is not associated with Kaiser Permanente or Kaiser Industries.

House (2005) reports that the average twelfth-grade African American student reads and does mathematics at around the level of an average eighth-grade white or Asian student. Hispanic students are close behind. Both African American and Hispanic college students earn diplomas at half the rate of white and Asian students. Inner-city schools that serve low-income minority and immigrant populations graduate fewer than half their students. In too many cases, those students who have managed to complete high school have had their academic careers badly mishandled, have been tracked into oblivion, or have been mislabeled into mediocrity (House, 2005).

Socioeconomic differences play a significant role in determining how a person acts, thinks, lives, and relates to others. Differences in values between students and educators basically represent social class differences, because many minority-group learners come from the lower socioeconomic classes. Educators coming from middle- or upper-class backgrounds may have difficulty understanding the social and economic problems facing children and adolescents from lower-socioeconomic homes. Many educators are far removed from poor people's experience of poverty, low wages, lack of property, and indeed of the most basic needs. The accompanying differences in values, attitudes, behaviors, and beliefs among the various socioeconomic groups warrant the professional's consideration.

A person's social class is sometimes thought to indicate his or her ambitions or motivation to achieve. It is a serious mistake, however, to stereotype people by social class—to assume, for example, that people from the lower classes lack ambition and do not want to work or improve their education status. It is not unreasonable to suggest that lower-class families, regardless of cultural background, want to improve their social status in life but meet with considerable frustration when faced with poverty and its accompanying conditions.

Social class differences, in some cases, may be more pronounced than differences resulting from cultural diversity. For example, lower-class African Americans may have more cultural commonalities with lower-class European Americans than they do with middle- or upper-class African Americans.

Language

Language diversity is one of the most significant challenges facing U.S. schools. The number of students who speak a language other than English has grown dramatically. Almost simultaneously, the number of English-only advocates has increased. This section looks at the number of non-English-speaking students and the challenges both they and their supporters face. Since Chapter 2 focuses mainly on diversity and related challenges, Chapter 11 will focus on English-language learners (ELLs), bilingual programs, and school models that work.

The increase in the number of students who speak a language other than English should be seen as a call for planned action. Consider these facts:

- The number of ELLs increased 72 percent between 1992 and 2002. Nearly 4 million ELLs attended K–12 schools in 2001–2002. At the same time, 357,325 of these students received some type of special-education services (Sandefur, Watson, & Johnston, 2007).
- Sixty percent of ELLs reside in five states: California, Texas, New York, Florida, and Illinois (Perkins-Gough, 2007).
- These students also represent a growing proportion in school districts that have rarely encountered them in previous years (Perkins-Gough, 2007).

The U.S. Census Bureau (2007) offers more specific information, especially on the languages students speak at home. The languages spoken at home can be a good indication of language difficulties experienced at school. The data from three large cities reveal the following:

◆ New York City has 1,695,000 students who speak English less than "very well" and 1,758,000 who speak Spanish in the home.
◆ Los Angeles has 1,111,000 students who speak English less than "very well" and 1,574,000 who speak Spanish in the home.
◆ Houston has 445,000 students who speak English less than "very well" and 674,000 who speak Spanish in the home (U.S. Census Bureau, 2007).

Denver, Fort Worth, and Phoenix also have significant numbers of students who do not speak English "very well" and who speak a language other than English at home (U.S. Census Bureau, 2007).

With these increasing numbers, one would think that additional programs are being implemented to meet the language needs of these students. In reality, quite the contrary is true. In some states, measures have been proposed to eliminate or cut back on ELL programs. In 1992, Massachusetts voters took away immigrant students' right to bilingual education (Berriz, 2006). In 1998, Proposition 227 in California's K–12 schools virtually eliminated bilingual education. Since then, ballot initiatives in Arizona and Massachusetts have created even more restrictive English immersion programs. In Colorado, backers of a failed ballot initiative are campaigning for a constitutional amendment (Hamilton & Krashen, 2006). In some cases, these challenges probably result from legitimate concerns that the United States needs to maintain its allegiance to English, from people who want educational revenue spent on programs to raise academic achievement (which sounds strange since increased language skills result in higher academic achievement), and, unfortunately, from racism, prejudice, and discrimination.

Again, parts of Chapter 11 will look at the actual instruction of ELLs, bilingual education, and English as a second language. In the meantime, readers should remember that students speaking a language other than English often experience academic difficulties, problems with socialization, and lower self-esteem.

Identity Formation

Identity formation involves questions such as Who am I? and Who am I to be? Identity is our sense of place within the world or the meaning that we attach to ourselves in the broader context of life. It is important that educators show children and adolescents that people may have several identities at once; that is, an individual might be Hispanic American, a member of any of the Spanish-speaking cultures, someone's brother, a Catholic, and an inhabitant of a specific geographic region in the United States.

The educator's first challenge is to view students as different and unique individuals rather than as a homogeneous group. Educators who assume too much homogeneity among students often fail to address individual and cultural differences and then fail to provide experiences that lead to forming positive cultural identities.

The second challenge for multicultural educators becomes clear as they understand that all individuals need to clarify personal attitudes toward their cultural and ethnic backgrounds. Educators' goals can be to teach self-acceptance, to instill in learners an acceptance and understanding of both the positive and negative attributes of their cultural groups, and to teach learners the importance of working toward social justice and an equitable environment. Students both desire and have the ability to take actions that will support and reinforce the values and norms of their ethnic, national, and global communities.

In some situations, people of differing cultural backgrounds might feel a need to forsake their identities in order to feel accepted and to experience success. Still, people of differing cultural backgrounds might not view the attitudes and behaviors of the dominant group appropriate for them. People who adopt the attitudes and behaviors of the dominant group might experience an identity crisis or an internal opposition to giving up their cultural beliefs.

To prevent students from feeling they must like any specific culture, educators need to design teaching–learning experiences in such a way that students feel they can maintain their cultural identities and still experience school success. While such a task will be difficult, educators need to demonstrate their respect for students' cultural identities, understand that students' perceptions of motivation may vary with culture, allow students to learn in the way they consider culturally relevant (i.e., working collaboratively, rather than competitively), provide curricular content and learning materials that show the contributions of

Points to Ponder 2.3

Clarifying Multiple Identities

Ask children and adolescents to consider their identities. For example, a child or an adolescent may have a number of different and changing identities, such as the following:

◆ African, Asian, European or Hispanic American or American Indian (just to mention cultures mentioned in this book)
◆ a person of the specific cultural background
◆ a member of a minority group
◆ male or female
◆ gay, lesbian, or bisexual or heterosexual
◆ a member of a particular school and grade
◆ a son, grandson, or nephew
◆ a best friend
◆ a person with disabilities

various cultural groups, and help students to feel they are accepted in the majority culture school system.

Exceptionalities

Nationwide, between 4 and 6 percent of students are classified as having a learning disability, as defined by federal statutes, while approximately 12 percent of all students have a disability of some kind (U.S. Bureau of the Census, 2007). Although each state must comply with federal mandates, the level of inclusiveness and support varies with the will of and budget of the local school district as well as the degree of parental advocacy.

There is a broad range of disabilities, such as specific learning disabilities, speech and language impairments, mental retardation, emotional disturbances, hearing disabilities, and several others covered by the Individuals with Disabilities Education Act (IDEA). We will look at the challenges in this chapter and then explore curricular and instructional strategies in Chapter 11.

Exceptional students (also referred to as *special-needs students*) include those with disabling conditions in any one or more of the following categories: mental retardation, hearing, speech or language, visual, emotional, orthopedic, autism, traumatic brain injury, other health impairment, and specific learning disabilities. To the maximum extent possible, students with special needs must be educated with their peers in the regular classroom, whether for the entire school day (full inclusion) or for part of the day (partial inclusion). General and special educators collaborate to provide instruction in the regular classroom. Providing effective instruction to special-needs students requires more attention to individual needs, better diagnosis of the child's strengths and weaknesses, and an understanding of the child's characteristics, especially those that affect instruction.

Sometimes educators are challenged to have their curricular and instructional experiences reflect the objectives stated in the student's individualized education program (IEP). With the reauthorization of the Individuals with Disabilities Education Act comes additional pressure for schools to demonstrate that all students, including students with disabilities, are meeting established learning outcomes. However, there has been some concern over both the failure to link specially designed instruction with the general education curriculum and the inadequate attention given to documenting the effectiveness of services specified on the IEP.

Among the students with exceptionalities are those who are gifted and talented. These students are sometimes neglected in the regular classrooms because there is no singular method to identify them. Gifted students can be very diverse and characterized as antisocial, creative, high achieving, divergent thinkers, or perfectionists. They can also have some special-needs characteristics, such as attention-deficit disorder, dyslexia, and other learning disorders (Kellough & Kellough, 2008). A number of developmental characteristics that apply to most other students apply to gifted students, as well, particularly rapid physical growth, varying levels of cognitive operation, sporadic brain growth, affective ambivalence, and capacity for introspection. Like all adolescents, gifted students have to deal with achieving independence, discovering identity as a person, exploring and accepting sexuality, developing meaningful interpersonal relationships, and establishing personal values and philosophies (Rosselli & Irvin, 2001).

Students who are exceptional and diverse may face even more challenges. Building an identity influenced by both exceptionality and diversity could create a feeling of double jeopardy. Also, some people in society equate language differences (e.g., speaking English as a second language or a dialect) with limited intelligence, while others equate physical exceptionalities with deficient mental abilities. Writing of white privilege and the disproportionate number of African American students in special-education classes, Blanchett (2006) notes that African American students are disproportionately referred for and placed in special classes for mental retardation, emotional and behavioral problems, and learning disabilities. Plus, African American students who make achievement gains exit special-education programs considerably less often than students of other racial and ethnic groups. Such treatment too often leads to segregation of students by race and ethnicity as well as to African American students receiving a general education or one that might be less challenging. We recommend the Blanchett (2006) article for readers who are concerned about the treatment that many African American students experience.

Challenges to Diversity

Historical perspectives reveal that the many people have been the recipients of cruel and inhumane treatment, mainly because of their differences. Just a few examples include the injustices imposed on American Indians in seizing their land and destroying their culture; the racism and discrimination in education, employment, and housing that have affected the progress of African and Hispanic Americans for centuries; and Asian Americans' cruel treatment upon immigrating to the United States. Educators have the challenge of molding a more humane and equitable society by providing responsive multicultural education programs that reduce racism, prejudice, and ethnocentrism and promote social justice, as discussed in Chapter 1.

Racism and Prejudice

Often defined as the domination of one social or ethnic group by another, *racism* is an ideological system used to justify the discrimination of some racial groups against others. Although we continue to hope for greater acceptance and recognition of cultural diversity, we must report that socioeconomic and societal inequities, racism, prejudice, and ethnocentrism continue in the United States. White privilege, discussed later in this chapter, also continues. Whether due to overt racism and discrimination or the more covert forms often found in employment and housing, many minorities continue to experience inequities and inequalities. Although overt acts of discrimination and Jim Crow attitudes are not as visible today as they were several decades ago, racial injustice continues to affect people's progress and well-being. Educators of all cultures may have to deal with problems resulting from these realities in the United States and may have to sort through their own personal biases and long-held cultural beliefs.

Racism and its negative effects have been with us for centuries, and unfortunately, little evidence suggests this evil will ever be eliminated. Educators are challenged to implement effective multicultural education programs that reduce the ignorance that breeds racism and to develop the understanding and actions people need to become antiracist. Undoubtedly, students of all cultures benefit when educators focus on reducing racial and ethnic prejudice and discrimination; teach certain humanistic values, such as the negative effects of racism, prejudice, and discrimination; provide appropriate educational experiences; and continue efforts toward realizing social justice.

White Privilege

White privilege has been described as the resulting benefits that accrue to those who have been constructed as possessing "whiteness" or who are seen as white (Manglitz, 2003). White privilege can also be defined as the belief that only white people's standards and opinions are accurate (to the exclusion of all other people's standards and opinions) and that these standards and opinions are defined and supported by whites in a way to continually reinforce social distance between groups (Hays & Chang, 2003).

Within the social science literature, there are two general perspectives about white being a racial category and associated with unequal access to resources and opportunities. One perspective equates whiteness with privilege and oppression and calls for the renunciation and abolition of the concept of whiteness. The second perspective calls for serious efforts to rearticulate whiteness into a progressive, antiracist white identity. Both perspectives share similarities

and assumptions about whiteness—namely, an awareness that all racial categories are racially constructed, fluid, and affected by changing historical, societal,
and political conditions; the recognition of the impact of interlocking oppression and privilege, including the assertion that whiteness and white privilege
are used to position others as inferior, with compelling effects on people's lives;
the importance of examining whiteness within the contexts of power and societal systems; and the need to address systemic and institutionalized racism by
creating spaces for whites to examine their identity and how it is implicated in
racism (Manglitz, 2003).

Privilege can also be considered in terms of power, access, advantage, and
majority status. Power is having control, choice, autonomy, and authority or
influence over others. Access is having money, opportunities, and/or material
possessions. Advantage is having connections, favorable treatment, entitlement,
social support, and lack of concern for others. Majority is simply being part of
the majority in number, social standing, and/or social norms. The opposite of
privilege, oppression, is the lack of privilege, power, access, and majority status
(Hays, Chang, & Dean, 2004). Blanchett (2006) writes about special education
and white privilege and concludes that white privilege can contribute to and
maintain the disproportionality in special-education results from (1) insufficient
funding of schools attended primarily by African American and poor children;
(2) offering culturally inappropriate and unresponsive curricula; and (3) inadequate training of teachers to teach African Americans and other minorities.

White guilt describes the dysphoria felt by European Americans who see
their group as responsible for illegitimate advantages held over other racial
groups. White guilt can include white people feeling good about their favored
social position. Some evidence suggests that the advantaged can experience
something akin to pride when they see themselves as superior to members of
other groups. Still, even feeling a sense of pride, these people might also feel bad
when systemic inequality illegitimately favors their group and penalizes others. For example, European Americans can feel guilty about the ways in which
racial inequality creates advantages for them and disadvantages for other groups
(Iyer, Leach, & Crosby, 2003).

Writing about the inclusion of white privilege in the social work curriculum, Abrams and Gibson (2007) recommended the inclusion of white privilege
and white identity. They maintain that white privilege is fundamental to understanding the systematic oppression of minorities and raising self-awareness
about practitioners' roles and responsibilities with culturally diverse groups
and communities. An additional benefit is that white students would have an
opportunity to explore their own racial and ethnic backgrounds. Stoesz (2007)

disagrees with Abrams and Gibson (2007) and maintains that, while it might be convenient to portray the world in dualistic terms, American society is too complex to have such categories. For example, white men earned more than any income group until they were surpassed by Asian men at the beginning of the twenty-first century.

What does all this have to do with educators developing multicultural education programs and working toward an overall sense of social justice? White educators respond to white privilege and oppression with varying levels of awareness. Depending on their level of awareness, white professionals report anger, guilt, confusion, defensiveness, sadness, and a sense of responsibility and need for advocacy when discussing these topics. Other counselors might not have such a sense of awareness. Because whiteness remains invisible to whites, they might look at racial discrimination with detachment and feel little responsibility for changing the status quo (Hays, Chang, & Dean, 2004).

Stereotypes

A *stereotype* can be defined as an attitude toward a person or group that supposedly characterizes or describes an entire group, gender, race, or religion. A stereotype produces a generalized mental picture that usually results in a judgment (negative or positive) of a person or an entire culture.

Although a stereotype might be partially valid, it is imperative that educators approach all stereotypes with skepticism and acknowledge that most result in prejudice, like or dislike, or approval or disapproval of a cultural group. Recognizing that stereotypes all too often contribute to people being beneficiaries or victims of racism, sexism, ageism, and so on, effective multicultural educators seek to understand and respond appropriately to others' and their own beliefs about people.

How can educators counter biases and stereotypes? How can teachers design multicultural education programs that respond to U.S. schools' diverse population?

1. Educators should be aware of their own biases and stereotypes.
2. Educators should expect achievement of all students, regardless of diversity.
3. Educators should examine and confront biases and stereotypes that students hold.
4. Educators should ensure that library materials and other instructional materials portray characters in a realistic, nonsexist, nonracist, nonstereotypical manner.

5. Educators should provide heterogeneous classes that allow students opportunities to build interethnic and interracial relationships with one another.
6. Educators should provide role-playing situations and simulation activities that help students gain better understanding of stereotyped groups.

Stereotypes and other generalizations that surround cultures have the potential for severely damaging interpersonal counseling and the outcomes of educational efforts. Whether one believes that all learners from different cultural backgrounds are underachievers or that all adolescents are involved in drugs and sex, stereotypes and generalizations can be detrimental to learners and educators, as well as teaching and learning relationships. For example, a teacher who bases educational decisions on the images the mass media present might conclude that all African Americans are dealing in drugs or survive only as welfare recipients. Too often, cultural stereotypes and generalizations are considered rooted in facts and become the basis for professional decisions affecting personal lives.

Points to Ponder 2.4

Clarifying Stereotypes

List several stereotypes that people might harbor about cultural groups. How do you think these stereotypes originated? Is there any objective basis for these stereotypes? How might such stereotypes affect educational decisions? List several ways educators can gain a better understanding of people, rather than rely on stereotypes.

Ethnocentrism

Ethnocentrism is the belief that one's own culture is superior to that of others. People also use ethnocentric beliefs to evaluate and judge human behavior. Persons with strong ethnocentric attitudes and beliefs may have difficulty appreciating and accepting the range of cultural differences that exist in society. Because our culture influences the way we think, feel, and act, it becomes our means of judging others and their actions. Our own ethnic background becomes the norm or the expectation for other cultures of the world. The result is that we evaluate other people by our cultural standards and beliefs, thus making it virtually impossible to view another culture as separate from our own. In essence, ethnocentrism is a universal characteristic in which one's own culture is viewed as natural, correct, and superior while others' culture is perceived as odd or inferior.

The challenge for educators in multicultural situations is to understand ethnocentrism and to realize we judge others by our own values and beliefs. For example, textbooks and other instructional materials can perpetuate ethnocentrism in subtle ways that educators may find difficult to recognize. Since we will likely accept without question a perspective consistent with our own vantage point, attitudes, and values, educators might not even be aware that another cultural perspective exists.

These educational accommodations can be made to address ethnocentrism:

◆ Instill in children and adolescents the idea that they should not consider cultural differences as right or wrong, superior or inferior.
◆ Arrange teaching and learning situations (e.g., cooperative learning and cross-age tutoring) so learners of varying cultures can have first-hand experiences with each other.
◆ Model acceptance and respect for all people.
◆ Respond appropriately to statements indicating a lack of understanding or acceptance of cultural differences.
◆ Encourage respect for all differences—cultural and ethnic, socioeconomic, sexual orientation, disabling conditions, gender, and other characteristics that contribute to diversity among individuals.

Responding appropriately to ethnocentrism is a significant challenge, because one of the primary goals of any multicultural program is to encourage and instill an acceptance of others' cultures and cultural backgrounds. First, it is crucial for educators to recognize their own ethnocentrism and its potential for clouding their objectivity. A second challenge is to convince children and adolescents that while they view their cultural beliefs as right, people from other cultures also consider their beliefs to be right. Convincing learners of the dangers of ethnocentrism and teaching them to perceive others' cultural differences and beliefs in a more positive light may be a major undertaking. In some cases, the educator may be challenging long-held beliefs that the learner's family may have taught or encouraged.

Cultural Models

Educators and other professionals need to examine their perspectives toward diversity and to determine if diversity appears as a *cultural deficit* (implying the need for change), a *cultural mismatch* (implying that learners from different cultural backgrounds fail because their traits are incompatible with schools' teaching practices), or as *culturally different* (implying that differences enrich the classroom and make individuals unique). This is more important than just an academic question; educators' perception of diversity determines their philosophical beliefs toward learners and toward their own instructional practices.

The Cultural Deficit Model

In the cultural deficit model, students who are culturally different are thought of as "deprived," "disadvantaged," and "socially deprived" only because their behavior, language, and customs are different from those the middle class values. The notion that some cultures do not seek to advance themselves because of a cultural deficit results in "blaming the victim." The individual is at fault for not being more successful (educationally, socially, etc.). The cultural deficit model has failed to address the implicit cultural biases that shape negative perceptions and inhibit the understanding of the roles of sociopolitical forces.

The Cultural Mismatch Model

In contrast to the cultural deficit model, the cultural mismatch perspective assumes that cultures are inherently different but not necessarily superior or inferior to one another. It assumes that people from culturally different backgrounds fail to achieve academically because their cultural traits do not match those of the dominant culture reflected in schools. Thus, in the mismatch model, the educational performance of diverse groups is related to the degree of incongruence between group values and traits and those of the educational system: The better the match, the greater the likelihood of academic success.

The Culturally Different Model

The culturally different model recognizes differences as strengths that are valuable and enriching to schools and to society as a whole. Its proponents believe nonetheless that all children and adolescents need to learn mainstream cultural values and knowledge. Researchers have begun to establish a research base documenting that differences in learning styles and language are not deficiencies. The differences can be a foundation to facilitate learning.

A certain degree of cultural compatibility is necessary as teachers and students become increasingly aware of each others' cultural differences, whether differences relate to school or home expectations. The situation for children and adolescents might be even more acute than for teachers, especially because learners must switch from home to school cultures and vice versa.

Points to Ponder 2.5

Determining School Opinions toward Differences

Visit an elementary or secondary school to learn about its educational philosophy, grouping practices, curricular and library materials, and extracurricular activities. Do you think the school's practices and policies indicate an acceptance of a cultural deficit, mismatch, or difference model? What are the implications of the model the school has chosen?

Case Study

Reducing Ethnocentrism

All too often, people believe that their culture and cultural traditions are correct, while those of others are wrong. Dr. Farnsworth, a high school principal, is one of these people. He either does not understand or is unwilling to accept that people from culturally diverse backgrounds have different opinions of what is important, different perceptions of immediate and extended families, and different degrees of allegiance to the elderly. Dr. Farnsworth's opinions and perceptions may have become ingrained in him early in life, and he has never considered his ethnocentrism objectively.

Educators who have these views or who teach children and adolescents with ethnocentric views should take action: First, educators must address their (and their colleagues') ethnocentrism, and second, they must seek ways to reduce ethnocentrism in their colleagues and students. Although reducing ethnocentrism is difficult, educators can use several approaches to further this goal with children and adolescents.

Questions for Discussion:

1. We must not give up on Dr. Farnsworth (and others like him). How can he be convinced of his ethnocentrism? What approach can be used to at least make him aware of his ethnocentrism and its harmful effects on others?
2. How could you design a lesson plan or unit to teach about ethnocentrism and its effects? Will such a lesson plan be most useful in the elementary, middle, or secondary school (or all three school levels)? Will you use a single-subject approach (e.g., social studies) or an interdisciplinary approach?
3. If you heard Dr. Farnsworth make an ethnocentric or derogatory comment, would you address the statement or think it might be best ignored? Why?

Summing Up

Educators who wish to plan an appropriate response to our nation's cultural diversity and to provide effective multicultural education programs should:

1. Understand the melting pot ideology and the more realistic contemporary perspectives toward cultural diversity.
2. Understand that cultural differences have value and are enriching to the United States.

3. Understand terms such as *culture, ethnicity, race, social class, gender,* and *sexual orientation.*

4. Address and stand against racism in all forms, regardless of the victim's cultural and racial backgrounds.

5. Form a perspective on culture and cultural diversity that perceives differences as positives rather than disadvantages that must be eliminated.

Suggested Learning Activities

1. Suggest several methods of helping children and adolescents develop positive individual and cultural identities. What would be your response to an educator who stated, "My work is teaching content—improving cultural identities is not my job!"

2. Give at least four examples of racist acts and offer a solution (a difficult task indeed) to each racist act. To what extent should reducing racism be a role of the school?

Implementing Research

Economic Status among Racial and Ethnic Minorities

Chong and Kim (2006) proposed and tested a theory of opportunities that explains the conditions in which economic status affects African Americans, Hispanic Americans, and Asian Americans. The study of racial politics in the United States can no longer be confined to analyzing contrasts between blacks and whites. Population changes in the last 40 years have resulted from the massive influx of immigrants from Latin America and Asia that followed the Immigration Act of 1965. Although whites still constitute a numerical majority, minority groups now wield considerable potential power in electoral politics because of their concentrated population in several parts of the country.

The socioeconomic barriers created by racial prejudice and discrimination have led scholars to question whether these most recent immigrants to the United States will follow the classic pattern of assimilation exhibited by earlier generations of European immigrants, in which ethnic identities faded as individuals were structurally assimilated into society. In some cases, socioeconomic mobility has created opportunities for equal status in workplaces and neighborhoods. In other cases, minorities have reported that economic achievement has not erased the racial and ethnic boundaries that limit opportunities. In the housing market, for example, middle-class minorities do not have access to the more desirable suburbs that are available to nonminorities with similar economic resources.

The Chong and Kim (2006) article reports on findings among and between African, Asian, and Hispanic Americans. For example, compared to Hispanic and Asian Americans, African Americans are the least responsive to changes in economic circumstances because they are, on the whole, more pessimistic about their life prospects and more likely to experience discrimination.

Implementing the Research

1. While we should understand differences among minority groups' socioeconomic achievements and challenges, it is just as important to recognize *intergroup* differences. We cannot assume that all members of a culture enjoy the same economic benefits or disadvantages. In addition, we need to understand how being poor affects the availability of housing and medical care and how it impacts identity development and motivation to succeed.

2. The Chong and Kim research provides additional evidence that some minorities continue to experience discrimination and dismal life prospects.

Source: Chong, D., & Kim, D. (2006). The experiences and effects of economic status among racial and ethnic minorities. *American Political Science Review, 100*(3), 335–351.

Suggestions for Collaborative Efforts

Form groups of three or four that, if possible, represent our nation's cultural and gender diversity. Working collaboratively, focus your group's attention on the following:

1. Survey a number of elementary, middle, or secondary schools to determine the cultural composition of the student body. What has been the school's response to meeting the needs of students' cultural differences? What efforts has the school made to teach majority cultures about minority cultures and vice versa?

2. Increasingly, gender and gender differences are important topics in multicultural education programs. Does your group feel gender should be a minor or major emphasis in multicultural education programs? Does your group feel that there is a "culture of gender" or that there is an overemphasis of gender differences? What role should educators play (or not play) in making gender an integral component of multicultural education programs?

3. How inclusive should multicultural education be? Originally, the idea prevailed that the term *multicultural education* included only culture, ethnicity, and race. Now, it has been expanded to include cultures of gender, sexual orientation, and ability/disability. How inclusive does your group think multiculturalism should be? Have scholars taken the inclusiveness idea too far? Or do we need to make multiculturalism even more inclusive?

Expanding Your Horizons

Additional Journals, Books, and Internet Sites

Abrams, L. S., & Gibson, P. (2007). Reframing multicultural education: Teaching white privilege in the social work curriculum. *Journal of Social Work Education, 43*(1), 147–160.

> These authors propose a strong emphasis on white privilege in the social work curriculum.

Crawford, J. (2007, June). A diminished vision of civil rights. *Education Week, 26*(39), 30–31.

> In this commentary, Crawford maintains that No Child Left Behind increases achievement gaps.

Information Center for Individuals with Disabilities. www.disability.net/conditions.htm

> This site provides an extensive listing of disabling conditions and specific illnesses.

Lalas, J. (2007). Teaching for social justice in multicultural urban schools: Conceptualization and classroom implication. *Multicultural Education, 14*(3), 17–21.

> Lalas maintains that although most people share opinions on social justice and supportive learning environments, many do not embrace these terms for educating students in urban school settings.

Mahoney, A. S. The Gifted Identity Formation Model. www.counselingthegifted.com/articles/insearchofID.html

> Mahoney looks at identity formation, especially as it relates to gifted learners, and suggests that family can have the most crucial influence on the development of a child's cognition.

Shin, R., Daly, B., & Vera, E. (2007). The relationships of peer norms, ethnic identity, and peer support to school engagement in urban youth. *Professional School Counseling, 10*(4), 379–388.

> These authors look at peer norms, ethnic identity, and peer support in their investigation of school success and educational resilience.

Stoesz, D. (2007). Letter to the editor. *Journal of Social Work Education, 43*(2), 347–349.

> In a response to the previous Abrams and Gibson (2007) article, Stoesz provides a new perspective on white privilege, especially in light of the financial success of some minorities.

Van Galen, J. (2007). Late to class: Social class and schooling in the new economy. *Educational Horizons, 85*(3), 156–167.

> Van Galen looks at social class during new economic times and suggests how we can transform schools to reflect new demands.

part 2

Understanding Learners and Their Cultural Backgrounds

Understanding, accepting, and respecting learners from all cultural backgrounds is of primary importance, as is providing them with culturally relevant educational experiences. Part II includes Chapters 3, 4, 5, 6, 7, and 8 and provides a portrait of children and adolescents in African, American Indian, Arab, Asian, European, and Hispanic American cultures.

Understanding African American Children and Adolescents

Understanding the material and activities in this chapter will help the reader to:

◆ Describe the cultural, gender, socioeconomic, familial, and language characteristics of African American children and adolescents.

◆ List several stereotypes of African American children and adolescents, and explain how these beliefs affect curriculum and school practices.

◆ Describe the educational achievement of African American children and adolescents, and be able to explain the importance of self-esteem to learning achievement.

◆ Understand African American English dialect as a valued cultural trait, and be able to explain its importance to achievement in school.

◆ List several points educators should remember when planning educational experiences for African American children and adolescents.

◆ Incorporate practical activities and suggest appropriate children's literature for situations involving African American learners (see the Appendix).

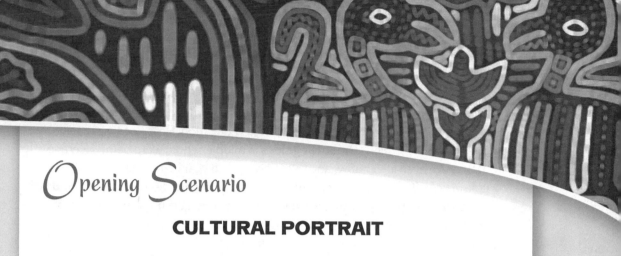

Opening Scenario

CULTURAL PORTRAIT

Paul: An African American Learner

Paul J., a sixteen-year-old African American learner, lives with his mother, father, grandmother, one older brother, and two older sisters in a lower-middle-class neighborhood in a large city. Several aunts and uncles and six cousins also live in the immediate neighborhood. William, Paul's father, has completed eleven years of schooling and works in a local manufacturing plant. His mother, Sheila, has had a similar education. She works as a hospital aide.

Paul attends a large urban school, which is approximately 50 percent African American, 30 percent European American, and 20 percent Hispanic American. He is a low achiever and speaks a dialect of English. Paul's neighborhood is pre-dominantly African American, although several Puerto Rican and Cuban families have recently rented houses in the area. Paul already realizes that people of different ethnic backgrounds have different customs and lifestyles.

Paul's teachers are predominantly middle-class African Americans, but he also has Mrs. Smith, a teacher who is middle class and European American. Although Paul tries hard in school, his achievement scores and performance place him below average. His teachers assume that his problems stem from a poor home environment, and they blame Paul and his parents for his difficulties. Although his dialect works well with his parents and in his neighborhood, it is not viewed favorably at school. Sometimes, he does not understand his teachers or the class materials. Mrs. Smith frequently corrects Paul's speech because, she says, students will need to use correct English when they enter the real world.

Paul has experienced several identity crises. He has questioned his success in developing from childhood to adulthood, and he has also questioned the signifi-cance of being African American in a predominantly European American society. Although he has learned much about his cultural heritage and is proud to be African American, he also realizes the harmful effects of racism and discrimination. Also, being an adolescent has not been easy. Even though Paul's parents and siblings view him as not yet grown, his peers think he is ready for adult activities. Should he listen to his family, or should he go along with his friends?

Another problem confronting Paul is his education. He is not sure that he will graduate from high school. His grades in middle school were below average, but they are even lower now, and this is his second year in the ninth grade. Paul thinks he can do the work, but his recent academic record discourages him and he admits to having many outside interests. He does not have many behavior problems in school (except perhaps talking with his friends too much at times), but he thinks his teachers are not too interested in him. Also, although he has both African American and European American teachers, he doubts whether any of them really understand what it is like being an African American adolescent in a large urban school. His parents talk with him often about the importance of education and encourage him to do his best work.

When speaking of Paul's lower academic achievement, Mrs. Smith, one of his teachers, feels he does not listen. She says, "I have tried to get him to look at me, but he looks away when I talk to him." Paul claims he is listening, even though he does not look directly at Mrs. Smith as she speaks. Regarding his language, Paul knows Mrs. Smith does not approve of his dialect, but his language works fine at home and with his friends, so he doesn't see any need to change.

Paul feels he is in a bind: He tries to make higher grades, but he just can't seem to do it. He sees himself in the middle. Some African American students make better grades than he does, and others make worse grades. Paul feels the frustration of coping in a school that appears to cater to white students and to expect African Americans to conform to European American expectations.

Although Paul has not confided in his friends, he has several concerns: What will he do if he cannot improve his grades? If his teachers insist that he speak a more standard form of English, will he be able to maintain his cultural heritage? Will he be able to accommodate his parents' insistence on academic achievement, his own motivation, and the expectations of his peers? Sometimes, Paul actually wishes that the adolescent years would end so that he could begin his adult life. ◆

Overview

A responsive multicultural curriculum recognizes the cultural diversity of African American children and adolescents and provides appropriate educational experiences based on an understanding of both the individual and the culture. The culture of African American children and adolescents as well as socioeconomic class, family, and language play significant roles and interact in a complex fashion to create unique learners with individual strengths and needs. Providing appropriate teaching and learning experiences for African American learners requires an understanding of the individual's development, achievement level, and self-esteem. This chapter examines African American children and adolescents and explores educational issues germane to them as learners.

Origins

African American people have lived in the United States for many centuries. Arriving in North America either as explorers or as slaves, African American people have experienced a long history of struggle. The first Africans in the Americas were explorers: Columbus's last voyage to the Americas included an African man, Balboa's crew brought an African man, and an African explored the territory that is now Kansas with Coronado. Africans were among the first non-native settlers. African people were part of the ill-fated South Carolina colony, San Miguel de Guadalupe, in 1526, and African people helped to establish Saint Augustine, Florida, in 1665.

One important distinction deserves understanding: Many multicultural groups elected to immigrate to the United States in hopes of improving their lives, to seek religious freedom, or to get away from oppressive conditions or war-torn areas. Most Africans, on the other hand, were transported against their will to a foreign land and forced to work and live in cruel and inhumane conditions.

African Americans Today

The latest annual population estimates indicate that African Americans total nearly 40 million. Most African Americans live in metropolitan areas, but the number of suburban African Americans today stands at about 7 percent of the U.S. suburban population. Educators in city schools work with significant numbers of African Americans, but educators in suburban schools will increasingly work with African Americans as more and more move away from the inner city.

Decades after the civil rights movement forced the United States to confront racial inequities, disturbing disparities remain on one of the most basic human levels: Blacks get sick more easily, stay sick longer, and die sooner than whites. From birth, a black baby's life expectancy is six and one-half years shorter than a white baby's. Blacks are more likely to be born weighing too little and less likely to survive their first year. Blacks face a higher risk of asthma, hypertension, and cancer. They are nearly twice as likely as whites to die of a stroke, more likely to die of heart disease, and they face a higher cancer rate than whites.

Blacks are more than twice as likely to be without health insurance. People cite many reasons for blacks' health predicament: Blacks face extra stresses, blacks have an unhealthy diet (it can be difficult to find fresh vegetables and produce in many inner-city grocery stores), and blacks often mistrust doctors and other health care providers.

African Americans have not shared equally in the nation's prosperity. They earn less than whites, and they possess far less wealth. The black-to-white median income ratio has hovered in the mid-50 to mid-60 percent range for the past twenty years. Fluctuations have been minor. In some respects, Americans have grown accustomed to this benchmark of inequality or are not sure how to correct the problem.

Stereotyping of African American Children and Adolescents

To be a child or adolescent as well as an African American in a predominantly European American society is to bear a double stigma. Stereotyping has produced negative images of the African American culture and its young people. Youth is the time of identity formation; for this reason, it is especially important that everyone objectively accept social, cultural, and age differences among young people. Young African Americans need fair opportunities to develop identities appropriate for their culture and age. Categorizing African American young people as language deficient because they speak dialectical English or as low achievers with behavior problems negates diversity and individual differences.

Educators must take a closer and more objective look at the child and the adolescent in the African American culture to improve their understanding of the learner and the world in which she or he lives. Such knowledge and understanding give educators an objective and sound foundation for a multicultural curriculum.

As you recall from A Note of Caution at the beginning of Chapter 2, we must always consider the *individual* child or adolescent. Chapter 3 makes the same point. As we look at African American children and adolescents, we have a professional obligation to consider the individual. As you consider cultural characteristics, gender, socioeconomic status, and other differences, remember that cultural and intracultural differences exist. We cannot speak of a typical African

American any more than we can discuss a typical Asian American or Hispanic American. Generalizing about the African American culture requires extreme caution and avoidance of stereotypes. The opening Cultural Portrait described Paul, an African American adolescent. Paul, like all other students, is unique and deserves to be considered as an individual.

Cultural Characteristics

African American children and adolescents are considerably diverse. Differences exist between lower, middle, and higher socioeconomic groups; between younger and older generations; between African Americans residing in the various geographic locations of the United States; and between urban and rural African Americans. An educator who understands this diversity among African American children and adolescents can make a valuable contribution to the multicultural curriculum and base choices on objective and factual information.

African American children daily face two cultures: the African American culture of the home and neighborhood and the cultures of schools and other social institutions. African American children and children from other cultures need opportunities to learn about one another's cultures and to understand that *different* does not imply *wrong*.

Education has focused for many years solely on historical and contemporary whites. Educators sometimes justifiably complain that their education did not provide them with examples of the contributions of African Americans. During the past several decades, attempts to instill pride and a better understanding of the African American culture have given rise to learning materials that emphasize the many positive aspects and leaders of the culture.

Although educators should make cultural generalizations cautiously, African Americans *tend* to have large families and respect for immediate and extended families. They also *tend* to have a non-verbal communication style that differs from that of the European American culture. (For example, an African American feels comfortable interrupting a speaker to show support and does not find it necessary to look the speaker in the eye.) African American children are generally highly expressive emotionally, assertive, and verbal in dealings with peers and adults. African American children and adolescents are taught respect for the elderly, kinship and extended family bonds, and

> **Points to Ponder 3.1**
>
> **Identifying Cultural Differences**
>
> Make a list of the cultural differences of African Americans. Then, keeping in mind the characteristics you listed, make another list of social class differences. How are the two alike and different? Are the social class differences more alike or different?

authoritarian child-rearing practices. Once again, we remind readers that individuals within a culture differ and that cultural characteristics vary with socioeconomic status and geographic region.

A difficult situation exists when African Americans want to retain their cultural heritage, the culture of their ancestors, and the culture with which they can relate and feel comfortable. Some African Americans, however, may also feel that some acculturation with the European Americans is necessary for economic and psychological survival. It is important to attain a middle ground on which African American adolescents can not only retain their African heritage but also feel successful in contemporary society.

Gender

The recent emphasis on gender differences and gender-appropriate education suggests educators should consider African American females and males from different perspectives. Undoubtedly, educators need to consider females' different learning styles, perceptions of motivation, and ways of responding to educators' efforts. Females, however, may need to give special attention to socially acceptable behaviors such as modulating their voices, proper grooming, and developing assertive demeanors. Such a proposal does not suggest that African American males (as well as males from other cultures) do not need educational experiences in similar areas; when addressing these points, however, educators need to consider the female perspective.

Teachers also should consider gender differences when planning actual educational experiences for African American females. For example, African American females might learn better through cooperative efforts rather than in competitive atmospheres. Also, they might benefit more from behavior management systems promoting positive consequences rather than negative ones. Positive environments also contribute to African American females' academic achievement and social development.

Mitchell, Bush, and Bush (2002) maintain that the plight of African American males calls for alternative schools to address their specific needs.

Points to Ponder 3.2

Helping African American Urban Males

Design a strategy to help African American urban boys in either elementary or secondary school. First, decide on a method of determining their needs (either a case study, some diagnostic device, interviews, or observation); second, select instructional methods that reflect their learning styles; third, select curricular materials to which they can relate; fourth, select culturally appropriate assessment devices; and fifth, decide what other guidance or advising topics might address their needs. In addition to these five approaches, what else might you suggest to help African American urban boys?

They offer disturbing statistics about African American males: The leading cause of death for black males between the ages of fifteen and twenty-four is homicide; one in twenty black males is in federal or state prison; black males' unemployment rate is sometimes twice that of white males; and African American males have higher suspension, expulsion, retention, and dropout rates and dramatically lower grade-point averages (Mitchell et al., 2002).

As early as 1790, Africans in the United States created alternative ways to school themselves. Reasons included lack of access to public schools, a threat of miseducation, and a belief that they were responsible for their own education. More recent impetuses to the independent schooling tradition and the black studies movement of the 1960s and 1970s included the black power, civil rights, and pan-American movements. The result has been an emergence of schools designed to focus on African American students, such as African-centered public schools, African American immersion academics, and black male academies (Mitchell et al., 2002).

The National Urban League (2007) calls for greater experimentation with all-male schools, longer school days, and mentoring. All-male schools, such as the Eagle Academy and Enterprise School in the New York City area, combined with mentoring and longer school days, help keep young boys focused on education and away from distractions that might lead to trouble. Mitchell et al. (2002) also recommend alternative schools for African American males. Such schools emphasize academic achievement, study skills development, cultural enrichment activities, counseling and mentorships, parent-education workshops, and sports-related activities to promote healthy development and adult mentors.

Gender Perspectives 3.1 in this chapter looks at African American males and programs to develop their leadership ability.

Socioeconomic Status

Six factors are used to determine socioeconomic status: income, wealth, occupation, education, prestige, and power (Gollnick & Chinn, 2006). The discrimination African American people experience has resulted in a lack of educational and employment opportunities and has prohibited significant social mobility. Because they have long been deprived of equal opportunities and the chance to improve themselves educationally and economically, African American people are disproportionately represented in the lower socioeconomic classes.

Socioeconomic status (SES) continues to be a powerful indicator of academic success for American children. Children from higher SES backgrounds score higher on standardized achievement tests, are more likely to finish high

Gender Perspectives 3.1

AFRICAN AMERICAN MALES

Bonner and Jennings (2007) discuss the research that documents African American males' underrepresentation and underachievement in U.S. schools. The authors maintain that African American males have been disproportionately placed in special-education classes and underrepresented in gifted classes. Presently, African American students are underrepresented in gifted classes in as many as half of U.S. schools.

Bonner and Jennings look at various definitions of *giftedness* and how the term has changed over the decades. Then, they offer comments specifically on gifted African American males and suggest that educators should start leadership programs. The authors discuss the RITES program, which is designed specifically for young African American males. They also briefly discuss the efforts of the Boy Scouts, 100 Black Men of America, Concerned Black Men, and other organizations. While these organizations have done some fine work, unfortunately, they too often work in isolation.

Bonner and Jennings make several recommendations:

◆ Involve civic, clergy-based, community, and historically black Greek letter organizations in the planning process when designing curriculum emphasizing leadership ability.

◆ Infuse "authentic" experiences into leadership ability curriculum and training opportunities.

◆ Create a more seamless connection between youth leadership behavior and adult leadership performance.

◆ Refrain from treating African American males as a monolithic group.

◆ Establish clear criteria in how leadership ability is to be used in the evaluation of giftedness.

Source: Bonner, F. A., & Jennings, M. (2007). Never too young to lead: Gifted African American males in elementary school. *Gifted Child Today, 30*(2), 30–36.

school, and are more likely to attend college and do postgraduate work than their less advantaged peers. Because poor children are less likely to pursue higher education, it is difficult to break them out of the cycle of poverty. The relationship between poverty and academic achievement is complicated by ethnicity; a disproportionate number of the poor are members of ethnic-minority groups.

The State of Black America 2007, published by the National Urban League (2007), reports a grim economic picture for many African Americans. Their economic status—based on annual median income, employment issues, poverty, housing and wealth information, and transportation—increased only slightly to 57 percent in 2007, up from 56 percent in 2006. (We want to note that the National Urban League uses the term *black* in its publications. We chose to use the term *African American* to maintain consistency in this textbook and because we think the latter is far more descriptive.)

In terms of annual median income, African American men earned less than three-quarters of what white men earned ($33,443 versus $46,807), roughly a $12,000 gap. African American women made 87 percent of what white women made and $5,000 less than African American men ($29,588 per year). Unemployment was highest among African American men: 9.5 percent compared to 4.0 percent of white men, a 5.5 percent gap. African American women had an unemployment rate of 8.5 percent, 4.4 percent above the 4.1 percent of their white counterparts (National Urban League, 2007).

Among people under the age of twenty-five, a higher percentage of whites are in the workforce, compared to African Americans. Among whites between the ages of twenty and twenty-four, 76.5 percent are employed compared to 68.7 percent of African Americans. However, with increasing age and education, African Americans are more likely than whites to be employed. For example, for African Americans over twenty-five years who have less than a high school diploma, only 40 percent are part of the workforce, compared to 47 percent of whites. That rate rises to 82.1 percent when African Americans have college degrees, which is 5 percent above the 77.5 percent participation of their white counterparts (National Urban League, 2007).

Poverty, much like unemployment, also tends to affect African Americans at a higher rate than whites, especially those under eighteen. Nearly 25 percent live below the poverty line, three times the percentage of whites. Of African Americans under eighteen, 33.5 percent live in poverty compared to 10 percent of white youths. Similarly, home ownership among African Americans is substantially lower than among whites (47.9 percent compared to 75.8 percent) and African Americans are more likely to get high-priced mortgage loans (54.7 percent of African American versus 17.2 percent of whites) (National Urban League, 2007).

Regardless of these facts, there are many African American success stories. Many disadvantaged parents—of minority as well as majority cultural groups— are successful in translating their high academic aspirations for their children into reality. Along this line of thinking, it should be noted that although economic hardship and social discrimination provide difficult obstacles to overcome, parents' behaviors, beliefs, attitudes, and goals may circumvent the detrimental effects of poverty.

When working with African American learners, elementary and secondary educators should understand the following:

1. the effects of being a member of a lower socioeconomic group
2. that children from lower socioeconomic groups might not understand words like *physician, lavatory, wraps,* and *pens* (*pens* for writing versus *pens* for confining animals)
3. that language differences are "differences"—not "deficits"
4. the need to work first on concrete learning and then move on to abstract learning
5. the need to provide positive reinforcement during the learning process, rather than expect learners to stay motivated by focusing on some faraway goal
6. the need to involve parents and extended families in the learning process
7. each learner's individual strengths and needs and how to plan teaching and learning experiences that always challenge and instruct

Today, African Americans have more equality of opportunity, better access to education, and more equitable salaries. Through civil rights legislation, affirmative action programs, and equal employment opportunity, African Americans are able to obtain an education and seek employment. We hope such gains will result in improved conditions for children. The problem of poverty, however, continues for many people and requires the attention of government, school, and other organizations concerned with the welfare of children.

Families

Educators who work with African American learners need a historical understanding of and perspective on the African American family. To gain such knowledge might prove difficult, because U.S. scholarship has mistreated, ignored, and distorted the African American family. Often, the misconceptions of majority-culture educators may cause them to question African American cultural traditions. Throughout centuries of cultural oppression and repression, for example, African Americans have developed, perhaps as much through necessity as choice, a network of "significant others" who have close ties to and are willing to assist the individual family. Understanding and accepting this African American family tradition continues to be a prerequisite for educators to help students make effective educational decisions.

Many African American children grow up in homes that are very different from the homes of children and adolescents from other cultures. Minority extended families function on the principles of interdependence and an extensive reliance on networks of people, including blood relatives and close friends called *kinsmen.* A young African American child might be taken into the household of elderly grandparents. In such arrangements, children have a sense they belong to an extended family clan, not merely to their parents. Uncles, aunts, cousins, and grandparents have considerable power within the family unit and may take responsibility for the care and rearing of children and for teaching appropriate skills and values.

Religion

Religion is a powerful aspect of the African American family orientation that has almost never had empirical documentation. Rather than study the church and religion in relation to children, writers usually focus attention on the role of religion in the civil rights movement, economic leadership, and the quest for equal opportunity. Children, however, undoubtedly perceive the African American church as a socializing and peer-group institution, a hub of social life, and a means to aspire to community leadership. Rather than simply a Sunday-morning experience, church membership for children is an integral aspect of African American family life (Hale-Benson, 1986).

The most rapidly growing religion in the United States is Islam. In 1960, there were no mosques in this country; in 1998, there were over 1,000. Muslims are a rapidly increasing part of the American religious scene. The United States needs to appreciate the gifts—their culture, their music, their food, and their philosophy—they bring to U.S. society. It is in the schools that people first start adapting to Muslim cultures and Muslims begin adapting to other U.S. cultures (Hodgkinson, 1998).

Language

The language of African American children is a function of their culture and plays a significant role in their cultural identity, school achievement, and social and psychological development. Although the child may not experience communication difficulties at home or in the neighborhood, language differences may cause problems when significant variations exist between home and neighborhood and school languages. Children's language skills are crucial in their education, and much of what educators measure as intelligence and achievement is actually skill in language and communication (Hale-Benson, 1986).

Aspects of African American oral tradition are observable in African American student behavior. In telling stories, African Americans render abstract observations about life, love, and people in the form of concrete narrative sequences that may seem to meander from the point and to take on an episodic framework. In African American communication styles, we often find overt demonstration of sympathetic involvement through movement and sounds; a prescribed method for how performer and audience react; total involvement of the participants; the tendency to personalize by incorporating personal pronouns and references to self (African American students tend to use first-person singular pronouns to focus attention on themselves); and the use of active verbs coupled with adjectives and adverbs with potential for intensification (called *features of elongation* and *variable stress*). Prosodic structure of speech often reflects the way information is organized for presentation. All of these observable aspects of the African American communication style provide leads for teaching innovations (Anokye, 1997).

Educators can benefit from objective and reliable information about African American language. Although the child may not experience difficulty at home or in the neighborhood, language differences may cause problems when the child gets to school. The dilemma for African American children is that their language, which is worthy at home, may be different and unworthy in school.

Considerable diversity exists in the degree to which children speak an English dialect. Dialect use varies with socioeconomic status, geographic location, and the acculturation of the child and the parents. Children of educated and socially mobile urban African American parents may not speak the dialect of rural and less fortunate parents. African American English is used in varying degrees depending on the individual and the situation.

African Americans have developed effective nonverbal communication that other cultures may question. For example, African American children may learn early that active listening does not always require looking the speaker in the eye. Neither is it necessary to nod one's head or make little noises to show that one is listening.

The language of African American children, albeit an excellent means of communication in the African American culture, may result in communication difficulties and other problems generally associated with not being understood outside one's social community. Furthermore, children who hear negative statements about their language and who are urged to change to a more standard form of English will undoubtedly have a lower self-esteem and opinion of cultural backgrounds.

The grammatical structure of African American speech patterns frequently leads listeners to conclude that a genuine structural pattern does not exist. Linguists acquainted with the various vernaculars of African American English realize the fallacy of such thinking. African American speakers who say "Carl hat" and "she book" might have knowledge of possessives in grammar like the speaker who says "Mary's hat" and "his book."

Achievement Levels

Objectivity is fundamental in considering the African American child's achievement. There is no room for stereotypes of achievement expectations. Still, the National Urban League (2007) reports some disturbing (but improving) levels of academic achievement. The educational status of African Americans (quality, attainment, scores, enrollment, and risk factors) improved slightly in 2007 to 79 percent of that of whites, up from 78 percent in 2006. Early in life, African American children excel until the middle grades and high school years, when their achievement falls off significantly. More than two-thirds of young African American children are enrolled in early childhood education programs such as Head Start, compared to slightly more than 64 percent of white children. African American children have also improved in the area of school readiness, scoring at 94 percent the rate of whites, up from 81 percent in 2006. They have even surpassed or nearly matched white children in terms of some home literacy activities: 81 percent are taught words or numbers three times a week, compared to 76 percent of whites, and 54 percent are read a story once a week, compared to 56 percent of whites (National Urban League, 2007).

A major disconnect begins to occur after elementary school as African American students, especially males, begin to fall behind or drop out completely. The disparities in writing proficiency scores widen as African Americans grow older. At the fourth grade, they score 87 percent of the proficiency of whites, a 13 percent deficit. By the time they get to the twelfth grade, the gap doubles to 26 percent with African Americans scoring 74 percent of the level of whites. By the time they are in their teens, African Americans are more likely to have dropped out of high school than white students—15 percent compared to 12 percent for whites. For African American males, the percentage rises to 18 percent, compared to 14 percent of white males (National Urban League, 2007).

The reasons for the widening achievement gap between African American and white students are likely related to differences in teacher quality and educational spending. Twenty-one percent of teachers in predominantly African American districts have had less than three years' teaching experience, compared to 10 percent in predominantly white districts. Also, in predominantly African American districts, 49 percent of teachers in the middle grades teach subjects outside their college major or minor, compared to 41 percent of middle grade teachers in mostly white districts. Moreover, the spending per African American student was only 82 percent of that per white student (National Urban League, 2007).

Selected instructional strategies for African Americans include these:

◆ Validating the African American culture and worldview, moving away from a cultural deficit model and supporting a sense of social justice

◆ Showing appreciation for the African American dialect and for its tradition of oral discourse

◆ Showing children and adolescents the value of African Americans' informal language interactions and writings

◆ Instilling a sense of trust, community, and social justice among students and teachers

◆ Using group projects that demonstrate an appreciation for collaborative efforts

◆ Fostering a school and class climate of cooperation, collaboration, empathy, and social consciousness

African American children's lower performance in the academic areas may be evidence of blaming the victims instead of examining the underlying causes of the problem. On national assessments in reading, writing, mathematics, and science, African American students' performance continues to lag behind that of white students, with uneven progress in closing the gap. Several possible reasons exist for this gap, ranging from increased family and community stresses (e.g., poverty, poor health, family difficulties, and community violence) to lower rates of in-school and out-of-school reading among learners and the declining quality of urban areas where most African American students attend school. Another possibility is that the curriculum in inner-city schools is outdated, inadequate to meet the demands of new curricula experiences and assessment.

Despite the rhetoric of equality and efforts of many involved in school desegregation and finance reform, problems continue to plague schools attended by many African Americans. Some African Americans have school experiences substantially separate from and unequal to those of other groups; the physical condition of many schools is poorer; and shortages of funds make it more difficult for rural and urban schools to employ qualified teachers and to provide the equipment that students need.

Although statistics reveal lower academic achievement among African Americans, it is important to understand the situation in its historical perspective. For years, many African Americans attended segregated schools in which instruction and materials were often substandard. Substantial progress has been made toward the provision of educational resources to African Americans, but educational opportunities are still not always equal.

African American learners face a brighter and more optimistic future. First, African Americans now receive more equitable educational opportunities. Second, more opportunities in employment, education, and housing will allow their families an improved standard of living. Third, educators are better trained in diagnostic and remediation approaches and individualized education. Fourth, educators are translating the research on effective teaching, which has grown considerably during the past twenty years, into practical application.

Here are some suggestions for working with elementary and secondary learners:

1. Get to know individual children and their strengths and weaknesses. Hold high expectations for *all* your students.
2. Disregard stereotypes about African American behavior and academic achievement.
3. Administer interest inventories to determine needs and areas in which instruction might be most effective.
4. Administer culturally appropriate diagnostic tests to determine which areas require remediation.
5. Work to convince learners that they can learn and achieve.
6. Work to improve learners' attitudes about the African American culture.
7. Teach, evaluate, and reteach basic skills.

CampbellJones and CampbellJones (2002) explain that African Americans often feel "a crisis of credibility" (p. 133) due to many broken promises. African American children continue to face teachers with low expectations and schools where covert discrimination is common. In school, more than any other place in society, African American children are socialized that their culture is unimportant. This often results in African American children disidentifying with school—for example, not participating in school activities and academics and eventually dropping out of school.

CampbellJones and CampbellJones (2002) encourage teachers to engage in self-reflection in

Points to Ponder 3.3

Instructional Strategies for African Americans

Consider the instructional strategies just mentioned for African Americans. What other methods do you suggest for developing a sense of trust, community, and social justice? How can we develop classes and schools that do not reflect the cultural deficit model? This effort should not be a matter of improving self-esteem; it should be an effort to change the mindsets of both students and teachers.

order to improve their teaching. Teachers often face the intense challenge of reflecting on behavior, feelings, and attitudes that affect their perceptions of others. Such reflection is one of the best ways to gain a better understanding of oneself and others.

CampbellJones and CampbellJones (2002) offer several strategies to improve teaching practices and create a more credible education system for African American students:

- ◆ Videotape instruction for critical analysis of teacher interaction with African American students—for example, look for wait times, expectations, and opportunities for higher-level thought.
- ◆ Visit the homes of African American students to establish relationships and to become knowledgeable about their lives.
- ◆ Use parents as resources to learn about their children, and use their expertise to provide a culturally relevant curriculum.
- ◆ Consider classroom materials to ensure that students are honored with literature that reflects positively on their culture.
- ◆ Facilitate learning by increasing variety, space, and opportunity for social interaction and movement.
- ◆ Build on the students' use of dialect in the classroom as a means of teaching language flexibility.

School Practices Promoting African Americans' Progress

Educators sometimes develop and implement curricula that either overlook or ignore cultural diversity. African American learners may find themselves in a world of unfamiliar rules, expectations, and orientations. Rather than recognize cultural diversity and teach learners as individuals, educators often treat learners as groups with homogeneous characteristics.

Conversely, school practices should promote learning achievement and appropriate behavior such as the following:

1. Understanding African American learners and expecting all learners to conform to specific standards and expectations
2. Grouping by heterogeneous ability, which does not result in the segregation of learners by culture and by social class
3. Providing sufficient and appropriate positive reinforcement

4. Understanding learners who speak English dialects
5. Basing academic and behavior standards and expectations on objective expectations

Howard (2001) maintains that research examining African Americans' perceptions and interpretations of learning environments has been minimal. In his article, the author explains the findings from a study that sought to assess African American elementary students' interpretations of culturally relevant teachers in urban contexts. Student responses indicated that culturally relevant teaching strategies had a positive affect on student effort and engagement in class content and were consistent with culturally relevant pedagogy. The students' perceptions and interpretations of their teachers' pedagogy reveal critical insights into the dynamics of young African American learners.

School practices related to the assessment of children and adolescents are another area that can impede African American learners' progress. Assessment devices designed primarily for middle-class learners do not always provide an accurate assessment of African American learners.

Promoting Cultural Identities

Several studies have sought to ascertain the effects of minority group status on personality development during identity formation. These studies provide concrete evidence for long-held opinions that the society and the culture in which African Americans live adversely affect their personality development and educational achievement.

The African American child or adolescent's self-perception influences not only his or her academic achievement but also many other social and psychological aspects of development. Distinctive aspects affecting self-esteem include children's perception of themselves, how others perceive them to be, and how they perceive others. Historically, African Americans have experienced much to lower their self-esteem, but civil rights efforts and recent decades of progress have helped raise it.

The identity formation of the African American adolescent has been a source of considerable concern, especially in poverty-ridden households and single-parent homes. New evidence, however, indicates that this concern may be ill founded, that the African American adolescent might not be as detrimentally affected as once believed. Specifically, single mothers do not usually perceive their families as "broken," because fathers and the extended family and kinship network continue to play a role in their lives. The physical presence or absence of adult males in the home says little about the availability of other male models. Adolescent males living in single-parent households often identify male role models in their neighborhoods and classrooms and even in instruction from their mothers (Bell-Scott & McKenry, 1986).

Suggestions for educators working with African American children and adolescents include the following:

1. Be open and honest in relationships with African American children.
2. Seek to respect and appreciate culturally different attitudes and behaviors.
3. Take advantage of all available opportunities to participate in activities in the African American community.
4. Keep in mind that African American children are members of their unique cultural group and are unique individuals as well.
5. Implement practices that acknowledge the African American culture.
6. Hold high expectations of African American children, and encourage all who work with African American children to do likewise.
7. Develop culture-specific strategies, mechanisms, techniques, and programs to foster the psychological development of African American children.

Gay African American youths (ages 14–19) have a unique set of stressful life events, low self-esteem, emotional distress, and multiple problem behaviors (alcohol use, drug use, and risky sexual behavior). Admitting their sexual orientation or having it discovered by others can expose a gay or lesbian to ridicule. Gay and lesbian youths cannot anticipate how others may respond to knowledge of their sexual identity. Stressful events related to being gay or lesbian have been shown to cause significant emotional distress and multiple problem behaviors.

Case Study

Responding to Parents' Demands

A vocal group of African American parents presents to the school board a list of demands for improving the school. They feel that the education their children are receiving does not meet the needs of African Americans. Two of their demands are to create all-male African American classes and to have African American male teachers for kindergarten through grade 3. Concerns also include the high rate of special-education placements of African American students.

Clearly, some action is necessary to change the attitudes of these parents toward the schools and to create schools that better meet the needs of African American learners. Failing to listen and respond appropriately to the parents' concerns will only result in frustration for the parents, school officials, and children attending the schools.

Recall from the Gender section of this chapter that the National Urban League (2007) has also recommended separate schools for African American females and males. Another concern focuses on students like Paul in the opening scenario—African American males who do not seem to fit in the public school system. Also, as we look at this Case Study, we should recall Bonner and Jennings's (2007) concern that African American boys are too often placed in special-education classes yet underrepresented in gifted classes.

Questions for Discussion:

1. As a school board member, how would you respond to the parents' concerns? If you intend to give them what they want, then what will you do will another cultural group wants gender-specific and cultural-specific classes (which can lead to segregation)? If you cannot give them what they want, how will you somehow compromise to help the students and their parents?
2. What do you think about all-male and all-female schools? What are the advantages and disadvantages? What would be the likely effects on academic achievement and social development?
3. Why do you think African Americans are overrepresented in special-education classes and underrepresented in gifted classes? Think beyond the cultural deficit model and consider social justice (discussed in Chapter 1). Is this a violation of social justice? How can we resolve these placement problems and promote social justice?

Summing Up

Educators planning a culturally responsive curriculum and school environment for African American learners should:

1. Understand the African American culture and its people from both historical and contemporary perspectives.

2. Understand the close correlation between socioeconomic status and academic achievement among African American learners (and learners of other cultures).

3. Address the dilemma of African American English, which needs understanding and appropriate action: African Americans understand one another in home and community situations, yet they sometimes experience difficulty in school and teaching and learning situations. Remember that *different* does not equate with *wrong* or *inferior.*

4. Promote cultural identities that are crucial to African American learners' academic achievement, psychosocial development, and general outlook on life.

5. Consider and address African American students' learning styles when planning teaching and learning experiences.

6. Consider intracultural, geographic, socioeconomic, urban and rural, and other differences that result in individuality, rather than categorizing all African American learners as a homogeneous group.

7. Understand several factors (appropriate diagnostic and remediation procedures, improving self-esteem, basic skills instruction) that have the potential for improving African American academic achievement.

8. Adhere to the commitment that educators should not stereotype African American learners or label them as slow learners. Educators also must not group learners in organization patterns that result in segregation by either culture or social class.

Suggested Learning Activities

1. Complete a case study of two African American learners, each from a different social class—for example, one from a lower class and one from a higher social class. Compare and contrast differences in culture, language, familial traditions, food, and life expectations.

2. The family, both immediate and extended, is a valued aspect of the African American culture. How can educators use this resource? What can educators do to involve African American families? What special concerns should educators keep in mind during parent conferences?

3. Consider the following Implementing Research, which focuses on African American students being placed in special-education classes. Williams (2007) maintains that placement is often unnecessary and unjustified.

Implementing Research

African Americans and Special Education

Williams (2007) maintains that the disproportionate number of students of color in special education has been an issue for decades. She shares the results of a qualitative study that explored the perceptions of one group of parents who challenged the school system on both the placement of students in special-education programs and the quality of services delivered to African American students.

Williams explains the shifts in theories about special-education delivery systems (i.e., models and practices that are more complementary in the notion of culturally relevant teaching than former perspectives). Former perspectives encouraged separate, pull-out service delivery models. Holistic, collaborative, inclusive approaches embrace a sense of consciousness rather than the deficit models of the past.

The study Williams describes has many quotes from parents regarding their dissatisfaction with the placement process and the quality of the programs. Williams writes about *cultural disconnect,* describing how African American students are relegated to classes because teachers do not understand their culture. Other concerns include the misidentification of students; the use and misuses of protocol, or the process used to place students; and students receiving a certificate of completion rather than a diploma.

Implementing the Research

1. Special-education placement should be a carefully monitored process for all students. While Williams only addresses African Americans, many students from all cultures are subject to misplacement and poor educational practices.

2. The tests and other assessments used to identify special-education students should be culturally relevant. For example, Hispanic and Asian American students should not be tested and placed with instruments designed primarily for African or European American learners.

3. Once placed, students of all cultures should be reassessed on a periodic basis and transferred to regular classrooms if they are capable of completing the work.

4. Parents and caregivers need to accept some responsibility for their children and adolescents attending specific classes and schools.

Source: Williams, E. R. (2007). Unnecessary and unjustified: African American parental perceptions of special education. *Educational Forum, 71*(3), 250–261.

Suggestions for Collaborative Efforts

Form groups of three or four that, if possible, represent our nation's cultural and gender diversity. Working collaboratively, focus your group's attention toward the following efforts.

1. Conduct an in-depth study of English dialects. Divide learning assignments in such a manner that each group member has an individual task, such as providing specific examples of dialectical differences, providing names of textbooks and other curricular materials that positively reflect dialects, and reviewing the literature on dialects. Working collaboratively, discuss how children and adolescents who are able to communicate in home and community situations may experience difficulties communicating in school.

2. Design a study (case studies, interviews, anecdotal records) to learn more about several African American families. Determine cultural, intracultural, and socioeconomic differences. How do these families differ in dress and food preferences, customs, and family behaviors? What other evidence can you find of tremendous diversity among African American families? How can the school provide a curriculum that responds to the African American family?

3. Reread the opening scenario about Paul and his academic difficulties. Also review the section on Gender, in which the National Urban League (2007) suggests all-male schools for African American boys, and reconsider the Case Study, in which parents want all-male schools and all-male teachers in kindergarten through grade 3. In your group, make a list of the advantages and disadvantages of all-male schools for African Americans. Why would the National Urban League make this recommendation? Does this sound like just another form of segregation? Will such schools prepare African Americans to live and work with people of other cultures?

Expanding Your Horizons

Additional Journals, Books, and Internet Sites

Barack, L. (2006). HS gender gap studied. *School Library Journal, 52*(6), 22.

> Barack reports that females graduate from high school at a substantially higher rate than males, but the gender gap is twice as large for African Americans and Hispanic Americans.

Connor, C. M., & Craig, H. K. (2006). African American preschoolers' language, emergent literacy skills, and use of African American English: A complex relation. *Journal of Speech, Language, and Hearing Research, 49*(4), 771–792.

> Using wordless book prompts, these authors examine African American English (AAE) and conclude, among other things, that African American preschoolers

may be switching dialects between African American English (AAE) and Standard American English (SAE).

Fitzpatrick, K. M., Dulin, A. J., & Piko, B. F. (2007). Not just pushing and shoving: School bullying among African American learners. *Journal of School Health, 77*(1), 16–22.

These authors examine the prevalence of bullying—a serious problem in U.S. schools—and recommend that educators and parents address its causes and consequences.

Fryer, R. G. (2006). Acting White. *Education Next, 6*(1), 52–59.

Fryer defines "acting white" as a set of social interactions in which minority adolescents who get good grades in school enjoy less social popularity than white students who do well academically.

Krezmien, M. R., Leone, P. E., & Achilles, G. M. (2006). Suspension, race, and disability: Analysis of statewide practices and reporting. *Journal of Emotional and Behavioral Disorders, 14*(4), 217–226.

These authors examine suspension data in a Maryland district, pointing to the disproportionate number of minorities (mainly African American and American Indians) and students with disabilities.

Lewis, A. (2006). Student health. *Education Digest, 72*(2), 72–73.

Lewis addresses the problem of obesity, which is at almost an epidemic level among African American and Hispanic American males.

Monroe, C. R. (2006). African American boys and the discipline gap: Balancing educators' uneven hand. *Educational Horizons, 84*(2), 102–111.

Monroe looks at African American boys and the problems they face at school.

About.com: African American history. http://afroamhistory.about.com

Major topics on this Internet site include Arthur Ashe, radical reconstruction, *Brown v. Board of Education,* Louis Armstrong, and the Montgomery bus boycott.

AfricanAmericans.com. www.africanamericans.com

This Internet site focuses on African Americans and their history, health, civil rights, demographics, and education.

Biography.com/black history. www.biography.com/blackhistory

As the name implies, this Internet site focuses on African American biographies.

Understanding American Indian Children and Adolescents

Understanding the material and activities in this chapter will help the reader to:

- ◆ Describe the cultural, socioeconomic, and familial characteristics of American Indian children and adolescents.

- ◆ Explain special problems and challenges that confront American Indian children and adolescents.

- ◆ Describe American Indian learners and their development, achievement levels, and language problems.

- ◆ List several educational practices that impede the American Indian learners' educational progress.

- ◆ Offer several suggestions and strategies for improving American Indian learners' cultural identities.

- ◆ List several points that educators of American Indians should remember when planning teaching and learning experiences.

- ◆ Suggest appropriate children's literature for American Indian learners (see the Appendix).

Opening Scenario

CULTURAL PORTRAIT

Fourteen-Year-Old John

John attends a school off the reservation. The student population is a mixed group of American Indians, some Hispanic Americans, a few African Americans, and some European Americans. Although the school includes several culturally diverse groups, most of the teachers are European American, and the school environment and educational program are oriented toward traditional white expectations.

John has several problems that result, at least in part, from his lack of proficiency in English. He must be able to function in a bilingual world. While his family continues to use the native language it has spoken for centuries, he must speak English at school. (Some of his friends have been punished for not speaking English.) Meanwhile, his grades are failing, he does not always understand the teacher (and vice versa), and he experiences difficulty as he ventures outside the social confines of his native culture.

John also has several academic and social problems: He makes below-average grades, feels he does not have many friends, and generally feels uncomfortable while in school, perhaps due to his language problems. Everything seems rushed, and cooperation is second to competition. His teachers feel he is not trying, and the overall curriculum makes little sense to him. John is interested in the ancient traditions of his people, yet his teachers rarely address his cultural interests or, in fact, any of his interests. He realizes that his grades need to improve, yet he does not always understand the teachers or the way they teach. Although John has American Indian friends, he has few friends among the students of other cultures. School is often frustrating for John, as he strives to make it through another day.

One of John's teachers, Ms. Lawler, recognizes his problems and potential and has made an effort to help. She has decided to do the following:

1. Arrange for John to visit the language specialist or a bilingual teacher, who can determine the extent of his difficulty and plan an appropriate course of action.

2. Arrange for John to visit the guidance counselor, who may be able to help him widen his circle of friends.

3. Spend some time alone with John to determine his strengths, weaknesses, and interests.

4. Reassess her teaching to see whether her methods match John's style of learning and knowing.

5. Build on John's interest in his cultural heritage through appropriate reading and other curricular materials.

Ms. Lawler also has another idea that she wants to try. Having John read and study about his own cultural background might show him that the curriculum values his American Indian culture and recognizes his individual needs and interests. Just as important, Ms. Lawler will provide a curriculum that gives other learners an appropriate multicultural understanding of the American Indian culture. There are many possible ways to help John and improve his feelings about school and himself. All John's teachers should recognize the importance of showing interest in him and providing first-hand and individual help in improving his academic and social progress. ◆

Overview

American Indian children and adolescents have special needs that warrant educators' understanding: cherished and unique cultural characteristics, language problems, familial traditions, and learning problems, all of which present schools with special challenges. Yet teacher-education programs traditionally have not prepared prospective teachers to understand multicultural populations and the special characteristics and learning problems of American Indian learners or, in reality, any other multicultural group. This chapter examines American Indian learners—their culture, language issues, families, achievement levels, and overall school programs.

Origins

Scholars do not know exactly when people first came to the Americas. While many archaeologists have concluded that the lack of fossils rules out the possibility of men and women having evolved in the Western hemisphere, some American Indians believe that they originated in the Americas. Archaeologists believe that the ancestors of American Indians came from Asia.

Portman and Herring (2001) offer an excellent description of American Indian history. (It is important to note that Portman and Herring preferred the term *Native American Indian* rather than *Native American* or *American Indian*.) The long history of interaction between Native American Indians and European Americans can be divided into five time periods, which have been determined largely by the interaction of the federal government with Native American Indians: (1) removal (seventeenth century to the 1840s), characterized by the saying "The only good Indian is a dead Indian" (Portman & Herring, 2001, p. 186); (2) reservation (1860s to 1920s), characterized by the saying "Kill the Indian, but save the person"; (3) reorganization (1930s to 1950s), when schools were allowed on the reservation, which eased cultural repression; (4) termination (1950s to1960s), characterized by attempts at sociocultural integration and end of dependence on the federal government, which led to the sale of large tracts of Native American Indian lands and increased poverty; and (5) self-determination (1973 to present), characterized by increased tribal sovereignty due mainly to the militant struggles of many Native American Indians in the early 1970s. Portman and Herring (2001) maintain that these time periods cannot be considered exclusive of each other because of the oral histories that were passed from one generation to the next in Native American Indian cultures. The experiences of past generations are continued in some degree by those Native American Indians who have maintained cultural and familial ties (Portman & Herring, 2001).

American Indians Today

American Indians number more than 500 tribes of varying sizes. The larger tribes include the Cherokee, Navajo, Chippewa, and Sioux. Fourteen tribes have populations between 10,000 and 21,000. Many tribes have less than 10,000. Nearly one-half of American Indians today live west of the Mississippi River. In fact, more than half of the American Indian population lives in just six states: Oklahoma, California, Arizona, New Mexico, Alaska (with large numbers of Aleuts), and Washington (U.S. Bureau of the Census, 2007).

The U.S. Bureau of the Census provides some interesting facts about the American Indian population. First, it is a young and growing population. In 2005, there were 792,000 school-age (from five to nineteen years old) American Indians, which indicates that the population will continue to increase. Second, American Indians' educational attainment continues to improve, although educators' jobs are far from done. Three, the population is diverse in terms of tribes, clans, reservation and off-reservation, and socioeconomic status. The typical American Indian does not exist. Fourth, many American Indians live below the poverty line.

Points to Ponder 4.1

Learning about American Indians—Their Tribes and Individuals

The American Indian population represents many different tribes and peoples—it is difficult to offer generalizations and conclusions. Bearing in mind tribal and individual differences, suggest four or five ways you could learn about the American Indian students in your class.

Over the past several decades, American Indians have been progressively moving off reservation lands. As a result, many American Indians live in non-Indian communities. Movement from reservation to off-reservation settings can harm family relationships and increase the likelihood of risk-taking behaviors that endanger health and well-being. Because educational behaviors and attitudes may result from other stresses in students' lives, off-reservation adolescents may be even more prone to educational problems than their on-reservation peers.

 ## Stereotyping of American Indian Children and Adolescents

Although stereotypical images often accompany the term *American Indian*, this culture and its developmental periods constitute a highly diverse group. Differences in developing children and adolescents vary significantly. Not all American Indians are slow learners, shy, and undependable; likewise, not all adolescents are rebellious and experience difficult and stressful times. Although some common characteristics emerge from the study of American Indian children and adolescents, we must use caution not to oversimplify or ignore individual differences.

As we have emphasized thus far, we need to be careful to speak of *individuals* in a culture. While some American Indians experience poverty on a daily basis, others have been successful in their educational and financial endeavors. A multitude of differences exists among tribes, clans, and geographic regions, as well as among American Indians living on reservations and off reservations. For too long, American Indians have been stereotyped without regard for differences in gender, social class, and sexual orientation. As we explore the American Indian population, we want readers to always remember the diversity of this culture.

Fleming (2007) suggests that American Indians are the most misunderstood cultural group in the United States, mainly because many people have such limited knowledge of the American Indian culture. Even in areas where the concentration of American Indians is high (e.g., the West), most people do not know much about American Indian history and culture. Thus, many people adopt negative stereotypes, such as that American Indians are drunks, get free money from the government, and receive large sums of money from their casinos.

Others assume all American Indians are at one with nature, deeply religious, and wise in ways of spirituality. Fleming echoes the point that we have tried to make in this book—namely, that educators should avoid basing educational decisions on stereotypical generalizations.

Cultural Characteristics

American Indian culture plays a major role in the shaping of children and adolescents. Educators must make the extra effort to seek accurate information and to understand American history and the American Indian culture from the point of view of the American Indian and from the child and adolescent's perspective. Educators should also think through their own cultural beliefs and realize the dangers of *cultural substitution*, in which American Indian learners are expected to change cultural viewpoints.

American Indians have some values and beliefs that differ from those of other cultures. Some Americans believe that individuals have freedoms as long as their actions remain within the law; American Indian children are taught that all actions must be in harmony with nature. Other values conveyed to children and adolescents include a degree of self-sufficiency and being in harmony with knowledge they gain from the natural world. Adults teach youth to respect and protect the aged, who provide wisdom and acquaint the young with traditions, customs, legends, and myths.

Societal and cultural beliefs and traditions of the American Indian people particularly influence developing adolescents and their evolving identities. Adolescents living in American Indian families and attending European American schools, whether on or off the reservation, experience degrees of cultural confusion and often question allegiance to a cultural identification. Such a dilemma can pose a particularly serious problem for adolescents who want to retain their rich cultural heritage while seeking acceptance in European American schools and society.

American Indian adolescents must also resolve cultural differences surrounding the concept of sharing. Sharing represents a genuine and routine way of life in the American Indian culture. Yet this cultural belief, which is so deeply ingrained in the American Indian culture, does not equate with the European American custom of accumulating private property or savings. The accumulation of material possessions is the measure of most people's worth and social status, but the American Indian considers the ability and willingness to share to be most worthy. While younger children may wish to share only with adults, acceptance of and allegiance to the cultural tradition of sharing increase as the child or adolescent develops. Adolescence is a unique time to develop a concept

Points to Ponder 4.2

The American Indian Concept of Sharing

Mrs. Jason was upset with eight-year-old Bill, an American Indian, when she learned that he had taken a pencil off another child's desk. The week before, he had taken a pencil off her desk. What's wrong with Bill? she wondered. She asked a friend, "I told him about taking other people's things. I just cannot understand him. Why does he continue to take things that do not belong to him?"

How would you handle Bill's situation? Is he stealing or sharing? What would you say if a teacher accused him of stealing yet he said he was just borrowing it? This can be a complex issue because of the cultural differences on what constitutes *sharing* versus *stealing*.

of sharing that is congruent with American Indian cultural expectations.

Several reasons exist for adolescents' becoming increasingly cognizant and accepting of this cultural expectation. Adolescents have more advanced intellectual abilities that enable them to recognize that it is possible for two people to want the same thing at the same time, that shared possessions often return, and that sharing can be reciprocal. Developing intellectual skills allows an adolescent to understand the difference between sharing temporarily and donating permanently. The adolescent can understand, as well as make clear to others, his or her intent. Other notable cultural characteristics of American Indians that become an integral part of children's and adolescents' evolving identity are the tendencies toward patience and passive temperaments. American Indians are taught to be patient, to control emotions, and to avoid passionate outbursts over small matters. As the American Indian adolescent develops an identity, cultural characteristics such as poise and self-containment become ingrained.

Such characteristics often lead to a mistaken perception that the American Indian is lazy, uncaring, and inactive. This demeanor or personality trait is also demonstrated in American Indians' tendency to lower their voices to communicate anger, unlike European American adolescents, who learn to raise their voices to convey a message.

Noninterference with others and a deep respect for the rights and dignity of individuals constitute basic premises of American Indian culture. Although such practices may have allowed people of other cultures to think of American Indians as uncaring or unconcerned, the actual case is quite the contrary. American Indians are taught early to respect the rights and privileges of other individuals and the responsibility to work together toward a common goal in harmony with nature.

Gender

Gender is another difference that makes American Indian children and adolescents unique. As in other cultures, American Indian females differ from males in their ways of thinking, behaving, and learning. Undoubtedly, American Indian females are also taught certain cultural and tribal beliefs from birth that influence their roles. Educators working with American Indians need to address females' particular gender differences, rather than assuming too much homogeneity between males and females. While research studies focusing specifically on American Indian females are virtually nonexistent, it is obvious that gender differences exist. As with other differences that multicultural educators work to address, gender differences also deserve consideration.

Portman and Herring (2001) offer several generalizations about American Indian women today. While these generalizations are useful in providing a glimpse of Native American Indian women, it is also important to consider tribal and other differences.

First, Native American Indian women continue to maintain a respect for power of words. They are socialized to use words positively (e.g., to inform, think, reconcile others) as well as negatively (e.g., insult or threaten). Many also use disclaimers to their humbleness and limitations prior to expressing an opinion. Native American Indian women also are encouraged to be strong and resilient in the face of tragedy.

Second, Portman and Herring (2001) also maintain that there are some indications of a positive correlation between the number of Native American Indian women in the labor force and the suicide rate of Native American Indian women. As more American Indian women entered the labor force, their suicide rates increased.

Third, the effects of forced assimilation have destroyed the complementary nature of female–male relations and have resulted in a general increase of Native American Indian male control over women. Women held many complementary positions in the tribes, as did men. When European men colonized the New World, they imposed a male-dominated system of "gynocide" (Portman & Herring, 2001, p. 193).

Gender Perspectives 4.1 looks at resiliency among American Indian youth.

Socioeconomic Status

Statistically, American Indians in the United States are among the poorest economically, the least employed, and the unhealthiest. Their education and income levels are low, and they are among the worst-housed ethnic groups. There are, however, signs of improvement in each area.

Civil rights legislation and the strong will and determination of the American Indian population are enabling these people to improve their lot in life. Some

Gender Perspectives 4.1

RESILIENCY OF AMERICAN INDIAN HIGH SCHOOL STUDENTS

A study by Thornton, Collins, and Daugherty (2006) focused primarily on American Indian girls living in Nevada (although the title says "high school students"). Participation for girls was 62 percent with good attendance records. We liked this article because the variables were predictive of gender. In fact, there was a significant relationship between resiliency and gender.

Resiliency can be defined as the capacity to bounce back or recover from disappointment, obstacle, or setback. *Resilient individuals* have the ability to adjust and adapt to the changes, demands, and disappointments that occur in the course of life. Resiliency includes eight characteristics in children:

◆ having stable relationships with peers

◆ possessing well-developed problem-solving skills

◆ considering realistic future plans

◆ having a positive sense of being able to achieve

◆ experiencing success in one or more life areas

◆ being able to communicate effectively

◆ having a strong attachment to at least one adult

◆ accepting responsibility for oneself and one's behaviors

The research suggests that resiliency of youth is affected by three major factors: family influences, school influences, and community influences. The research also suggests that male American Indian/Alaskan native students have lower levels of resiliency than female students.

Source: Thornton, B., Collins, M., & Daugherty, R. (2006). A study of resiliency of American Indian high school students. *Journal of American Indian Education, 45*(1), 4–16.

of their lands contain rich energy resources. Specifically, the Southern Utes in Colorado, the Uinta-Ouray Utes in Utah, and the Blackfeet in Montana have gas and oil reserves, as do the Shoshones and Arapaho in Wyoming. Similarly, the Bannocks and Shoshones, whose reservations are in Idaho, own one of the largest phosphate deposits in the West. The Navajo and Hopi reservations in the Southwest contain vast oil and gas fields as well as uranium reserves.

Attempting to break the bonds of poverty, other American Indians today are making notable achievements. Some American Indians have engaged in business ventures that have had considerable successes. The Navajo Nation produces electronic missile assemblies for General Dynamics; the Choctaws of Mississippi build wire harnesses for Ford Motor Company; the Seminoles in Florida own a 156-room hotel; and the Swinomish Indians of Washington state plan a 60-acre boat basin, an 800-slip marina, and a three-story office and commercial headquarters.

Families

American Indian adolescents place a high priority on both the immediate and the extended family. The immediate and extended families, tribe, clan, and heritage all contribute to the child's cultural identity and play a significant role in overall development.

Grandparents retain an official and symbolic leadership in family communities. Children seek daily contact with grandparents, who monitor children's behavior and have a voice in child-rearing practices. Although the adolescent's social consciousness and awareness doubtlessly cause a transition from a family-centered to a more peer-centered environment, the traditional American Indian respect and commitment to the family continue.

Adult perceptions of childhood and child-rearing practices also influence the developing person significantly. The American Indian family considers children to be gifts worthy of sharing with others, while the white perception holds that children constitute private property to be disciplined when necessary. In essence, children in the American Indian family have few rules to obey, but white children have rules with strict consequences.

American Indian parents provide children with early training in self-sufficiency. Whereas European Americans prize individualism, the American Indian family places importance on group welfare (Axelson, 1999).

Any crisis in the home or within the family precipitates an absence from school until the crisis ends and the family situation returns to normal. American Indian children and adolescents are taught obedience and respect for elders, experts, and those with spiritual power. They also learn the importance of the family as well as responsibility to family members. In fact, supportive nonfamily members are often considered to be an integral part of the family network.

American Indian child-rearing practices and differing cultural expectations for behavior can result in confusion and frustration for the children. American Indians who confront an incompatibility with their European American counterparts appear to demonstrate growing feelings of isolation, rejection, and anxiety, which can result in alienation, poor self-image, and withdrawal. Such feelings undoubtedly affect the behavior and aspirations of American Indian children and adolescents.

Young people seek social acceptance and approval from older members of the family as well as from younger family members. Unlike adolescents in the European American culture, which emphasizes youth and the self, American Indian adolescents place family before self and have great respect for elders and their wisdom. The wisdom of life is received from the older people, whose task it is to acquaint the young with the traditions, customs, legends, and myths of the culture.

The early training in self-sufficiency that American Indians receive from their families and other significant adults continues to have an impact during the adolescent years. Although the adolescent continues to recognize the loyalty and dependence on the immediate and surrounding family, adolescents develop independence and confidence in their abilities to deal with the world outside the family. We must consider this attitude of self-sufficiency, however, from the American Indian point of view. For example, not sharing with one's fellows and accumulating great wealth and possessions would not be included in the American Indian self-sufficiency concept.

Religion

According to American Indian belief, the world is interconnected and everything, including humankind, lives according to the same process. Each being has its power, function, and place in the universe. Every part of nature has a spirit that many tribes believe possesses intelligence, emotion, and free will. Praying, in fact, is praying to one's own power. Because the Great Spirit is everything in all of nature, there is no need to question the existence of a god. Because nature is the essence of God, nature would stop if God no longer lived (Axelson, 1999).

God is the great power above everything. God created man, nature, and the universe, and God instructs on how to live on the land. The inner spiritual power, or the word *God*, was *orenda* to the Iroquois, *manitou* to the Algonkian tribes, *alone* to the Powhatans, and *wakan* or *wakonda* to the Sioux. The Sioux also used the expression *wakan tanka*, meaning all of the *wakan* beings.

The spiritual God of the American Indians is positive, benevolent, and part of daily living. God's knowledge and advice are transmitted through traditional American Indian wisdom. Ideal action toward God is accomplished by helping others understand and get along with people and by comprehending the natural world of which everything (living and nonliving) is a part. The American Indian respects all of nature's objects equally as both physical and spiritual entities (Axelson, 1999).

As in any other culture, the American Indian culture contains norms and standards for behavior, but American Indians are inclined to judge each person as a separate individual, taking into consideration the reasons for actions ahead of the norms of the society. Some societies judge behavior as right or wrong, good or bad, and consider how things "should" be and not necessarily how they are.

For American Indians, there exists a close relationship between spiritual realization and unity and their cultural practices. Catholic and Protestant clergy have sought to Christianize American Indians, but there has been a continuation of indigenous religious rituals and beliefs in the healing power of nature. Natural forces are associated with the life process itself and pervade everything that the believing American Indian does.

Community religious rites are a collective effort that promote this mode of healing and increase inward insight and experiential connection with nature. American Indian individuals can utilize the positive experiences resulting from ceremonial events, power-revealing events (omens, dreams, visions), and contact with a tribal medicine man in the healing process.

Language

Language and communication, whether verbal or nonverbal, may constitute the most important aspects of an individual's culture and characterize the general culture, its values, and its ways of looking and thinking. Educators should develop a consciousness and appreciation for the many American Indian languages and recognize the problems that may result when educators and school children have differing language backgrounds.

The cultural mannerisms and nonverbal communication the American Indian child demonstrates add another personal dimension to both culture and language. Professionals should recognize communicational differences (both verbal and nonverbal). American Indians tend to speak more softly and at a slower rate, to avoid direct identification between speaker and listener, and to interject less frequently with encouraging communicational signs such as head nods and verbal acknowledgements.

American Indian adolescents, like adolescents of all cultures, need the security and psychological safety that a common language provides, yet they experience significant language problems during this crucial period of development. Self-esteem and identity are formed during the transition from the family-centered world of the immediate and extended home. No longer is communication possible only with elders, parents, and siblings. American Indian adolescents' ability to reach out to a wider world depends greatly on the ability to speak and understand the language of the majority and other cultures.

American Indian children and adolescents often have to decide which language to speak. This may be an even more difficult task for American Indians than for other cultures, because American Indians view language as a crucial aspect of the culture and a cherished gift that should be used whenever possible. Such a belief conflicts with the European American opinion that English is American Indians' means to success and that English should be the predominant language.

That American Indians speak about 2,200 different languages further complicates language use. This broad and diversified language background, albeit personal and sacred to American Indians, has not provided the rich cultural and language experiences that contribute to European American definitions of school success. Wide-scale differences exist in American Indians' ability to speak English. In some cases, as few as 4 percent of American Indians speak "excellent" English; a far greater percentage speak either "good" or "poor" English. Children who have attended English-speaking schools, of course, speak better English than their elders.

Achievement Levels

As stated earlier, several studies suggest that tests and teacher reports show that American Indian children function at the average-to-superior range until the fourth grade. After the fourth grade, academic functioning typically declines each year so that by grade ten, American Indian learners' academic achievement falls below the norm. Several complex factors may contribute to this predicament, such as growing feelings of isolation, rejection, and anxiety that American Indian learners feel as they confront the incompatibility of their cultural value system with peers. These feelings contribute to alienation, poor self-image, and withdrawal.

Teachers sometimes view some behaviors that American Indian students exhibit as rude or insulting. For example, if these students avoid the teacher's gaze, do not volunteer answers, or delay response, as their cultural background has taught them to do, they are seen as lazy or uncomprehending.

American Indian students are sometimes thought to lack time-management skills or to be self-centered because of their present-time orientation. The American Indian concept of time is that what is happening now is more important than what is not happening now; that what is happening now deserves full attention; and that what one will be doing at this time tomorrow will be more important than what one is doing now or what one will not be doing tomorrow.

Whether or not the educational problems American Indian adolescents experience are caused by *cultural teachings* or the *cultural differences* in European American schools, the result is the same: Americans Indians continue to have one of the highest dropout rates. The reasons for dropping out of school include (1) school rules are not enforced uniformly; (2) factors pertaining to teacher–student relationships, for example, teachers' not caring about students and not providing sufficient assistance; (3) disagreements with teachers; and (4) the content of schooling, which the students perceive as not important to what they want to do in life.

Perceptive educators should demonstrate genuine care, understanding, and encouragement with which American Indian learners can identify; ensure that the curriculum addresses American Indian needs and provides culturally relevant experiences; and understand the home problems of some American Indians, such as separations and divorces, unemployment, alcoholism, and child abuse.

Educators who understand American Indians' cultural characteristics can help prevent school failure in American Indian learners. A significant factor in American Indians' academic underachievement appears to be feelings of isolation, anxiety, and rejection as they confront the incompatibility of their cultural values with those of their mainstream classrooms. Often forced to renounce their own culture, these learners are torn between two worlds and often withdraw as a result.

Morris, Pae, Arrington, and Sevcik (2006) argue that American Indian children experience an education system that is distinctly different; have a history of child-rearing and educational practices that is not congruent with the education system; experience shortages of sociopolitical and socioeconomic resources; and often are forced to learn a different language.

Powers (2005) offers several suggestions for educating American Indian students:

1. Teachers should strengthen connections with American Indian students. Having strong relationships between students and teachers promotes a sense of belonging, freedom to take academic risks, and investment in academic learning and may help American Indian students negotiate cultural discontinuities between school and home.
2. Teacher training in native cultural competencies is a positive step toward increasing teachers' understanding and commitment to forming positive relationships with their students.
3. Schoolwide antibullying, anger-management, and substance abuse programs also may contribute to academic achievement.
4. Schoolwide screening may be effective in identifying American Indian students when they first begin to fall behind in achievement or attendance. An

individualized intervention plan can be devised based on factors such as individual assets, native cultural affiliation, and parental support for learning.

Nel (1994) offers several American Indian cultural characteristics that often conflict with mainstream school systems. Educators should be able to address the following:

◆ American Indians often place emphasis on generosity, sharing, and cooperation. These cultural characteristics sometimes conflict with mainstream school systems, which emphasize competition. Educators can take two directions: (1) reassure American Indian learners that mainstream society accepts and encourages personal achievement and that peers will not blame them or think less of them for excelling in classwork or even in the playground and (2) provide teaching and learning experiences that emphasize teamwork and cooperation.

◆ American Indians often experience discomfort when teachers single them out for praise for accomplishments, because they often do not want to excel at others' expense. Educators can (1) let students know that praise is a form of acknowledging accomplishments and mainstream schools' students expect it and (2) offer private recognition and praise for those learners who continue to feel uncomfortable.

◆ American Indians' sense of generosity and cooperative efforts makes it difficult not to help a friend in need, for example, a fellow student needing help on a test or graded exercise. Educators should understand American Indians' concept of generosity and should take special care in handling these situations. Educators can (1) avoid situations in which they strictly prohibit lending assistance and, for situations in which individuals must work alone, (2) try to explain the necessity of working alone, so they can determine individual achievement.

◆ American Indians have more flexible concepts of time than do some other cultures; that is, students might not arrive at class on time and might be late with assignments. They often do not regard time and punctuality as important concerns. Educators need to take several directions: (1) avoid judging American Indians using middle-class white perspectives, by realizing that students being late or submitting assignments late might not be signs of laziness or unconcern, and (2) help students to understand that their cultural orientations are not wrong but that mainstream U.S. schools and society expect punctuality in many cases.

Educational and societal factors, as well as the clash of cultures, during these crucial developmental years have the potential for developing feelings of frustration and hopelessness that often result in alienation. Such alienation may have been a factor to the American Indians' general loss of confidence and decline in motivation. These feelings during adolescence may also result in considerable confusion in the classroom. The American Indian adolescent may demonstrate behavior that teachers perceive as excessive shyness, inactivity, or lack of motivation. Adolescents whose teachers misunderstand or culturally misconstrue these characteristics (along with the adolescent's usual steady decline in achievement) may develop feelings of hopelessness and alienation.

Educators can benefit from understanding these common characteristics of American Indians:

1. American Indians often harbor significant feelings of suspicion and distrust of professionals and institutions.

2. Communication problems may result in an inability to understand, trust, and build rapport with peers and professionals of other cultures. Differences in home language and school language or American Indians' nonverbal communication might hinder educational efforts. American Indian learners may appear to be unconcerned with educational progress when, in fact, they may be painfully shy and oversensitive to strangers because of language problems.

3. American Indian adolescents develop in an often unique and difficult situation. They must reconcile allegiance to the values and customs of both the American Indian and other cultures. They also encounter the usual problems of adolescence, for example, the possibility of experiencing role confusion or differences associated with building a positive identity.

4. American Indian learners have to decide whether the Indian, other culture, or European American culture (or some "cultural combination") should provide the basis for the identity. They need to attempt proficiency in both the Indian language and English and learn how to maintain harmony with family and nature while surviving in the European American world.

Many American Indian students who are gifted are either not identified or not served in schools. Montgomery (2001) maintains that the underrepresentation of American Indians in gifted programs can be attributed to several factors: need for appropriate measures, need for cultural responsiveness, need for appropriate language and relevant cultural responsiveness, need to accommodate predominantly rural schools providing education to American Indian children, and need to address alternative

Points to Ponder 4.3

Promoting American Indians' Academic Achievement

Consider several ways to promote American Indians' academic achievement. Remember, American Indians generally meet academic expectations until the fourth grade. Then, many of them (just like John in the opening Cultural Portrait) begin a downward trend in academic achievement. What might cause this downward trend for American Indians? What can educators do to help American Indians maintain satisfactory academic achievement?

learning styles. Montgomery (2001) also maintains that rural schools traditionally have had difficulty offering a range of programs necessary to meet the needs of gifted American Indians. The main reasons for this difficulty include the heavy reliance on standardized achievement tests and the limited number of culturally and linguistically diverse school professionals. Increasing the number of American Indian teachers, administrators, paraprofessionals, and psychologists may provide American Indian children with greater access to educational opportunity.

To address the challenges facing American Indians in gifted programs, Montgomery (2001) explains Project Leap, which includes four program initiatives: Leadership, Excellence, Achievement, and Performance. The program focuses on collaboration, identification, curriculum, and community and parent involvement, all designed to help gifted American Indian students discover and nurture gifts, talents, or high potential.

School Practices Promoting American Indians' Progress

Because some techniques taught to educators are incompatible with American Indian cultural traditions, it is imperative that educators use strategies that are appropriate for the culture. What specifically should educators avoid?

1. Methods that increase positive self-talk, such as "something I like about myself" or "a sport I can play well," often work well with white and African American children but not with American Indian children.
2. Attempts to convince American Indians to be competitive (such as being the first, best, fastest, or smartest) are incompatible with their cultural values.
3. Educators often expect eye contact and perceive the American Indian's tendency to look the other way as a sign of withdrawal, embarrassment, or discomfort.
4. Educators and counselors often rely extensively on verbal participation by children in the class. Although verbal interaction is valued by Anglo, African, and Hispanic cultures, it is not valued by American Indians.

Promoting Cultural Identities

Educators working with American Indian learners readily recognize the many personal and social factors that affect children's and adolescents' self-esteem and cultural identities. Injustice and discrimination, poverty, low educational attainment, and perhaps growing up on reservations, in foster homes, or in a predominantly white society may cause American Indian learners to question their self-worth and the worth of their culture.

What specific methods might educators use to promote cultural identities? Ask young American Indian children to make a drawing or a silhouette of an Indian child. Ask them to write words or draw symbols to illustrate their favorite foods, favorite games, favorite sports, and perhaps some things they like to think about.

Ask the American Indian children to explain their pictures to the other children in the group. Indian children may prefer to simply look at their pictures, together, as a group. They may look for some similarities in their pictures to identify their group's favorite foods or some things their group likes to think about.

After sharing, the children may combine their pictures to create a "group personality" collage. The purpose of this type of self-disclosing activity for American Indian children is twofold: First, they see a type of collective group personality emerge, and second, they begin to think of themselves as a part of the group. They do not compare themselves individually with other members of the group. Instead, they gain a sense of their contribution to the group and of the ways in which they belong and identify, not with individuals in the group but with the group as a whole.

Case Study

Mr. Thomas and Low-Achieving Students

Mr. Thomas pondered his class—the achievers, the low achievers, and those who seemed to be in a constant struggle just to make passing grades. As Mr. Thomas thought about his students, he also wondered whether his lack of knowledge of how American Indians learn actually contributed to their learning difficulties. He did not understand American Indians' short-term orientation, their concern for nature, and their sometimes strange cultural mannerisms. Mr. Thomas asked himself, "What should I know about the way American Indians learn, and how can I help to improve their academic achievement?"

Mr. Thomas went to several authorities on American Indian children and adolescents to seek advice on how he could better understand these learners, make his teaching more effective, and maximize teaching and learning efforts. The advice he received included the need to understand the short-term time orientation of many American Indians; to understand families and involve them in school activities and their children's learning; to understand how to improve American Indian learners' belief in their ability to learn; to understand the importance of genuinely positive and caring relationships between teachers and students; to understand the importance of designing curricula that reflect American Indians' backgrounds and contemporary needs; and to understand American Indians' ways of receiving and using knowledge.

Questions for Discussion:

1. After the fourth grade, American Indians' academic achievement typically begins to decline. While understanding the reasons for the decline is important, it is even more important to think of strategies for preventing it. Suggest a number of steps (e.g., culturally appropriate diagnostic tests, curricular materials, and instructional procedures) that educators might take to increase American Indians' academic achievement.

2. Realistically speaking, what should Mr. Thomas do? Should he pursue another teaching job with students from his own socioeconomic group and culture? What is the possibility of his finding a teaching position with less diversity? If he continues at this predominantly American Indian school, what methods should he use to learn more about American Indian students?

3. Consider this suggestion: "Understand the importance of designing curricula that reflect American Indians' backgrounds and contemporary needs." How can such a suggestion be made a reality? What would be the first steps in designing such a curriculum? What are specific aspects of American Indians' backgrounds? Contemporary needs?

Summing Up

Educators who plan teaching and learning experiences for American Indian children and adolescents should:

1. Remember that American Indian people have a proud history of accomplishments and notable contributions and that these should be part of school curricula.

2. Avoid providing curricular and instructional practices that indicate only white, middle-class expectations and that might seem alien to American Indian learners.

3. Remember that educators who understand American Indians and the possible cultural basis for educational problems must address achievement levels and school dropout rates.

4. Promote positive self-images and cultural images among American Indian learners, which may be one of the most effective means for improving academic achievement and school-related problems.

5. Adapt teaching styles and other school practices to meet American Indians' ways of knowing, demonstrating that educators are caring and interested in improving school achievement and overall school success.

6. Understand the American Indian culture and the learners' cultural characteristics, religious orientations, and socioeconomic backgrounds.

7. Provide learning experiences so that learners of other cultures can develop a better understanding of their American Indian peers.

8. Understand the learner's development, and provide school experiences based on developmental and cultural characteristics.

9. Consider American Indians as individuals who come from different nations, tribes, socioeconomic levels, and levels of educational attainment.

Suggested Learning Activities

1. Observe an American Indian learner and record the cultural mannerisms that might be contrary to the behaviors that schools expect. How might a teacher misinterpret the behavior of American Indians? How might educators better understand American Indian learners and their behaviors?

2. List several stereotypical beliefs about American Indians. What is the basis of these beliefs? How might these beliefs affect educators' perceptions of these learners? What steps can multicultural educators take to lessen the effect of stereotypical beliefs?

3. Consider the following Implementing Research section, which looks at a review and analysis of the research on American Indian students.

Implementing Research

American Indian Students

Demmert, Grissmer, and Towner (2006) reviewed the research on minority and disadvantaged youth—mainly American Indians. They concluded that while considerable research has been done on the achievement of minority and disadvantaged white students, far less has focused on American Indians due to their lower population numbers.

These authors maintain that two issues are predominant in American Indian education. First, widespread concern exists among American Indians about the preservation and revitalization of their traditional languages and cultures and how to incorporate them into the educational process. Second, to make economic and educational progress, it is important for American Indians to participate successfully in the larger society.

Demmert et al. (2006) offer three explanations for the American Indian achievement gap. First, cultural differences between the minority group and majority group affect early development, motivation, and educational expectations. A second reason is the past and present unequal treatment of American Indians. Third, American Indians and other disadvantaged groups share several characteristics, such as poverty and high levels of teen pregnancy and single-parent families.

Implementing the Research

Usually in this section, we offer suggestions for implementing the research; however, in this situation, we want to offer the suggestions given by Demmert, Grissmer, and Towner (2006):

1. Recognize and use American Indian (or Alaska Native, Native Hawaiian) language as the language of instruction, as a bilingual approach to learning, or as a part of a second language.

2. Stress traditional cultural characteristics and adult–child interactions as a foundation for education.

3. Teach strategies that are congruent with the traditional culture along with contemporary ways of knowing and learning.

4. Develop a curriculum that is based on traditional culture, that recognizes American Indian spirituality, and that places the education of children in a context of visual arts, oral histories, and fundamental beliefs.

5. Encourage the American Indian community to participate in educating children and in the planning and operation of school/community activities.

6. Know and use the social and political mores of the community.

Source: Demmert, W. G., Grissmer, D., & Towner, J. (2006). A review and analysis of the research on Native American students. *Journal of American Education, 45*(3), 5–23.

Suggestions for Collaborative Efforts

Form groups of three or four, which, if possible, represent our nation's cultural and gender diversity. Working collaboratively, focus your group's attention toward the following efforts:

1. Talk with several teachers of American Indian learners to see what first-hand experiences they have to offer. Specifically, learn their perceptions of cultural characteristics, the influence of families, achievement levels, and language problems. What advice can these teachers offer?

2. American Indians experience academic problems, including low academic achievement, low reading scores, and high dropout rates. Design a remediation plan to address American Indians' academic problems. Specifically, look at learning styles, curricular materials, instructional strategies, classroom environments, and motivation. (Be sure to consider that American Indian indicators of motivation might differ from others'.) In other words, how does your group believe schools can better address the needs of American Indian learners?

Expanding Your Horizons

Additional Journals, Books, and Internet Sites

August, D., Goldenberg, C., & Rueda, R. (2006). Native American children and youth: Culture, language, and literacy. *Journal of American Education, 45*(3), 24–37.

This article reviews the research on the influence of culture (mostly discourse and interaction) and then examines instructional approaches to promote literacy.

Demmert, W. G., Grissmer, D., & Towner, J. (2006). A review and analysis of the research on Native American students. *Journal of American Education, 45*(3), 5–23.

As stated in Implementing Research, these authors conducted a review of the research and offer suggestions for improving academic achievement.

Demmert, W. G., McCardle, P., Mele-McCarthy, J., & Leos, K. (2006). Preparing Native American children for academic success: A blueprint for research. *Journal of American Education, 45*(3), 92–106.

> These authors look at federal reports, legislation, and mandates and considerations for improving academic achievement.

Ingalls, L., Hammond, H., Dupoux, E., & Baeza, R. (2006). Teachers' cultural knowledge and understanding of American Indian students and their families: Impact on a child's learning. *Rural Special Education Quarterly, 25*(1), 16–24.

> This article focuses on educational practices in K–12 school systems and maintains that these practices are not compatible with American Indian culture and values.

Mohatt, G. V., Trimble, J., & Dickson, R. A. (2006). Psychosocial foundations of American performance in culture-based education programs for American Indians and Alaska native youth: Reflections on a multidisciplinary perspective. *Journal of American Education, 45*(3), 38–59.

> These authors recommend a multidisciplinary approach and culture-based program for improving educational achievement.

Starnes, B. A. (2006). What we don't know can hurt them: White teachers, Indian children. *Phi Delta Kappan, 87*(5), 384–392.

> Starnes suggests that white teachers are unprepared to teach American Indian children and offers suggestion for them.

Thornton, B., Collins, M., & Daughterty, R. (2006). A study of resiliency of American Indian high school students. *Journal of American Education, 45*(1), 4–16.

> These authors look at measures associated with student success and conclude resiliency is a major factor.

Trafzer, C. E., & Keller, J. A. (2006). *Boarding school blues: Revisiting American Indian educational experiences*. Lincoln: University of Nebraska Press

Indians.org. www.indians.org

> This Internet site provides various resources, such as indigenous literature, a tribal directory, and information on activism.

Iowa State University, Diversity and Ethnic Studies. www.public.iastate.edu/~savega/amer_ind.htm

> This Internet site provides selected American Indian resources useful for academic research and informational purposes.

Native American Resources. www.kstrom.net/isk/mainmenu.html

> Covering over 300 Internet sites, this site provides maps, stories, art, astronomy, and herbal knowledge, just to name a few topics.

Understanding Arab American Children and Adolescents

Understanding the material and activities in this chapter will help the reader to:

◆ Understand the Arab American people, their origins, and what they are like today.

◆ List several stereotypes of Arab American children and adolescents.

◆ Describe Arab Americans' cultural, gender, socioeconomic, familial, religious, and language diversity.

◆ Suggest appropriate children's literature and provide culturally appropriate educational experiences for Arab Americans (see the Appendix).

◆ Name several culturally responsive educational practices that promote Arab Americans' educational progress, self-esteem, and cultural identities.

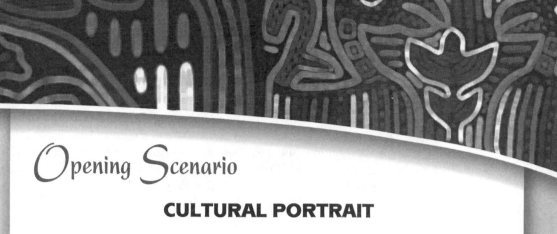

Opening Scenario

CULTURAL PORTRAIT

Abdullah Salaam

Abdullah Salaam is a thirteen-year-old Arab American boy whose parents had moved to the United States from Saudi Arabia. Abdullah's father worked for a company that wanted to expand its international operation. His family was reluctant to move to the United States, but then they realized the economic and other benefits of doing so. The family hated to leave behind their family and friends, as well as their cherished religious customs and traditions. Still, they knew their family could visit. Plus, places existed in the United States where they could practice their religion.

Abdullah faced several challenges, which his school addressed with varying degrees of success. First, his English-speaking skills were good, but he still had difficulty understanding the teacher and communicating with other students. Second, he received a little abuse from the other middle school students, who sometimes mocked his language. They spoke to him using what they considered an Arab accent. Third, Abdullah's social development was lacking, perhaps because of his language proficiency and fear of others mocking him. He had few friends and usually stayed alone.

Most of the teachers, unfortunately, ignored Abdullah's school situation, but two realized that he needed help. After enlisting the aid of the guidance counselor to come up with a plan, they decided on a four-prong approach. First, they asked the language specialist to work with Abdullah to improve his language abilities. Second, they decided to address mocking and other forms of harassment in the advisor–advisee program (an essential middle school concept) to try to show the effects of such negative behaviors. Third, they decided to try cooperative learning activities that would bring Abdullah into social contact with other students. Fourth, they agreed to work informally with him to improve his self-esteem.

Admittedly, the teachers had doubts about whether these approaches would have positive and long-term effects, but they thought Abdullah's problems deserved to be addressed in some way. ◆

Overview

Although articles, books, and instructional materials may deal with the cultural heritages of African American, American Indian, Asian American, European American, and Hispanic American children and adolescents, Arab American learners and their cultures are often ignored. "The kids from the Middle East are the lost sheep in the school system. They fall through the cracks in our categories" (Wingfield & Karaman, 1995, p. 8). We agree wholeheartedly that Arab American children and adolescents are still often forgotten or ignored in U.S. schools.

Origins

Arab people emigrate from twenty-two countries in the Middle East and northern Africa. They possess a shared heritage, which typically includes Arabic as their native language, and they identify with key features of Arab culture, including the centrality of family and religion. Nevertheless, important social, political, and religious differences exist both within and among people from Arab countries. Notably, considerable variability exists among families in terms of the degree of acculturation to both Western and Arab countries. The Arab population is also young; 25 percent of the population is under eighteen years old (Haboush, 2007).

According to Haboush (2007), the U.S. Census Bureau identifies as Arabs those people whose ancestry originates in Arabic-speaking countries, even though not all these individuals consider themselves Arabs. In the Middle East, Arab countries include Lebanon, Syria, Jordan, Iraq, Yemen, the United Arab Emirates, Kuwait, Saudi Arabia, Bahrain, Oman, and Qatar. These countries differ in terms of racial and ethnic mix, religious composition, and economic development. The racial/ethnic diversity of Arab American families is not well reflected in the U.S. Census because Arabs are considered white (Haboush, 2007).

Like Hispanic Americans, Arab Americans are a linguistic and cultural community, rather than a racial or religious group. Arabs speak Arabic as their primary language and share in the culture and history of the Arab world, which stretches from Morocco to the Arabian Peninsula. Most Arabs are Muslim, which means they believe in the religion of Islam. However, most of the largest Muslim countries—including Indonesia, Pakistan, Bangladesh, Iran, Turkey, and Nigeria—are not Arab. Worldwide, the more than 200 million Arabs make up only a relatively small percentage of the more than 1 billion Muslims (Wingfield, 2006). Table 5.1 provides a list of definitions to assist educators in understanding Arab Americans and the Arab culture.

table 5.1

Terms and Definitions

Allah—means God and is used by Arabic-speaking Christians, Muslims, and Jews.

Arab—a person whose native language is Arabic and who lives according to Arab cultural traditions and values.

Arab Americans—immigrants and their descendants with ethnic roots in Asian and African Arabic-speaking lands.

Arab Nation—all peoples who speak the Arabic language and claim a link with the nomadic tribes of Arabia, whether by descent, affiliation, or by appropriating the traditional ideals of human excellence and standards of beauty.

collective or *collectivism*—people who are more oriented toward the group.

Bedouin—a nomadic desert-dwelling Arab.

fundamentalist—one who follows the fundamentals of a religion.

galabiya—a body-length robe.

hadith—the Prophet's own traditional sayings.

hajj—the pilgrimage to Mecca made by millions of Muslims once each year; for men it is called *hajji,* and for women it is called *hajjah.*

hijab—a scarf worn to cover the hair on a woman's head.

imam—the leader of prayer at the mosque; he is sometimes called a *sheik.*

individualistic or individualism—people who are more oriented toward individual concerns.

Islam—the Arabic word means "submission" and is derived from the word meaning "peace."

jihad—a Muslim's strenuous intellectual, physical, and spiritual efforts for the good of all.

Muslim (not *Moslem*)—a believer in the religion of Islam, who may or may not be an Arab.

Pillars of Islam—(1) oral testimony that there is only one God and that Mohammed is His prophet; (2) ritual prayer practiced five times a day with certain words and certain postures of the body; (3) the giving of alms; (4) keeping a strict fast of no liquid or food from sunrise to sundown during the month of Ramadan; and (5) holy pilgrimage to Mecca once in a lifetime at a specific time of year.

Quran—the holy book for Muslims, who believe it is the literal word of God revealed by the prophet Mohammed.

Ramadan—the ninth month of the calendar year, the month of fasting, self-discipline, and purification.

sunna—the Prophet's own traditional practices.

umma—a belief that all Muslims are brothers and sisters.

Arab Americans represent a wide range of diverse cultures, languages, religions, and ethnic and racial backgrounds. An Arab can be Muslim, Christian, Jew, or of some other belief. Although most Arab Americans are generally categorized as Caucasian, ethnic and racial diversity are two salient features of this unique group. For example, Arab Americans can be black, interracial, or white. Also, not everyone who comes from the Arab countries is an Arab. For example, people can originate from Kildanis, Kurds, Druze, Berbers, and other ethnic groups.

Arab Americans Today

Erroneously perceived as a unified, single ethnic group, Arab Americans' diversity is grossly overlooked. Arabs in the United States come from different countries with different allegiances and interests.

Recent estimates suggest the number of Americans of Arab descent ranges between 1 million and 3.5 million. Some Arab organizations place the figure closer to 3.5 million. Increasingly, Arab Americans are being recognized as an ethnic minority in the United States (Haboush, 2007). Miller (2007) reports that 54 percent of the Muslim population is male and 46 percent female. Among U.S. Muslims, 30 percent are eighteen to twenty-nine years old, 26 percent are thirty to thirty-nine years old, 31 percent are forty to fifty-four years old, and 13 percent are fifty-five or older. In terms of educational achievement, 10 percent have done graduate study, 14 percent are college graduates, 23 percent have some college, 32 percent are high school graduates, and 21 percent are not high school graduates.

Arab American Christians' tendency to enrich their lives through effective interaction with others appears to have assisted them as they entered mainstream U.S. culture. However, in contrast to Arab Christians, assimilation was much more difficult for the Arab Muslims because of their strong adherence to Islamic faith and law.

Stereotyping of Arab American Children and Adolescents

The Arab community is one of the most heterogeneous in the United States, yet it is likely also the most misunderstood. It is the negative images and stereotypes of Arabs that are the most prevalent. The popular images of Arabs as rich sheiks, religious zealots, and terrorists are gross stereotypes. Stereotypes also surround the roles of Arab American men and women.

The 1992 cartoon fantasy *Aladdin* proved immensely popular with American children and their parents and is still one of the few U.S. films to feature an Arab hero or heroine. However, a closer look provides disturbing evidence of stereotyping. The film's light-skinned lead characters, Aladdin and Jasmine, have Anglicized features and Anglo American accents. This is in contrast to the other characters, who are dark-skinned, swarthy, and villainous—cruel palace guards and greedy merchants with Arabic features, Arabic accents, and grotesque facial features. The film also characterizes the Arab world as alien and exotic.

Other offenders also use negative images to cast Arabs. For example, children and adolescents develop negative images of their culture when they see Arab women dressed as belly dancers and harem girls and Arab men as violent terrorists, oil sheiks, and marauding tribesmen. Even on Saturday-morning cartoons, Arabs are portrayed as fanatic and dark complexioned, with sabers and rifles, allies of some force plotting to take over the world. Comic books are equally troubling. Tarzan battles with an Arab chieftain who kidnaps Jane, Superman foils Arab terrorists hijacking a U.S. nuclear carrier, and the Fantastic Four combat a hideous oil sheik supervillain. Computer games often feature cartoon Arab villains, and children rack up high scores and win games by killing Arabs (Wingfield, 2006).

Because many Arabs are Muslims, their dress and traditions are sometimes misunderstood. People sometimes stereotype men with a *galabiya*, or body-length robe, and women wearing a *hijab*, a scarf covering the head, as religious fundamentalists. As with robes, wearing *hijab* is a personal choice. Many women wear *hijab* because of cultural traditions. A devout Muslim woman does not necessarily wear a *hijab*. Wearing the *hijab* is a religious practice rather than a cultural practice and is rooted in the Islamic emphasis on modesty. Interestingly, some Arab women say veiling denigrates women; others say the practice liberates them. Covering is not universally observed by Muslim women and varies by region and class.

Points to Ponder ◆ 5.1

Consider Your Images of Arab Americans

Think about your images of Arab Americans. Be honest with yourself and admit possible stereotypical images. Second, determine the basis for your beliefs. Third, ask yourself, "How true is the image?" Last, decide what you can do to dispel your stereotypical images and gain a more accurate perception of this cultural group.

Schools should recognize other Arab American religious practices. Many Arab Americans adhere to restricted diets—for example, Islamic law forbids eating pork and drinking alcohol. Teachers should recognize the month of Ramadan, in which many Muslim students participate in fasting.

Cultural Characteristics

It is difficult to generalize about any group of people, but it is particularly difficult with Arab Americans because of the many different countries from which they come. Still, some generalizations can be made, provided one considers factors such as generational status, socioeconomic status, commitment to religion, and the actual country of origin.

Haboush (2007) suggests that Arabs are more collective or more oriented toward the group and that Americans are more individualistic or more oriented toward individual concerns. In other words, many Arab Americans believe that individuals have the right to take care of themselves. They are self-oriented and emotionally independent, and their emphasis is on individual initiative, the right to privacy, autonomy, and individual decisions. Arabs believe in a more collectivist orientation.

Educators who understand Arab American learners and the Arab culture quickly realize the importance of the individualism–collectivism issue and of the necessity to learn about individual Arab American students. Generally speaking, the U.S. school system has focused on individualism. Educators expect learners, both elementary and secondary, to fend for themselves. Students are expected to have goals, to work individually toward those goals, to compete with others for academic achievement and for the teacher's time, and to claim personal and individual pride in their accomplishments. That individualistic mindset changed somewhat with the inception of cooperative learning, but still, the U.S. school system is individual oriented.

Educators working with Arab Americans (as well as some American Indians and Hispanic Americans) might see more tendencies toward collectivism. Such a statement does not imply, however, that all Arab Americans are collective. To some, when considering education, the theory of collectivism does not make sense, and therefore, they feel a need to compete.

Even considering the research on individualism–collectivism, educators who are sensitive to cultural concerns realize the need to consider students' individuality. Undoubtedly, there are Americans who have orientations toward collectivism and Arabs who prefer to work individually toward learning goals. Perceptive educators see the need to know individual students and then to plan culturally responsive educational experiences.

Gender

Gender roles differ for Arab Americans. Some factors affecting gender roles include country of origin, whether the family came from a rural or urban area, and how long the family has been in the United States. Rather than assume a gender stereotype, it is better to ask the person about his or her own experiences.

Arab American women and girls sometimes experience "double jeopardy" for being young and female and almost constantly feel victimized by stereotypical images in the media. Females often feel obligated to fight the media images in positive ways, showing a more accurate context of their religious and social climate.

Boys and girls are treated differently in Arab cultures. Also, as explained later in the Families section, Arab parental discipline and child-rearing methods are often gender specific. While child-rearing methods vary among Arab cultures and among parents, a great deal of unconditional love usually accompanies discipline, especially for sons. Differential treatment of boys and girls is not uncommon. Educators working with Arab Americans need to remember that their equal treatment of boys and girls, as well as the school's efforts to promote egalitarianism, might be misunderstood by children and parents. While some acculturation might have occurred toward more equal sex roles, it is a mistake to assume that children and adolescents who have lived in the United States for a number of years have adopted Western norms of gender and equality.

In Gender Perspectives 5.1, Ajrouch (2004) looks at gender, race, symbolic boundaries, and Arab American adolescents. Ajrouch completed her study in Dearborn, Michigan, the city with the largest concentration of Arab Americans living in the United States. The community in Dearborn is composed of immigrants who entered the United States at different times and who have varying educational, economic, and social backgrounds. The largest group of immigrants is from Lebanon, and many of the most recent of these immigrants are well educated and prosperous; in addition a small number have come from the rural villages of Lebanon.

Socioeconomic Status

Although many early Arab immigrants were peddlers and merchants, the new immigrants reflect a greater variety of professions. Whereas the average household income for Arab Americans tends to be higher than the national average, there is a greater percentage of Arab American households below the poverty level than for the U.S. population as a whole. Household incomes vary among Arab Americans, just as they do for people of all cultures. Some people achieve socioeconomically, while others have difficulty earning a living and moving up to the next socioeconomic level. Miller (2007) provides these figures on Arab Americans' annual earnings: over $100,000 (16 percent), $75,000 to $99,000 (10 percent), $50,000 to $74,999 (15 percent), $30,000 to $49,999 (24 percent), and $29,000 or less (35 percent).

Gender Perspectives 5.1

GENDER, RACE, SYMBOLIC BOUNDARIES, AND ARAB AMERICAN ADOLESCENTS

Ajrouch (2004) has examined identity formation among second-generation Arab American adolescents from the immigrant culture, along with their relationship with the so-called white culture. In her detailed examination, she offers interpretations of religious teachings and how they shape identity formation, and she also discusses cultural gender-controlling behaviors.

The subjects in Ajrouch's study were all adolescent females and all Muslims. They were the children of Lebanese and Palestinian immigrants, an ethnic group that is understudied. Eight of the ten participants were of Lebanese descent. One identified herself as Palestinian, and one's mother was born in Palestine and her father was from Tunisia. All the adolescent females knew one another.

Interestingly, the term *boater* emerged as a word describing students who spoke only Arabic or who spoke English with an Arabic accent and wore ethnic clothes. *Boater* is the term used to refer to children of Arab immigrants to describe a purely Arab identity—that part of ethnicity that represents the originating immigrant culture. The term *boater* is rooted in the history of immigration to the United States, as immigrants from various locations across the Atlantic arrived in boats. The study's participants had an embarrassing dislike for the term. They wanted to make it clear that they were of Arab descent but they were different.

Ajrouch offers several useful conclusions, but some are particularly interesting in our study of Arab Americans:

1. Religion played a major role in the young women's lives. Religion was more powerful than nationality.

2. Male adolescents were given more freedom and responsibility than female adolescents.

3. Cultural resentment was evident (e.g., feelings toward the boaters) based on the young women's speaking Arab, speaking English with an Arab accent, or dressing differently (probably what was customarily worn in their originating country).

4. Arab girls occupy a precarious position in that conforming to Arab traditions and values requires them to negotiate between Arab culture and the culture of the United States.

Ajrouch maintains that interpretations of gender roles and relations are often derived from religious doctrine and frequently shaped by societal realities. For example, the traditional Arab belief that the man is the breadwinner and the woman is the homemaker has changed because the economic downturn has drawn women to the workplace in order to maintain a middle-class standard of living.

Source: Ajrouch, K. J. (2004). Gender, race, and symbolic boundaries: Contested spaces of identity among Arab American adolescents. *Sociological Perspectives, 47*(4), 371–390.

Financially successful Arab Americans cannot be considered victims of exploitation and marginalization. They are not powerless in terms of economics or social standing. Middle- and upper-class professionals are ensured privilege and empowerment. Despite their affluence, however, some middle-class Arab Americans encounter job discrimination in hiring and firing, promotions and tenure, access to certain jobs and fields, and exclusion, harassment, and hostility in the workplace (Wingfield, 2006). More recent immigrants with lower income and educational levels face the problems of poverty, prejudice, neighborhood tensions, and cultural adjustment similar to those of other non-European immigrants. In contrast to middle-class professionals, these individuals are less likely to be treated with respect (Wingfield, 2006). While we respect Wingfield's (2006) opinion, we feel he neglects the influence of affirmative action programs and other efforts to help minority immigrants. Plus, we think that people at all lower socioeconomic levels experience problems similar to what Wingfield describes.

Families

Arab Americans value the family and take pride in extended family members. They share several familial traits, such as generosity, hospitality, courage, and respect for the elderly. Most important, Arab Americans invest in their children through education, which is seen as a social asset and religious duty necessary for the survival of both individuals and groups.

Arab American families are, on the average, larger than non–Arab American families and smaller than families in Arab countries. Traditionally, more children meant more pride and economic contributors for the family. The cost of having large families in the United States, however, and adaptation to American customs seem to encourage smaller families.

If the Quran is the soul of Islam, then the family can be described as the body. Islam focuses on the *umma* and considers all Muslims as brothers and sisters belonging to the same *umma*. With the *umma*, families are given importance as units.

Although differences exist among Arab Americans, the importance of the family unit is the central unifying feature. Arab culture is collectivistic, or focused on the welfare of the group. Unlike Western culture, which stresses independence and individual autonomy, Arab culture stresses the collective good of the family. This value underlies Arab society and permeates all religious groups. Decisions are made with the ultimate goal of maintaining family stability, honor, and cohesiveness. Children are taught to look within the family for solutions, rather than to develop their own coping strategies, and separating from the family is not encouraged. In fact, many children continue to reside with their parents even after marrying. Strong emphasis is also placed on not shaming the family by one's behavior. Shame, which implies a sense of external exposure, is associated with guilt, which implies an internal issue that one has not lived up to individual standards of behavior. The emphasis on maintaining family honor also means that expressing emotions is discouraged (Haboush, 2007).

Traditional Arab culture is patriarchal, or male dominated. A woman's main roles are those of wife and mother. Unmarried women often reside in the parents' home. The father is the dominant authority although older brothers can exert control over mothers and sisters. Although mothers have some power within the family, dominance by males (greater property rights and custody of children) is established by law in some Arab countries. Under Islam, the importance of women's roles as wives and mothers has been strengthened. In Arab countries such as Saudi Arabia, widespread gender segregation occurs in work, school, and social settings (Haboush, 2007).

How can educators best respond to Arab American families? Arab Americans from different countries differ from each other in culture, socioeconomic status, religion, and newly arrived second and third generations. To accommodate the individuality of Arab families, it is important for teachers and counselors to take the lead from students and their parents when discussing school and other related issues and to be knowledgeable about Arab culture. Educators also can recognize that family life and harmony are crucial to Arabs and demonstrate respect for the sanctity of the nuclear and extended family and the familial role of elders. When Arab American students seem troubled, it may be productive to determine whether their problems stem from intergenerational differences within their family or another source. Inviting parents' input in problem solving can be helpful. Because Arabs are sensitive to public criticism, teachers should be careful how they express concerns to Arab American students and parents. Last, helping families cope with varying levels of acculturation, language differences, and conformity to tradition can enable students to develop a positive identity that is both personally satisfying and respectful of their heritage.

Religion

Arabs belong to many religions, including <u>Islam, Christianity, Druze, Judaism,</u> and others. There are additional distinctions within each of these, and some religious groups have evolved new identities and faith practices in the United States. Educators should be careful to distinguish *religion* from *culture*. Although Arabs are connected by culture, they have different faiths. Common misperceptions are that all Arab traditions are Islamic and that Islam unifies all Arabs. Most Arab Americans are Catholics or Orthodox Christians, but this is not true in all parts of the United States. In some areas, most Arab Americans are Muslim.

The Arab culture has been shaped by numerous historical disputes over religion, territorial boundaries, and political dominance. Beginning with the Crusades, many Arab countries were under the rule of various foreign powers, such as the Ottomans, English, French, and Italians. Colonization by the Europeans and the accompanying devaluation of Arab culture endured into the mid-twentieth century and contributed to long-standing feelings of mistrust toward the West. Since the Crusades, there have been strong divisions between Christian and Muslim groups, who view each other as a threat, as well as internal divisions within each group (Haboush, 2007).

The two main religions with which Arabs identify are Christianity and Islam. There are also Arab Jews, Hindus, and other groups, but their numbers are small. The proportion of individuals practicing Islam and Christianity varies among Arab countries. Muslims constitute more than 90 percent of the population in Syria, Egypt, Saudi Arabia, Qatar, Algeria, Bahrain, Jordon, Morocco, Libya, Tunisia, the United Arab Emirates, and Yemen. However, being Arab is not synonymous with practicing Islam, because Muslims are found in countries throughout the world (Haboush, 2007).

One cannot assume that all Arab Americans are Muslims or that all Muslims are Arab. Miller (2007) provides the following breakdown of religious beliefs of foreign-born Muslims in the United States: Sunni (53 percent), Shiite (21 percent), and other (26 percent). Miller also categorizes the religious commitment of foreign-born Muslims as high (22 percent), medium (49 percent), and low (29 percent).

Points to Ponder 5.2

Religious Beliefs

Educators have a professional responsibility to avoid promoting one religion over another. How can teachers teach about Arab Americans' religions without offending members of other religious groups? Or should these topics be avoided altogether to avoid offending someone? Remember that any discussion of religion must be done with respect and objectivity. What specific teaching strategies might you use to teach Arab Americans' religions (or any religion)?

Religious diversity is characteristic of both the Arab world and the Arab American population. In the United States, where the majority of Arab Americans are Christians, there are still several thousand who belong to the Jewish faith. On the other hand, a Muslim is an adherent to Islam and may or may not be an Arab. Arabs are a minority in the Muslim community. Muslims are from many different parts of the world, including China, Indonesia, Turkey, Russia, and even the United States. To label all Arabs as Muslim is a sweeping false generalization.

The essence of Islam, as preached by the Prophet Mohammed, was transmitted through the Quran, which is believed to be the literal word of God. In addition to the Quran, religious guidance also includes the Prophet's own traditional sayings (*hadith*) and his practices (*sunna*). Except by implication, the Quran does not contain explicit doctrines or instructions; basically, it provides guidance. The *hadith* and *sunna*, however, contain some specific commands on issues such as marriage. They also address such daily habits as how often the believer should worship God and how all people should treat each other.

Language

The Arabic language is one of the great unifying and distinguishing characteristics of Arab people. Arabic is spoken by 130 million people and is the fourth most widely spoken language in the world (tied with Bengali). Although spoken Arabic is as varied as the different parts of the Arab world, classical Arabic and written Arabic are the same in all Arab nations. While many people feel an affection for their native language, Arabs' feelings for their language are much more intense. The Arabic language is one of the greatest Arab cultural treasures. Plus, because of its complexity, a good command of the Arabic language is highly admired (Abudabbeh, 1996).

Arab schools usually teach more than one language. It is more common for Arab Americans to speak more than one language than it is for non–Arab Americans. Many immigrants come to the United States having learned two or three languages in their country of origin.

Achievement Levels

Arab American students are among the newest of the sizable ethnic groups comprising the student population in the United States. Arab American students have generally been an invisible minority in many ways. Their immigration to the United States has been relatively smooth. Still, elementary and secondary school educators should not assume that Arab Americans have experienced easy success in U.S. schools. Arab Americans' academic progress has not undergone the scrutiny that other cultural groups have experienced. Because the cultural group has been an invisible minority, data to prove or disprove their academic achievement are not available.

Flanagan, Gill, Cumsille, and Gallay (2007) found that, regardless of age, gender, or cultural background, youth were more likely to perceive the United States as a just society and to commit to democratic goals if they felt a sense of community. This was especially true if they felt that teachers practiced a democratic ethic at school. Educators may promote the Arab American and Muslim communities in several ways: speaking out when discriminatory attitudes are expressed, reaffirming school antidiscrimination policies, and publicly sending messages of support. When crises erupt, it is time to call friends and contacts at Arab American organizations and mosques to inquire about needed support (Wingfield, 2006).

Some evidence suggests that social justice can be promoted for Arab Americans (and we hope all Americans):

- A network of institutions and organizations has emerged in the recent decades, offering teacher training and a rich collection of classroom materials on Arabs and Muslims.
- More efforts are being made to reach out to the local Arab Americans and Muslim communities and establish ongoing working relationships.
- Textbooks are being reviewed to detect errors of fact, emphasis, and interpretation and to eliminate Eurocentric and Israeli-centric bias.
- Educators are beginning to overcome the prevalent monocultural approach to education that favors the perspectives of dominant groups.
- Educators are moving toward a genuine acceptance of and respect for these communities (Wingfield, 2006).

> **Points to Ponder 5.3**
>
> **Promoting Social Justice**
>
> Working in groups, discuss what social justice might mean to Arab American students. While Wingfield (2006) offers some suggestions, offer specific ways teachers can promote social justice, such as by making sure procedural (daily routines, disciplinary problems, solving disputes) justice occurs, reducing oppression (harassment, bullying, name-calling), and acting as advocates for others.

School Practices Promoting Arab Americans' Progress

Teachers and curriculum designers should integrate culturally relevant materials about all ethnic and cultural groups. Although a lot has been written about various ethnic groups, schools have little information about Arab Americans, their culture, school experiences, or learning styles. At the same time, teachers must engage in the unteaching of myths, stereotypes, and false images of Arab Americans.

Arab American students are often confronted by a biased curriculum and literature. As a result of negative media images, perceptions of Arab American students and their families range from the overly romanticized to the harmfully negative. Schools can make sure that Arabs are accurately and fairly represented in the curriculum and school activities.

Schools can take action against prejudice, discrimination, and incidences of racism. They can also provide professional training for staff and teachers and provide accurate textbooks and curricular materials. As for Arab American students, knowledge of their culture and history should help educators to construct a more realistic picture of their students. For example, by being aware of food taboos, dress codes, and restrictions on male and female interaction, teachers can reach out to their students in a meaningful way. Teachers can enhance pride in Arab American students by learning about Arab contributions in fields such as algebra, science, linguistics, astrology, art, and architecture.

Promoting Positive Cultural Identities

It is recognized that the more positive a student's cultural identity, the higher her or his achievement level. Teachers can use various techniques to make students feel worthwhile and capable of handling everyday academic and social tasks. Arab American students need to see positive images of their culture and cultural backgrounds.

One special challenge to educators of Arab American learners is how to provide appropriate educational activities that acknowledge and respect students' Arab culture and cultural traditions. One approach is to attempt to employ counselors and teachers from Arab cultural backgrounds, but that may be difficult in some areas. Another approach is to provide training sessions focusing on Arab cultural characteristics, worldviews, and perceptions of school success and motivation. As a result of the training, educators might learn that all students do not perceive events through a European American (or whatever the majority culture) lens. With the increasing number of learners from Arabic cultures, educators should understand students' cultural orientations and worldviews and use culturally responsive teaching–learning strategies that promote social justice.

Case Study

A School Faces a Language Dilemma

The educators at the K–5 school in this medium-sized southern city were somewhat startled when they learned that twenty-eight to thirty Arab American children planned to enroll in their school in less than a week. An international corporation was sending a group of Arab Americans to this city for nine months of training. This middle- to upper-class school was predominantly European American but had a handful of African and Asian American students. The school had neither planned nor implemented language services for Arab American students because there had never been a need. Still, the school had a commitment to diversity, and it now faced a problem: How would it accommodate the language needs of some thirty Arab American students who would be entering in less than a week? The children, ranging from ages five to nine, had differing English-language skills. None was fluent, but some had a basic knowledge of the English language.

A committee of teachers, administrators, and counselors met to decide how to meet the challenge. Fortunately, one teacher knew someone who had grown up in the Arab country from which the children were coming and could speak the language. The committee made several quick decisions. First, they decided to see if this individual would volunteer as a translator several mornings a week. Second, they contacted the local university to see if its student services expert (who had considerable experience working with diverse populations) would come to the school to discuss Arab cultural mannerisms and traditions. Third, they had the foresight to ask a local religious leader to speak to the teachers about religious customs. He agreed but cautioned them to avoid making assumptions about the new students' religious allegiances.

Questions for Discussion:

1. The school made a commitment to address the challenge of having thirty Arab American students enter, forming a basic plan to address language and religious differences. What could the educators have done to learn about other critical differences, such as families and socioeconomic status (although this was a fairly affluent group)?
2. Stereotyping is a major ill in the United States and probably other nations, as well. What stereotypes might these teachers and administrators have harbored? What could the administrators have done to help the teachers develop a positive and objective perception of these new students?
3. The United States has the reputation of a being a gender-equitable society. Although progress toward this goal has been made, most people think we still

have challenges. Consider the gender differences between these Arab American girls and boys. How could the teachers address gender differences without making false assumptions about Arab American girls?

Summing Up

Educators who plan teaching and learning experiences for Arab American children and adolescents should:

1. Remember that Arab Americans are not a unified single ethnic group; making such an assumption will grossly overlook their tremendous diversity.
2. Clarify stereotypes, myths, and misconceptions about Arabic culture.
3. Avoid letting Arab American children and adolescents be overlooked by the school system.
4. Consider acculturation factors among Arab Americans; for example, the length of U.S. residence, age at immigration, visits to one's homeland, and being Christian all affect acculturation.
5. Remember differences—cultural, gender, generational, and socioeconomic—that contribute to Arab American children's and adolescents' diversity.
6. Recognize the essential need for Arab American learners to develop positive self-esteem and cultural identity.
7. Provide a learning environment that respects Arabic American cultural backgrounds and languages.
8. Provide curricular and instructional practices that reflect the Arab American culture as well as their accomplishments, art, and literature.

Suggested Learning Activities

1. Choose an Arab American learner with a language problem. Evaluate the extent of the problem, list several ways educators might address the language difficulty, and devise a plan to remediate the language problem.
2. Make a list of specific ways you can improve Arab Americans' self-esteem, especially students who are not doing well academically, students with language difficulties, and maybe girls who feel inadequate in a predominantly white and male-dominated classroom. As you compile your list, how can you make it as culturally responsive as possible, that is, as responsive to the Arab culture as possible?
3. Consider the following Implementing Research, which focuses on working with Arab American families.

Implementing Research

Working with Arab American Families

In her excellent article, Karen Haboush (2007) provides a comprehensive look at the growing Arab American population. She emphasizes the ethical considerations involved in working with diverse populations; provides an overview of the Arab culture (e.g., cultural demographics, religion, family); and offers implications for school psychologists (which are also appropriate for elementary, middle, and secondary educators).

Since Haboush's information was examined in the appropriate sections of this chapter, we will look now only at selected topics and suggestions for implementing her research:

Religion
◆ Show respect for Arabs' religions. The importance of religion cannot be overestimated, because religion permeates all aspects of Arab culture, influencing family life, child rearing, and views regarding education. In fact, identification with one's religious group often precedes identification with one's nationality or country.
◆ Demonstrate knowledge and acceptance of a family's religion.
◆ Expect that a professional might be greeted with a cautious attitude, since many Arab Americans consider non-Arabs as outsiders who do not understand or respect their worldview.

Family
◆ Understand the importance of the family as the central, unifying unit.
◆ Support family stability by accepting and showing respect for traditional familial customs.

Implementing the Research
Haboush's article is so comprehensive that many ideas and suggestions can be sifted from the comprehensive review. Selected ideas include the following:

1. Teacher-education programs and school districts need to take planned approaches to teaching prospective and in-service teachers about Arab Americans and their families.

2. All teachers should appreciate the ethical considerations associated with teaching students of differing cultural backgrounds.

3. We know a great deal about African Americans and European Americans, but far less is known about Arab Americans and American Indians. Efforts should focus on these groups.

Source: Haboush, K. L. (2007). Working with Arab American families: Culturally competent practice for school psychologists. *Psychology in the Schools, 44*(2), 183–198.

Suggestions for Collaborative Efforts

Form groups of three or four that, if possible, represent our nation's cultural and gender diversity. Working collaboratively, focus your group's attention toward the following efforts.

1. Design a plan to reduce harassment and bullying of Arab American students. Identify your goals or objectives, methods, and materials for this effort. Will you consider your plan an instructional plan or a disciplinary plan? Will you take a cultural deficit approach or an objective plan for learning about cultures and promoting social justice? How will you evaluate your plan's effectiveness?

2. Design a one-hour school orientation program that can be presented to Arab American parents and families. Brainstorm in your group what these parents might need to know about the U.S. public school system—for instance, its egalitarian treatment of both genders, the emphasis on individualism, teacher and school expectations, parents' responsibilities and rights, and student rights. Let each person in your group take one aspect and tell what will benefit Arab American parents the most.

3. Interview a first-, second-, and third-generation parent (only two will suffice, if your group cannot locate three) to determine the challenges they face in dealing with the school and society in general. Make a chart that lists the challenges on the left and what your group thinks will help the parents on the right.

Expanding Your Horizons

Additional Journals, Books, and Internet Sites

Al-Hazza, T., & Lucking, R. (2005). The minority of suspicion: Arab Americans. *MultiCultural Review, 14*(3), 32–38.

> The writers discuss Arab Americans, a minority that is currently facing increased suspicion and discrimination. They also look at the diversity of Arab Americans, their history, and their current demographics.

Gorski, P. C. (2006). Beyond propaganda: Resources from Arab film distribution. *Multicultural Education, 13*(3), 56–57.

> As the title implies, this article looks at films that provide accurate and objective views of Arab culture.

Haboush, K. L. (2007). Working with Arab American families: Culturally competent practice for school psychologists. *Psychology in the Schools, 44*(2), 183–198.

> In this excellent article, Haboush looks at Arab American families and considers the ethical considerations of working with minority cultural groups.

Hackman, H. (2006). I exist: Voices from the Middle Eastern lesbian and gay community. *Multicultural Education, 13*(3), 56–57.

> Actually a video, this resource provides a heartfelt journey into the experiences of Arab and Arab American gays and lesbians living in the United States.

Wingfield, M. (2006). Arab Americans: Into the multicultural mainstream. *Equity and Excellence in Education, 39*(3), 253–266.

> The writer examines the place of Arab Americans in society, identity and discrimination in Arab American history, and the development of anti-Arab discrimination and violence.

Sarroub, L. K. (2005). *All American Yemeni girls: Being Muslim in a public school.* Philadelphia: University of Pennsylvania Press.

> This interesting book looks at the challenges of being Muslim in a public school.

Arab American Institute. www.aaiusa.org

> This organization promotes the welfare and overall progress of Arab Americans.

National Council of Arab Americans. www.arab-american.net

> This organization provides political analyses, resources, and information on Arab culture and history.

Tolerance.org. www.tolerance.org/teach/current/event.jsp?cid=249

> This Internet site provides information on Arab Americans and encourages tolerance, especially in times when tolerance is needed.

Allied Media Corporation. www.allied-media.com/Arab-American/Arab%20american%20Demographics.htm

> This organization maintains that the vast majority of Arab Americans are very much like other Americans, except that they are younger, more educated, more affluent, and more likely to own a business. Arab Americans want to enjoy the United States' riches while preserving the important parts of their native culture.

Understanding Asian American Children and Adolescents

Understanding the material and activities in this chapter will help the reader to:

◆ Describe the cultural, gender, socioeconomic, familial, and language characteristics of Asian American children and adolescents.

◆ Explain the "model minority" stereotype and its effects on Asian American children and adolescents.

◆ Describe Asian American learners and their development, achievement levels, language problems, and learning styles.

◆ List several practices that impede Asian American learners' educational progress.

◆ Offer several concrete suggestions for improving Asian American learners' self-esteem and cultural identities.

◆ List several points that educators of Asian Americans should remember.

◆ Suggest appropriate children's literature for Asian American learners (see the Appendix).

Opening Scenario

CULTURAL PORTRAIT

Chinese American Mina

Mina, a ten-year-old Chinese American girl, attends a large urban elementary school. The student population is approximately half European, one-fourth African, and one-fourth Asian and Hispanic. Although Mina makes about average grades, she does not make the high grades that her family and teachers expect. Her difficulty with the English language is probably the major reason for her grades, but other factors also contribute to the situation: Her family and teachers have expectations of her that are unrealistically high; she does not want to volunteer for special assignments; she does not want to raise her hand to answer; and she does not always understand the European American learner's attitude toward school, teachers, and people.

Mina feels a little lost. Her teachers are either European or African American. They are friendly and appear to want to help her, but they do not seem to understand her and the way she feels children should act around adults, especially teachers. Mina perceives the school as being oriented toward European American expectations, and perhaps a little toward the African perspective, yet very little toward the Asian or Hispanic view. While she feels somewhat frustrated with this arrangement, she also realizes that she has to do her best school work and that her behavior must be exemplary. Otherwise, her family might feel shame or disappointment.

Responding to Mina's psychosocial and intellectual needs first requires understanding her as an individual learner and then as a member of the Asian American culture. Mina's teacher, Mrs. Daniels, has responded by doing these things:

1. Help Mina to understand both the Asian culture and the American culture.
2. Maintain high but not unrealistic expectations for Mina, and avoid relying on cultural stereotypes.
3. Understand that Mina's reluctance to volunteer or raise her hand during class reflects her cultural background, not indifference or low ability.

4. Provide appropriate multicultural experiences that teach learners of all cultures about the Asian culture, including its diverse characteristics and many contributions.

5. Assign a professional in the school to be an advisor or mentor who will help Mina deal with daily school routines.

6. Meet with Mina's family to explain the philosophy and expectations of American schools and work to gain the understanding, respect, and support of Mina's family.

7. Decide how special service personnel (that is, guidance counselors, speech and language specialists, and other school support personnel) can assist Mina. ◆

Overview

Planning teaching and learning experiences for Asian American learners requires an understanding of their developmental characteristics, achievement levels, language problems, learning styles, and cultural characteristics. The diversity among Asian American learners also requires a consideration of their geographic, generational, and socioeconomic differences, as well as intracultural and individual characteristics.

Stereotyping, which plagues learners from all cultures, is a particular problem for Asian Americans. The notable success of the Asian American people has resulted in a "model minority" stereotype that sometimes leads educators to expect exemplary achievement and behavior of all Asian American learners. This chapter examines the cultural characteristics of Asian American children and adolescents and then focuses attention on these learners in teaching and learning situations.

Origins

Asian Americans include a number of national, cultural, and religious heritages and more than twenty-nine distinct subgroups, each with unique language, religion, and customs. The four major groups of Asian Americans include East Asian, such as Chinese, Japanese, and Korean; Pacific Islander; Southeast Asian, such as Thai and Vietnamese; and South Asian, such as Indian and Pakistani. Undoubtedly, similarities exist among these cultures, but educators working with Asian Americans need to remember Asians' different origins, ecological adaptations, and histories.

The term *Asian American* is an artificial one, originating as an imposed entity by non-Asians and later adopted by Asian American activists in the 1960s. Since the Immigration Act of 1965, the Asian American population has become more diverse ethnically, and with immigration legislation giving preference to those with more schooling, Asian Americans have been more fragmented socioeconomically.

Asian Americans have lived in the United States for over one-and-a-half centuries: Chinese and Asian Indians since the mid-nineteenth century, Japanese since the late nineteenth century, and Koreans and Filipinos since the first decade of the twentieth century. An earlier group of Filipinos settled near New Orleans in the late eighteenth century. Because of exclusion laws that culminated with the 1924 Immigration Act, the Asian American population was relatively small before the mid-twentieth century. As late as 1940, Asian immigrants and their descendants constituted considerably less than 1 percent of the U.S. population. With the passage of the 1965 immigration law, the United States opened its doors to formerly excluded groups. As a result, East Asians, South Asians, and Southeast Asians began arriving in increasing numbers.

Individual differences also exist in reasons for immigration and related hopes and expectations. Some immigrants are refugees from war-torn countries, and others are from the middle class of stable countries. Some came with nothing, and others came with skills and affluence.

Asian Americans Today

According to the U.S. Bureau of the Census (2007), 12,687,000 Asian Americans lived in the United States in 2005, compared to 10,589,000 in 2000. Among the 2005 population, 4,141,000 were twenty-four or less years of age; the median age was thirty-four and one-half years. We think the fairly young age of the Asian American population will result in an increasingly larger population.

Several indicators provide a portrait of Asian Americans today: 54 percent lived in the West in 1990, compared to 21 percent of the total population; their educational attainment varied widely by group; 67 percent of the Asian population, compared with 65 percent of all Americans, were in the workforce; and many work in higher-paying occupations, partly because of higher educational attainment (U.S. Bureau of the Census, 1993a).

There are several unique characteristics of the cultures of Southeast Asian countries that professionals working with children can misunderstand. Many people refer to any Southeast Asian child as "Vietnamese" without realizing that they may be insulting him or her because of a different cultural heritage. Such labeling fails to realize the bitter feelings among various nationalities and ethnic groups.

Stereotyping of Asian American Children and Adolescents

Asian Americans are often called the model minority because of their remarkable educational, occupational, and economic successes. The media like to portray Asian Americans according to this image. For example, some reports applaud the educational achievements of Asian Americans and generally stereotype them as successful, law-abiding, and high-achieving minorities. The success of many Asian students has created the model minority stereotype. The popular and professional literature often labels them as "whiz kids" and as "problem free." Some claim that Asians are smarter than other groups; others believe there is something in Asian culture that breeds success, perhaps the Confucian ideas that stress family values and education.

Other stereotypes include viewing Asian Americans as proficient in mathematics and not competent with verbal tasks. Such stereotypes might lead educators to hold high expectations of their Asian American students in some areas and low expectations in others. Both kinds of expectations can produce bored, frustrated students who are afforded few opportunities to learn at their ability and motivational levels. Educators must remember to view each child as an individual with unique strengths and weaknesses.

The academic successes of some Asian Americans have led to a perception that all Asian Americans are exceptional in all pursuits. To assume, however, such scholarly expertise on the basis of culture alone does not have any greater validity than does saying that all African Americans are incapable of high academic achievement or that all American Indians live on reservations. Cultural misconceptions of oneself can have a detrimental effect on the forming identity and can result in undue and unrealistic pressures and demands.

Cultural Characteristics

Teachers often think of Asian American children as studious, high-achieving, well-behaved students, whom educators expect to excel in the U.S. culture yet retain Asian American cultures, values, and traditions. Conforming to both Asian American and European American cultures results in high expectations and considerable problems for developing personalities and identities.

Differences between the European American culture of the United States and the many long-accepted traditions, customs, and values of Asian American families (both immediate and extended) contribute to the developing child's sense of confusion regarding role expectations. Children growing up in such a multicultural setting may develop an ethnic identity problem as two major role expectations confront them. Developing children can, indeed, become confused as their identities form. Educators who work with Asian Americans should remember the personality differences between these children and European American children. These differences deserve recognition as cultural variations and should be in proper perspective. For example, people have described Japanese Americans as quiet, reticent, and aloof in interethnic situations and as more dependent, conforming, and obedient to authority and more willing to place family welfare over individual wishes (Feng, 1994).

Several other cultural differences also warrant educators' attention: (1) Physical contact between members of the same sex is permissible but is not acceptable between members of the opposite sex, and (2) Vietnamese rarely touch their heads, either because of a religious belief or the fear of damaging their heads (West, 1983).

Recently arrived Asian children and adolescents may experience particularly acute conflicts. They are caught between their parents' culture and the school and have little power to influence either. These young people often serve as translators, and adults may call on them to complete forms, applications, and licenses.

Points to Ponder 6.1

Understanding Asian American Families

Meet with a group of Asian American parents and extended family members to discuss their perceptions and expectations of educators and schools. Allow sufficient time for questions and discussions. Do not be dismayed if parents do not express themselves, because they sometimes perceive teachers as authority figures or place teachers on a pedestal.

Gender

As in all cultures, particular differences distinguish females from males in the Asian cultures. First, in Asian families, females do not receive the respect that males receive; they are valued less than males. Similarly, they do not receive the opportunities afforded to males. Although these differences are only in cultural *expectations,* they can have far-reaching effects on Asian females' worldviews, motivation, and perception of their place in the world and their ability to perform in the home, community, and society.

Second and related, Asian females might show less motivation to succeed in ventures outside the home; they might be more reluctant to participate in class discussions and less willing to excel academically when the opportunity arises. In summary, just as we cannot classify all Asians in a single cultural group, it is equally dangerous to label all males and females as one homogeneous group.

Gender Perspectives 6.1 looks at gifted Asian American males and cultural dilemmas.

Gender Perspectives 6.1

GIFTED ASIAN AMERICAN MALES

With the growing Asian American population, schools need to be prepared to address the needs of this increasing cultural group. Unfortunately, the research on Asian American students is limited.

Kao and Hebert (2006) look at the success myth of Asian Americans—for example, that they are well behaved and demonstrate high motivation and high academic performance. Such stereotypical beliefs add to the pressure and create a potential crisis for Asian Americans. Their problems in U.S. schools result in some failing to achieve and some experiencing feelings of loneliness and disgrace.

In addition to facing the model minority stereotype, Asian students in this country must address the conflict between their ethnic identity culture and the dominant American cultural system. The Asian cultural system is rooted in Confucianism and Buddhism, whereas the American cultural system is influenced by capitalism, democracy, and Christianity.

Kao and Hebert (2006) present the cultural dilemmas of two gifted Asian American males and then offer suggestions for supporting these students:

- ◆ Understand the intergenerational conflicts that might occur between Asian and American parents and children. Some parents want their children to adhere to Asian values and expectations, while the children might feel obligated to (or simply want to) adopt American values.
- ◆ Have high expectation for students' academic achievement and behavior.
- ◆ Develop students' interests and talents during the early childhood years.
- ◆ Understand the ethnicity issues that underlie being Asian, male, and gifted.
- ◆ Avoid being too critical of the acculturated behaviors of children and the excessive pressure to follow family traditions and beliefs.

We recommend the Kao and Hebert (2006) article for anyone teaching Asian American males, especially those students who are gifted.

Source: Kao, C., & Hebert, T. P. (2006). Gifted Asian American males: Portraits of cultural dilemmas. *Journal of the Education of the Gifted, 30*(1), 88–117.

Socioeconomic Status

Asian Americans' socioeconomic status as a group shows the financial success of some and the dismal accomplishments of others. For example, in 2004, 145,000 families earned less than $10,000, while 152,000 earned more than $200,000. The greatest number of Asian American families (438,000) earned from $75,000 to $99,999. Disturbingly, in 2004, 9.8 percent lived below the poverty level and 17.1 percent lived at 125 percent of the poverty level. Of these, 10 percent were under the age of eighteen (U.S. Bureau of the Census, 2007). Some Asian Americans' socioeconomic status is indeed impressive and indicates many have overcome (or successfully coped with) racism and prejudice. Others have not been as fortunate and deserve better educational opportunities.

The accumulation of wealth allows people more options, opportunities, and increased amounts of leisure time. A change in economic circumstances also influences a person's social expression, values, and patterns of thinking and behaving. A learner's socioeconomic status is undoubtedly one of the most significant factors affecting his or her learning and achievement. Educators can readily understand the educational and social implications of a learner's socioeconomic status and the danger of basing curricular and instructional decisions on stereotypical beliefs and assumptions.

Trying to determine the socioeconomic level of Asian Americans proves difficult at best, because of the diversity among the Asian cultures and the lack of current information on their earning power and social class. Educators must be careful not to rely on the model minority stereotype by assuming that all Asian Americans experience social and economic success—at least not according to the common U.S. perception of success as the accumulation of material wealth. In all likelihood, some Asian Americans—like members of other cultures—have achieved socioeconomic success and others have not

Families

In 2004, there were 1,618,000 Asian American families in the United States. Of these, 1,409,000 were two-parent families and 209,000 were one-parent families. Of the one-parent families, 159,000 were headed by the mother and 50,000 were headed by the father (U.S. Bureau of the Census, 2007).

Child-rearing techniques of Asian American families, founded in cultural expectations, emphasize loyalty to the family. The culture sends a powerful message of the importance of not bringing embarrassment or shame to the family. The inculcation of guilt and shame is the principal technique that controls the behavior of family members. Parents emphasize their children's obligation to the family and their responsibility for abiding by family expectations. Adults consider children who act contrary to the family's wishes as selfish, inconsiderate, and ungrateful. The behavior of individual members is a reflection on the entire family. For example, aberrant behavior is great shame and is usually hidden from the public and handled within the family. Outstanding achievement in some aspect of life is a source of great pride for the child and for the entire family as well. Such a standard of morality sometimes causes confusion for children who are attempting to satisfy the expectations of two cultures, but it emphasizes the importance of unity and honor in the Asian American family.

Asian American children and adolescents learn early in life that the family is the primary unit and that considerable value should be placed on family solidarity, responsibility, and harmony. Communication with adults is usually one with way, primarily adults speaking to children. Children also learn loyalty to authority (Mathews, 2000). In summary, the family is central to the Asian culture. Individual conflicts may arise, because parents and family reflect traditional ways and children see another way of life.

Family allegiance and respect for parents and family play a significant role in the value system, achievements, and behavior of the developing Asian American child. In many Eastern and Southeast Asian cultures, Confucian ideals, which include respect for elders and discipline, are a strong influence. Most Asian American parents and families teach their children to value educational achievement, respect authority, feel responsible for relatives, and show self-control. Asian American children tend to be more dependent, conforming, and willing to place family welfare ahead of their own individual wishes than are other American children (Mathews, 2000).

Asian American parents seem to structure their children's lives for academic success more than Caucasian parents do. Asian parents are more likely to decide whether their children should go to college, to discuss SAT/ACT plans and preparation with their children, and limit television and video games. In general, it appears that Asian parents organize and structure their children's lives to facilitate academic success. Another important point, however, needs to be explained. People often have an authoritarian image of Asian parents. That is, Asian parents are less likely to be involved in children's actual academic activities.

Points to Ponder 6.2

Helping Asian American Families Understand U.S. Schools

Asian American families, especially first generation, might not understand U.S. schools. These families have traditionally placed greater value on sons than on daughters and feel considerable shame when children's achievements or behavior does not meet the family's expectations. List several ways—such as parent-education programs or orientation sessions—in which you can help Asian American families to understand U.S. schools better.

For example, they are less likely to decide what classes their children should take and to check on the completion of homework. They help their children with homework less often and discuss school progress less.

In the traditional family, age, sex, and generational status are the primary determinants of the child's role behavior. Ancestors and elders are greatly revered and respected and are actively involved with child rearing. Families are patriarchal. The primary duty of the son is to be a good son, and his obligations as a good husband or father come second to his duty as a son. The role of the female in the family is that of subservience to the male, the performance of domestic chores, and the bearing of children. Such generalizations may vary depending on socioeconomic class and generational status (Mathews, 2000).

What can educators do to support Asian American families?

1. Arrange small-group sessions with families (both immediate and extended), perhaps at Parent–Teacher Association (PTA) meetings or other school functions, to learn what families expect of schools and children and to explain school expectations to parents.
2. Learn about families from a variety of Asian cultures for a better understanding of intracultural and individual differences.
3. Learn about generational differences among families, for example, variations in first-, second-, and third-generation immigrant families in the United States.
4. Learn about families from differing socioeconomic groups to gain an understanding of values, traditions, and beliefs.

Religion

The recent influx of Indochinese, Chinese, Koreans, and other groups has increased the religious pluralism in the United States. Laotians and Cambodians are primarily Buddhists, as are the Vietnamese. Some Vietnamese, however, are Taoists or Roman Catholic. Some embrace the philosophy of Confucianism, as do the majority of Korean immigrants. Most Koreans are likely to be Buddhists. A minority, however, are Protestant, and a smaller, but still significant, group are Roman Catholic. The majority of Hong Kong immigrants are Buddhists; some are Taoists. Many of these immigrants are also likely to adhere to the teachings of Confucius (Gollnick & Chinn, 2006).

Asian Americans tend to practice values such as respect for ancestors, filial piety, and avoidance of shame. These moral principles define a person's obligation, duty, and loyalty to others. Good performance and achievement bring honor to the family. Shame and dishonor are powerful preventives to unacceptable behavior. This standard of morality may seem harsh and rigid to the outsider, but to many Asian Americans, it maintains honor and harmony in the family (Mathews, 2000).

Language

For a better understanding of Asian American learners, educators should recognize the problems Asian Americans have with English. Without doubt, the language barriers and problems confronting Asian American learners make achievements and educational attainments even more significant. Although many Asian American parents encourage the use of English, many adolescents still live in homes where the native language is the primary language. This results in learners who speak and understand two languages.

Understanding the spoken word and being understood while speaking English often pose difficult situations for Asian American learners, especially in school systems that forbid learners from speaking their native languages. For example, of the 4.1 million Asians five years and older, 56 percent did not speak English "very well," and 35 percent were linguistically isolated.

Japanese American and Chinese American boys and girls scored lower than European American children on the verbal sections of an achievement test. The reasons for language difficulties may include that Asian Americans often come from bilingual backgrounds and that cultural traditions and customs often restrict or impede verbal communication. Many Asian American families, for example, encourage one-way communication; that is, parents speak to children.

Educators working in multicultural settings with such children can avoid several of the pitfalls that may lead to stereotypical thinking. Educators must remember that Asian American students may be communicating in a second language. Although English may be the predominant language, these children may continue to hear their parents' native language.

Educators who work with Asian American learners readily recognize the language and communication problems. One of the authors taught a Japanese American learner who excelled over all others in the class. Her language problems, however, required that she study far longer and more diligently than her classmates. During tests and other written work, she relied extensively on her Japanese–English dictionary and requested extra time. Despite all her language difficulties, her persistence and determination overcame her deficiencies in English.

Not only must educators in multicultural settings understand (and be understood in) verbal interactions with Asian Americans, but they must also make an equal effort to understand nonverbal communication. Several examples of non-verbal behavior that adolescents learn show the distinctive differences among cultures. First, the forward and backward leaning of the body indicates feelings: A backward lean indicates a withdrawal from a conversation or topic, and a forward lean lets the speaker know that the listener is polite, concerned, and flexible. For educational efforts to be most effective, educators and Asian American learners should work actively to understand each others' verbal and nonverbal behaviors.

Achievement Levels

Although some Asian American students do not fare well educationally, many of them do (Maxwell, 2007). In 2005, 54 percent of Asian American males and 46 percent of Asian American females were college graduates (or higher). These numbers are up from 2000, when the numbers were 47.6 and 40.7 percent, respectively (U.S. Census Bureau, 2007).

Although Asian Americans undoubtedly have attained enviable accomplishment in U.S. schools, it is unrealistic to expect all Asian Americans to attain such achievement levels. Not all Asian immigrant children are superior students who have no problems at school. Some have learning problems; some lack motivation, proficiency in English, and financial resources; and some have parents who do not understand the U.S. school system because of cultural or language barriers.

When they first enter the United States, children often experience a clash between their cultures and the expectations of their new homes and schools. Several distinct differences exist between Asian and European American expectations and attitudes toward schools and teachers. First, teachers in Asia are accorded a higher status than teachers in the United States. The informality between American teachers and students may seem confusing to Southeast Asian children and appalling to their families. Second, their cultural backgrounds and values cause Asian children to expect considerable structure and organization.

One of the obvious differences in values is the high value of self-effacement and saving face; students wait to be answered or to participate unless the teacher requests otherwise. Having attention drawn to oneself—the teacher putting a child's name on the board for misbehaving, for example—can bring considerable distress. Another difference is that Asian social values call for children to listen more than they speak and to speak in a soft, well-modulated voice. In the United

States this characteristic is often perceived as shyness. Asian adults teach children to be modest in dress, manner, and behavior (Feng, 1994).

The European American emphasis on individualism may present challenges for Asian American learners, who seek to satisfy the demands of contemporary society while feeling loyalty to Asian American family traditions. Educators need to understand the Asian American's strong regard for the father as head of the family, the value placed on sons rather than daughters, and the respect for the older family members. Maintaining loyalty to family tradition while building an identity and life in a European American society that emphasizes individuality may prove troublesome for Asian American children and adolescents.

It is important that educators understand Asian American parents' perceptions of school behavior and achievement. Asian Americans come from cultures that often view children's behavior as the result of a lack of will or attributable to supernatural causes. Cases of school failure have resulted in parents' complaining that children are lazy and lack character.

Rather than look for educational reasons, parents often believe that the solution lies in increasing parental restrictions, more homework, and other negative sanctions designed to promote character development. Asian parents consider hard work, effort, and developing character the best avenues to improving behavior or school work. As educators quickly realize, such beliefs can be particularly acute for Asian American children with limited intellectual (or other) abilities.

Lee and Manning (2001) maintain that educators increasingly will be called on to work with Asian students and families. They also remind educators to remember the tremendous diversity among Asian Americans and to avoid stereotypes and generalizations. Whether through parent conferences, parent-involvement programs, or parent-education programs, Lee and Manning (2001) suggest that teachers and administrators must have knowledge of Asian cultures, positive attitudes toward Asian people, and skills to conduct successful conferences as well as involve and educate Asian parents and families.

Educators' openness to Asian cultures and commitment to working with Asian parents will contribute to teachers and parents developing a collaborative partnership that improves academic achievement and provides a more equitable learning environment for Asian students. Suggestions for achieving that are as follow:

1. Respect both immediate and extended-family members; consider Asian parents' English proficiency and their nonverbal communication; and prepare education programs for Asian parents.

2. Understand diversity within Asian ethnic groups.
3. Recognize Asian traditions of respect toward teachers.
4. Encourage children to be bicultural.
5. Eliminate the stereotype that all Asians are automatically smart in academics.

School Practices Promoting Asian Americans' Progress

Educators who understand Asian Americans' cultural backgrounds and school-related problems may actually contribute to their academic and social success in U.S. schools. Looking at Asian Americans from any other cultural perspective may promote learning experiences and expectations that are not compatible with Asian American expectations. The tendency toward generalizing across Asian customs and assuming too much homogeneity among learners negates or overlooks the tremendous cultural diversity between groups and ignores generational and socioeconomic differences.

What school practices might promote Asian American academic achievement and psychosocial development?

1. Provide teaching and learning experiences that place Asian American learners at an advantage.
2. Make school expectations clear to both students and parents.
3. Don't expect Asian American students to participate in discussion and sharing times, during which they may say something construed to shame their name or reputation.
4. Have realistic academic and behavioral expectations of Asian American learners, recognizing that some are academic achievers and some are lower achievers.

Suggestions for understanding and teaching Asian American learners include the following:

1. Avoid reprimanding or disciplining Asian American learners in front of peers. Having one's name written on the blackboard or on other public displays may be far more damaging to the Asian child than to the European American child (West, 1983).

2. Avoid thinking that all Asian Americans are high achievers who reach excellence in all academic areas and who model impeccable behavior.

3. Help the Asian American family to understand the U.S. school system and its expectations of learners and their families. Also try to understand how the Asian family perceives teachers—that is, with high respect. As the teacher earns the family's respect, the teacher gains its assistance and support.

4. Understand that behavior (at least to European American teachers) that may seem to indicate indifference or lack of interest (for example, looking the other way or not volunteering to answer) is appropriate for Asian learners. For example, Asian culture teaches learners to listen more than they speak and to speak in a well-modulated voice.

5. Understand other culturally specific traits: Asian American learners may be modest in dress; girls might be quieter than boys; girls might not want to reveal their legs during physical education activities; and problems might result when assigning girls and boys as cooperative learning partners (West, 1983).

Chiang (2000) maintains that given the increasing number of Asian immigrant children, educators need to recognize Asian students' cultural characteristics as well as learn to work with them effectively. In her article, she looks specifically at the relationship between teaching styles and Asian cultures, communication patterns, cognitive activities, and social support. Overall, she finds that Asian American students adjust well to U.S. schools academically. Still, some might need psychological support and understanding from teachers and administrators—for example, they might need more assistance and encouragement and less pressure from teachers and schools.

Chiang (2000) makes these recommendations:

1. Help Asian American students by giving clear directions, allowing choices of projects and peers, communicating on an individual basis, and providing peer tutoring.

2. Help parents of Asian students by developing an understanding of commonly accepted gender roles in the United States, an understanding of school systems and how they function, and being involved in their children's education.

3. Help policy makers assist Asian American students by recruiting Asian American teachers, revising the curriculum to reflect more positive images of Asian people, and providing in-service training for teachers to better acquaint them with school structures and family expectations.

Promoting Cultural Identities

Asian American children have special needs that responsive educators should address. In a school system that might seem different and perhaps even oblivious to their needs, these learners need teaching and learning experiences that reflect their cultural and social experience. Learners in formative developmental stages may begin to question their self-worth and their cultural worth. Responsive multicultural educators need to focus their efforts in several directions that will improve the self-esteem of Asian American learners.

First, the actual effect of the school experience on the Asian American learner deserves consideration. Attending a school that appears to direct attention toward the majority culture can cause Asian Americans to question their place in the school. Educators can focus attention in several directions: recognizing Asian Americans as integral and worthy learners in the school system; recognizing the Asian culture as worthy; and directly addressing the concerns of Asian Americans, for example, teachers who often have high expectations based on the model minority stereotype.

Second, educators can respond by understanding the cultural differences that affect Asian Americans and their academic and social progress in U.S. schools. For example, Asian Americans strive toward the accomplishment that brings pride to the family, in contrast to European Americans, who work for individual acclaim. The custom of many European Americans is to question the teacher, volunteer for an academic activity, or assertively raise their hands to answer a teacher's question. Such traits are in opposition to Asian beliefs. Teachers need to understand these cultural differences and then respond with appropriate teaching behaviors, rather than expect learners of all cultures to respond in a similar fashion.

Specifically, educators can do the following:

1. Read aloud culturally appropriate children's books about Asian Americans.
2. Convey a sense of welcome that makes children feel wanted, a part of the class, and an integral presence in the classroom.
3. Encourage them to make a "Me" collage that demonstrates both the individual and the Asian culture.
4. Encourage learners to engage in *open-ended writing* in which they can probe their feelings and express them without fear of sharing.
5. Teach learners to write about "What I Like about My Life" (and perhaps culture) or "Ten Things about Me," in which learners can feel free to express opinions and emotions.

Third, responsive multicultural educators need to engage in direct activities to improve the self-esteem of Asian American learners. Such activities include specifically addressing their needs, asking about their families (using extreme caution not to make the learner feel uncomfortable or think that the teacher is prying), genuinely and truthfully conveying to the learner that other students would benefit from knowing more about the Asian culture, and letting the students know that their presence is understood, accepted, and appreciated by both school personnel and other children and adolescents.

Educators should remember the importance of the family in efforts to improve cultural identity. Asians generally have close-knit families, and Asian people's feelings about themselves usually include a consideration of their feelings about the family (and vice versa).

Case Study

The Language Problem

Keigo, an Asian American fourth-grader, has a language problem that interferes with several aspects of her school life. She often cannot understand her teachers, and she has difficulty making friends. Her language at home and in her community does not pose a problem. Her parents and neighbors either speak their native language or a form of English not much better than Keigo's. Yet at school, Keigo's language results in her having to study harder and having few friends.

Keigo's teacher, Mr. Ottom, can take any of several approaches to help her improve her language, make better use of her study time, and improve her friendships. It is important at the outset for Mr. Ottom to avoid a blame the victim perspective, in which Keigo would be at fault for her lack of fluency in English. Mr. Ottom and the school as a whole should understand Keigo's situation and try to help her overcome the language barriers.

First, Mr. Ottom should make arrangements with the school's language specialist to meet with Keigo, determine the extent of her problem, and suggest possible remediation. Second, Mr. Ottom might consider placing Keigo in a cooperative learning team, in which other students can help her understand. Third, he might place Keigo and other children with language difficulties in a group that receives extra attention. Regardless of what means Mr. Ottom uses to help Keigo, it is important that he understand her and her problem rather than hope the problem will simply disappear.

Questions for Discussion:

1. What specific actions should Mr. Ottom take?
2. Reflect on this statement: "Her parents and neighbors either speak their native language or a form of English not much better than Keigo's." Perhaps Keigo's language works at home and in the community, but it does not work at school. The difference between home language and school language often causes a problem. What should the school's policy be toward this type of language difference?
3. What other resources might Mr. Ottom seek for more specialized assistance?

Summing Up

Educators planning educational experiences for Asian American learners should:

1. Reflect on both historical and contemporary Asian cultural experiences, and plan teaching and learning experiences accordingly.

2. Undertake objective assessments, rather than believe all learners are members of a model minority.

3. Understand that language warrants understanding because of its cultural basis (and its cultural value) and because of the problems many Asian Americans have with the English language.

4. Understand that positive self-esteem and cultural identities are crucial to Asian learners' psychosocial development and general outlook on life. Plan appropriate activities.

5. Recognize that students have their distinct culture with its unique cultural characteristics, rather than group all Asian American learners into one "Asian" culture.

6. Consider the tremendous diversity among learners—individual, generational, socioeconomic, urban, and rural—rather than categorize all Asian American learners into one homogeneous group.

7. Exercise extreme caution by not expecting all Asian American learners to be high achievers.

8. Recognize the family and its powerful influence (e.g., the injunction against bringing shame and embarrassment on the family) on children and adolescents.

Suggested Learning Activities

1. Complete a case study of a high-achieving Asian American student. Specifically, (a) outline outstanding accomplishments, (b) address how the family has contributed to successes, (c) describe any problems or frustrations the student may experience, (d) explain how one can account for outstanding achievements, even though language problems exist, and (e) ask how schools can address the student's problems. Show why it is imperative that educators not base teaching and learning experiences on the model minority stereotype.

2. Survey several educators who have taught Asian American students. Develop a survey designed to determine the strengths and weaknesses of Asian American learners, the educators' opinions of Asian American attitudes and achievements, and how schools respond to meet the individual needs of Asian American learners. What efforts can be made to educate parents and gain their support? Generally speaking, what approaches can you suggest to educators who work with Asian American learners of varying cultural backgrounds and individual differences?

3. Consider the following Implementing Research, which looks at an *Education Week* article that says Asian Americans often outperform their peers and are left out of the debate on the achievement gap.

Implementing Research

The "Other" Gap

Maxwell (2007) maintains that the debate about student achievement and how to close the gap for Asian Americans is often ignored. People too often assume that Asian Americans are outstanding academically. Such a stereotypical assumption results in educators trying to improve the academic achievement of Hispanic and African American students but not Asian American students. Altough there is little difference between the performance of whites and Asian Americans in the early grades on the National Assessment of Educational Progress, there is a gap by high school. Still, Asian Americans enroll in colleges and universities in a far higher proportion than their overall share of the U.S. population. At some elite universities, they make up 25 percent of the undergraduate student population.

Maxwell (2007) says Asian cultural traits are used to explain academic success. Such an attitude masks family income, parental educational levels, and how recently families immigrated to the United States, which affects all students. Educators should not base educational decisions on stereotypical myths. Not all Asian American students are high achievers, and this must be considered in closing the academic gap.

Implementing the Research

Although some might not consider Maxwell's article as research, it will be informative to educators and anyone believing the model minority stereotype.

1. Asian Americans should be considered as individuals, not as a high-achieving cultural group.

2. The achievement gap for Asian Americans needs to be examined, just as it should for all students.

3. Successful Asian Americans should be respected for their intelligence, determination, and hard work—again, like all students.

Source: Maxwell, L. A. (2007). The "other gap." *Education Week, 26*(23), 26–29.

Suggestions for Collaborative Efforts

Form groups of three or four that, if possible, represent our nation's cultural and gender diversity. Working collaboratively, focus your group's attention toward the following efforts.

1. Have each member of your group select an Asian American learner: a Japanese American, a Chinese American, a Filipino American, and a Korean American. After getting to know these learners and their families, show similarities and differences among the four cultures. Specifically consider cultural characteristics, families, academic achievement, socioeconomic accomplishments, and any other area in which similarities and differences are evident.

2. Suggest several ways educators can address Asian Americans' language problems. What language programs will most effectively help Asian Americans? What other efforts might educators implement to help Asian Americans overcome language obstacles?

3. Educators often experience difficulties locating children's books that focus on Asian American learners and themes. Consult recent publishers' catalogs and make a list of current children's books that appear to provide accurate descriptions of the Asian American culture. Check with textbook publishers to determine what efforts are being made to make textbooks more reflective of our increasingly multicultural society. (Also see the Appendix.)

Expanding Your Horizons

Additional Journals, Books, and Internet Sites

Alvarez, A. N., Juang, L., & Liang, C. T. H. (2006). Asian Americans and racism: When bad things happen to "model minorities." *Cultural Diversity and Ethnic Minority Psychology, 12*(3), 477–492.

> Professionals should understand racial identity theory and the manner in which Asian Americans are socialized to perceive racism.

Asian Americans.com. www.asianamericans.com

> This site defines an Asian American as a person of Asian ancestry and American citizenship, although that definition may be extended to include noncitizen resident Asians as well. The term *Asian American* was used informally by activists in the 1960s as an alternative to the term *Oriental,* arguing that the latter term was derogatory and colonialist.

Asian Nation. www.asian-nation.org/index.shtml

> This Internet site is a one-stop information resource and overview of the historical, demographic, political, and cultural issues affecting today's diverse Asian American community.

Doan, K. (2006). A sociocultural perspective on at-risk Asian American students. *Teacher Education and Special Education, 29*(3), 157–167.

> Asian students at risk are rarely mentioned, but Doan looks at teachers' perception and society's perception of Asian American students and offers suggestions for the field of education.

Duffy, J. (2007). *Writing from these roots: Literacy in a Hmong-American community.* Honolulu: University of Hawaii Press.

> This is an interesting book for those interested in the Hmong culture and community.

Infoplease. www.infoplease.com/spot/asianhistory1.html

> May is Asian Pacific American (APA) Heritage Month—a celebration of Asian and Pacific Islanders in the United States. This site includes these topics: Origins of APA Heritage Month, Asian-American History, Timeline of Asian-American History, and Japanese Relocation Centers.

Iowa State University, Diversity and Ethnic Studies. www.public.iastate.edu/~savega/asian_am.htm

> This site includes selected Asian American web resources useful for academic research and information purposes. (If you are doing library research, please see

the *Asian American Studies Library Research Guide.*) Only websites that contain realistic information about Asian Americans were considered; sites that are exclusively Asian in origin or focus are only rarely included. The recommended websites were evaluated for breadth, perceived authority, stability, usefulness, and accuracy.

Liang, C. T. H., Alvarez, A. N., Juang, L. P., & Liang, M. X. (2007). The role of coping in the relationship between perceived racism and racism-related stress for Asian Americans: Gender differences. *Journal of Counseling Psychology, 54*(2), 132–141.

These authors conclude that the more Asian American men perceive racism, the more likely they are to use support-seeking coping strategies.

Witkow, E. R., & Fuligini, A. J. (2007). Achievement goals and daily school experiences among Asians, Latino, and European American backgrounds. *Journal of Educational Psychology, 99*(3), 584–596.

Witkow and Fuligini suggest experiences in adolescents' daily lives help explain the relationship between goals and achievement outcomes.

Wong, F., & Halgin, R. (2006). The "Model Minority": Bane or blessing for Asian Americans. *Journal of Multicultural Counseling and Development, 34*(1), 38–49.

As the title implies, Wong and Halgin examine the prevalence, accuracy, and implications of this label and discuss problems associated with this characterization.

Understanding European American Children and Adolescents

Understanding the materials and activities in this chapter will help the reader to:

- ◆ Describe European Americans, their origins, and who they are today.
- ◆ Identify several stereotypes of European American learners and how these stereotypes adversely affect peers' opinions as well as educators' perceptions of their propensity toward academic success and behavior.
- ◆ Describe European Americans' cultural, gender, socioeconomic, family, religious, and language diversity.
- ◆ Describe European American learners, and show how teaching and learning practices can reflect knowledge of cultural differences and learning styles.
- ◆ Suggest appropriate readings for European Americans (see the Appendix).

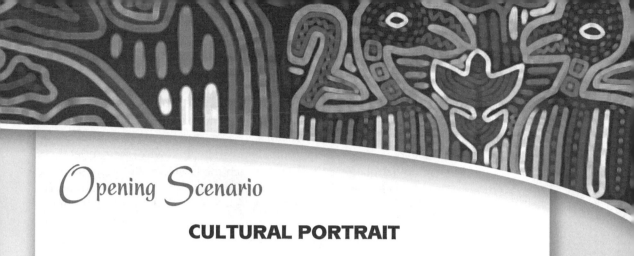

Opening Scenario

CULTURAL PORTRAIT

Greek American Helen

Helen, an eleventh-grader, is a second-generation Greek American female. She is personable and intelligent, speaks excellent English, and is an all-around good student. She talks of wanting to teach in an elementary school when she finishes college. While Helen is sociable and others like her, she does not have any close friends. In fact, she perceives several of her teachers as friends and talks with them at length whenever she can.

While Helen is Americanized in many ways, her parents and extended family members maintain Greek values, customs, and traditions. They continue to speak Greek in the home on many occasions. One of Helen's teachers, Ms. Jacobs, once telephoned Helen at home and asked to speak with her. Helen's father spoke English with such an accent and with such difficulty that Ms. Jacobs could not understand why Helen could not come to the phone. The next day, Helen asked Ms. Jacobs whether she had called and then explained that she was not at home. Ms. Jacobs perceived that Helen was uncomfortable that she had called and did not call her at home again.

Helen's family owns a fast-food restaurant, which has been in business for nearly twenty-five years, since her father brought his family from Greece. All family members work at the restaurant at some time; Helen probably works the least because she commits so much of her time to her school work.

Ms. Jacobs has genuine respect for Helen's Greek background, but she wonders how Helen considers her diversity. Does she feel accepted? Does her parents and family members' continuing to speak Greek bother her? Does she intentionally avoid working in the restaurant? Ms. Jacobs will not take any specific action, but she wonders about Helen's feelings and questions her decision not to discuss Helen's diversity with her. ◆

Overview

The African, American Indian, Arab, Asian, European, and Hispanic cultural groups make up a sizable percentage of our nation's diversity. Likewise, their differences, traditions, customs, language, and dialects enrich the United States in many ways. Another cultural group, however, also contributes to the nation's diversity. The various European American cultures bring a plethora of differences that perceptive educators will want their students to understand and appreciate. Just as Asian and Hispanic Americans originate from many places, European Americans originate from scores of locations, such as France, Germany, Greece, Hungary, Ireland, Italy, Poland, and Portugal, as Chapter 1 indicated. This chapter focuses on European Americans and their cultural, gender, socioeconomic, family, religious, and language diversity. To avoid overgeneralizing, we will discuss specific cultural groups, such as Helen's Greek American culture, whenever possible.

Origins

The hundred-year period from 1830 to 1930 was a century of mass immigration in the history of the United States. Many millions of people uprooted themselves, primarily from crowded places of Europe, and flowed outward to less crowded areas such as the United States. About 32 million left Europe for the United States, contributing enormously to the nation's expansion and industrial growth. The primary reason for this massive transfer of people from the Old World to the New World was the social and economic strain on the rural systems of Europe. More specific causes included large populations; the lack of farming land for all people; and the abolition of feudalism, which ended peasant privileges (Alba, 1985).

In the colonial days, most of America's immigrants came from Great Britain and Ireland, and a few came from Germany, France, the Netherlands, Belgium, and Luxembourg. During the early nineteenth century, Germans (mainly tradesmen, farmers, weavers, tailors, shoemakers, and carpenters) began coming in ever-increasing numbers. French, Norwegians, and Swedes also began moving to the United States, feeling the push of economic pressures at home and the pull of prospective free land and good wages in the New World. Italians began arriving in 1890, and from 1900 until the start of World War I, about a quarter of all immigrants were Italians. After World War II, many Germans arrived in the United States.

European American people came from a wide array of places—western and southern portions of Europe as well as the eastern portion and the Soviet Union.

Greeks, Italians, Poles, Irish, French, and Germans are well known in the United States, but other people from the Netherlands, Portugal, Spain, and Switzerland are less known. Each cultural group brought its own cultural characteristics, language, traditions, and customs, which contributed to the already rich diversity of this nation. They came to the United States for a number of different reasons: Some planned to earn money and return to their home country, whereas others planned to make the United States their home.

Although the number of European cultures makes it impossible to discuss them all, it is interesting to examine a few cultures and immigrants' reasons for coming to the United States. Such a discussion is limited to census information and recent books written on the European people; the same information is not available for all cultural groups.

Greek immigration began in the 1880s, when the Greek economy failed to show signs of improvement. These early immigrants came from the Peloponnesus and Tripoli, both agricultural and pastoral regions that were economically depressed. In fact, the Greek government actually encouraged young men to emigrate so they could send money back to Greece.

The majority of Poles came to the United States as a result of mass migration during World War II. The immigrating Poles were a diverse group. Some were women and children without an occupational designation; others were blacksmiths, carpenters, locksmiths, miners, dressmakers, shoemakers, and tailors. There was concern about how Polish immigrants would sustain themselves in their new land. Three percent entered with fifty dollars in their possession, having spent most of their money on transportation. Only about one-fourth had others, usually relatives, to cover the cost. Another problem, language, confronted Poles as they entered the English-speaking nation. They worked in the steel mills and coal mines of Pennsylvania, Ohio, and Indiana; in the automobile factories of Detroit; and in the stockyards of Chicago. Many changed their names to survive and hide their native origins.

More than 5 million immigrants from Italy arrived in the United States between 1820 and 1870, and more than 4.5 million came during the century of mass immigration, 1830–1930. Only the number of arrivals from Germany was larger. The Italian immigration was concentrated tightly into a small period of time—more than 4 million arrived between 1890 and 1921, and in fact, 2 million arrived during a single decade, 1901–1910. The peak year of Italian immigration was 1907, when nearly 300,000 came to the United States. Although it is difficult to pinpoint exact regions from which they came, many Italian immigrants came from Mezzogiorno. Between 1899 and 1910, when more than 2,200,000 immigrants came, perhaps as many as 80 percent came from the Mezzogiorno region (Alba, 1985).

Abrams (1993) reported that significant numbers of Jews migrated to Israel and to the United States from the former Soviet Union. With the crumbling of the Soviet economic system came a resurgence of anti-Semitism. Although the majority of Jewish people are choosing Israel as their new home, 40,000 immigrated to the United States in 1989.

These Jewish people, however, are not the first to arrive in the United States from the former Soviet Union. In the 1970s, some Jewish people arrived in the United States from the Soviet Union after the Six Day War and the Leningrad Trial. At first, nearly all left for Israel, but after 1972, a rising proportion chose other countries. The majority of the 90,000 Soviet Jews who chose the United States came from Russia, Byelorussia, and Ukraine, those republics most heavily under the rule of the Soviet regime. These Jews had had their Jewish heritage systemically denied through the closing of synagogues, the banning of the study of Hebrew and Yiddish, and the virulent anti-Israel, anti-Zionist propaganda of the Soviet regime.

Points to Ponder 7.1

Will Whites Become a Minority?

In a group of three or four, discuss this question: Are whites really becoming a minority because whiteness is not a fixed racial category? A number of demographic studies suggest that whites will become a minority. What does your group think?

European Americans Today

European Americans today live in many geographic areas of the United States. Available data from the U.S. Census Bureau do not indicate the cities where European Americans have selected to live. Some evidence, however, suggests that immigrants to the United States tend to settle near their port of entry. More than two-thirds of those who came from Italy, for example, live in the northeastern part of the country, where they arrived.

According to the U.S. Census Bureau, during 2005, approximately 46,500 Europeans entered the United States as permanent residents. The largest numbers arrived from Bosnia and Herzegovina, and substantial numbers came from Russia and Poland. Even using the latest census information, it is difficult to specifically determine people's native countries because some become U.S. citizens and are classified as permanent and others are not. Still, the immigration rate does not rank with the Hispanic birthrate and immigration patterns. Interestingly, most European Americans locate in states in the West (35 percent) and the South (31 percent), with the fewest locating in the Northeast (15 percent). Plus, one can only guess at the number of illegal immigrants in the United States

(U.S. Census Bureau, 2007). Regardless of the actual numbers, the United States is a country of destination for many people of differing cultures, languages, and traditions.

 # Stereotyping of European American Children and Adolescents

European cultures are not immune to the stereotyping that has dogged American Indian, African, Asian, Arab, and Hispanic cultures. European groups have been considered in terms of undesirable characteristics. Italians have been stereotyped as being swarthy, bearing signs of physical degradation (such as low foreheads), having criminal tendencies, and being prone to passion and violence. Jews are stereotyped as stingy, shrewd, and intellectual. Germans are often characterized as evil, incompetent, or mad. Readers know that this unfair and dangerous list could continue.

Stereotyping, racism, and discrimination can affect European Americans, just as they affect people from all cultures. Plus, the basis for these insidious acts or feelings can result from reasons other than the color of peoples' skin or the language they speak.

> **Points to Ponder** **7.2**
>
> **European American Stereotypes**
>
> Unfortunately, stereotypical assumptions about people continue and are often the point of jokes. We are concerned that educational decisions are often made on the basis of one's skin color or socioeconomic status. What are some stereotypes of European Americans, such as the Polish, Germans, and Greeks, just to name a few? Is there a basis to any of these statements? Look at some textbooks (especially ones a little older). What stereotypes do you see? How do stereotypes affect people in their daily routines? How can we reduce stereotypes and gain a better understanding of people?

Cultural Characteristics

What constitutes the cultural characteristics of European Americans? European Americans comprise numerous subcultures that vary by country and language, economic status, generation in the United States, religious affiliation, and a host of other factors. Still, Kitano and Perkins (2000) suggest several common European American cultural values, such as beliefs, interaction and communication patterns, and behavioral expectations. Values include an emphasis on the individual, personal achievement, independence, and control over one's environment. European Americans can best be described as holding firm beliefs in support of inalienable rights (e.g., privacy), free enterprise, and private property. Interaction patterns are characterized by role specialization, self-sufficiency (as opposed to teamwork), competition, and communication that is direct, informal, and assertive. Overall, European Americans place importance on time, cleanliness, hard work, material comforts and material wealth, and an orientation toward work and the future. The most valid cultural descriptions of European Americans come from considering individual cultures.

In general, Greek Americans are confident that they alone know the causes of their problems and how best to solve them. If they feel powerless, they are likely to either overdo attempts to control their families or sink into fatalistic resignation. If misfortune comes their way, they assume that the causes of the problems come not from themselves but from somewhere outside the family, such as the malice of neighbors or the envy of competitors.

Greek Americans take tremendous pride in individual achievement and consider themselves as individuals. Greek Americans may have difficulty cooperating with others, especially in business deals. They prefer a competitive atmosphere and are usually unwilling to put aside their individual interests for the sake of the group.

Italian Americans have a strong allegiance to family and tend to live where they grew up. They believe that young people should learn from their elders and have an allegiance to a church. They are suspicious of strangers and expect filial obedience. Some of these tendencies (e.g., suspiciousness of strangers) decrease with education and advancing occupational position (Alba, 1985).

Greek Americans value frugality, careful saving, and wise use of financial resources; they often work two jobs. Scourby (1984) describes Greek Americans in several ways: They have clearly defined status and roles in work situations; they practice patriarchal control and have deeply binding extended kinship networks; they value interdependence among people (rather than individualism); and they demonstrate a strong need to defend family honor and, generally speaking, have a love of *philotimo,* or honor.

Gender

Although gender differences are not an area of extensive research, they exist in European American males and females, just as they do in all cultures. Girls and boys have different learning styles, worldviews, perceptions of motivation and school success, and learning strategies. For example, an educator cannot conclude that a cooperative, seemingly passive female is not motivated, because boys show different signs of motivation and competitive behaviors. The educator's challenge is to recognize that girls and boys are different, make an attempt to know individual females, and plan strategies to which females can relate.

Kitano and Perkins (2000) maintain that whereas European American parents value independence, achievement, individualism, and hard work in boys, the same is not always true with daughters. Parents' actions sometimes teach daughters to be dependent on others (perhaps a man) and to lack confidence in their abilities. For example, some daughters learn that they should not outperform men in academic or physical skills or they will end up isolated and unloved. Instead, daughters should channel their work into relationships and toward home-centered, family-oriented achievement.

Kitano and Perkins (2000) describe factors affecting achievement of fifteen highly accomplished European American women. As children and adolescents, most of the gifted European American participants read fervently, achieved in school, and lacked confidence about their popularity with peers. Consistent with the literature on Europan American culture, their communities valued hard work, achievement, and self-reliance and sometimes communicated confusing messages to women. Despite the group's high academic performance, half of the participants remembered K–12 schools as unchallenging, neglectful of their needs, and as providing poor or inadequate counseling. Still, many recalled individual teachers who encouraged and inspired them.

Implications for elementary and secondary schools include the following:

◆ Provide a more challenging curriculum, one that meets the academic needs of both girls and boys.
◆ Provide systematic and developmentally appropriate educational and career counseling.
◆ Provide constructivist coping strategies that have the potential to prepare gifted young women for success in a gendered and heterosexist society.

Gender Perspectives 7.1 looks at the gender gap in the National Assessment of Educational Progress (NAEP) over a four-year time period. The NAEP began in 1969 and has become the only nationally representative and continuing assessment of what U.S. students know in the various subject areas.

Socioeconomic Status

Describing the socioeconomic status of the many European cultures is nearly impossible. Just as with other cultures we discuss in this book, many variations exist among European cultures. There are both wealthy and poor European Americans, just as among all cultures. Many criteria determine a person's socioeconomic status: Is the husband or father present? Does the wife work? How many

Gender Perspectives 7.1

GENDER GAP IN NAEP SCORES

Klecker (2006) presents a secondary analysis of the NAEP reading scores in the fourth, eighth, and twelfth grades to determine gender differences in reading scores. In her brief discussion of the No Child Left Behind Act (NCLB), she argues that the "no child left behind" (p. 50) in reading is very likely to be a male—from elementary school through the university level. She explains that the No Child Left Behind Act requires state participation in the NAEP to receive funding.

Klecker explains that the NAEP includes differing reading contexts as well as comprehension questions developed to engage the different approaches readers may take to understand what is being read. According to Klecker, the research strongly suggests a positive relationship between being female and reading achievement. Her study clearly shows that school improvement efforts, including NCLB, should take a more careful look at males and reading across grades P–12.

While the Klecker study is well designed and written, we hope readers will avoid assuming the stereotype that females perform better in reading and that boys perform better in science and mathematics. Just as with cultures and social classes, educators need to examine individual males and females to determine reading motivation and reading abilities. Believing in the stereotype can result in students meeting lower expectations or sometimes failing to meet overly high expectations.

Source: Klecker, B. M. (2006). The gender gap in NAEP fourth-, eighth-, and twelfth- grade reading scores across years. *Reading Improvement, 43*(1), 50–56.

children are in the family? Are the people living in a part of the country where the cost of living is high or low? How well does the family manage its money?

Families

An educator should approach any discussion of family characteristics with considerable caution. Family patterns differ according to time of immigration, region of origin, economic class, and religious background. Many factors influence how a family lives, the roles of the husband and wife, perspectives on and treatment of children, and the importance of extended-family members. Although pre-service and in-service teachers need information about European families, providing a description of these families risks stereotyping. To avoid stereotyping, we attempt to use only the most objective information and the most widely accepted resources.

Parents and families are expected to be involved in their children's education and to work as partners with teachers. Education is highly regarded at all levels. Cultural emphasis on independence and achievement becomes manifested in parents' expectations for self-reliance on the part of children. In European American families, offspring frequently participate in decision making at early ages; have designated chores within the household; and, as adolescents, hold part-time jobs. Families expect youth to establish their own identities, leave the family home, and create their own families (Kitano & Perkins, 2000)

In the German American family, the husband or father is the head of the household and leader of the family. Traditionally, the father, although sometimes sentimental, has a stern side. He is usually self-controlled, reserved, strict, and stubborn. Somewhat distant, the husband or father is often less emotionally available to the children than their mother. The German American woman, regarded as hardworking, dutiful, and subservient, adopts her husband's family and friends and gains his social status. Her contributions center mainly around household and family duties. Today the wife's main tasks continue to focus on the house and the family. In fact, how her husband and children look can be a source of pride to her (Winawer-Steiner & Wetzel, 1996).

The Greek American family maintains strict sex roles. Men provide economic necessities, and women cater to men's desires and wish to be good wives. Men are authoritarian fathers and husbands. Often appearing emotionally distant, they are parsimonious with praise and generous with criticism. They often tease their children (some say to toughen them), and children learn that teasing is part of being loved. Other male characteristics include revering their mothers, valuing the family honor, and believing the women's place is in the home. Women expect to comply with tradition and view motherhood as a fulfillment. They prefer male children over female, even in urban areas of the United States. Having a son is a mother's main source of prestige. Parents feel that some emotions, such as uncertainty, anxiety, and fear, are weaknesses that should be hidden from their children (Welts, 1982).

Irish American women have traditionally dominated family life and primarily found their social life through the church. They have enjoyed a greater amount of independence relative to women in other cultures. More Irish women have immigrated to the United Stated than Irish men. Irish families often pay as much attention to the education of their daughters as of their sons. Traditionally, fathers have been shadowy or absent figures, and husbands have dealt with wives primarily by avoidance. Discipline is maintained by ridicule, belittling, and shaming. Children are generally raised to be polite, respectful, obedient, and well behaved. Parents rarely praise or center attention on their children (McGoldrick, 1982).

For Italians, the family is the training ground for learning to cope with a difficult world. The father has traditionally been the family's undisputed head, often authoritarian in his rule and guidelines for behavior. He usually takes his responsibilities to provide for his family very seriously. As the ultimate authority on living, he offers advice on major issues. The mother provides the emotional sustenance. While yielding authority to the father, she traditionally assumes responsibility for the emotional aspects of the family. Her life centers around domestic duties, and she is expected to receive her primary pleasure from nurturing and servicing her family. Concerning children, there is a marked difference between sons and daughters. Sons are given much more latitude in what they do. The family expects a daughter, rather than a son, to assume major responsibility for an aging or sick parent. The extended family plays a central role in all aspects of Italian family life, including decision making.

A major characteristic of the Polish American family is its respect for individual family members. The father and husband is the acknowledged leader of the household. The family is to respect and obey his wishes. Children are raised in a strict tradition of discipline, and they are to give their fathers unquestioned obedience. They are disciplined physically, sometimes harshly. Second-generation children have become acculturated, but the practice of physical discipline continues.

In the Portuguese American family, the man maintains great physical and emotional strength to combat life's difficulties. Family members tend to keep feelings to themselves to avoid the loss of respect or power. The father expects to receive respect and obedience from his children. Virtue and purity are desirable feminine qualities for the Portuguese woman. Her role includes loving, honoring, and obeying her husband and caring for her family's many needs. Children are to be seen and not heard. They receive most physical and emotional attention from their parents from infancy to about school age. Girls tend to receive overt displays of affection from both parents; the parents, especially the father, often don't give to boys in the same way.

Religion

As with other descriptors, European Americans' religion deserves careful consideration. A culture's religion often depends on its specific geographical origin and degree of acculturation.

Italian Americans are predominantly Catholic. One survey showed that 90 percent of the respondents had been raised as Catholics, and 80 percent called themselves Catholic at the time of the survey. Because the church has stood for tradition, family, and community, Italians continue to offer their support to the church (Alba, 1985). Similarly, Polish Americans have a powerful allegiance to the Catholic church.

By 1923, there were about 140 Greek churches in the United States. Each community of Greeks formed a board of directors whose function was to build a Greek Orthodox church. Some attempts were made to unite the Greek church with other Eastern churches into an American Orthodoxy, but this consolidation did not materialize. The church seems inextricably intertwined with its role as transmitter of the Greek heritage (Scourby, 1984).

For most newcomer Jews, their primary motivation in leaving the Soviet Union was fear of anti-Semitism rather than the desire for religious freedom. Most Soviet Jews view themselves as culturally Jewish. They are interested in the Jewish past expressed in history and literature, but they are not sure which religious practices have meaning.

Language

U.S. Census information suggests most learners from Germany and the United Kingdom have little difficulty with the English language. On the other hand, over half of the Italians living in this country experience difficulty with the language. (Census documents do not provide information on language for the other European groups.) Without doubt, considerable diversity exists within the three groups. Several factors influence learners' ability to speak English—for example, whether their parents and families live in *language enclaves* where people speak native languages, whether the parents speak the native language in the home, whether parents are trying to learn to speak English, and the school's efforts to provide programs in English as a second language (and show appreciation for native languages).

Remember Helen in the opening Cultural Portrait? She is a good example of a Greek American

Points to Ponder 7.3

Language Differences

We often hear about students with language difficulties, but some people think only about Asians and Hispanics. One of the authors of this text had a Greek student a few years back. Although she was fluent and articulate in English, her first-generation parents knew very little of the language. Trying to reach her via telephone was very difficult if she did not answer the phone. In the school district where you teach or plan to teach, what languages are spoken? How can professional educators plan for students speaking so many different languages? How should programs for students who speak European languages differ from those provided for Asian and Hispanic students?

who can speak fluent English. Some of her Greek friends, however, are not as fortunate. Considerable variation exists in European Americans' ability to speak English. Too often, we assume that European Americans are fluent in English. Such an assumption can lead to problems for both students and educators.

While definitions of literacy differ, we prefer the one adopted by the National Assessment of Adult Literacy, which defines *literacy* as "using printed and written information to function in society, to achieve one's goals, and to develop one's knowledge and potential" (National Assessment of Adult Literacy, 2007, p. 2).

The variety of languages spoken in American homes is a good indication of the language difficulties experienced in American schools. For example, in 2004, 783,000 Americans spoke Italian in the home, and 1,087,000 spoke German. A wealth of other languages (e.g., Russian, Polish, and Greek) are also spoken in U.S. homes (U.S. Bureau of the Census, 2007). While schools and geographical areas differ, educators still have a challenge to meet the language needs of European American children and their parents or caregivers.

School Practices Promoting European Americans' Progress

What school practices might impede European American learners' progress? It sounds ironic to even suggest that school practices would interfere with students' learning and overall school progress, especially because a major goal of schools is to teach. Schools, however, often have practices that do not contribute to the academic achievement and overall development of all learners.

First, policies toward language might be a detrimental factor. Some schools forbid learners to speak their native languages. For example, the school might not allow one Greek American child to teach another Greek American child their native language. Also, some schools fail to provide adequate English as a second language (ESL) programs. As a result, learners are taught in a language that they do not fully understand.

Second, perhaps because of language difficulties or teachers' perceptions, schools sometimes place European Americans in a group that is academically too high or too low for their abilities. Third, teachers sometimes fail to realize that learners in various cultures have differing learning styles and perspectives of motivation and school success.

Promoting Cultural Identities

As other chapters on the various cultures have indicated, perceptive educators, especially those teaching in multicultural settings, need to be aware of the importance to children and adolescents of the formation of positive cultural identities. Cultural differences play significant roles in a young person's degree of self-worth and self-image. For example, a student from a culture different from the teacher's and from a lower socioeconomic level may indeed consider his or her differences as inferior or wrong. Perceptive educators recognize the disastrous consequences such feelings can have on children's and adolescents' sense of personal worth.

Scholars can take special steps to promote positive self-esteem and cultural identities:

1. Educators, perhaps through academic and extracurricular programs, can help European American children and adolescents understand culture, recognize how culture affects people's lives, and understand that they cannot place values on culture.
2. Educators can work toward providing all children and adolescents with accurate and objective materials and lead discussions about culture and cultural differences that dispel as many myths, distortions, and stereotypes as possible.

Case Study

Anna—An Italian American Girl

Anna is a nine-year-old, second-generation Italian American girl living in a large urban area. She lives with her father, mother, and grandmother, who is her father's mother. Anna attends school in an overcrowded city school, which has a cultural composition that is fairly representative of that of the nation. While a number of European American cultures are represented, significant numbers of African and Hispanic American students also attend the school. Anna feels fairly safe in her school, except when fights break out, and the school's security guards have done a good job of curtailing fights.

Anna's teacher, Ms. Taylor, is a white American woman who has tried to understand her and her family traditions. Anna likes her and thinks Ms. Taylor likes her, although she does not want the teacher to meet her parents except when absolutely necessary. Anna has a conflict between her family and her school: Her parents do not understand what the school is trying to do. Their English is not very good; in fact, they continue to speak Italian at home. Sometimes, Anna's school work makes little sense to them, and they usually do not understand the written correspondence that comes from the school. Anna tries to interpret the English and explain the meaning of the correspondence to her parents.

Anna works very hard at her school work and usually does pretty well. She does all right in reading and the other school subjects, except mathematics. Although she studies daily, her grades in math are not as high as her other grades. She wants to improve, both to satisfy her teacher and her parents.

Anna has one or two friends but not anyone she can really call a best friend. She is sociable with people once she gets to know them, but at first, she is a little quiet (perhaps a little suspicious) around strangers.

Questions for Discussion:

1. What could Ms. Taylor do to assist Anna and her family with communication problems? How can Anna's parents gain a better understanding of important school correspondence and the school's roles and objectives?
2. When Anna's parents attend a parents' meeting, what can Ms. Taylor do to make them feel comfortable and let them know she wants to help Anna? How can Ms. Taylor address Anna's family's suspicious view of the school and individual teachers?
3. What can Ms. Taylor do to help Anna in mathematics? Is motivation the problem? Is the level of curricular content the problem? Generally speaking, what can Anna's teacher do?
4. How can Ms. Taylor help Anna to make closer friends with whom she can speak and socialize? Or is socialization the teacher's role? If it is the teacher's role, what curricular materials and instructional methods might improve Anna's socialization?

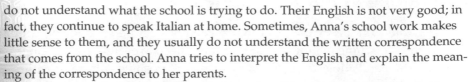 Summing Up

Educators planning educational experiences for European American learners should:

1. Perceive European American learners as an integral part of our nation's diversity, even though little attention and research have been focused toward this group.
2. Recognize the futility of past educational practices, in which language programs were inadequate and cultural differences in motivation and learning went unrecognized.

3. Recognize that girls and boys have different perceptions of motivation and school success and perceptions of learning strategies.

4. Realize that cultural characteristics vary among European Americans and that people also differ according to generational status and age, socioeconomic status, and gender.

5. Understand that European Americans vary widely in their ability to speak English and that the need is strong for methodically planned language programs.

6. Consider European American language differences, learning styles, perceptions of motivation and school success, cooperation versus competition, and differences in behavior expectation and management.

7. Be aware how important it is for European American children to develop positive self-esteem and cultural identities.

Suggested Learning Activities

1. Interview a first- or second-generation Greek, French, or German American student to determine the problems or special challenges he or she faces in school. If possible, meet with the family as well to learn what problems they experience with the schools. Then, list problems on the left side of your paper and possible solutions on the right.

2. Language problems continue to plague many European American learners: They cannot speak the language of the school but are forbidden to speak their native languages in school. Their parents cannot understand the school's language, and the school might show little appreciation for native languages. Yet, in all candor, educators feel they should use the language of the nation or the language most students speak. The dilemma challenges many schools in our nation. Think about and write a brief proposal (no matter how radical and forward looking!) to address this challenge.

3. Consider the following Implementing Research, which looks at a teacher's efforts to help students rethink the line between Mexico and the United States.

Implementing Research

Rethinking the Line

Bigelow (2007) maintains that studying the U.S.–Mexico immigration issue helps students to understand the global economic and social forces that affect us all. He also maintains that the standard curriculum in U.S. schools fails to help students think historically and critically about immigration issues. Two key questions need to be addressed: What is the origin of the U.S.–Mexico border? Why are so many people fleeing Mexico and coming to the United States? Answering such questions will provide students with a fuller perspective about the line between these two nations and peoples.

According to Bigelow (2007), in his students' minds, "the line dividing Mexico and the United States is as clear as if it had been decreed by some border deity" (p. 47). Bigelow prepared a unit on the relationship between the two countries for his class of mostly European American, working-class eleventh-grade students. He reports on the success of the unit with some students, noting that other students held onto stereotypical ideas and perspectives.

Reexamining Mexican Americans' migrant roots shows a lack of curiosity by students about why an enormous number of people risk their lives to enter the United States. While stories abound about daring attempts and the border patrol, few stories look at topics such as why the majority of Mexicans are poorer and more economically insecure than they were just a few years ago. Bigelow blames this condition partly on the North American Free Trade Agreement (NAFTA), which greatly reduced tariff and nontariff trade barriers between Mexico, the United States, and Canada. According to Bigelow, manufacturing wages throughout Mexico have declined by 9 percent and poverty has increased from 54 percent in 1989 to 81 percent in 2001. Air pollution has increased as well.

In his article, Bigelow explains his curricular unit and some of the successes and challenges. We recommend the article to readers who want to produce a similar unit.

Implementing the Research

1. Students need to learn about the two sides of the Mexico–U.S. border controversy and the results of NAFTA, so they will be better able to make informed decisions.

2. Teachers need to work toward changes in students' attitudes toward immigration issues as well as gains in knowledge.

3. Teachers need to help students of all cultures examine the economic perspectives of other people.

Source: Bigelow, B. (2007). Rethinking the line between us. *Educational Leadership, 64*(6), 47–51.

Suggestions for Collaborative Efforts

Form groups of three or four that, if possible, represent our nation's cultural and gender diversity. Work collaboratively and focus your group's attention on the following efforts:

1. Have each member of your group interview four or five students from different European cultures, preferably first and second generation. As a group project,

design an interview to learn about differences in cultural characteristics, language, family (be careful, some cultures may feel you are prying), social class, and gender. What differences do you find among cultures? Did you find intracultural differences? Were there significant gender differences? What role does social class play in determining what a person is like? Last, what differences did you find between first- and second-generation European Americans?

2. We hear that people from different cultures are "lazy," others "dumb," some "swarthy," and others "stingy." Some are "model minorities," and others are prone to passion and violence. Being careful to respect class members' feelings and cultures, make a list of stereotypes (perhaps on the board as a class project). To show stereotypes are myths and often the result of hate mongering, hypothesize how these stereotypes might have begun. How can stereotypes affect the person being stereotyped and the person harboring the stereotype? How should we as educators respond when we hear someone describe another person in stereotypical terms?

3. In Klecker's (2006) discussion of No Child Left Behind, she argues that the "no child left behind" (p. 50) in reading is very likely male. Working collaboratively and assuming Klecker is correct, discuss why this achievement gap persists. Have actual gender differences been inherited or socialized? We have often read that schools cater to European American males. If this is true, why do boys have more difficulty with reading than girls? What can educators do to address this reading problem?

Expanding Your Horizons

Additional Journals, Books, and Internet Sites

Birenbaum, M., Nassar, F., & Tatsuoka, C. Y. (2007). Effects of gender and ethnicity on fourth graders' knowledge states in mathematics. *International Journal of Mathematical Education in Science and Technology, 38*(3), 301–309.

These authors look at the achievement gap between cultural groups on a national mathematics test.

Cohall, A. T., Cohall, R., Dye, B., Dini, S., Vaughn, R. D., & Coots, S. (2007). Overheard in the halls: What adolescents are saying, and what teachers are hearing. *Journal of School Health, 77*(7), 344–350.

This study examines the role played by general academic teachers in facilitating adolescent health promotion efforts.

Consedine, N. S., Sabag-Cohen, S., & Krivoshekova, Y. S. (2007). Ethnic, gender, and socioeconomic differences in young adults' self-disclosure: Who discloses what and to whom? *Cultural Diversity and Ethnic Minority Psychology, 13*(3), 254–263.

> These authors look at the self-disclosure of feelings, thoughts, and experiences among young people and maintain that self-disclosure has numerous implications for relationships and health.

Farver, J. M., Yiyuan, X., Bakhtawar, R., Narang, B. S., & Lieber, E. (2007). Ethnic identity, acculturation, parenting beliefs, and adolescent adjustment. *Merrill-Palmer Quarterly, 53*(2), 184–215.

> These authors consider how child-rearing beliefs change as immigrant families adapt to the host culture.

Johnson, L., & Joshee, R. (2007). *Multicultural education policies in Canada and the United States.* Vancouver, British Columbia: UBC Press.

> Learning about the similarities and differences among multicultural education policies in Canada and the United States can be both interesting and beneficial.

Wadsworth, D., & Remaley, M. H. (2007). What teachers want. *Educational Leadership, 64*(6), 23–27.

> These authors examine what parents want in school, focus on standards and classroom atmosphere, and suggest that teachers and parents have similar concerns.

Wolfsberg, J. S. (2007). Successful prevention of underage drinking and other drug use: An integrated approach. *Independent School, 66*(2), 104–107.

> Wolfsberg discusses alcohol use among underage students and calls for a new approach to addressing the problem.

Chicago State University. http://webs.csu.edu/~amakedon/articles/GreekAmerican .html

> This Internet site provides excerpts from *The Social Psychology of Immigration: The Greek-American Experience*, by Alexander Makedon.

www.italianamericans.com/home.html

> This website chronicles the rich Italian culture, heritage, and traditions that have been passed down to the current generation from parents, grandparents, and great-grandparents.

Quagliata Family Genealogy Project. http://home.comcast.net/~m.quagliata/iahistory .html

> The site focuses on Italian history, culture, and traditions.

WLIW Television. www.wliw.org/productions/greek1.html

The ongoing odyssey of the Greek American experience—a story inspired by the muses and infused with an enthusiasm of mythic proportions—is explored in *The Greek Americans*. This tribute to Greek culture and tradition shares the collective memory of an extraordinary group, from the untiring efforts of the first Greeks to land on American shores to some of their most famous American achievers.

Understanding Hispanic American Children and Adolescents

Understanding the material and activities in this chapter will help the reader to:

- ◆ Describe the cultural, gender, socioeconomic, familial, and language characteristics of Hispanic American children and adolescents.

- ◆ Understand the dangers of stereotyping Hispanic American learners and know how to respond appropriately in teaching and learning situations.

- ◆ List and describe the educational characteristics and problems of Hispanic American learners.

- ◆ Name several practices that impede the educational process of Hispanic American children and adolescents.

- ◆ List several points that educators of Hispanic American children and adolescents should remember.

- ◆ Suggest appropriate children's literature involving Hispanic American learners (see the Appendix).

Opening Scenario

CULTURAL PORTRAIT

Teaching Hispanic American Students

Mr. Donaldson, an elementary school teacher, faces two major challenges in teaching Hispanic students. First, he has little patience with Hispanic students experiencing difficulty with English, and second, he has low academic expectations for these students. He just doesn't think they can learn English and follow English-language instruction.

Mr. Donaldson has a fourth-grade student, Maria, whose lack of proficiency in English has left her virtually unable to learn. Rather than providing a meaningful learning experience, the school day is a time of boredom and frustration. Devastating consequences await Maria and other similar learners with limited English proficiency, who feel stupid. Some feel as though teachers have forgotten they are there, and others wish they were not there. Even though achieving language proficiency takes time and effort, Maria needs to feel that her teachers and other school personnel care and want to help her. Mr. Donaldson is convinced Maria cannot learn and was overheard saying in the hall, "Hispanic students always experience learning problems in American schools. They have so many problems—language, poverty, and those big families! What more can I expect of these students?"

Mrs. D'Angelo, another teacher in the school, overheard Mr. Donaldson's remark and pondered whether she should talk with him about his attitudes toward Hispanic students' English and learning ability. Expecting poor academic achievement as a result of language problems (and poverty) may well set the stage for students' failure. Without a doubt, Mr. Donaldson needs a better understanding of Hispanic cultural heritages, more recognition of the differences within the Hispanic culture, and more objectivity toward his students. Mr. Donaldson should also understand individual differences resulting from generational factors, geographic origins, and socioeconomic factors.

Mrs. D'Angelo went to talk with Mr. Donaldson about Hispanic students and Maria, in particular. She approached the subject gingerly because she did not want Mr. Donaldson to get defensive. Somewhat surprisingly, Mr. Donaldson was openminded about the discussion. The two teachers decided to do these things:

- ◆ Ask the bilingual teacher or language expert to meet with Maria to create an immediate plan of action.
- ◆ Arrange for a professional (perhaps a paraprofessional) to work closely with Maria to show a sense of caring and concern.
- ◆ Call on or talk to Maria about a range of topics: school, home, the Hispanic culture, or playground activities.
- ◆ Administer an interest inventory to learn about Maria's interests, likes and dislikes, and then plan instruction and communication accordingly.

In some ways, this school was fortunate: One teacher overheard another making negative remarks and had the commitment to assist the teacher and student. While we hope these instances are few, we are sure there are others in which the student is ignored and continues to feel frustrated. ◆

*O*verview

Understanding Hispanic American children and adolescents requires knowledge of their families, their religion, their language, and their culture's contributions. Knowing, understanding, and appreciating Spanish-speaking learners are prerequisites, yet not enough: Educators must also understand the relationship of the cultural characteristics of Hispanic learners, their differences as learners, and their school-related problems. Educators' emphasis should be on understanding cultural diversity and demonstrating genuine appreciation of and respect for Hispanic cultures.

Origins

Hispanic Americans as a group include people who are Mexican Americans, Central and South Americans, Chicanos, Spanish Americans, Latin Americans, Puerto Ricans, Cubans, Guatemalans, and Salvadorans. All these Hispanics share many values and goals but are different in many aspects. In some ways, Hispanics are a single cultural group with a fairly common history and the sharing of language, values, and customs, but in other ways, they are a significant heterogeneous population that is an aggregate of distinct subcultures.

Tremendous cultural diversity exists among Hispanic Americans, such as the differences between Mexican Americans and Cuban Americans, among generations, and among people living in different geographic locations in the United States. Although this section examines only several Hispanic cultural characteristics, educators should learn about individual students and their respective cultural characteristics.

The 1848 Treaty of Guadalupe Hidalgo, which ended the war between the United States and Mexico, promised to respect Hispanic people's civil rights, Catholic heritage, and cultural traditions. Although in theory, the treaty promised Mexicans the same rights and privileges as all other U.S. citizens, in practice, they were forced to live in segregated communities, to attend segregated schools, and to face discrimination in church and society (Espinosa, 2007).

Hispanic Americans Today

No other ethnic or racial group will do more to change the makeup of U.S. schools over the next quarter-century than Hispanics. They are already the nation's largest minority group among children under eighteen. In fact, projections suggest that in twenty-five years, one in every four elementary students will be Hispanic (Zehr, 2000).

The Latino population of the United States has grown dramatically in the past few decades, surpassing the African American population as the largest minority group (Kelly & Kelly, 2005). The Latino community has only attracted national attention because its population grew from 22.4 million in 1990 to 44 million in 2007. It is expected to climb to 103 million by 2050 (Espinosa, 2007).

Stereotyping of Hispanic American Children and Adolescents

As with other learners, Hispanic American children and adolescents may experience "double jeopardy" if educators label learners and base teaching and learning decisions on cultural stereotypes. In essence, teachers may perceive children and adolescents erroneously as exhibiting undesirable behavior, while feeling Hispanic Americans have tendencies toward emotional and violent behavior.

Educators do learners a terrible injustice when educational decisions are based on such stereotypes as the Hispanic American learner is not as "well behaved" as the Asian American learner, is not as "intelligent" as the European

American, or is not as "docile or peaceful" as the American Indian learner. In fact, such stereotypes become self-fulfilling prophecies; Hispanic learners may achieve and behave in accordance with the educator's stereotyped academic and behavior expectations.

What action should educators take? All school personnel should seriously examine the validity of their cultural "baggage" and work toward an objective understanding of Hispanic American children and adolescents. Educators can acquire a more enlightened picture of Hispanic American learners by meeting Hispanic Americans first-hand, learning their proud and diverse history, becoming acquainted with their parents and extended families, understanding the culture's contributions, and understanding their allegiance to the Spanish language. It is also helpful to understand what being a Hispanic American child or adolescent is really like and to realize the potentially disastrous consequences of basing educational programs on cultural misperceptions.

Resiliency theory identifies factors present in the families, schools, and communities of successful youth that are missing in the lives of troubled youth. Four common attributes of resilient children include social competence, problem-solving skills, autonomy, and sense of purpose and future. When at least some of these factors are present, researchers report the successes of many resilient youth (Chavkin & Gonzalez, 2000). The literature on resiliency identifies five key protective factors of families, schools, and communities:

1. Supportive relationships, particularly encouragement from school personnel and other adults
2. Student characteristics such as self-esteem, motivation, and accepting responsibility
3. Family factors such as parental support/concern and school involvement
4. Community factors such as community youth programs
5. School factors such as academic success and prosocial skills training

Cultural Characteristics

Educators who plan and implement a multicultural curriculum can benefit from knowledge, understanding, and appreciation of Hispanic learners and their culture. Studies of Hispanic youngsters do not differentiate sufficiently among the different Spanish-speaking ethnic groups. Differing cultures, generational, socio-economic, and acculturation factors exist that educators must consider to understand Hispanic American learners.

A cultural description of Spanish-speaking peoples should include an understanding of certain values and traits. Educators can gain considerable insight into the culture by understanding several unique characteristics. Hispanic Americans tend to avoid any competition or activity that will set them apart from their own group. To stand out among one's peers is to place oneself in great jeopardy and is to be avoided at all costs.

Machismo plays a significant role in the Puerto Rican culture and significantly influences the behavior and attitudes of adolescent males during this time of identity formation. It suggests a clear-cut distinction between the sexes: Males can enjoy rights and privileges denied to females. Used as a flattering term among Hispanic Americans, Hispanic American boys and girls learn that *machismo* refers to the male's manhood, to the courage to fight, to the many traits of honor and dignity, to keeping one's word, and to protecting one's name. On a more subtle level of analysis, *machismo* also includes dignity in personal conduct, respect for others, love for the family, and affection for children. Many children are taught early on that European Americans are not trustworthy. Mexican Americans, for example, often teach their children to look toward European Americans with fear and hostility.

Educators have realized for many years the advantages of knowing as much as possible about learners. When teaching students from culturally different backgrounds, however, educators must understand learners' cultural backgrounds so as to make the most of learners' opportunities to improve learning experiences and self-esteem. What can educators do to learn about Hispanic learners' cultural backgrounds?

> **Points to Ponder 8.1**
>
> **Understanding the Hispanic Culture**
>
> It is important that educators of Hispanic children and adolescents understand and appreciate important concepts of the Hispanic culture. On understanding these cultural characteristics, try to identify related behaviors in Hispanic learners.
>
> *corazon:* heart
> *sensibilidad:* sensitivity
> *afecto:* warmth and demonstrativeness
> *dignidad:* dignity
> *respecto:* respect
> *machismo:* biological superiority
> of the male

1. Read objective literature about the Hispanic culture to learn about its historical background.
2. Understand Hispanic people's contributions and cherished cultural traits and how they are different from and similar to the majority culture and other minority populations.
3. Learn about Hispanic families—both immediate and extended—and understand the value Hispanic people place on the family.
4. Get to know individual Hispanic learners. Don't just generalize about them.
5. Visit Hispanic learners in their homes to learn first-hand about their home lives.

Gender

In Hispanic American culture, just as in other cultures, females' roles differ from those of their male counterparts. Although males and females both experience similar frustrations, such as discrimination and prejudice and sometimes poverty and lower standards of living, Hispanic American females are different from males in other ways. For example, Hispanic American females usually prefer cooperative learning environments over competitive classrooms in which many boys learn best. Likewise, Hispanic American females, because of their families' adherence to strict gender roles, are often less vocal and take less assertive stands than males do.

It is important to note, however, that because of acculturation and females taking steps to improve themselves economically and socially, some Hispanic American females are adhering less and less to traditional gender expectations. In any event, perceptive educators who work with Hispanic American females will want to bear in mind the gender-role differences among Hispanic cultures and among individual females.

Gender differences also exist in language acquisition and development. Gender Perspectives 8.1 looks at English-language anxiety in Mexican girls.

Socioeconomic Status

Over 1 million Hispanic American families live in poverty—just over two of every ten Hispanic families, compared with less than one of every ten non-Hispanic families. About 30 percent of Puerto Rican families, 33 percent of families from the Dominican Republic, about 10 percent of families from Spain, 11 percent of Cuban families, 23 percent of Mexican families, and 21 percent of Central American families were below the poverty level in the United States in 1990. About 22 percent of Hispanics lived in poverty in 2004 (U.S. Bureau of the Census, 2007). Two interrelated factors contribute to this cycle of poverty among Hispanic Americans: The unemployment rate among Puerto Rican males is twice that of European Americans, and the number of female-headed households continues to increase.

Hispanic children are more likely than other children to live in very poor neighborhoods. The percentage of Hispanic children at or below 100 percent of the poverty line declined between 1996 and 1999, but Hispanic children are still twice as likely as European American children to live in poverty. Plus, Hispanic children are less likely to have health insurance than either African or European American children (Williams, 2001).

Hispanic Americans' socioeconomic status is a result of their educational attainment, as is true of people from other cultures. Fewer Hispanics age twenty-five

Gender Perspectives 8.1

ENGLISH-LANGUAGE ANXIETY IN MEXICAN GIRLS

The process of moving from an English as a second language (ESL) class to a mainstream class with no supplementary English support can be very traumatic for many ESL students. This article describes the results of a study that shows how Mexican adolescent girls often experience more anxiety in the mainstream classroom than boys, due to differing types of English-language anxiety associated with the two differing learning environments.

Suggesting classroom implications, Pappamihiel (2001) suggests that educators can take several directions:

1. Adolescent girls need more help developing affective strategies to deal with social interactions with other students. Females often mentioned they feared speaking English with native English speakers because they were afraid of being laughed at or socially rejected.

2. Teachers can incorporate more cooperative learning groups, in which students will have more opportunities to interact positively with each other and reduce anxiety.

3. Mexican females often withdraw from social interaction and allow more vocal speakers to speak. Teachers can battle this avoidance by ensuring that all female students interact in safe groups in which they feel comfortable.

Pappamihiel concludes that her work and the work of others suggest affective evaluations must be taken into consideration when mainstreaming ESL students, especially when dealing with female students. Teachers should consider social competence along with academic and linguistic competence in order to best meet Mexican girls' needs.

Source: Pappamihiel, N. E. (2001). Moving from the ESL classroom into the mainstream: An investigation of English language anxiety in Mexican girls. *Bilingual Research Journal, 25*(1 & 2), 1–8.

or older have completed high school than have African Americans and European Americans. Latinos with a median family income of $28,000 lag behind the $39,000 income of the population as a whole. While 36 percent of Latino children live in poverty, only 26 percent attend Head Start programs, which are designed to remedy the effects of poverty on academic achievement (Latinos in school: Some facts and findings, 2001).

Are there indications that the socioeconomic status of Hispanic American children and adolescents will improve? One could provide an affirmative answer to this question if Hispanics work to improve their educational levels and English skills. These improvements will allow them to venture from Spanish-speaking communities into mainstream U.S. society. Although educators should recognize (and respond appropriately to) the effects poverty often has on academic achievement, it would also be a serious mistake to categorize all lower-socioeconomic Hispanics as unmotivated or underachieving.

Points to Ponder 8.2

Getting to Know Hispanic Families

Learning about the Hispanic learner's family may be one of the best ways to improve the child's academic achievement and self-esteem. Educators can do several things to learn about Hispanic families.

1. Invite families to school on special occasions just to visit. While the family learns about the school and its policies and expectations, teachers can become acquainted with the families.
2. Request that students write a story or essay about their families. Be sure to emphasize including parents, grandparents, brothers and sisters, cousins, and other relatives living in the home. Keep an open mind, and remember the importance of the extended family. Tell students before they write the story whether or not their stories or essays will be shared with the class.
3. Educators who teach in areas with great numbers of Hispanics may want to schedule a day for only Hispanic families to visit. Have individual meetings to determine how the family influences school achievement and attitudes toward school. (If possible, speak Spanish to families with limited English-speaking skills.)
4. Schedule individual meetings with Hispanic students to discuss their families, but be careful that students understand the purpose of these discussions. Allow and respect a learner's privacy.

Families

A basic feature of the Hispanic American family is the extended family, which plays a major role in each family member's life. These are families with strong bonds and frequent interaction among a wide range of kin. Grandparents, parents, and children may live in the same household or nearby in separate households and visit one another frequently. A second feature is the emphasis on cooperativeness and on placing the needs of the family ahead of individual concerns. This aspect of Hispanic family life has led to the erroneous conclusion that the family impedes individual achievement and advancement. Generally speaking, Hispanic American children and adolescents learn to show respect for authority, the patriarchal family structure, and extended family members.

Hispanic American children learn early the importance of (1) a deep sense of family responsibility, (2) rigid definitions of sex roles, (3) respectful and reverent treatment of the elderly, and (4) the male's position of respect and authority in the family. Although some of the male's authority appears to be relaxing as the woman's role is redefined, women in the

Hispanic American culture continue to occupy a subordinate position. Fathers have prestige and authority, and sons have more and earlier independence than do daughters. Hispanic families value the extended family structure and interaction in their daily lives. Parents often arrange for godparents or companion parents for the child, thus demonstrating the value Hispanics place on adults other than the immediate parents. These *compadres* also have a right to give advice and correction and should be responsive to the child's needs.

Schwartz (2001) maintains that educators need to understand and work closely with Latino families. For example, educators need to understand that while Latino families want their daughters to have a good education, many have personal problems with which to deal. Plus, they should work to increase parental involvement in children's education, for example, invite them to school functions, asking for their input on curricular and instructional activities, and suggesting specific ways they can promote their children's education.

Religion

Religion plays a central role in the lives of Hispanic Americans. The Spanish colonial experience brought about a distinct culture of which the Catholic faith was an important part. Catholicism was brought by the Spanish to the United States. The first mass on what is now U.S. soil was celebrated at Saint Augustine, Florida, in 1565. Spanish missionaries were active in the Southwest as early as 1539, and California missions were founded between 1770 and 1782.

The stereotype that the Latino population is overwhelming and immutably Catholic is inaccurate and misleading. While scholars of American religion have become aware of Latinos' declining attachment to the Catholic Church, political scientists have paid little attention to this trend. While non-Catholic Latinos are mostly evangelical, data suggest that an appreciable number are mainline Protestants or have no religious affiliation. According to Kelly and Kelly (2005), religion is not a constant factor among Latinos. These authors also report that Roman Catholics are the most strongly Democratic group (actually 65 percent), whereas evangelicals identify most strongly with the Republican party and the unaffiliated also tend to be Democrats.

Armitage and Dugan (2006) write about Hispanic females in a youth-based religious group that has abandoned some church restrictions to create a form of church (p. 217) while still fulfilling spiritual needs. Activities include sleepovers, movie nights, and youth-led prayer activities. The congregants are provided community role models, positive images, and cultural pride, while the church gains more followers, grows stronger, and cultivates prospective male leaders.

Gender distinctions also appeared in the youth-based ministries. Women and men, both adults and teens, followed gender models with clear behavioral expectations and limitations. Males were primarily leaders and pastors, whereas females were wives, mothers, devout participants, and other less central positions in the ministry. Men expressed their acceptance of God and Christ through leadership and authority; women expressed their acceptance through outward physical appearances (Armitage & Dugan, 2006).

Language

Hispanic people in the United States speak many Spanish dialects, depending on where the speakers live, how long they have lived in this country, and where they came from originally. Spanish in the Southwest is different from Spanish in the Midwest, the Northeast, and Florida. Even in New York City, there are important cultural and linguistic differences between speakers from Puerto Rico, Cuba, the Dominican Republic, Colombia, Ecuador, Peru, Mexico, Venezuela, Bolivia, and other South American areas.

Some Hispanic American learners' language poses a problem outside the immediate neighborhood, because they tend to retain the native tongue rather than make a cultural transition to English. Instead of making an attempt to learn English, many do not perceive a need to develop proficiency in English and continue to risk survival in a predominantly English-speaking country. Language difficulties that learners experience may have a major impact on self-esteem and the developing identity.

As in other cultures, nonverbal language also plays a major factor in the Hispanic American culture, and professionals of other cultures must recognize and understand this. Although a complete list of nonverbal behaviors is impossible and would deny individual and intracultural differences, several examples will serve to indicate their significance. Many Hispanic Americans stand close together while communicating, touch to communicate, and often avoid eye contact.

Undoubtedly, many of the problems Hispanic American learners experience stem from their difficulties with English. Hearing Spanish spoken at home yet feeling pressure to communicate in English at school often results in academic and behavioral problems, lower self-esteem, negative cultural identities, and a general pessimism toward teachers and schools.

Hispanics comprise three-quarters of all students enrolled in limited English proficient (LEP) programs, although not all Hispanic students have limited English proficiency ("Latinos in School: Some Facts and Findings," 2001).

One especially important factor is the failure of some public schools to provide a meaningful education that builds on students' native language and culture while also helping them to develop good English-language skills. Schwartz (2000) summarizes effective bilingual strategies for Hispanic students, although most strategies are appropriate for the education of all students with immigrant and limited English-speaking backgrounds. The author focuses attention toward several directions: educational policy; teacher training and performance; effective elementary, middle, and secondary bilingual programs; instructional strategies, and effective tutoring. Schwartz (2000) offers these suggestions:

1. Schools continually revise their approaches as new strategies are proven effective and new student needs are identified.
2. Schools embrace the philosophy that true bilingualism means proficiency in both Spanish and English, and they include Hispanic culture in the curriculum.
3. Schools offer individualized instruction and other aids to ensure that students learn English and other subjects that will enable future career fulfillment.
4. Schools, with the full participation of their teachers and staff, maintain an atmosphere that supports the beliefs that all students are equally valuable and bring to the school equally valuable cultures, and the expectation that all will succeed.

Children who feel pressure to speak Spanish at home and English at school may develop problems in both languages, may become bilingual, or may avoid English-speaking situations. This may result in dual cultural identification, additional language conflicts, and chronic anxiety. In the southwestern United States, many Hispanic American people live in Spanish-speaking communities isolated from English-speaking communities. In fact, children often enter the English-speaking world for the first time when they begin their public school education. Then, to make matters worse, these children are often threatened with punishment in school environments for speaking Spanish.

Achievement Levels

The news media periodically raise several issues concerning the level of educational achievement of Hispanic American students, such as the relatively low number of Hispanic American students eligible for college. By the senior year, only 31 percent of Hispanic American high school students are enrolled in college-preparatory courses.

On reaching an understanding of the social and cultural characteristics of Hispanic American children and adolescents, educators can proceed with understanding the learner in the Hispanic culture. What special school-related problems do Hispanic learners experience? Do European American expectations and stereotypes penalize Hispanic learners? Are Hispanic learners labeled? How do learning styles of Hispanics differ? What school practices might impede Hispanics' progress? As we explore these and other questions, we caution readers to consider the intracultural, generational, and socioeconomic differences between individual learners when reaching educational decisions.

Hispanics have had much lower high school completion rates than African and European Americans, which leaves many Hispanic youth less prepared. Plus, Hispanic youth are more likely than European American youth to neither attend school nor work (Williams, 2001). The dropout rate among Hispanic youth is unacceptably high; nearly one in three students fails to graduate from high school.

There are a number of reasons Hispanic students drop out. Many youth attend overcrowded, instructionally inferior, and inadequately staffed schools that do not meet their educational needs and are breeding grounds for antisocial activities. Many also live in the most economically distressed areas of the United States; they witness their elders' limited employment opportunities; and they experience debilitating stereotyping, prejudice, and bias. In essence, Hispanic youth do not believe that remaining in school will materially improve their lives (*School practices to promote the achievement of Hispanic students*, 2000). The dropout rate for Hispanic Americans is partially attributed to the relatively greater dropout rate for Hispanic immigrants: 44 percent, as compared with 21 percent for the U.S.-born. The high school completion rate for Hispanic Americans is increasing, but continues to be low (Latinos in school: Some facts and findings, 2001).

Only about 4 percent of public school teachers are Latinos, whereas Latinos constitute 15 percent of the student body (Latinos in school: Some facts and findings, 2001). Still, teachers should not let stereotypes and erroneous conclusion interfere with their academic and behavior expectations of Latino learners.

Recommendations for promoting the achievement of Hispanic American students include the following:

◆ Each Hispanic student should have an adult in the school committed to nurturing a personal sense of self-worth and supporting the student's efforts to succeed in school.
◆ Schools should be safe and inviting places that personalize programs and services that succeed with Hispanic students.

◆ All students should have access to high-quality, relevant, and interesting curricular experiences that treat their culture and language as resources, convey high expectations, and demand student investment in learning.

◆ Schools should replicate effective programs and continually try to improve programs with more reliable strategies.

◆ Schools should emphasize the prevention of problems and be aggressive in responding to early warning signs that a student is disengaging from school.

◆ Schools and alternative programs should be coordinated.

◆ Teachers should teach content so that it interests and challenges Hispanic students. They should understand the roles language, race, culture, and gender play in the educational process.

◆ Schools should recruit Hispanic parents and extended families into a partnership of equals for educating Hispanic students ("School Practices to Promote the Achievement of Hispanic Students," 2000).

Disproportionately fewer Hispanic American students than European American students take challenging academic courses. Some schools rigidly track students into such courses, using test scores or previous grades to weed out those considered less able. Other schools might open their tough academic courses to anyone, but minority students choose not to enroll (Viadero, 2000).

Scribner and Scribner (2001) explain what research tells educators about creating schools that better support the success of Mexican American students. These authors investigated three elementary schools, three middle schools, and three secondary schools. Each school had an enrollment of 66.6 percent or more Mexican American students. A pilot study was conducted and data analysis and interpretation were conducted by research teams trained in multicultural research, qualitative analysis, and interpretation techniques.

Scribner and Scribner (2001) offer suggestions in four areas:

1. Collaborative relationships with parents and communities:

   Building on cultural values of Mexican American parents

   Stressing personal contact with parents

   Fostering communication with parents

   Creating a warm environment for parents

   Facilitating structural accommodations for parent involvement

2. Collaborative governance and leadership:

   A clear, cohesive vision and mission shared by the school community

Humanistic leadership philosophies

Current and appropriate professional development

An ethic of caring

The belief that all students can succeed

A culture of innovation

3. Student-centered classroom environments:

Consistent, productive, and intensive collaboration among teachers

The encouragement of collaborative learning

Student access to a wide variety of learning materials

Utilization of both Spanish and English, as needed, to enhance learning

4. Advocacy-oriented assessment practices:

Efforts to avoid premature referrals for special services, especially for students whose first language is not English

Intensive language development, team planning/teaching, and coordination of instruction

A philosophy that stresses collaboration and familiarity with ESL student needs, which resulted in an advocacy-oriented approach to assessment

Points to Ponder 8.3

Teaching Hispanic American Students

How can educators best improve the achievement of Hispanic Americans? Should efforts focus on textbooks and other curricular materials, instructional efforts, organizational patterns, or teacher attitudes? Should Hispanic Americans be placed in cooperative learning groups or continue in the competitive atmosphere of many U.S. schools?

Teaching practices alone do not make effective schools. Recent research confirms the importance of inclusive leadership that creates a sense of community, drawing everyone into the learning process and preventing alienation of faculty, students, parents, and the larger Mexican American community.

School Practices Promoting Hispanic Americans' Progress

Is it possible that well-meaning teachers, either European American or of another culture, actually encourage school practices that may prove detrimental to Hispanic students? A look at many U.S. schools causes one to answer in the affirmative. The already somewhat overwhelmed Hispanic child or adolescent may be even more startled at the verbal emphasis in U.S schools. The extreme verbalism that characterizes U.S. schools can have profound consequences for learners with limited English-language skills.

A second, related detrimental practice is well-meaning teachers' forbidding Hispanic students to speak Spanish and actually punishing them for it. Understanding such a situation is difficult for learners who are proficient in Spanish but are experiencing considerable difficulty with their second language.

A third practice involves an entanglement of values and cultural orientations. Believing in the American cultural tradition of excelling among one's peers, teachers often motivate learners by encouraging Hispanic learners to excel above others in the class. Causing oneself to stand out among one's peers goes against Hispanic cultural traditions and expectations.

The educational challenges of Latinas (i.e., Latino women and girls) are compounded by the high rate of poverty in their communities, the learning problems caused by a lack of English-language proficiency, racism, and sexual harassment. Schwartz (2001) presents a range of strategies that serve Latinas and promote their academic achievement. These strategies will likely be most relevant for Latinas whose families have been in the United States for only a few generations, are poor, less fluent in English, and are more culturally isolated, although all Latinas can benefit from them.

Some challenges facing Latinas are common to all students from poor and/or immigrant backgrounds. These families may lack communication skills, knowledge, and experiences to take advantage of educational, cultural, and social opportunities; and they may not have school readiness skills. Additional challenges to Latinas' education ironically relate to their strong and rich Hispanic culture. The belief that the welfare of the family and community supersedes individual aspirations is fairly fixed in the various Hispanic communities. For example, it can be strong enough to convince an adolescent to drop out of school to make money for the family, or it can hamper efforts to succeed if achievement requires competition rather than cooperation with other students. Also, Latina adolescents often assume adult roles in the home, for example, taking caring of younger children as well as elders.

In general, Schwartz (2001) maintains that schools need to individually tailor supports they offer to Latinas and their families to accommodate their diverse needs and perspectives. Recommendations are as follow:

1. Educators need to convey the message that all students are expected to graduate and to succeed academically.

2. Educators can help Latinas understand how it is possible to value familial independence without subverting personal goals, because individual achievement reflects well on their community.

3. Schools can help Latinas develop the contacts and access to the community resources that will increase their opportunities for future fulfillment and are readily available to their more advantaged peers.

4. Schools can facilitate Latinas' learning and increase their feelings of attachment to the school community by providing the educational services needed to ensure their educational preparedness and by developing a fully multicultural curriculum.

5. Schools can create an environment in which students believe that their requests for help will receive a positive response.

Promoting Cultural Identities

The educator's role in promoting positive cultural identities among learners will always be of paramount importance. There is a clear relationship between self-esteem and school achievement. Emphatically stated, a student who feels "worthless," "not so good," and "inferior" will experience academic difficulties despite the teacher's most conscientious efforts. Drill, memorization, and worksheets cannot overcome learners' feeling that they (or their culture) are inferior. Although the problems associated with speaking one's mother tongue in a predominantly English-speaking environment deserves consideration, allowing (or even encouraging) Hispanic children to read appropriate children's literature written in Spanish might enhance their self-esteem and cultural identities.

Specifically, what can educators do to promote positive feelings of self-worth and cultural identity? First, all efforts should be genuine and honest; learners will detect hypocrisy if teachers say one thing but demonstrate another. Second, educators should plan programs that teach about the Hispanic culture and the proud history and accomplishments of the Spanish-speaking people. Third, rather than having "Spanish Art, Music, and Foods Week," educators must develop a curriculum that shows an appreciation for cultural diversity and that fully incorporates the Hispanic culture into all areas of the school curriculum. Last, educators can use literature and any other method or activity that improves learner self-esteem, enhances cultural identities, and increases the appreciation of cultural differences.

Case Study

Carlos—A Hispanic American Learner

Carlos S., a twelve-year-old boy of Spanish origin, is one grade level behind in his public elementary school. The student population is composed predominantly of African and Hispanic American children; a small percentage of Anglo students also attend the school. While the majority of the teachers are Anglo, a few are African American and one is Hispanic.

Carlos lives in a lower-socioeconomic, Spanish-speaking neighborhood near the school. He has several problems: His family speaks Spanish at home, but he is forbidden to speak Spanish at school; his difficulty with the English language has resulted in low reading grades and achievement test scores (thus, the grade level deficit); and he sees older boys dropping out of school and wonders when he can end his frustration with school. Carlos admits his frustrations to his best friend, another Hispanic American boy: Why does his teacher, Mrs. Little, keep asking him to excel? Why doesn't she allow him to speak Spanish when his family (including his grandparents, aunts and uncles, and cousins) all continue to speak Spanish? Carlos knows he has problems, and he thinks Mrs. Little has almost given up on him.

Mrs. Little understands that Carlos's situation calls for immediate attention. First, whenever possible, Carlos needs to be allowed to speak Spanish. This is the language in which he is most proficient, and he cannot understand why he is not allowed to speak the language that both his family and friends speak. Second, Carlos needs English-language instruction from qualified professionals who understand second-language instruction and who understand the problems Hispanic learners face. Third, Carlos needs appropriate diagnostic testing to determine his strengths and weaknesses, followed by carefully planned remediation to address his weaknesses.

Equally important is for the teachers in Carlos's school to understand the Hispanic culture and the situations of students like Carlos. Additionally, because the cultural diversity of the school population is not reflected in the teaching staff, the curriculum and learning environment probably reflect an Anglo perspective. More effort should be directed toward making Carlos's school more multicultural in nature and, in this case, more understanding and accepting of Hispanic American learners.

Questions for Discussion:

1. Should Carlos be allowed to speak Spanish in an English-speaking school, as his teacher thinks? Can Carlos survive in an English-speaking society if he is allowed to speak Spanish in school? Consider that English is the primary language spoken and taught in U.S. schools. Also, if Carlos cannot learn in English,

should he be allowed to learn in his native language? These are difficult questions that are fundamental to honoring the English language, yet accepting and appreciating another's language.

2. We will probably all agree that Carlos needs diagnostic testing to determine his strengths and weaknesses. Should Carlos be tested with English or Spanish diagnostic tests?

3. The case study says that "the curriculum and learning environment probably reflect an Anglo perspective." Should the curriculum and learning environment be modified to fit Carlos's cultural background, or should Carlos be expected to adapt to Anglo perspectives? If the former, suggest three tactics for changing the curriculum and learning environment.

Summing Up

Educators who plan teaching and learning experiences for Hispanic American children and adolescents should:

1. Provide an educational environment in which Hispanic American children and adolescents feel that educators and other significant adults and peers respect their Spanish culture and background.

2. Allow Spanish to be spoken in schools, because it is the language spoken at home and in the neighborhoods; learners should be taught to speak English as well.

3. Understand that language problems and differences are partly responsible for most academic problems.

4. Consider differences in learning styles when planning and implementing education programs.

5. Promote positive feelings toward learners' selves and their culture, because learners' self-esteem and cultural identities influence school achievement and social development.

6. Understand and appreciate cultural diversity to the degree that Hispanic learners do not feel their culture, socioeconomic status, families, religion, and language are wrong or inferior.

7. Use utmost caution not to label Hispanic learners on a basis of myth, stereotypes, prejudices, racism, or any other form of discrimination.

8. Use test data carefully, and remember that achievement tests, intelligence tests, and other measurement instruments might have a cultural bias toward European American standards and cultural expectations.

⬥ Suggested Learning Activities

1. Choose a typical Spanish-speaking student (from any of the Spanish-speaking cultures) and write a case study that explores individual and cultural characteristics. Consult with the school guidance counselor to better understand the child and his or her culture. After listing specific individual and cultural characteristics, plan an educational program that will meet the needs of this child.

2. Choose a low-achieving Hispanic American student and assess his or her language proficiency. To what extent is the student's lower academic achievement a product of poor English skills? Interview the student to determine whether the immediate and extended families speak Spanish or English. In what ways can the school's speech correctionist (working with language development specialists) assist this child? Plan an instructional program that addresses the student's problems with language and academic achievement.

3. Consider the following Implementing Research, which looks at dispelling myths about Latino parent participation in schools.

Implementing Research

Latino Involvement in Schools

Quiocho and Daoud (2006) intended to discuss and dispel commonly held myths about Latino parents' involvement in their children's education. The authors found that some teachers promote negative perceptions of Latino parents. They also found that Latino parents had high expectations of their children's academic performance and wanted to be involved in their education.

Quiocho and Daoud (2006) examined two schools in large, unified school districts in southern California, where teachers, administrators, and school staff had low expectations of Latino children and their parents. Specifically, the authors examined the differences in perceptions of Latino families and the educators.

The results of this study challenged popular yet negative perceptions of Latino parents and their participation in their children's education, including the following:

- Latino parents are responsible for the problems of low-performing schools.
- Declining student performance, as measured by standardized test scores, is due solely to the changing demographics of the neighborhood.
- Low student performance is due to an influx of uneducated families who are not supportive of or interested in their children's education.
- Latino parents do not participate in the life of the school and thus do not contribute positively to the education system.
- Latino immigrant and migrant parents do not have high academic expectations.

Another concern among teachers is that the children of immigrants cannot or will not assimilate into American culture. Quiocho and Daoud (2006) found that although Latino parents wanted their children to have a better life than their own, they also wanted them to maintain their native culture and identity, which is sometimes perceived as not wanting to assimilate into American culture. The former concern (that parents do not want to be involved in their children's education) and the latter (that children do not want to assimilate into American culture) are both based more on assumptions than facts.

Many assumptions can be dispelled when teachers have a first-hand understanding of their Latino students' families. Results from the Quiocho and Daoud (2006) study suggest several more mistaken beliefs:

- ◆ Latino parents are not only unreliable, but they refuse to volunteer in the classroom.
- ◆ Latino parents did not support the school's homework policy because they felt unable to assist their children.
- ◆ Latino parents did not care about schooling.

Implementing the Research

1. Educators need to be objective and have accurate perceptions of Latino learners, just as they should of all children and their families.

2. Educators should invite parents and families into schools to learn about American schools and what they can do to help their children.

3. Educators should plan and implement a parent-education program designed especially for Latino parents and families so they will know what to do and realize that educators care about their children's progress.

Source: Quiocho, A. M. L., & Daoud, A. M. (2006). Dispelling myths about Latino parent participation in schools. *Educational Forum, 70,* 255–267.

 ## Suggestions for Collaborative Efforts

Form groups of three or four that, if possible, represent our nation's cultural and gender diversity. Working collaboratively, focus your group's attention toward the following efforts.

1. Develop a two-part approach to understanding Hispanic families and teaching them about U.S. schools. For example, plan an approach for understanding Hispanic American families (e.g., school meetings, home visits, and other first-hand contacts) and teaching Hispanic American families about U.S. schools (e.g., parent-education programs).

2. With the growing Spanish-speaking population, it is becoming easier for Hispanic people to live in sections in which Spanish continues to be the mother tongue. Have each member of your group examine a specific language aspect. What language is spoken during recess, lunch time, and other breaks during the school day? Do teachers allow Spanish to be spoken in the classroom? Do teachers see the advantages of having one learner help another while speaking in Spanish? What language is spoken in the home? When parents and guardians speak to children in school, what language is spoken? Does the learner live in a predominantly Spanish-speaking neighborhood? What attempts have you made to understand the beauty of the Spanish language and to realize the language problems some students might experience?

3. Increasingly, the Spanish language will be spoken in the United States, especially because all demographic predictions suggest the Hispanic population will continue to increase. Some people feel that the United States should accept Spanish as the official second language; other people argue that English should be the only official language of the nation. In your group, discuss issues related to Spanish being increasingly spoken in the United States: whether Spanish should be accepted in an English-speaking country; whether schools should teach Spanish as well as English; whether instruction should occasionally be in Spanish; the implications for U.S. society and schools; and other issues that your group feels are significant.

Expanding Your Horizons

Additional Journals, Books, and Internet Sites

Abalos, D. T (2007). *Latinos in the United States: The scared and the political.* Notre Dame, IN: University of Notre Dame.

This informative book will appeal to professionals planning multicultural education programs as well as those just interested in the Latino culture.

Altshuler, S. J., & Schmautz, T. (2006). No Hispanic student left behind: The consequences of "high stakes" testing. *Children and Schools, 28*(1), 5–14.

The authors review the impact of traditional assessment approaches and discuss the influence of culture and ethnicity on standardized test results, especially for Hispanic students.

Clark, A. A., & Dorris, A. (2006). Welcoming Latino parents as partners. *Principal Leadership, 7*(3), 22–25.

Clark and Dorris examine school–family partnerships and ways to understand the community and build such partnerships.

Kettler, T., Shiu, A., & Johnsen, S. R. (2006). AP as an intervention for middle school Hispanic students. *Gifted Child Today, 29*(1), 39–46.

> This article focuses on two education-related topics: sense of belonging and composition of the student's peer group.

Quiocho, A. M. L., & Daoud, A. M. (2006). Dispelling myths about Latino parent participation in schools. *Educational Forum, 70,* 255–267.

> While these authors make some powerful (and disturbing) assumptions at the beginning of their article, they still offer several excellent suggestions for helping Latino children and their families.

Trevino, A., & Mayes, C. (2006). Creating a bridge from high school to college for Hispanic students. *Multicultural Education, 14*(2), 74–77.

> The authors look at ways to help Hispanic high school students by helping educators create more effective transitions for minority students from high school to college.

Infoplease. www.infoplease.com/spot/hhmbioaz.html

> This site provides an A–Z list of topics for Hispanic Heritage Month, plus notable biographies.

National Library of Medicine. www.nlm.nih.gov/medlineplus/hispanicamericanhealth .html

> This site looks at Hispanics' health basics, such as genetics, environmental factors, access to care, and cultural factors.

Penn State. www.personal.psu.edu/faculty/c/s/csr4/PSU3/Hispanic-Latino-Americans/Hispanic-Latino-Americans.html

> This Internet site looks at Hispanic and Latino Americans who have made significant historical contributions.

Unbeatables. www.unbeatables.com/HHeroes.html

> This site tells about renown Hispanic scientists, poets, educators, athletes, lawyers, doctors, and businesspeople as well as many other Hispanic notables.

Teaching and Learning
in a Diverse Society

Part III focuses on what educators should consider when planning and implementing programs that teach acceptance and respect for cultural diversity. Chapters 9, 10, 11, 12, 13, and 14 focus on curriculum, instruction, individual and cultural differences, parents and families, administrators and special school personnel, and twenty-first-century issues, respectively. The emphasis continues to be on promoting multiculturalism and social justice and implementing effective multicultural education programs.

Curricular Efforts

Understanding the material and activities in this chapter will help the reader to:

◆ Understand how the school curriculum can convey acceptance for all students, promote a sense of social justice throughout the school day, and move away from cultural deficit approaches and perspectives to a more social justice approach.

◆ Distinguish between the purported changes and the actual progress people from culturally different backgrounds have achieved in U.S. society.

◆ Prepare a multicultural teaching unit that addresses the needs of learners from culturally different backgrounds and teaches European American learners about diversity.

◆ State several reasons a school needs a multicultural education program that emphasizes an across-the-curriculum approach and encompasses the total school environment.

◆ List and describe several methods for extending the multicultural education curriculum to the community and having it pervade extracurricular activities.

◆ Understand the importance of having school administrators, faculty, and staff reflect the cultural diversity of the student body.

Opening Scenario

The Hidden Curriculum

Mrs. Brunson, a teacher at Calhoun Middle School, knows she will have to take a stand at the faculty meeting. No longer can she let injustice prevail. Her only decision is how to make her point in such a way that positive action will result.

"We have a hidden curriculum," she says calmly and matter of factly. Although the school's philosophy purports to promote equality and equitable treatment for all students, it does not act on that belief. Young adolescents learn from a so-called hidden curriculum that teaches as much as or more than the planned curriculum.

Mrs. Brunson has numerous examples to substantiate her point: school policies that recognize only middle-class European American expectations; a media center that is oriented predominately toward European Americans; instructional practices and academic expectations that address European American learning styles; and extracurricular activities in which participants are mostly European American. What message is the school sending to learners of diverse cultural backgrounds? While the curriculum seeks to show acceptance and respect for social justice, the hidden curriculum conveys an almost totally opposite picture. Learners from different cultural backgrounds often feel unaccepted and perceive that they must adjust to middle-class, white values and customs.

The faculty expresses some skepticism over Mrs. Brunson's remarks. Clearly, they have not considered the impact of the hidden curriculum. In fact, the school is not as multicultural as some believe.

Mrs. Brunson feels better for having expressed herself. Accomplishing genuine change will be slow and supporters of the status quo will challenge efforts, but at least the faculty now recognizes the problem. This is a first and significant step. ◆

*O*verview

The tremendous cultural diversity that characterizes U.S. school systems sends a strong message to educators and curriculum developers at both elementary and secondary levels. They must develop a curriculum that addresses the needs of learners and creates a school environment that reflects cultural diversity. To implement such an across-the-curriculum approach, they must carefully select bias-free teaching materials, choose evaluation instruments that take into account cultural differences, encourage appropriate community involvement, and provide extracurricular activities that involve all learners.

Educators such as Mrs. Brunson who are planning a curriculum that reflects acceptance for diversity and social justice should focus on these goals:

- Developing a school curriculum that reflects multiculturalism and diversity
- Providing textbooks and other curricular materials that reflect multiculturalism in an accurate manner—free of stereotypes and cultural generalizations
- Including all cultural groups and providing accurate information about their histories, cultures, contributions, and experiences
- Offering curricular experiences at a level that students can understand and comprehend in an honest, meaningful manner

Sleeter (2000) explains that a good multicultural curriculum is an ongoing process. Educators and multiculturalists are never finished with the multicultural curriculum, because they continually learn as they deal with various issues. In fact, the curriculum that educators teach is only as good as their understanding of the content and issues being taught, about diverse people, about the society in which we live, and about knowledge of the various academic disciplines.

Toward Cultural Diversity and Social Justice

Overall school curriculum and teaching and learning situations should reflect the cultural diversity of our nation. Although the *Brown* desegregation case and the civil rights legislation of a number of years ago contributed to better treatment and acceptance of groups from culturally different backgrounds, there is much room for improvement. Educators should place change and progress in proper perspective. Hindrances to progress include the following:

- Deficit ideologies that limit access and opportunity
- Testing and assessment issues, for example, extensive reliance on tests

- ◆ IQ-based definitions and theories
- ◆ Achievement-based definitions and theories
- ◆ Inadequate policies and practices (Ford & Harmon, 2001)

 # The Illusion of Change and Progress

Without a doubt, U.S. education is making progress toward better relations between groups of people. The accomplishments of people of differing cultures and of women are recognized; many educators welcome youngsters with disabilities into their classrooms; most teachers work to reduce racist and sexist behavior in their classrooms; and many work to develop or obtain curricular materials free from bias and prejudice.

Consider, however, the racism and nonacceptance that continue to plague society—the growing popularity of "skinheads" and neo-Nazi groups, for instance. In addition, school practices often document either a lack of understanding of learners from culturally different backgrounds or a lack of acceptance and respect for their cultural differences.

> **Points to Ponder 9.1**
>
> **Determining Significant Change**
>
> Undoubtedly, the U.S. education system has made progress toward providing a culturally relevant curriculum—more materials reflect diversity and provide objective portrayals of females, people from culturally different backgrounds, and people with disabilities. Visit several schools to determine the extent of the changes—how far have we come? What still needs to be done? Are changes superficial or do they show genuine commitment?

The Continuing Need for Change in Educational Practices

There continues to be much room for genuine change in teaching and learning situations, compatible treatment of people who are disabled or from culturally diverse backgrounds, improvement of the cultural and ethnic compositions of school faculty and staff, and equitable representation of all people, regardless of culture, in textbooks and other curricular materials. This discussion and the accompanying recommendations do not downplay the significant progress that our society and schools have already made. It is necessary, however, to perceive society and schools objectively and to plan an appropriate agenda for positively reconstructing society and schools during the twenty-first century.

Schools should accept responsibility for translating illusion into reality and recognize that they can serve as a significant force in countering discrimination and the various "-isms" that affect people from culturally diverse backgrounds, women, and the disabled.

From Illusion to Reality: Responding to Racism, Discrimination, and Stereotypes

Racism has many damaging and long-lasting effects on the lives of children and adolescents, the character of society, the quality of our civilization, and people's prospects for the future. Before an illusion of racial harmony and justice for all can become a reality, schools must take a powerful and pivotal role in teaching about racism and in working toward acceptance and respect for all people, regardless of racial and cultural background. Schools can play a powerful role in combating racism and educational inequities by confronting and challenging racism, hiring teachers from diverse cultures, developing and implementing a genuine multicultural curriculum, and improving pedagogical practices that address the needs of all learners.

Ethnocentrism occurs when some people hold that their group is better than other groups. Some ethnocentrism is good, but too much group pride can result in a negative force. A society and its schools must seek to understand the many forms of ethnocentrism and work toward keeping ethnocentrism under control among individuals and student groups.

Schools' responsibilities in our multicultural society extend to countering the dangers of stereotyping, from which even educators are not exempt. What steps can educators take to transform illusions of equality and justice into reality?

First, teachers should be aware of their own biases and stereotypes. Through self-examination or cultural awareness workshops, educators can gain a better understanding of their attitudes toward people who are culturally different, women, and people with disabilities. Second, as cultural understandings clarify stereotypical beliefs, educators see the need for expecting as much from learners of differing cultural backgrounds as they do from other students. Although educators should recognize the plight of minorities, they must encourage minority students to excel in all areas of academic pursuit.

Third, educators should examine curricular materials for evidence of stereotyping. Specifically, does the material present females and minorities in a realistic, nonstereotypical manner? Does the material accurately reflect a holistic view of the past in terms of the contributions of females and people of differing cultural backgrounds in U.S. history? Fourth, educators should strive to diversify classes of homogeneous ability levels, which have the potential for segregating students by race or socioeconomic group. Heterogeneous classes and cooperative learning activities are very important.

Because of landmark court decisions, civil rights legislation, and overall improved race relations, U.S. society is not as divided racially and culturally as it was several decades ago. We must not, however, allow illusions of grandeur to overshadow reality. Discrimination, social injustices, and stereotypes continue to exist and to take a heavy toll. Rather than accept the status quo as the most equitable we can achieve, school curricula should deliberately instill in children and adolescents a sense of respect and acceptance for all people, regardless of their cultural and individual differences.

Planning and Implementing Curricula Promoting Social Justice

The Total School Environment

Multiculturalism should extend to and permeate all aspects of the school. In fact, multiculturalism should be such a basic part of the school that it becomes a natural and accepted aspect of the daily routine.

One way that multiculturalism can permeate the curriculum is through an approach that incorporates literature that is culturally appropriate for children and adolescents in teaching the various areas of the curriculum. Multicultural literature is essential to all areas of the curriculum to help students grow in understanding themselves and others. Through careful selection and sharing of multicultural reading materials, educators help students learn to identify with the people who created the stories, whether of the past or present. Folk tales, myths, and legends clarify the values and beliefs of people. By reading the great stories on which cultures have been founded, learners can discover the threads that weave the past with the present and the themes and values that interconnect people of all cultures.

Reform Efforts

As stated earlier, teaching units are an appropriate and viable means of reaching specific objectives. Serious reform efforts toward a more realistic portrayal of all people, however, will require a major overhaul of elementary and secondary school curricula. What steps can educators take to ensure that elementary and secondary school curricula reflect the cultural diversity of U.S. society?

Proposals for improving the achievement of all students are often doomed to failure, largely due to their allegiance to a deficit orientation—that is, concentrating on what ethnically, racially, and linguistically different students do not have and cannot do. Much more cultural content is needed in all school curricula about all ethnic groups. The need is especially apparent in math and science for

Points to Ponder **9.2**

Researching Cultural Diversity

Separate into small groups and have each group select a different cultural group to research. The following questions may serve as guidelines:

1. Where did the racial, religious, or ethnic group you are studying originate?
2. Why did they leave their homeland?
3. Where in the United States did they originally settle?
4. What kind of work did they do when they first came here?
5. What was their native language?
6. What was their dominant religion?
7. What is a popular myth or legend from their culture?

ethnic groups other than African Americans. This is true for those subjects in which some initiatives are already underway as well as those that have not changed at all. This means designing more multicultural literacy programs in secondary schools and more math and science programs at all grade levels; teaching explicit information about gender contributions, issues, experiences, and achievement effects *within ethnic groups*; and pursuing more sustained efforts to incorporate content about ethnic and cultural diversity in regular school subjects and skills taught on a routine basis.

Sleeter and Grant (2007) offer these guidelines for developing multicultural curricula:

1. Reform the curriculum in such a way that it regularly presents diverse perspectives, experiences, and contributions. Similarly, present and teach concepts that represent diverse cultural groups and both sexes.
2. Include materials and visual displays that are free of race, gender, and disability stereotypes and that include members of all cultural groups in a positive manner.
3. Embrace concepts, rather than fragments of information, related to diverse groups.
4. Emphasize contemporary culture as much as historical culture, and represent groups as active and dynamic. The curriculum, for example, should include not only the women's suffrage movement but also more contemporary problems confronting women.
5. Strive to make the curriculum a "total effort," with multicultural aspects permeating all subject areas and all phases of the school day.
6. Make sure the curriculum uses nonsexist language.
7. Support a curriculum that endorses bilingual education and the vision of a multilingual society.
8. Draw on children's experiential background in teaching and learning. Base community and curricular concepts on children's daily life and experiences.
9. Insist on a curriculum that allows equal access for all students. All students, for example, should have the freedom to enroll in college-preparatory courses and other special curricular activities.

Diversity comes in many forms, all of which need to be addressed in the curriculum. We maintain that sexual orientation should be included in a definition of multicultural education as well as reflected in curricular efforts. Gay and lesbian adolescents confront many of the same biological, cognitive, and social developmental changes as their heterosexual counterparts. Fear of and misunderstandings about homosexuality can result in negative consequences for adolescents struggling with identity formation that differs from that of the majority of their peers.

By learning about the concerns of gay and lesbian youth, middle and secondary educators can break the barrier of silence that contributes to the difficulties and hurt these teens face. Gay and lesbian adolescents bear a double burden: They experience harassment, violence, and suicidal tendencies because of their age and their sexual preference. They sometimes feel fearful, withdrawn, depressed, and full of despair. Curricular efforts should address the needs of gay and lesbian adolescents by including age-appropriate literature to explain sexual orientation as well as others' experiences with being gay or lesbian. Such books help readers develop self-understanding and gain insight into the special developmental needs of gay and lesbian youth.

The Hidden Curriculum

Although some aspects of the curriculum are readily discernible to children and adolescents attending a school, other aspects are more subtle and may be equally influential. For example, we have little difficulty determining whether people of differing backgrounds are represented honestly and adequately in textbooks and other curricular materials. We can also ascertain with relative ease whether tracking and ability grouping have resulted in the segregation and relegation to second-class status of all people from different cultural backgrounds and lower-socioeconomic students.

There is, however, another equally important curriculum, one that has a powerful influence on children and adolescents. This very subtle *hidden curriculum* affects learners of all races and cultures. Mrs. Brunson in the Opening Scenario takes a stand against the hidden curriculum in her school.

What specific aspects might be included in a hidden curriculum? It might comprise any number of events, behavior expectations, and attitudes that might appear relatively unobtrusive to some learners but might appear out of character or context to other learners. Representative examples might include teacher behaviors and expectations conveyed both verbally and nonverbally; textbooks and other curricular materials that portray white, middle-class values and orientations; segregation due to tracking or ability-grouping policies; educators' and other students' degrees of acceptance and attitudes toward learners from different cultural backgrounds; and the degree of acceptance of language differences. In other words, middle- or upper-socioeconomic European American students might expect their teacher to encourage them to compete and excel above others in the class; this same teacher expectation, however, might be anathema to American Indian learners. Educators must make a deliberate effort to examine all their behaviors (both conscious and unconscious) to determine what hidden messages they are conveying and to assess carefully every aspect of the curriculum and the total school environment.

Guidelines for Developing a Multicultural Curriculum

As with all curricular efforts, a multicultural curriculum should be carefully matched with goals and objectives and use established guidelines. Although each program should reflect the needs and goals of the respective school, the following guidelines can serve as a basis for multicultural curricular development:

1. Consider students' individual socioeconomic status, religion, gender, sexual orientation, culture, and language, and whenever possible, use these differences (or at least show respect for) when designing curricula.
2. Use an interdisciplinary approach, in which topics are addressed in more than one curricular area. Relate the topic to as many other topics as possible across the curriculum.
3. Use a variety of instructional approaches—ones that reflect how students think, organize learning, and compete or cooperate in learning activities.
4. Focus on affective and psychosocial gains, rather than only cognitive gains. Learning facts in isolation is insufficient. Forming positive attitudes toward others and showing respect for social justice among all people are paramount.
5. Make maximum use of community resources, cultural support groups, and social service.

Several other important implications for culturally responsive pedagogical practices are embedded in the nature and effects of culturally diverse curriculum content examined thus far. One is the need to regularly provide students with more accurate cultural information to fill knowledge voids and correct existing distortions. This information needs to be capable of facilitating many different kinds of learning—cognitive, affective, social, political, personal, and moral.

No single content source is capable of doing all of this alone. Therefore, curriculum designers should always use a variety of content sources from different genres and disciplines.

Assessing the Need for Curricular Change

Before planning to adopt a multicultural curriculum, the school must assess its needs to determine the direction and extent of the change. Here are some questions a school should consider in conducting a needs assessment:

1. Do multicultural perspectives permeate the entire school curriculum and environment?
2. Do the attitudes of teachers, administrators, and staff members indicate a willingness to accept and respect cultural diversity?
3. Do textbooks and other curricular materials recognize the value of cultural diversity and gender and social class differences?
4. Do curricular activities and methods provide learners with opportunities to collaborate and cooperate?
5. Do extracurricular activities reflect cultural diversity?
6. Do curricular planning efforts reflect the views and opinions of parents and other community people?
7. Do curricular efforts include bilingual perspectives or provide assistance for students with limited English-speaking skills?

Selecting Bias-Free Curricular Materials

Over the years, a great deal of research has been done to determine if textbooks are dealing adequately with diversity issues. The inadequacies of textbook coverage of cultural diversity can be avoided by including accurate, wide-ranging, and appropriately contextualized content about different ethnic groups' histories, cultures, and experiences in classroom instruction on a regular basis. The efforts need not be constrained by lack of information and materials. Plenty of resources exist about most ethnic groups and in such variety that all subjects and grades taught in schools can be served adequately. Since this information is not always in textbooks, teachers need to develop the habit of using other resources to complement or even replace them. Students also should be taught how to critique textbooks for the accuracy of their multicultural content and how to compensate.

Other equally important concerns related to bias in textbooks are omissions and distortions. *Omission* refers to information left out of a textbook, and a *distortion* is a lack of balance or systematic omission. Because of omissions, members of some cultural and ethnic groups are virtually unrepresented in textbooks. Hispanic Americans, Asian Americans, American Indians, and women continue to be underrepresented in educational materials. The invisibility of a group implies that it has less value or significance in U.S. society than others. Invisibility applies most often to women, culturally diverse people, people with disabilities, and the elderly (Gollnick & Chinn, 2006).

Distortions result from inaccurate or unbalanced impressions. History and reading materials too often ignore the presence and realities of certain groups in contemporary society, or they confine treatment to negative experiences. In some cases, they provide a single point of view about events that may be technically correct but is nevertheless misleading.

Sexism and sexist language are other factors to consider when selecting textbooks and other teaching materials. Gollnick and Chinn (2006) have called attention to the sexism that often occurs in children's and adolescents' textbooks, especially at the elementary school level. Children who were asked to draw an early caveman drew only pictures of cavemen. In contrast, when instructed to draw "cave people," the children generated drawings of men, women, and children. In classrooms, teachers can point out sexist language to students. When words appear to exclude women as full participants in society or limit their occupational options, teachers can provide alternatives—for example, *mail carrier* and *police officer* as alternatives to *mailman* and *policeman* (Gollnick & Chinn, 2006).

The challenge facing multicultural educators is to select textbooks and other materials that objectively represent various groups and people who have been traditionally either ignored or misrepresented. Table 9.1 provides educators with a means of evaluating written material to determine its suitability in our increasingly multicultural schools.

Gender Perspectives 9.1 (page 199) looks at diversity and social justice in the curriculum.

Evaluating Curricular Efforts

Evaluating the multicultural curriculum to determine overall program strengths and weaknesses and to assess how well it meets individual learner needs is as

table 9.1

How to Analyze Books for Racism and Sexism

These guidelines provide a starting point and are designed to help educators detect racist and sexist bias in children's story books, picture books, primers, and fiction.

1. *Check the illustrations.* Look for stereotypes, oversimplified generalizations about a particular group, race, or sex that generally carry derogatory implications. Look for variations that in any way demean or ridicule characters because of their race or sex.

   Look for tokenism. If there are culturally diverse characters, are they just like Anglo Americans but tinted or colored? Do all culturally diverse faces look stereotypically alike, or are they depicted as genuine individuals?

   Look at the lifestyles of the people in the book. Are culturally diverse characters and their settings depicted in such a way that they contrast unfavorably with an unstated norm of Anglo American middle-class suburbia? For example, culturally diverse people are often associated with the ghetto, migrant labor, or "primitive" living. If the story does attempt to depict another culture, does it go beyond oversimplifications of reality to offer genuine insights into another lifestyle?

2. *Check the story line.* Civil rights legislation has led publishers to weed out many insulting passages and illustrations, particularly in stories with black themes, but the attitudes still find expression in less obvious ways. The following checklist suggests some of the various subtle forms of bias to watch for:

   Relationships: Do Anglo Americans in the story have the power and make the decisions? Do culturally diverse people function in essentially subservient roles?

   Standard for success: What does it take for a character to succeed? To gain acceptance, do culturally diverse characters have to exhibit superior qualities—excel in sports, get A's, and so forth?

   Viewpoint: How are problems presented, conceived, and resolved in the story? Are culturally diverse people themselves considered to be the problem? Do solutions ultimately depend on the benevolence of an Anglo American?

   Sexism: Are the achievements of girls and women based on their own initiative and intelligence, or is their success due to their good looks or to their relationships with boys? Are sex roles incidental or paramount to characterization and plot? Could the same story be told if the sex roles were reversed?

3. *Consider the effects of the book on the child's self-image and self-esteem.* Are norms established that limit the child's aspirations and self-esteem? What does it do

continued

table 9.1

Continued

to African American children to be continuously bombarded with images of white as beautiful, clean, and virtuous and black as evil, dirty, and menacing? What happens to a girl's aspirations when she reads that boys perform all the brave and important deeds? What about a girl's self-esteem if she is not fair of skin and slim of body?

4. *Consider the authors' or illustrators' qualifications.* Read the biographical material on the jacket flap or on the back cover. If a story deals with a culturally diverse theme, what qualifies the authors or illustrators to deal with this topic? If they are not members of the culturally diverse group being written about, is there anything in the authors' or illustrators' backgrounds that would specifically recommend them for this book? Similarly, a book that has to do with the feelings and insights of women should be more carefully examined if it is written by a man, unless the book's avowed purpose is to present a male viewpoint.

These observations do not deny the ability of writers to empathize with experiences other than those of their own sex or race, but the chances of their writing as honestly and as authentically about the experiences of other genders and races are not as good.

5. *Look at the copyright date.* Books on culturally diverse themes—usually hastily conceived—suddenly began appearing in the mid-1960s. There followed a growing number of "culturally diverse experience" books to meet the new market demand, but they were still written by Anglo American authors and reflected an Anglo point of view. Only in the late 1960s and early 1970s did the children's book world begin even to remotely reflect the realities of a multiracial society, and it has only just begun to reflect feminist concerns.

Source: Adapted from www.osi.hu/iep/Workshops/anti_bias/ten_ways.html, www .birchlane.davis.ca.us/library/10quick.html, and www.misf.org/educatorstoolkit/mce/ evaluatingbooks.html. Retrieved October 17, 2002.

important as the actual content and teaching methods the teacher uses. One basic criterion is to determine whether teaching and learning situations reflect multi-culturalism (Sleeter & Grant, 2007).

Other measures of program effectiveness include oral and written tests (teacher-made and standardized), sociograms, questionnaires, surveys, student projects, interviews, anecdotal information, and discussion groups. Indicators such as attendance records, class participation, and incidence of disruptive

DIVERSITY AND SOCIAL JUSTICE

Aberle, Krafchick, and Zimmerman (2005) maintain that diversity and social justice issues have profound effects on individual development and societal health, including forming positive self-images, developing strong relationships with others, and contributing to fairness in society. Ideally, social justice is introduced to children when they are young and is then continued during middle and secondary school.

The authors explain FAIR (Fairness for All Individuals through Respect), an experiential curriculum that invites children to learn about social justice and diversity. The curriculum includes five experiential activities that address diversity of race, gender, and socioeconomic status. The program not only celebrates diversity, but it also builds awareness of social injustice and fosters critical thinking.

After providing an overview of multicultural and social justice education literature, the authors explain the five experiential activities:

1. *Images in Our Minds*—This activity focuses on stereotypes that are often based on gender, race, and socioeconomics. A story is told, and children are asked about their images of the participants involved.

2. *Toy Sorting*—A variety of toys traditionally considered girl toys and boy toys are provided. Children are given one blue box and one pink box. They place each toy in what they perceive as the appropriate box. The facilitator discusses with the children their placement of the toys and their reasons for doing so.

3. *Image Collage*—A collection of magazines is provided, along with scissors and glue. The children make a collage consisting of "Jack-in-the-Box" and "Jill-in-the Box." A discussion follows that focuses on traditional perceptions of male and female roles.

4. *Build a House*—Collect house-building materials, both good and bad or sturdy and weak, and have the children build their own houses with what they can afford. Children learn the differences between being poor and wealthy and the differences between socioeconomic levels.

5. *The Marine Life Story*—The children discuss a shark, carp, crab, and dolphin and the role each plays in the ocean. Comparisons are then made to people—for example, the shark fears there will not be enough food to go around, and the crab walks sideways and is afraid to take a stand.

We recommend this article to educators promoting social justice. Although the FAIR curriculum was designed for young children, it could easily be adapted for middle school or secondary school.

Source: Aberle, J. M., Krafchick, J. L., & Zimmerman, T. S. (2005). FAIR: A diversity and social justice curriculum for school. *Guidance and Counseling,* *21*(1), 47–56.

behavior also provide clues about student acceptance of and interest in the program. Many of these procedures are conducive to staff, parent, and student involvement. Whatever evaluation is used, the information collected should be well documented, relevant, and useful. The validity of evaluation depends on the questions asked, behaviors observed, and efforts made to sample randomly and to apply common standards.

Lee and Johnson (2000) propose that effective multicultural education programs require well-written multicultural literature and curricular materials that represent all students, including interracial children. To accept and affirm the pluralism in our schools, educators should recognize interracial children and integrate interracial literature in the school curriculum.

The benefits of using interracial literature include the following:

◆ Interracial literature, both fiction and nonfiction, can help build a sound personal identity in interracial children.
◆ Interracial literature changes the way children look at their world by offering different perspectives of people and events.
◆ Interracial literature shows people who traditionally have been denied realistic images of themselves, their families, community, and culture.

A Multicultural Education Unit

Our premise in this book is that multicultural education should be a total-school curriculum and environmental approach, rather than an occasional unit. We do, however, recognize that the situation should not be "either/or," nor should it become a battle of multicultural education curriculum versus the unit approach. We firmly believe that a once-a-year (or even an every-semester) effort in the form of a multicultural week or perhaps a two- or three-week unit is insufficient to teach knowledge of and respect for cultural diversity. We remind readers, therefore, to consider units as a part of a total curriculum effort, perhaps as a means of addressing one or more specific objectives.

Considerations

Before examining a unit designed to convey knowledge and understanding of cultural diversity, it is important to define the unit approach and to look briefly at what units usually include. First, *units* (sometimes called *modules*) are designed to teach a specific body of information over a time lasting more than a class meeting or two. For example, might the unit last one, two, or three days or weeks or years or longer in some instances?

Second, units contain goals, objectives, content, activities, materials, enrichment resources, and evaluational instruments. Although educators may differ about what the unit should include, generally speaking, it is a comprehensive guide that differs from the one-day lesson plan.

Example

The next several pages provide an example of an instructional unit. It is important to remember that this unit serves only as an illustration. Educators should assess their students' developmental needs, levels of knowledge, and attitudes and assess the planned instruction accordingly.

THE UNIT: *Unjust Treatment of People of Culturally Diverse Backgrounds*

Rationale

African Americans were brought to the United States to be sold into slavery. American Indians were forced off their lands. Asian Americans, especially Chinese Americans, worked on the railroad linking the Missouri River to the Pacific Coast in 1862. Hispanic Americans worked in "sweat factories" or as migrant workers. Japanese Americans were relocated to internment camps after the bombing of Pearl Harbor.

Objectives and Activities

1. Have students define the terms *racism, social justice, discrimination,* and *injustice* and identify examples of each that have harmed several groups from culturally different backgrounds.
2. Have students identify three books or songs that describe the injustices that groups from different cultural backgrounds experienced.
3. Have students develop a time line showing culturally diverse people's responses to unjust treatment—for example, African Americans' march on Washington in 1963.

4. Have students identify three examples of contemporary racism, discrimination, or injustice and list possible solutions for each.

Individuals, cooperative learning groups, or interest-established pairs or triads may work on these activities.

Language Arts

◆ Have students prepare short stories, poems, skits, and plays on the unjust treatment many people received.
◆ Ask students to write and give a speech that an American Indian might have given regarding land being taken away.
◆ Keep a class scrapbook of unjust practices that currently exist in the United States.
◆ Help students write a letter to the editor of a newspaper proposing a solution to an injustice people suffer today.

Mathematics

◆ Compile a "numbers" list with students: acres of land taken away from American Indians, numbers of African Americans brought to the United States to work as slaves, numbers of Asian Americans who worked on the railroad, and numbers of Hispanic Americans who worked as migrant workers. Compute estimates of money saved by having workers work in low-paying jobs in poor working conditions.
◆ On a bar or pie graph, ask students to show numbers of workers from culturally different backgrounds in minimum-wage jobs.
◆ Have students estimate the value of land taken from American Indians, and compare the estimate with the amount received (if any money was actually paid).

Science

◆ Study terrain as part of your lesson plan—for example, land taken away from American Indians and farming land on which migrant workers grow produce.
◆ Have students examine climate conditions necessary for growing various types of produce and determine the effects these conditions have on people.

◆ Study with students the climatic conditions (e.g., temperature, humidity, heat index) of many "sweat shops" and the effect these conditions have on people.

Social Studies

◆ Examine with students the concepts of racism, injustice, and discrimination, and pinpoint historical and contemporary examples.
◆ Ask students to gather information on immigration patterns by decade or some other time frame.
◆ Review with students Americans' resistance to immigrants entering the United States.
◆ Have students write an essay explaining the "melting pot" concept and its limitations and how we currently support the "salad bowl" concept.
◆ Ask students to write a position paper for or against the resistance or unjust treatment people received on arrival to the United States.
◆ Develop a time line with students showing each cultural group's important dates or events—the Emancipation Proclamation, for example.
◆ Ask students to develop a chart listing injustices and offer possible solutions.

Art

◆ Introduce students to works of art depicting injustices people have suffered and struggled to overcome.
◆ Assign students to create collages, dioramas, and mobiles showing injustices: the bonds of slavery, the plight of American Indians, and the menial jobs many Asian and Hispanic Americans have been forced to accept.
◆ Study art of various cultures and ask students to look for common themes and areas.
◆ Examine American Indian art with students and the relationship between the art and the history of American Indians.

Music

◆ Listen to songs of various cultures that have helped people to survive, provided a ray of hope, and communicated pain and suffering.
◆ Ask students to write lyrics for a familiar melody that deal with a contemporary injustice and offer hope.
◆ Research musical instruments that slaves and other people in bondage used.

This partial unit can serve as a beginning point or skeletal unit. Teachers working on interdisciplinary teams can tap their professional expertise in particular content areas and offer many exciting and productive activities and ideas. Readers are also reminded that the appendix, Literature for Children and Adolescents, provides titles of current books for children and adolescents of each cultural group discussed in this book.

Other topics for multicultural units include the following:

◆ Contributions of people from culturally different groups (or a specific cultural group)
◆ Cultural traditions: family and society (in general or for a specific cultural group)
◆ Books, poems, and short stories (or music or art) by writers from culturally different backgrounds, such as *Native People of the Southwest, African American Scholars: Leaders, Activists, and Writers,* and *Martin Luther King: A Lifetime of Action.*
◆ Contemporary contributors from culturally different backgrounds: civil rights activists
◆ Influential women and their contributions (women in general or women in a specific cultural group)
◆ Coming to the United States: immigration in the 1990s to the present

Expanding the Multicultural Education Curriculum

Involvement of Parents, Caregivers, Families, and Communities

Efforts to provide multicultural education curricula and environments must extend beyond the confines of the school. Children and adolescents need to perceive evidence of recognition and respect for cultural diversity in the home and in the community. The home and the community can serve as powerful and positive forces to help reinforce the efforts of the school. Parents and other community members and organizations are valuable resources to help support the school's efforts to promote respect for cultural diversity. They should be made aware of school efforts and should feel that the school seeks and respects their advice and opinions. These two entities can also provide considerable financial and volunteer support for the multicultural education program.

As parents become involved in their children's education and learn more about the school's goals (especially in relation to the goals and materials of the multicultural education curricula), they are more likely to give overall support for school programs. Parents in all likelihood will become more interested in their children's school success and be better able to assist the school in its efforts.

Parents and educators should ask whether the community supports the school and its academic and social tasks. Is the leadership of the community concerned with school effectiveness? Does the community support efforts toward school improvement? Are the achievements of all students and teachers celebrated in the community at public occasions? Are the role models in the community educated people? If the community is not strongly positive, bring the matter to the attention of progressive community leaders with the suggestion that they sponsor a determined effort to improve the community environment.

Extracurricular Activities

Perceptive educators readily recognize the need for equitable representation of all races and ethnic groups in extracurricular activities. Guidelines are as follows:

1. Athletic programs should include minority students and women, and cheerleading teams should include both sexes as well as students of culturally different backgrounds.
2. Clubs and organizations should not perpetuate racial or gender segregation, and one group should not dominate positions of student leadership.
3. Females should participate in all sports and there should be special arrangements for students who are unable to participate for financial or other reasons (Gollnick & Chinn, 2006).

Table 9.2 provides a checklist for evaluating extracurricular activities for racial and ethnic equity.

table 9.2

Extracurricular Activity Checklist

1. Do all the school's racial and ethnic groups participate in extracurricular activities?
2. Are financial resources equitably distributed among extracurricular activities?
3. Are extracurricular activities segregated along racial lines?
4. Do sponsors or advisers of extracurricular activities encourage learners from culturally different backgrounds to participate in the activities they sponsor?
5. Are arrangements available to support students who lack the financial or other (e.g., travel) resources to participate in extracurricular activities?
6. Are conscious efforts made to include students of differing socioeconomic groups and to involve both boys and girls in the school's extracurricular program?
7. Do the efforts to involve all children and adolescents in extracurricular activities receive the wholehearted support (not just token support) of all administrators, teachers, special service personnel, and staff members?

Case Study

Community Involvement

The school personnel at HS 170, an urban secondary school, has reached basic agreement on their multicultural education program. They have established specific objectives for the program, one of which is to involve the community. Extending the program outside the school will show their genuine commitment. Also, doing so will give parents, families, and other community members a chance to provide input and become involved.

The group has decided on several approaches to achieving this goal. They have sent notices home with the students explaining the basic premises of the program and how parents, families, caregivers, and the community can respond. They have also asked local radio and television stations to donate brief airtime to inform the community of the effort. Finally, they have placed student-designed posters in businesses and other public places.

The planning group, recognizing the varying work schedules of community members, called meetings at different times and locations. The purposes of the meetings were to do the following:

1. Explain the purposes of the program and how it will fit in with the existing academic program.

2. Explain the phases of implementation and the rationale and objectives for each phase.
3. Explain that all aspects of the program will be subject to evaluation and review for changes and revisions.
4. Form a committee to review library and media acquisitions.
5. Explain that the program will be interdisciplinary and permeate all areas of the school: curriculum, instruction, materials, teaching and learning environment, and teacher attitudes and behaviors.

Perhaps of greatest importance, during the meetings, the planning group demonstrated the objectives of the program itself: recognition, acceptance, appreciation, and respect for all people regardless of differences.

Questions for Discussion:

1. Consider additional objectives for HS 170's multicultural education program. Although they did not mention social justice, suggest several objectives, especially for social justice.
2. How might these educators involve parents, guardians, and caregivers in the program? Suggest three or four specific objectives for involving people from outside the school. What assessments could be used to measure the success of the involvement of parents, families, caregivers, and community members?
3. To what extent should HS 170 address gender, sexual orientation, and socioeconomic status? Some think that multicultural education should be considered in narrow terms (e.g., *culture*), but there are cultures of gender, sexual orientation, and social class.

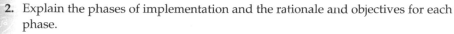 Summing Up

Multicultural educators planning and implementing culturally responsive curricula should:

1. Reflect and recognize that the United States has experienced considerable progress toward acceptance of cultural diversity; that racism, discrimination, and prejudice continue to exist in the United States; and that curricular efforts and overall school environment should demonstrate an emphatic respect for cultural diversity.
2. Place reform efforts on an across-the-curriculum approach and on the overall school environment, rather than on a once-a-year or unit approach.

3. Have a sound multicultural basis: a careful assessment of overall needs, established guidelines, the selection of bias-free curricular materials, and the provision of evaluative procedures for both learners and curricular efforts.

4. Include extensive involvement of community resources, and permeate extracurricular activities as well as the academic curricular aspects.

5. Respect and build on, as much as possible, individual learners' native languages.

Suggested Learning Activities

1. Interview a curriculum coordinator of a large school (or school district) with a large percentage of students from culturally different backgrounds. What approach is the school taking to implement a multicultural education program? What mechanism is in place to ensure that all levels of educators are involved in the program? After the interview, carefully consider your findings, and write a brief paper that summarizes your findings and offers what you think are appropriate suggestions.

2. Prepare a multicultural unit (designed for perhaps two or three weeks) that a school could integrate into an overall multicultural education program. In this unit, be sure to include goals, objectives, activities, curricular materials, provisions for evaluation (of both students and the unit itself), and provisions for children and adolescents with limited English-speaking abilities.

3. Consider the following Implementing Research, which looks at how schools can respond to diversity by implementing five phrases of professional development.

Implementing Research

Embracing Diversity

Howard (2007) points out that many school districts are experiencing rapid growth in the number of students of color, culturally and linguistically diverse students, and students from low-income families. While many schools have a "Welcome to America" attitude, other schools unfortunately do not. Some teachers view their schools' increasing diversity as a problem, rather than an opportunity.

Continuing with business as usual will mean failure or mediocrity for too many students. Rapidly changing demographics demand that educators engage in a vigorous, ongoing, and systemic process of professional development to prepare them to function effectively in a highly diverse environment.

Many educational leaders in diversity-enhanced schools are moving beyond blame and befuddlement and working to transform themselves and their schools to serve all students. From observing and working with them, Howard (2007) has learned that this transformation proceeds in five phases: (1) building trust, (2) engaging personal culture, (3) confronting issues of social dominance and social justice, (4) transforming instructional practices, and (5) engaging the entire school community.

Implementing the Research

1. Some educators (certainly not all) need to change their mindset to view diversity as an opportunity and challenge, rather than a hurdle or obstacle.

2. Rather than tackle too many issues at one time, educators should set clear goals and then work diligently to meet them.

3. Educators should celebrate successes but never forget the overall goals: acceptance, recognition, and social justice for all students.

Source: Howard, G. R. (2007). As diversity grows, so must we. *Educational Leadership, 64*(6), 16–22.

Suggestions for Collaborative Efforts

Form groups of three or four that, if possible, represent our nation's cultural and gender diversity. Working collaboratively, focus your group's attention toward the following efforts:

1. Have each member of your group select a type of curricular material, for example, textbooks, workbooks, worksheets, audiovisuals, and any other curricular materials that elementary or secondary schools commonly use. Prepare an evaluation form (on textbooks as an example here) to answer such questions as: Is the portrayal of children and adolescents of culturally different backgrounds filled with stereotypes and myths? Of the materials on your list, consider the actual numbers of learners of culturally different backgrounds in the school, the accuracy and objectivity of their portrayal, and whether the material addresses differences among people within cultural groups (e.g., Are all Asian Americans alike? Are all Spanish-speaking people alike?).

2. As a group, visit a school to determine its efforts to help children of limited English-speaking capability. What special considerations are made for these learners? What language programs are in place? What professional staff is available to offer help? What remedial programs are available? Are learners allowed to speak their native languages in schools?

3. Evaluating the school curriculum for relevance, objectivity, and accuracy should be a major part of planning any multicultural education program. In your collaborative groups, suggest eight to ten criteria for evaluating the curriculum

to determine whether it recognizes and shows respect for cultural diversity and promotes social justice for all people.

Expanding Your Horizons

Additional Journals, Books, and Internet Sites

Brown, P. L., & Abell, S. K. (2007). Cultural diversity in the science classroom. *Science and Children, 44*(9), 60–61.

> These authors suggest inquiry learning to foster student success in science.

Chan, E. (2007). Student experiences of a culturally-sensitive curriculum: Ethnic identity development and conflicting stories to live by. *Journal of Curriculum Studies, 39*(2), 177–194.

> Analyzing the experiences of students in an inner-city middle school, Chan focuses on what a culturally sensitive curriculum includes.

Leiding, D. (2007). Planning multicultural lessons. *Principal Leadership, 8*(1), 48–51.

> Leiding looks at effective multicultural curricula, prepares teachers for the challenges, and makes suggestions for planning lessons.

Parameswaran, G. (2007). Enhancing diversity education. *Multicultural Education, 14*(3), 51–55.

> Although this article focuses on the college classroom, the elements for an effective curriculum apply to other levels.

Phillion, J., & He, M. F. (2005). *Narrative and experience in multicultural education.* London: Sage.

> Basing multicultural education on narratives and experiences in students' lives can be an excellent curricular-planning technique.

Wassermann, S. (2007). Dare to be different. *Phi Delta Kappan, 88*(5), 384–390.

> Wassermann discusses the Charles Dickens Elementary School in the city of Vancouver.

White-Hood, M. (2007). Becoming culturally proficient. *Principal Leadership, 8*(1), 35–36.

> White-Hood writes about how to contribute to the development of pre-service teachers, enrich the pedagogy of new teachers, and inspire veteran teachers.

EdChange. www.edchange.org/multicultural/curriculum/characteristics.html

> This site looks at delivery, content, teaching and learning materials, cultural perspectives, critical inclusion, social responsibility, and assessment.

ERIC Digests. www.ericdigests.org/1992–5/perspective.htm

> Teaching with a multicultural perspective encourages appreciation and understanding of other cultures as well as one's own. Teaching with this perspective promotes the child's sense of the uniqueness of his or her own culture as a positive characteristic and enables the child to accept the uniqueness of the cultures of others.

In Time. www.intime.uni.edu/multiculture/curriculum/approachs.htm

> This site explores four approaches to multicultural curricula. For example, the contributions approach reflects the approach to multicultural education that requires the least amount of involvement. This is accomplished by selecting books and activities that celebrate holidays, heroes, and special events from various cultures.

National Council for the Social Studies. www.socialstudies.org/positions/multicultural

> This site looks at Curriculum Guidelines for Multicultural Education prepared by the NCSS Task Force on Ethnic Studies Curriculum Guidelines.

Instructional Practices

Understanding the material and activities in this chapter will help the reader to:

◆ State the importance of individual and cultural differences among learners, and explain how these differences affect the teaching and learning process.

◆ Explain the classroom teacher's role in providing teaching and learning situations that are beneficial to culturally diverse learners.

◆ State how socioeconomic conditions, social class, and parents and families affect culturally diverse learners.

◆ List the factors educators should consider in evaluating culturally diverse learners.

◆ List the items educators should consider during self-evaluation to determine teaching effectiveness in multicultural situations.

◆ Explain special considerations educators should address when planning teaching and learning experiences with African, American Indian, Arab, Asian, European, and Hispanic American children and adolescents.

◆ List the characteristics of teachers who are effective in multicultural situations.

◆ Explain the importance and necessity of ensuring that multicultural education permeates the total school environment, provides educational experiences that demonstrate acceptance of culturally diverse learners, and promotes positive self-concepts and cultural identities.

Opening Scenario

Knowledge, Attitudes, and Skills

The discussion continues in the teacher's lounge at Ocean View Middle School. When working in a multicultural situation, which characteristic does a teacher need the most: knowledge, attitudes, or skills? Although the discussion is professional in nature, it is growing increasingly intense.

"Knowledge is what it takes," says one teacher. "If we know about diversity and the cultural characteristics of learners, we can plan appropriate teaching and learning activities. Also, we will better understand how others' characteristics differ from our own."

"True," another teacher responds, "but knowledge is not enough. You need proper attitudes; you need to examine your attitudes toward diversity, and you need to respond to culturally diverse students and their needs. History is full of instances in which people had cultural knowledge yet failed to respond when injustices occurred."

"Your arguments are missing a vital point," states a teacher from another group. "Even with the appropriate knowledge and attitudes, you will still fail to provide the most effective educational experiences for culturally diverse learners unless you have skills."

The teachers consider the issue and decide that, perhaps, it takes all three—knowledge, attitudes, and skills—to provide an effective multicultural education. Some teachers recognize the shortcomings of their positions. Whereas some had tried to improve their knowledge, others had worked to develop more accepting attitudes. One had even taken a skills course to improve his ability to work with students of varying cultures.

The effective teacher in a multicultural education setting, however, needs knowledge, attitudes, and skills. As the educators file back to their classes, someone says, "Quite a challenge, but just think of the benefits for diverse learners—in fact, for all learners." ◆

Overview

Learners at both the elementary and secondary levels deserve the most effective educational experiences possible. In the past, however, educational experiences have all too often minimized the importance of minority viewpoints and issues. Cultural diversity has been an obstacle for learners to "overcome" or for teachers to "remediate." If teachers are to provide effective culturally responsive teaching, they need to understand how ethnically diverse students learn.

Viadero and Johnston (2000) noted an academic achievement gap that separates African and Hispanic American students from their European and Asian American counterparts in schools nationwide. On the average, these minority students start school trailing behind European and Asian children and never catch up, lagging on national tests in every subject—sometimes by as much as four grade levels. A new sense of urgency about the problem is prompting educators and policy makers around that nation to try a variety of tactics to narrow the academic disparities dividing racial and ethnic groups. In some cases, class sizes are being trimmed, teachers are receiving special training, and preschool programs for minority children are being expanded. Schools are opening access to high-level classes and encouraging minority children to enroll. Districts are looking for schoolwide-improvement models, and policy makers are raising the academic bar for students and teachers.

This chapter explores several teaching and learning contexts: learners' individual and cultural differences, characteristics of educators, organization and instruction, the teaching and learning environment, and cultural perspectives that influence the teaching and learning process in multicultural settings.

Learners' Individual and Cultural Differences

Perceiving All Learners Objectively

It is important that teachers perceive elementary and secondary learners objectively, regardless of cultural, ethnic, racial, sexual orientation, socioeconomic, or religious differences. Learners need the psychological security of feeling valued and accepted; therefore, all educational decisions should be based on objective evidence and should be made with the individual's welfare in mind. Because of the tremendous diversity among contemporary learners, educators cannot consider an entire class as a homogeneous group who need the same educational experiences. Students differ significantly in social class, geographic location, and family background. It is the school's responsibility to develop an understanding of each learner and to base teaching and learning experiences on reliable and objective information.

Recognizing and Accepting Diversity

It is an understatement to suggest that teaching and learning situations must demonstrate an emphatic acceptance of learners in all their cultural, ethnic, socio-economic, and religious diversity. An environment that promotes acceptance of diversity does more than pay lip service to the concept or have goal statements that are merely rhetorical.

For culturally diverse learners to feel genuine acceptance, the teaching and learning process must concretely demonstrate respect for cultural and ethnic differences (Are all cultures and ethnic groups represented in the curriculum?); it must recognize socioeconomic status (Do children come in contact with children from other socioeconomic levels? Do textbooks portray the various social classes of U.S. society?); and it must accept all religious groups (Do children feel their religious views are accepted?).

Sapon-Shevin (2000/2001) maintains that the diversity of our nation calls for schools for all students. For example, she lists growing signs of our schools' diversity: school-aged students who speak a language other than English; growing numbers of migrant families whose children attend schools intermittently; and inclusion, which brings increasing numbers of students with disabilities into mainstream classrooms.

Points to Ponder 10.1

Valuing Differences Among Learners

Learners have many differences—many that educators can see, and others more subtle. Also, as we have repeatedly stated, no one can consider an individual to be like others in his or her culture. Yet some educators consider all students of one race, for example, to be the same and fail to consider their many differences. Make a list of ways educators can learn about students and their differences (e.g., get to know individual students, meet their immediate parents and extended family members, and study the respective cultures).

Referring to instruction, Sapon-Shevin (2000/2001) looks at cooperative learning, peer tutoring, and multilevel teaching. First, she maintains that cooperative learning is an optimal way to teach students with different abilities in the same classroom. Research suggests that cooperative learning validates the importance of heterogeneous grouping as well as demonstrates that cooperative learning groups work best when they address differences in student status related to gender, race, and ethnicity. Second, peer tutoring allows teachers to address different skill levels and to respect differences. Still, teachers should use caution to avoid a situation in which a student is always being tutored and never has the opportunity to serve in a teacher or leader role. Third, multilevel teaching can be used to teach a wide range of students in one classroom. Teachers need to organize classroom learning activities so that all students can participate successfully.

Characteristics of Effective Educators in Multicultural Settings

Educators who seek a comprehensive understanding of cultural diversity and expertise in multicultural education should direct attention to both cognitive and affective factors. It will not suffice for educators to have knowledge of culturally diverse learners yet be unable to recognize learners' individual and cultural needs and the complex relationship between culture and learning. Educators also need to develop appropriate attitudes that show genuine concern and caring, as well as skills to plan and implement instruction that addresses cultural and individual diversity.

This section looks briefly at the knowledge, attitudes, and skills teachers need in multicultural settings. It is important to emphasize that these three attributes do not work in isolation. Teachers who work in multicultural situations are responsible for developing expertise in all three areas so they can provide learners with the most effective learning environment.

Knowledge

Teachers may lack factual information about ethnic, racial, and cultural differences; teacher education programs traditionally have not provided appropriate experiences to prepare teachers to teach in an increasingly multicultural classroom. A teacher's diversity knowledge base should include culture, race, ethnicity, and socioeconomic status, and the teacher should comprehend the implications for the teaching and learning process. Similarly, teachers must know and understand the ramifications of racism, discrimination, prejudice, and injustice and what it means to be a diverse learner. Teachers need sufficient knowledge to be able to understand culturally different learners and to plan both developmentally and culturally appropriate instruction.

Attitudes

Both elementary and secondary teachers need to acquire specific attitudes that will contribute to their ability to teach in contemporary multicultural classrooms: (1) a sense of democracy, in which differences are respected as well as students rights are respected; (2) an educational philosophy that includes recognition and respect for all types of diversity; (3) the ability to perceive events and situations from other cultural perspectives; (4) an understanding of the complexities of culture and ethnicity in U.S. society; and (5) the desire and willingness to work on a daily basis with people who are different.

Teachers, for the most part unknowingly, have long transmitted biased messages to students. Whether lining up students for lunch by sex or allowing ability grouping to result in racial segregation, teachers often send messages to students that one sex or race is entitled to preferential treatment. Most educators do not consciously or intentionally stereotype students or discriminate against them; they usually try to treat all students fairly and equitably. Nevertheless, teachers, like others in U.S. society, have learned attitudes and behaviors that are ageist, disability biased, racist, sexist, and enthnocentric. Some biases are so deeply internalized that individuals do not realize they hold them. Only when teachers can (and are willing to) recognize the subtle and unintentional biases of their behavior can they make positive changes in the classroom (Gollnick & Chinn, 2006).

Teacher educators are increasingly aware of the importance of preparing teachers to teach in a multiethnic, multilingual, economically stratified society. To better prepare teachers for these challenges, Allen and Labbo (2001) explored how inquiry into teachers' own cultural influences shaped their interactions with and reflections on students of diverse cultural backgrounds. If teachers begin to see cultures —their own and their students'—in complex, shifting terms, they might begin to apply their understandings to making their teaching culturally engaging.

Allen and Labbo (2001) explored practices with their teacher-education students that had the potential for building a self-reflective, culturally conscious community that maintains a balance between comfort in who we are and confrontation of ourselves as cultural beings in a multicultural society. Through building cultural memoirs, the teachers in this study gained a better understanding of their cultural backgrounds, and in essence gave their cultural backgrounds and lives a second thought.

Skills

Daily, teachers must understand many complicated areas: learning styles, the dangers of ability grouping, the benefits of cooperative learning, culturally different perceptions of motivation and competition, learners who may not want to excel at the expense of their peers, and stereotypical beliefs about a culture's ability to learn or not to learn. Generally speaking, teachers need the skills to teach children and adolescents in the various cultural groups and the ability to convey that teachers genuinely want what is best for learners, both as students and as people.

Points to Ponder 10.2

Knowledge, Attitudes, and Skills

Culturally appropriate knowledge, attitudes, and skills are essential for educators who deal with students of culturally differing backgrounds on a daily basis. But how can the appropriate knowledge, attitudes, and skills be acquired? List ways (such as reading, in-service workshops, college coursework) in which you can become an effective educator in multicultural situations.

Teachers, working in a position to speak for change, have a responsibility to do whatever is possible to reduce racism, prejudice, and injustice among children and adolescents and to instill attitudes of equality and democratic values, which may continue for life. Teachers, indeed, should be significant influences on the values, hopes, and dreams of their students. In a democratic classroom, teachers and students who are committed to human freedom should have the liberty to express their views, values, and beliefs with regard to democratic ideals such as human dignity, justice, and equality.

These teacher behaviors are essential in multicultural classrooms:

1. Provide learning experiences that reflect individual cultures' learning styles and perceptions of competition, group welfare, sharing, motivation, and success. For example, some American Indian learners may prefer sharing and helping peers to competitive learning activities, and Puerto Ricans may not wish to excel or be set apart from the group as being different or excelling.
2. Provide learning experiences that reflect gender differences. To confront gender bias in curricular materials, encourage gender integration through peer tutoring and other small learning groups. Encourage open dialogue and collaboration.
3. Encourage and support the development of bilingual programs.
4. Immerse students in a variety of written and oral language activities that are meaningful, relevant, and functional in a pluralistic society.
5. Treat all students fairly and establish a democratic classroom in which all students give and receive equal treatment.
6. Expect the best from *all* students. Encourage all of them to succeed academically; don't automatically assume that minority students will perform less well.
7. Group heterogeneously whenever possible, to enhance self-esteem and promote ethnic interaction.
8. Demonstrate daily the necessity of democratic values and attitudes, a multicultural education philosophy, and an ability to view events and situations from diverse ethnic perspectives and points of view.
9. Recognize as a myth the belief that culturally diverse parents and families do not care about their children's education.

10. Encourage cross-cultural friendships and social interaction, cooperation, and socialization among boys and girls in the classroom, on the playground, and in the community.

11. Address the special problems that culturally diverse parents and families may face, such as language difficulties and misunderstanding the U.S. school system.

12. Acquire factual knowledge about learner differences such as culture, race, ethnicity, socioeconomic status, and gender and commit to having educational experiences reflect these differences.

13. Arrange your classroom so that it reflects cultural diversity in bulletin boards and on the walls and in the selection of artwork and artifacts on display.

Educator Self-Evaluation

Educators of all grade levels and all cultures probably agree that some type of evaluation is necessary periodically to determine whether the school is meeting goals and objectives. Whether of an informal or formal nature, the evaluation instrument should focus on teachers' ability to plan and implement appropriate teaching and learning activities for children and adolescents.

Points to Ponder 10.3

Determining Other Needed Characteristics and Behaviors

Work in groups of three or four to identify other characteristics or behaviors that educators need to address in multicultural settings. Consider this task from several perspectives. What type of teacher do you want to be? What might parents from a culturally different background want for their child? How might a child or adolescent want his or her teacher to be?

Teachers should also use a self-evaluation instrument designed to measure their ability to provide the environment and learning activities that are responsive to culturally diverse learners. Such a self-evaluation should include several questions designed to provide insight into the teacher's knowledge, attitudes, and skills:

1. Have there been efforts to understand and respect cultural diversity among learners not as a problem to solve but as a challenging opportunity and a rich gift?

2. Have there been efforts to provide a classroom in which learners feel free to speak and express diverse opinions? Does the teacher repress them or allow other students to stifle diverse opinion?

3. Have there been efforts to have the classroom reflect cultural diversity? Do the walls, bulletin boards, and artwork in the classroom demonstrate respect for cultural diversity, or do the contents of the classroom indicate an appreciation or valuing of only one culture?

4. Have there been efforts to provide organizational patterns that do not result in segregation of some learners according to race, culture, ethnicity, or socioeconomics?

5. Have there been efforts to understand language differences and differing learning styles? Has the school developed organizational patterns and instructional methodologies that might be helpful to culturally diverse learners?

6. Have there been efforts to understand culturally different learners' perspectives toward motivation, excelling among one's peers, competition, group welfare, and sharing?

7. Have there been efforts to understand culturally diverse parents and extended families and to ensure their participation in learners' academic and social life at school?

8. Have there been efforts to treat each learner with respect, to consider each learner as equal to other students, and to treat each learner as a valued and worthwhile member of the class? Are all learners accorded similar academic assistance? Do all learners receive help from the school's special service personnel?

9. Have there been efforts to allow (and indeed encourage) all students to work in cross-cultural groups, to carry on conversation and meaningful dialogue, and to feel they are valued members of the group?

10. Have there been efforts to instill multiculturalism as a genuine part of the teaching and learning process and overall school environment?

Organization and Instruction: Cultural Considerations

Students are often organized for instructional purposes on the basis of test scores, previous grades, teacher recommendations, and other supposedly objective information. The basic rationale for grouping students is to narrow the abilities range and thus provide teachers with a homogeneous group that is supposedly easier to teach. Two dangers inherent in any grouping process are (1) placing students in the wrong group and (2) having an organization pattern that segregates students by race.

Whether considering race, socioeconomic status, or gender, organizational patterns should not result in segregation, whereby inferior teachers teach some students or teach in inferior schools and other students receive preferential treatment. Organizational patterns should result in a student population that is as representative as possible of the entire school population and, if possible, the composition of the community at large.

Ability Grouping

Ability grouping may result in a form of segregation. Ability-grouping patterns often parallel students' nonacademic characteristics, such as race or ethnic background, socioeconomic class, or personal appearance. Learners of low socioeconomic status and minority groups often find themselves in lower-ability groups. Such practices may be discriminatory, because the segregation of students is along ethnic and socioeconomic lines. These patterns of grouping appear to be related to ethnicity and socioeconomic standing, rather than purely academic abilities and achievement levels.

Cooperative Learning

People who help one another by joining forces to achieve a common goal generally feel more positively about each other and are willing to interact more positively when performing collective tasks. Rather than treat academic learning and social or intergroup relations as two distinct entities, cooperative learning has contributed positively to overall intergroup relations and particularly to improving relations with diverse students. Cooperative-learning procedures can reinforce the efforts of culturally diverse children to continue their schoolwork successfully. Children who work cooperatively in groups, rather than in isolation, are usually motivated to help each other carry out the assigned or chosen project.

Research on cooperative learning and intergroup relationships has concluded that students in cooperative learning situations had a greater appreciation for cooperative-learning classmates. Specifically, cooperative learning increases contact between students, provides a feeling of group membership, engages learners in pleasant activities, and requires that team members work toward a common goal (Slavin, 1996).

Students' working cooperatively can contribute positively to specific multiethnic populations. Both black and white students working in cooperative-learning situations liked school better than those of the same ethnic groups working in competitive classrooms. Working cooperatively seems to have particularly strong effects on Hispanic and black students, regardless of achievement levels. A study of Jigsaw II-related classes that included recent European and West Indian immigrants and white Canadians documented substantially more cross-ethnic friendships than in the control groups (Slavin, 1983).

Cooperation, collaborating, and community are prominent themes, techniques, and goals in educating African, Arab, and Hispanic American as well as American Indian students. Two major reasons help to explain these pedagogical trends. First, underlying values of human connectedness and collaborative problem solving are high priorities in the cultures of most groups of color in the United States. Second, cooperation plays a central role in these groups' learning styles, especially the communicative, procedural, motivational, and relational dimensions.

Language Differences

Language diversity is so great in some parts of the United States that sometimes classroom communication is virtually impossible. In addition, many schools are unable to provide appropriate learning experiences for children whose native language is not English. As a result, language-minority children do not learn the essential lessons of school and do not participate fully in the economic, social, and political life of the United States. As they decide on organizing students for instruction, culturally sensitive educators recognize the dilemma that learners with limited English skills often face.

Maintaining that language differences pose a major stumbling block for American Indian students, suggestions for American Indians include these:

1. Implement cooperative-learning techniques. American Indians, reared to value cooperation and sharing, are not accustomed culturally to working alone or to competing for grades and teacher approval.
2. Avoid large-group, formal lessons in the lecture–recitation mode. American Indian students tend to withdraw during formal patterns. These learners perceive more opportunity in student-to-student dialogues and group problem-solving efforts.
3. Liberally give encouragement and positive reinforcement. Include language-lifting techniques and modeling of correct language patterns. Avoid correcting pupils' oral language errors except during formal language lessons.

Other suggestions for educators working with language-minority learners include the following:

1. The use of formal language, teacher leadership and control of verbal exchanges, question-and-answer formats, and references to increasingly abstract ideas often characterize a classroom environment with which many minority children are unfamiliar. Whenever possible, communication is made easier if these ideas overlap with those the learners already know.

2. Language-minority learners should experience familiar communication styles to establish a basis for communication. This basis may include speaking in the child's primary language, using culturally appropriate styles of address, and relying on management patterns that are familiar to and comfortable for children.
3. The meanings of words, gestures, and actions may be quite different from culture to culture.

In an interesting study, Huguet and Regner (2007) examined gender stereotypes among women involved in mathematics tests. Unfortunately, for quite a few years, educators have believed gender stereotypes existed. See Gender Perspectives 10.1 for more on this aspect of the hidden curriculum.

$\mathcal{G}$ender $\mathcal{P}$erspectives 10.1

GENDER STEREOTYPES

Huguet and Regner (2007) wrote that sufficient evidence suggests that women and girls are influenced by gender-stereotyped expectations on standardized mathematics tests. Middle school girls exhibited a performance deficit when they were convinced a task involved mathematical skills. This deficit occurred in mixed-gender groups but not in same-gender groups. The research review concluded that women are expected to experience additional tension, over and above that associated with taking a difficult test, because they are preoccupied by fears of confirming a negative stereotype.

Huguet and Regner (2007) offered three conclusions:

1. A stereotype (or stereotype threat) exists when both genders are represented and the negative gender stereotype is presented.
2. Middle school girls are affected by this stereotype threat at school; the phenomenon is more problematic than once assumed.
3. The threat of gender stereotyping was eliminated in same-gender classes.

We like the Huguet and Regner (2007) article because we think many females have adopted gender stereotypes about mathematics ability.

Source: Huguet, P., & Regner, I. (2007). Stereotype threat among schoolgirls in quasi-ordinary classroom circumstances. *Journal of Educational Psychology, 99*(3), 545–560.

The School Environment

The school environment includes all experiences with which learners come in contact: content, instructional methods, the actual teaching and learning process and environment, the professional staff and other staff members, as well as the actions and attitudes of other students. This definition of environment is synonymous with curriculum itself.

Working toward a Multicultural School Environment

It is important that the multicultural environment demonstrate genuine respect and concern for all learners, regardless of their racial, cultural, or ethnic backgrounds. With a supportive school environment, culturally different children, along with other learners, can learn to take an active role in a democratic society, guided by relevant understanding, and develop skills in communication and computation, social attitudes and interests, and human appreciation. The school environment should support school learning and socialization for all students. A supportive school environment is one in which the morale of both teachers and students is high. Teachers believe in their mission to help guide and stimulate the learning activities of their students and are pleased with their students' responsive behavior.

Although it is impossible to describe in detail all the factors that make a school environment responsive to cultural diversity, briefly discussing several areas illustrates the environment in its broadest sense: the unconditional acceptance of diversity, the promotion of positive cultural identities, and a faculty and staff composition that represents the cultural diversity of the school population. The school environment is by no means limited to these three aspects. These three, however, have a powerful influence on how learners perceive others' opinions of cultural diversity.

Here are recommendations for creating a teaching and learning environment that reflects the cultural diversity of the school:

- ◆ As a part of the daily learning environment, provide and consistently update a variety of multiethnic, multicultural, and self-awareness materials.
- ◆ Plan learning experiences that are flexible, unbiased, and inclusive of contributions from diverse cultures.
- ◆ Find good people to serve as role models and material resources that focus on problems in a pluralistic society.
- ◆ Adopt instructional strategies relevant to the physical, emotional, social, and intellectual development of children of multiethnic heritage.

◆ Use instructional material that shows individuals from diverse cultural groups working in different occupational and social roles. Make sure all materials are free of bias, omissions, and stereotypes.

◆ Adopt flexible scheduling that provides ample time and space for children to share their uniqueness through role-play, art, conversation, and games.

◆ Continuously use ideas and materials that represent cultures throughout the year, not just during special holidays such as Black History Week, Christmas, Thanksgiving, Hanukkah, and Chinese New Year.

An educational setting should allow children to feel accepted, encouraged, and respected. Here are more ways of creating appropriate school environments in our diverse society:

1. The total school environment should undergo reform, not just the courses and programs. The school's informal hidden curriculum is as important as, or perhaps more important than, the formal course of study.

2. Cultural content should be part of all subject areas from preschool through grade twelve and beyond.

3. Learning centers, libraries, and resource centers should include resources for history, literature, music, folklore, views of life, and the arts of the various groups of people.

4. Cultural diversity should be reflected in assembly programs; classroom, hallway, and entrance decorations; cafeteria menus; counseling interactions; and, as we previously discussed, extracurricular activities.

5. School-sponsored dances and other such activities should reflect a respect for a diverse society.

6. Service learning should accompany multicultural education courses, so pre-service and in-service teachers can better relate to the content examined in multicultural education courses.

Table 10.1 provides additional ways of addressing diversity in educational settings.

Promoting Positive Cultural Identities

It is imperative that educators understand the school environment's influence (perhaps an unconscious or unrecognized influence) on a child's cultural identity. Without doubt, the school environment affects both the manner in which children perceive themselves and their cultural images.

table 10.1

Addressing Diversity in Its Many Forms

1. Check district and school policies, procedures, practices, curriculum guides, lesson plans, and instructional materials to be sure they are free of bias toward race, gender, religion, culture, and disabilities.

2. Make newcomers feel welcome through a formal program.

3. Be sure that assignments are not offensive or frustrating to students of cultural minorities. For example, asking students to discuss or write about their Christmas experiences is inappropriate for non-Christian students. Let students discuss their similar holidays.

4. Form a schoolwide planning committee to address the implementation of multicultural education.

5. Contact your district curriculum coordinators for ideas and assistance.

6. Let faculty knowledgeable about multicultural topics provide in-service for others or guest-teach their classes.

7. Take a cultural census of the class or school to find out what cultures are represented; let students be the ethnographers.

8. Form a multicultural club.

9. Select a theme to tie various multicultural activities together; hold school programs with art, music, and dramatic presentations; hold a multicultural fair or festival featuring music, art, dance, dress, and so on; adopt a multicultural theme for existing activities.

10. Hold a school cross-cultural food festival.

11. Have multicultural celebrations and teach-ins with schoolwide activities in all classes.

12. Decorate classrooms, hallways, and the library media center with murals, bulletin boards, posters, artifacts, and other materials representative of the students in the class or school or other cultures the class is studying. Posters and other information are available from foreign government travel bureaus and education agencies, private travel agencies, consulates, the United Nations, and ethnic and cultural organizations.

13. Designate a permanent bulletin board for multicultural news and displays.

14. Help students develop the skills necessary to locate and organize information about cultures from the library media center, the mass media, people, and personal observations.

15. Have students write to foreign consulates, tourist bureaus, minority organizations, and others for information and decorative materials.

table ◆ 10.1
Continued

16. Supplement textbooks with authentic materials on different cultures from newspapers, magazines, and other media of the culture. Such materials are available from the Department of Education Foreign Language Documentation Center.

17. Take advantage of community resources. Have representatives of various cultures talk to classes; actors portray characters or events; and musicians and dance groups, such as salsa bands or bagpipe units, perform.

18. Work with the library media center on special bibliographies, collections, displays, and audiovisuals.

19. Hold a mock legislature to debate current or historical issues affecting minorities and cultural groups.

20. Hold oratorical, debate, essay, poster, art, brain brawl, or other competitions with a multicultural focus.

Self-concept, or self-image, is a complex set of beliefs that an individual holds about himself or herself. A person may have more than one self-image and actually hold positive feelings in some areas and negative images in others. For example, a person might have a positive self-image in intellectual pursuits while harboring negative feelings toward his or her athletic abilities. The actions of others or the way in which learners think others perceive and treat them significantly influences their self-concepts.

The environment should allow culturally diverse people to feel a sense of being able to cope or to feel that they can control their lives at least to some extent. Youngsters who feel torn between two cultures may have a low self-image because they assume they cannot be successful in either society.

Self-concepts and cultural identities of learners relate not only to their race, culture, and social class but also to their feelings of power in the school environment. The task facing educators is to help students build positive perceptions about their reference groups and to develop confidence in actively participating in social discussion and change. The educators' goal should be to provide a school environment that either raises or contributes positively to racial and cultural pride of all people.

Promoting Diversity among Faculty and Staff

Diverse people must be an integral part of the school's instructional, administrative, and supportive staffs. School personnel—teachers, principals, cooks, custodians, secretaries, students, and counselors—make contributions as important to multicultural environments as do the courses of study and instructional materials. Students learn important lessons about culture and cultural diversity by observing interactions among different racial and cultural groups in their school; hearing verbal exchanges between the professional and support staffs; and observing the extent to which the staff is culturally representative of the student population.

Cultural Perspectives

Socioeconomic and Class Differences

The student's socioeconomic level and social class deserve consideration as elementary and secondary educators plan teaching and learning experiences. If a group of individuals has particular characteristics that are valued by a society, the group so identified will enjoy high status. The reverse is also true. Thus, when speaking of upper and lower classes, we are referring to groups of individuals who either have or do not have the qualities that are prized by a larger society.

In the United States, upper classes are those groups that have wealth, advanced education, professional occupations, and relative freedom from concern about their material needs. Conversely, lower classes are those groups that live in or on the edge of poverty, have poor education, are irregularly employed or employed in jobs requiring little or no training, often require assistance from government welfare agencies, and are constantly concerned with meeting the basic needs of life.

At least two perspectives stand out as being important for educators to consider: (1) some social classes may be able to provide their children with additional experiences that may be conducive to education and academic achievement, and (2) determination, hard work, and middle-class values are believed to pay rich dividends. The problem with the former is that many students do not bring to school experiential backgrounds that contribute to their education. The latter often causes poor people to be perceived as and feel like failures who lack the ambition or determination to pursue long-term goals.

Realistically, culturally diverse students often come from poorer financial backgrounds and homes in which language differences impede communication and upward social mobility. Such obstacles, however, do not mean that these social classes value education and school achievement any less. It is educators' responsibility to provide teaching and learning experiences that build on the strengths and backgrounds of all children and adolescents.

It is important to emphasize the economic advances and achievements of culturally diverse learners and their families during the past decade or two.

Educators should objectively consider each learner to determine individual strengths and weaknesses. To equate poverty with a particular culture, race, or ethnic group is a serious mistake and can jeopardize a learner's educational future.

What are the implications for educators working with children and adolescents from lower socioeconomic and social classes?

1. Teachers, counselors, and administrators should recognize the dangers of associating negative and harmful expectations with culturally diverse groups and lower classes. In fact, educators should periodically review their beliefs about children and adolescents as well as their behavioral and academic expectations (Gollnick & Chinn, 2006).
2. Educators should examine curricular and instructional efforts to determine whether they reflect only middle-class European American perspectives. Culturally diverse learners and students from low socioeconomic backgrounds need to see a reflection of their values and lifestyles in the educational content and in the instructional methods (Gollnick & Chinn, 2006).
3. Educators should be on a constant lookout for grouping patterns that segregate students along cultural, racial, or ethnic lines. Teachers often place students from lower socioeconomic classes or who are culturally diverse in lower ability groups. Such practices may be discriminatory, because students are segregated along ethnic and social class lines.

The Role of Parents, Families, and Caregivers

Parent involvement and cooperative relationships between parents and schools are essential. First, parental interest and participation in schools and classrooms has a positive influence on academic achievement. Second, parents involved in academic activities with their children gain knowledge that helps them to assess their children's education. They can help their children with areas of education in which they need assistance. Third, the results of parental involvement in tutoring students who are limited English proficient are consistent with those for native English-speaking students and their families. To be effective as home tutors, all parents need school support and direct teacher involvement.

Educators must employ special strategies to accommodate the unique cultural characteristics of Asian immigrant parents. Their agenda should include (1) educators asking themselves some difficult questions about their prejudices and stereotypical beliefs about Asian Americans, (2) understanding Asian beliefs about education, and (3) providing opportunities for Asian American parents to participate in school activities, to communicate through newsletters, and to serve on advisory committees.

Culturally diverse children and adolescents often perceive the roles of grandparents, aunts, and uncles as similar to those of the mother and the father. For this reason, educators should welcome extended families who are interested in the learner's educational progress. Culturally diverse parents and families may not understand the U.S. school system and its emphasis on competition and individual welfare and achievement over group accomplishments. Teachers may offer suggestions and directions to parents and families who are able to assist their children and adolescents. Teachers need a better understanding of culturally diverse families and their values, customs, traditions, and expectations. All too often, teachers view the benefits of parent involvement too narrowly. Not only do children benefit, but parents and teachers do as well.

Learner Evaluation

The evaluation of learners should include a consideration of individual and cultural differences, variations in learning and testing styles, and differences in motivation. Rather than evaluate only what paper and pencil can measure, evaluation efforts should also focus on student behaviors, attitudes, and everyday actions. For example, a student might be able to list examples of racist behavior and offer several valid reasons on paper why racism should be reduced. The evaluation process, however, should also include a consideration of actions. Do students make racist remarks? Do students demonstrate racial harmony? Do students engage in segregationist activities? Generally speaking, have students developed respect and acceptance for, as well as knowledge of, our increasingly culturally diverse world?

Sleeter and Grant (2007) offer several recommendations for educators planning and implementing programs that evaluate learners:

1. Evaluation procedures should not include standardized achievement tests that are monocultural in nature and that sort students into different groups that result in different and unequal opportunities.
2. Evaluation procedures should not penalize students by requiring skills that are extraneous to what is being evaluated. For example, a science teacher assessing science concepts should not require students to read and write about their skill level.
3. Evaluation procedures designed to assess students' English proficiency levels should take into account the different contexts in which school communication takes place and the different factors involved.
4. Evaluation procedures should be free of sexist or racist stereotypes.

Decisions concerning evaluation include both what should be evaluated and a determination of the evaluation methods. As with all curricular efforts, educators should closely match the evaluation with goals and objectives, should measure what was taught, and should measure attitudes and behaviors as well as cognitive knowledge.

Case Study

Teacher Self-Evaluation

The faculty at Public School (PS) High School 93 were accustomed to being evaluated by the principal, a central office evaluational specialist, and occasionally peer teachers. The teachers were beginning to realize, however, that something was missing. Evaluation forms indicated the degree of success, yet a teacher basically knew, better than the instrument could suggest, whether he or she had met the school's expectations and was working to maximum potential. There was yet another issue: While the existing instruments evaluated overall performance, they did little to determine the educator's efforts to address the needs of diverse learners.

In keeping with the research on evaluation, the counselor suggested a self-evaluation form for the teachers. Interested faculty members decided to work as a committee to develop a self-evaluation scale—a measure that each teacher might share with peers or administrators. (The decision to share the outcome was one the teacher could make at a later date.)

While the evaluation committee was to study the various possibilities and make final recommendations, broad categories for evaluation might include the following (with the specifics to be added later):

◆ Knowledge, attitudes, and skills
◆ Classroom environment
◆ Instructional purposes
◆ Curricular materials
◆ Management system
◆ Evaluation process

Questions for Discussion:

1. While a teacher's skills can be evaluated by direct observation, how can his or her attitudes toward individuals, as well as the increasingly diverse school population, be evaluated?
2. What other criteria should be included on the self-evaluation scale? For example, should the scale include a detailed list of teacher competencies or effective teacher behaviors?
3. With whom should the self-evaluation be shared? Anyone? In other words, should the self-evaluation scale be for *evaluation* or *improvement*?

Summing Up

Educators who plan teaching, learning, and classroom environments in multicultural settings should remember to:

1. Recognize and respect learner diversity: culture, race, ethnicity, sexual orientation, individuality, gender, socioeconomic status, and religion.

2. Develop the knowledge, attitudes, and skills to teach and relate to culturally diverse children and adolescents.

3. Recognize that some organizational practices contribute to exclusivity and segregation; therefore, educators should provide instructional methods to which culturally diverse children and adolescents can most effectively relate.

4. Plan a school curriculum and environment that reflect respect for all cultural, ethnic, social class, and religious differences among people and that promote learners' cultural identities.

5. Recognize and respond appropriately to cultural perspectives that influence the academic achievement and overall school progress of culturally diverse learners; for example, socioeconomic status and social class, parents and families, and learner evaluation.

6. Implement a teaching and learning environment that affects positively how children and adolescents feel about school, about being culturally different in a predominantly European American school, and about feeling genuinely accepted and cared about.

7. Provide culturally diverse learners with an administration, faculty, and staff that reflect the cultural diversity of the overall school population.

Suggested Learning Activities

1. Design a plan for involving culturally diverse parents and immediate families in the teaching and learning process. Explain specifically how you would address the following points: language barriers between culturally diverse parents and you; explaining school expectations to parents and families who might not understand how U.S. schools function; and ways you might involve parents and families.

2. Observe a teaching demonstration to determine a teacher's unintended bias. Did the teacher call on more girls than boys or more European Americans than Hispanic Americans, expect Asian Americans to answer more difficult questions, or tend to ignore students from lower socioeconomic groups? How might you help this teacher recognize bias? What items would you include on a teacher self-evaluation scale designed to help teachers recognize unintended bias?

3. Consider the following Implementing Research, which looks at how teachers should consider culturally and linguistically diverse learners as capable prior to engaging them in educational tasks.

Implementing Research

Understanding and Engaging Diverse Learners

Teaching is an ethical activity, and teachers have an ethical obligation to help all students learn. Based on this belief, Villegas and Lucas (2007) maintain that successfully teaching students from culturally and linguistically diverse backgrounds involves more than just applying specialized teaching techniques. It demands a new way of looking at teaching that is grounded in an understanding of the role of culture and language in learning.

These authors offer six qualities that can serve as a coherent framework for professional development:

1. Understanding how learners construct knowledge
2. Learning about students' lives
3. Holding affirming views about diversity
4. Being socioculturally conscious
5. Using appropriate instructional strategies
6. Advocating for all students

From a constructivist perspective, learners use their previous knowledge and beliefs to make sense of the new ideas and experiences they encounter in school. A central role of the culturally and linguistically responsive teacher is to support students' learning by helping to build bridges between what they already know about a topic and what they need to learn about it.

Implementing the Research

1. Teachers have an ethical responsibility to teach all students. This is a foundation of the profession. Teachers' responsibilities include gaining the knowledge they need, changing attitudes (if necessary), and developing the skills to teach culturally and linguistically diverse students.

2. Teachers need to understand culturally and linguistically diverse students' ways of knowing—how they construct learning and build current learning on previous learning.

3. Teachers will face increasing diversity in future years—cultural, social class, sexual orientation, and individual differences.

In sum, teachers cannot teach and engage students if they do not accept their diversity.

Source: Villegas, A. M., & Lucas, T. (2007). The culturally responsive teacher. *Educational Leadership, 64*(6) 28–33.

Suggestions for Collaborative Efforts

Form groups of three or four that, if possible, represent U.S. cultural and gender diversity. Working collaboratively, focus your group's attention toward the following efforts:

1. Have each member of your group survey elementary and secondary school teachers to determine their efforts to include multicultural perspectives in their teaching and learning activities. Look specifically at items such as curriculum content, teacher expectations for achievement and behavior, grouping strategies, testing and evaluation, and involvement of parents and extended family members. How does your group believe teachers could improve their efforts?

2. Devise a checklist to evaluate the degree to which the overall school environment reflects multicultural perspectives. Although your group should include perspectives it feels are important, the basic underlying question should be this: Does the overall school environment portray multicultural perspectives? Other questions might be these: Is there evidence that cultural, ethnic, social class, and religious diversity is accepted? Are there deliberate attempts to promote positive cultural identities? Is cultural diversity represented among faculty and staff and at all levels of administration?

3. List ten to twelve criteria for evaluating a teacher's (or any school professional's) performance in working with diverse students. Perhaps you will want to separate your list into three categories: knowledge, attitudes, and skills. Or you might just want to write down a list of characteristics or behaviors. Consider the perspectives of the educator, the parent, and the learner as you make your list.

Expanding Your Horizons

Additional Journals, Books, and Internet Sites

Castleman, B., & Littky, D. (2007). Learning to love learning. *Educational Leadership,* *64*(8), 58–61.

These authors look at the child-centered school, the importance of individualized attention, and the need for change in many schools.

Datnow, A. (2006). *Integrating educational systems for successful reform in diverse contexts.* Cambridge, England: Cambridge University Press.

Successful reform in diverse contexts requires more than simply a singular-focused approach.

Eisner, E. (2006). The satisfactions of teaching. *Educational Leadership, 63*(6), 44–46.

Eisner, a noted writer, discusses six satisfactions of teaching.

Huguet, P., & Regner, I. (2007). Stereotype threat among schoolgirls in quasi-ordinary classroom circumstances. *Journal of Educational Psychology, 99*(3), 545–560.

> These authors cite evidence of a stereotype threat by which women and girls are influenced by gender-stereotyped expectations.

Richards, H. V., Brown, A. E., & Forde, T. B. (2007). Addressing diversity in schools: Culturally responsive pedagogy. *Teaching Exceptional Children, 39*(3), 64–68.

> These authors explain the need to address diversity, define the term *responsive pedagogy,* and discuss what the educational system must do.

Shealey, M. W., & Collins, T. (2007). Creating culturally responsive literacy programs in inclusive classrooms. *Intervention in School and Clinic, 42*(4), 195–197.

> This article seeks to increase awareness of culturally responsive literacy instruction by describing the components of a literacy program that addresses the needs of diverse learners.

Education Place. www.eduplace.com/rdg/res/literacy/multi2.html

> This site looks at strategies to support multicultural instruction, such as questioning styles, role-playing, cooperative learning, exposure to different languages and cultures, group discussions, and active involvement.

Michigan State University. http://diversity.cas.msu.edu/index.html

> Infusing college classes with multicultural values and content remains a never-ending challenge, and educators, especially those at land-grant institutions such as Michigan State University, must continually strive to attain this important goal. This website is dedicated to helping university faculty and staff achieve excellence in multicultural instruction, but it will be helpful to other levels of educators as well.

National Association for Bilingual Education. www.nabe.org/education/index.html

> This site looks at teaching English, fostering academic achievement, acculturating immigrants to a new society, preserving a minority group's linguistic and cultural heritage, enabling English speakers to learn a second language, and developing national language resources.

University of Northern Iowa. www.uni.edu/coe/inclusion/standards/competencies.html

> This site provides a detailed listing of teacher competencies and should be helpful to both pre-service and in-service teachers.

Individual and Cultural Differences

Understanding the material and activities in this chapter will help the reader to:

◆ List individual and cultural differences and similarities, and explain their influence on learning and achievement.

◆ Develop positive orientations toward so-called cultural deficiencies and cultural differences perspectives, and understand the importance of providing educational experiences based on the differences perspective.

◆ List at least six individual differences (e.g., self-esteem, gender, development, motivation, socioeconomic status, exceptionalities) that affect learning and achievement.

◆ List several dangers associated with labeling exceptional learners (and, in fact, all children and adolescents), and demonstrate how their exceptionalities affect learning and achievement.

◆ Describe an educational program (e.g., bilingual education, teaching English as a second language [ESL]) that effectively addresses the needs of language-minority learners.

◆ Recognize the need for a celebration of cultural diversity and how diversity among learners can enrich elementary and secondary school programs.

◆ Understand the importance of positive cultural identities, and suggest methods to build positive identities among learners.

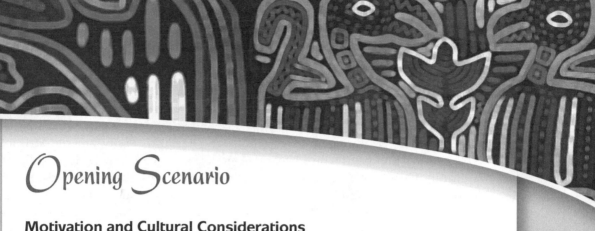

Opening Scenario

Motivation and Cultural Considerations

Carl, a thirteen-year-old American Indian middle school student, shows a lack of motivation, initiative, and competitive drive. He does not demonstrate any desire to set himself apart from or to rise above others in his class. His teachers see him as "different." Whereas most of the white students in Carl's school strive for success and good grades, he does his work but shows no desire to achieve more. The teachers who work together in Carl's unit wonder what to do and how to motivate him.

Although this pattern is typical of American Indians in this school, Mrs. Westerly, the special-education teacher, recognizes a crucial aspect of this situation that others either do not want to see or admit. Rather than look at Carl from a European American perspective, Mrs. Westerly suggests viewing him from the American Indian perspective. Perhaps, from Carl's cultural perspective, he is motivated. His family has transmitted a cultural heritage that does not emphasize competition or achievement that would set him apart from his peers. He does not value competing with other learners, because it seems far more logical to share ideas and work cooperatively.

The teachers begin to realize that they have evaluated Carl's motivation through a middle-class, European American lens. They have, in fact, been expecting Carl to conform to behaviors that are completely alien to his cultural heritage and background. ◆

Overview

Educators' positive responses to elementary and secondary learners' differences are crucial to celebrating cultural, ethnic, and racial diversity among African, Arab, Asian, European, and Hispanic Americans as well as American Indians. Cultural diversity is a strength—a persistent, vitalizing force in our lives. It is a useful resource for improving educational effectiveness for all students. Using the cultures and experiences of African, Arab, Asian, European, and Hispanic American students facilitates their school success. Learning experiences and achievement outcomes for ethnically diverse students should include more than cognitive performances in academic subjects and standardized test scores. Moral, social, cultural, and personal aspects are also important. All of these are essential to the healthy and complete functioning of human beings and societies.

No ethnic group is ethnically or intellectually monolithic. For instance, African Americans include people who are descendants of Africans enslaved in the United States, others whose origins are in the Caribbean, and recent immigrants from various African nations. Some are native speakers of English, some are dialect speakers, and others speak English as a second language. Some African Americans are academically gifted, some are average students, and some are failing in school. This kind of variability exists in all ethnic groups, and it affects the achievement of students in different ways. What these differences are must be more clearly defined if teachers are to further encourage those students who are already performing well and remediate those who are not.

Individual and cultural differences can provide an effective framework for teaching and learning experiences and can enrich and contribute to individual teaching and learning situations and to the total-school program. This chapter looks at individual and cultural diversities and examines their influence on student learning and overall development.

The Reality of Individual and Cultural Diversity

All too often, classroom teachers, special services personnel, and administrators assume too much homogeneity among learners' abilities, backgrounds, and interests. Some educators still subscribe to the belief that a purpose of the school is to homogenize students (along the lines of the melting pot idea) and to eradicate or "remediate" differences. The reality is that learners' many differences affect their perceptions of learning and achievement, their ways of learning and knowing, and their overall learning and school achievement.

Educational institutions, regardless of grade or academic level, have the responsibility for recognizing individual and cultural differences and planning appropriate educational experiences for all learners. Differences such as income level, home and family conditions, and some exceptionalities may appear difficult to overcome; nevertheless, students deserve an affirmative response to their differences and learning needs. It no longer suffices to plan educational experiences only for middle- or upper-class white learners and then expect students of other social classes and cultures to change perspectives on motivation and competition, learning styles, and attitudes and values that their homes and families have instilled in them.

Today, society increasingly considers differences among children and adolescents as entities to be appreciated and on which educational experiences can be built. Teachers should recognize and respect children's and adolescents' attitudes, customs, and sacred values. A positive perspective toward these differences must inform curricular decisions and instructional practices.

Recognizing Individual and Cultural Differences and Their Influence on Learning

Children's and adolescents' every difference—whether of intellectual, developmental, or gender origin—affects their academic achievement and overall school success. For too many years, educators have planned for the "learner in the middle" (e.g., white, middle-class, nondisabled, male, normally developing) and have expected other learners to conform and to use "middle" cognitive strategies to process information. Schools are challenged to take a more enlightened or multicultural approach and to recognize the multitude of differences among learners. Educators should offer an appropriate response to the increasing diversity in cultures and languages. Schools should reflect the perspective that diversity is not the problem but rather an opportunity for every American to experience other peoples and cultures.

Achievement, Intelligence, and Cognitive Processes

A definition of a *learner's achievement level* is previously acquired knowledge that relates to what is being taught. Most educators believe that what students already know affects their present and future achievement. The question the educator should always ask is To what extent and how can previous learning contribute to new learning? The learner who already knows numbers, who is fascinated with science, or who is interested in geography will have a head start over learners without special areas of expertise or interests.

The educational systems from which immigrant students come rarely match U.S. school systems, since culture determines the content of school curricula, assumptions about background knowledge, teaching approaches, classroom interaction, classroom routines, and parental participation (Quinn, 2001). Also, a school environment that takes multiculturalism to a level of quality and makes it a perspective rather than a once-a-month assembly demonstrates respect for different cultures in the life of the school.

Quinn (2001) maintains that most teachers of Hispanic students in rural areas are white American women from middle-class backgrounds. Therefore, most teachers are unfamiliar with Mexican traditions and lifestyles. Plus, some of these teachers graduated from institutions that rarely offer teacher candidates courses in teaching linguistically and culturally diverse students.

Often, when teachers are asked to educate non-native-English speakers, they believe that if the students acquire the language of the majority culture, the students' problems will be solved. Still, Quinn (2001) maintains that students who are living on the margins of school life cannot succeed academically and socially. In order to facilitate language learning, which begins with accepting the language and the need for literacy in a new language, teachers must bring the students who are different into the classroom community.

A learner's overall intelligence, abilities, or special expertise contributes to the degree to which he or she processes information. Learners organize their perceptions and experiences of the school and physical world into cognitive structures. Much is still to be learned about cognition, but it is known that cognitive development is an active process in which learners assimilate information into cognitive categories and adapt their previous categories to accommodate new information. These functions of assimilation and accommodation cause the change and growth in learners' thinking that constitute cognitive development. Educators who work with students from differing cultural backgrounds should plan educational experiences that recognize the developmental capabilities of children as well as their cultural perspectives.

Points to Ponder **11.1**

Dealing with Unfamiliar Behaviors and Customs

Name a number of ways in which educators can deal effectively with unfamiliar behaviors and customs in our schools. For example, what activities can you suggest for teaching students that how far people stand apart from others is a cultural mannerism? It is not a matter of right and wrong, and people are not necessarily being rude or overly presumptuous. Name several activities that might engage students that would teach them the concept of and acceptance of personal space.

The learners' cognitive development is of particular importance in multicultural situations, because teachers cannot assume that all learners process information in the same manner. Children's language, thinking strategies, ability to make comparisons and hypotheses, and skill at applying concepts and information depend on their overall cognitive development, which is grounded in their cultural backgrounds. Rather than assuming too much homogeneity among learners, educators have to consider cultural orientations toward achievement, cultural diversity among learning styles, and the learner's degree of active participation.

Cultural Identities

We have mentioned repeatedly throughout this text the importance of the learner's cultural identity and its effects on academic achievement. How learners perceive themselves is especially significant for those of differing cultural backgrounds. The learner who feels that others perceive him or her as inferior, deficient in some manner, or in stereotypical terms may begin to feel less than adequate or unable to cope with the U.S. school system. A child's cultural identity and the value he or she places on cultural heritage and background can plummet to a point where success in school and in other areas of life is in jeopardy.

Gender

Gender determines masculine and feminine differences—the thoughts, feelings, and behaviors one identifies as being either male or female. Culturally determined masculine and feminine behavior can differ significantly. For example, a boy demonstrating feminine traits might be called a "sissy" in one culture but be accepted in another (Gollnick & Chinn, 2006).

Educational experiences and outcomes differ for males and females:

◆ Lundeberg, Fox, and Puncochar (1994) report that, as early as the sixth grade, girls have less self-confidence than boys, and the differences increase with age. Both boys and girls lose self-esteem as they grow older, but girls show a far greater loss. For example, girls in elementary, middle, and secondary schools experience continuous decreases in self-esteem of 60, 37, and 29 percent, respectively ("Education and Gender," 1994).

◆ *Everybody Counts: A Report to the Nation on the Future of Mathematics Education* (National Research Council, 1989) indicates that girls and boys progress through the mathematics curriculum and, in fact, show little difference in ability, effort, or interest until the adolescent years. Then, as social pressures increase, girls' decisions to reduce effort in the study of mathematics progressively limit their future education and eventually their career choices.

◆ Focusing on risk taking and mathematics achievement, Ramos and Lambating (1996) examined females' reluctance to be risk takers and males' tendency to be greater risk takers. Females' reluctance to guess on multiple-choice tests and their tendency to leave more questions unanswered (true–false, multiple choice, and relationship analysis) contribute to their lower achievement.

How can educators address gender differences? How can educators provide females with an education that adopts feminine perspectives? First, women's studies should include consciousness-raising efforts and attempt to create a more enlightened view of women and their unique individual perspectives. Second, education should be as nonsexist as possible. Teachers should scrutinize all instructional materials and seek to eliminate sexist connotations and promote feminine learning styles. Teachers should understand and consider cognitive strategies whenever possible. Third, Title IX of the 1972 Educational Amendment addresses the discriminatory treatment of students based on their sex. Title IX (Gollnick & Chin, 2006) states that "no person shall, on the basis of sex, be excluded from participation in, be denied the benefits of, or be subjected to, discrimination under any education program or activity receiving federal financial assistance."

All too often, when educators and scholars think about gender, they only think about girls. Gender Perspectives 11.1 looks at boys and the education they receive.

Developmental Levels and Cognitive Readiness

The learner's developmental stage is perhaps the most significant individual difference affecting learning. Learners functioning at one developmental level simply cannot comprehend material that requires the thinking and cognitive skills of the next higher developmental level. Rather than assume that learners can succeed by trying hard or doing more homework, educators should understand that development and readiness, not effort alone, affect what youngsters can learn.

A youngster at the concrete-operations stage cannot master intellectual challenges that demand formal, abstract thinking abilities. Although some memorization might occur, learners will be unable to learn information that is beyond

Gender Perspectives 11.1

GENDER MYTHS AND BOYS

The so-called boy crisis in education has become a major media event, with tales of boys falling behind girls in academic achievement, lagging in college enrollment, and being at risk for failure in the new knowledge economy. Barnett and Rivers (2007) maintain that some boys might be going through a crisis but certainly not all boys. Overall, nonpoor, academically inclined boys are doing just fine.

Although middle-class boys are hardly free from academic problems, the real boy crisis is among disadvantaged boys—largely, African and Hispanic Americans in the inner cities. In fact, when looking at academic achievement, race and class are far more important than gender. Indeed, middle- and upper-class girls may be doing better than boys in valedictorian slots, club presidencies, and honor grades, and schools should strive to learn why. Still, when race and class are considered, the picture changes.

Barnett and Rivers focus on boys' verbal skills, the difference in how boys and girls see and hear things, and whether there is value in single-sex schools. The authors also say that no data support the idea that boys are destined to fail in school. As long as doing well in school is devalued and playing video games is much more popular to do than reading a book, many boys' academic performance will suffer.

Barnett and Rivers have written an excellent article, one that we highly recommend. While gender and gender differences always deserve recognition, it does appear that race and social class play far greater roles in determining who does and does not achieve academically.

Source: Barnett, R. C., & Rivers, C. (2007). Gender myths and the education of boys. *Independent School, 66*(2), 96, 98.

their cognitive ability at any given age. To assume that all learners can perform functions and master content at a level that a few precocious and intellectually advanced students attain ignores individual differences and what is known about cognitive readiness.

The challenge for educators is to determine developmental and readiness levels and to plan and implement appropriate instruction. Educators might raise some questions about theories that proclaim growth and development as cross-culturally valid. However, development as an individual difference affects learning and crosses cultural boundaries. Regardless of cultural backgrounds and when they reach certain developmental stages, learners cannot master material they are not developmentally ready to learn. The challenge for educators is to diagnose the learner's developmental stage and then provide developmentally appropriate curricular experiences and instructional practices.

Beliefs, Attitudes, and Values

Understanding children and adolescents from culturally different backgrounds requires knowing their beliefs, attitudes, and values. These idiosyncrasies are based in each learner's culture and influence all aspects of his or her life, whether in motivation, competition, perspectives toward the family, or perceptions of racism and its effects. Numerous illustrations provide evidence of the effects of attitudes: the Asian American student who is taught to revere teachers; the African American child who can listen to someone without looking the speaker in the eye; the American Indian learner who values cooperation and sharing as being more worthy than competition; or the Hispanic American adolescent who believes he or she should not stand out among peers.

Perceptive educators recognize the cultural "baggage" (prejudices, myths, and stereotypes) that children and adolescents bring to school, baggage that affects attitudes toward school, other learners, and learning achievement. The educator's challenge is to understand and to respect these personal aspects and, whenever possible, to provide school experiences that are culturally compatible. Curricular practices and instructional methods that are genuinely multicultural in both theory and practice reflect the values, attitudes, and beliefs of learners of culturally different backgrounds and do not require learners to participate in actions that contradict their cultural beliefs.

Motivation

It is important for educators in multicultural situations to understand motivation. Rather than perceive motivation through middle-class perspectives, educators must understand the complex relationship between motivation and cultural diversity. For example, some middle-class students might be motivated by competition, by an outstanding achievement that sets the individual apart from peers, or by the desire to work independently. Learners from culturally different backgrounds may not hold those same values and might appear unmotivated when they do not want to stand out among their peers or to excel at the expense of others or when they choose to work in cooperative-learning situations sharing expertise.

Closely related to learners' motivation and willingness to employ cognitive abilities is their expectation of success or failure. Beliefs related to the likelihood of success, to judgments about their ability, and to emotional reactions of pride and hopelessness all contribute to the extent learners are willing to use cognitive strategies. Over time, learners who believe that lack of ability causes failure are likely to feel a sense of helplessness. This theory of the relationship among motivation, feelings of self-worth, and the willingness to use cognitive strategies might be especially useful for educators who work with learners from culturally different backgrounds.

Educators should focus on the particular motivational problems of individual students. School learning requires active effort, and children are not likely to put forth the active effort if they do not see that their school work helps them to achieve their own purposes or to satisfy their own interests. They may respond to their parents' or teachers' pressures, but unless students have a personal reason to complete school assignments, motivation will be difficult to maintain. Educators need to understand motivation from its cultural perspective and then attempt to help learners understand qualities in their assignments that are either interesting or useful.

Socioeconomic Status

The socioeconomic differential that exists in the United States includes the family's absolute income, educational background, occupational prestige, place of residence, lifestyle, and relative autonomy and power. It is worth remembering, however, that wealth and material success are relative concepts; one family might consider ownership of a swimming pool a sign of success, whereas another family might perceive the addition of a porch to a mobile home as an indicator of success. In any event, a family's socioeconomic status and income level determine children's and adolescents' experiences, as do other factors (e.g., conditions of the home, the presence of books and other reading materials and computers, trips with educational significance) that have positive effects on educational progress.

An educator must remember to consider learners and their families individually. It is a serious mistake and an injustice to learners to make assumptions of wealth and social class based on culture, race, or ethnicity. Conversely, a teacher should never predict a learner's educational potential on the basis of socioeconomic level. Just as many higher-socioeconomic-class learners often fail to respond to their educators' efforts, students from lower-class homes and neighborhoods have achieved extraordinary educational successes.

Exceptionalities

The Dangers of Labeling and Erroneous Placement

Labeling learners has such potentially harmful effects that educators who assign labels may be placing children and adolescents at great risk. Although such educators probably have the learner's interest and educational welfare in mind, labeling learners as "slow" or "disabled" can sometimes cause irreparable harm, not only during school programs but throughout their lives. Educators should be cognizant of the disadvantages of labeling and should know when the practice is or is not in the learner's best interest. Disadvantages of labeling children and adolescents include the following:

1. Learners who are identified as disabled or exceptional may be permanently stigmatized, rejected, or denied opportunities for full development.
2. Learners labeled as "mentally retarded" (or the equivalent) may be assigned to inferior educational programs in school or illegally placed in institutions.
3. Large numbers of learners from culturally diverse backgrounds are inaccurately classified as mentally disabled on the basis of scores they earn on inappropriate tests.

The disadvantages of labeling are sufficient to cause alarm, but another problem may result from labeling: the overt segregation of learners. Grouping and placement practices have segregated learners racially. Using subjective means or teacher recommendations, labeling or placement policies can contribute (either intentionally or unintentionally) to the segregation of students along racial and ethnic lines. Such policies are both unethical and unprofessional and can condemn learners to "slow" groups or inferior materials and methods. Such situations may occur because educators want learners segregated or because educators erroneously equate race or ethnicity with achievement and ability.

When, if ever, should educators label learners? Teachers should give a learner a label when, and *only* when, it is in the student's best interest and when substantial objective data can document the learner's condition. The label should serve a

Points to Ponder **11.2**

Avoiding Erroneous Labeling

Name five or six ways in which educators can avoid the hazards of labeling learners. Your list might include getting to know individuals, talking with parents and extended family members, conversing with others in the culture, and using culturally relevant testing devices for assessment purposes.

meaningful purpose and provide a basis for assisting the learner's overall educational progress. Even when this is the case, educators have a moral, ethical, and professional responsibility to assess learners periodically, to diagnose accurately, to follow all due-process procedures, and to ensure that learners are placed in other groups or classes if the disabling or exceptional conditions change.

Disabling Conditions

Children and adolescents from culturally different backgrounds can experience the same disabling conditions that other children or adolescents experience, such as behavior disorders, mentally disabling conditions, visual impairments, communication disorders, and hearing and visual impairments. It is crucial, however, to ascertain that diagnostic tests accurately reflect the strengths and weaknesses of disabled youngsters from culturally different backgrounds and make decisions accordingly. When working with disabled learners, educators must identify the concept of behavior and its role in determining eligibility for special programs. Most important, professionals who make eligibility decisions should be sensitive to what is educationally best for the student.

Gifted and Talented

Some people continue to question the use of *gifted* in the same breath with *cultural diversity*. It has been difficult for some people to understand that a child or adolescent may be verbally gifted (although perhaps in a language other than English), that learners have higher-order cognitive processes in survival techniques (that do not reveal themselves on school assessments), and that the term *culturally different* does not imply that students are lacking in some areas.

Although many papers in the literature urge educators to be sensitive to the special characteristics of culturally diverse populations, most programs for gifted learners continue to use traditional methods of identification, which rely on popular notions of gifted characteristics. Identifying gifted learners from different cultural backgrounds may be difficult. Learners from culturally different backgrounds might be from a home environment that rewards certain types of behavior that are not consonant with conventional notions of giftedness. For example, some Hispanic American families may provide less reinforcement of highly verbal behavior. Children from such a family may be somewhat reticent on entering school and not stand out in screening for giftedness.

Points to Ponder 11.3

Determining Giftedness

Identifying gifted learners from culturally different backgrounds can pose challenges for educators who might be accustomed to looking for particular traits that might relate to a specific culture. Traits suggesting giftedness in learners from differing cultural backgrounds might go undetected. Name several ways educators might determine learners' areas of giftedness, remembering that learners in some cultures might be reluctant to reveal special talents at the expense of other students.

Gifted children are found in every socioeconomic and cultural group. Educators have been less than successful in identifying gifted learners from culturally different backgrounds, perhaps because they are more difficult to recognize and teach. Several factors have contributed to an increased emphasis on identifying gifted learners from culturally different backgrounds: First, broader definitions of giftedness and intellectual ability are contributing to the identification of more learners; and second, there is a new willingness among educators to use a variety of screening and evaluation techniques and instruments.

After educators have identified gifted learners, they must select programs that match the needs of gifted youngsters from culturally diverse backgrounds. These programs should have a design and method of implementation that consider the learner's psychological, cultural, and linguistic characteristics. Simply integrating learners into an established gifted curriculum may not be successful, because it requires learners to accommodate themselves to the school program, rather than have the program meet the needs of individual learners.

Language

Language differences continue to challenge educators in the twenty-first century:

1. Significant numbers of groups speak a language other than English at home and do not speak English very well.
2. Linguistic diversity (both limited English proficiency and use of dialects) is controversial, dividing much of the nation.
3. Inseparable relationships exist between language and culture.
4. Effective multicultural education programs place considerable emphasis on accepting linguistic diversity and encouraging learners to be bilingual and bidialectal.
5. Teaching linguistically different students requires effective strategies.

Some suggest that linguistically different learners forsake their native languages, and others suggest learning English as a second language. A genuine multicultural education program teaches learners to hold onto their native languages so they can be bilingual and have access to two cultures.

Dialects

Dialects and the issue of whether to require use of Standard American English in the schools are sensitive and controversial subjects. Because there is a close relationship between groups of differing cultural backgrounds and dialects that are often nonstandard, this issue also has civil rights implications. Some consider any requirement that standard English be spoken in schools discriminatory. They think that such a requirement places an additional educational burden on the non-standard-English-speaking students. Further, the insistence on standard English may hinder the acquisition of other educational skills, making it difficult for these students to succeed. Such a practice may deny non-standard-English-speaking students the same educational opportunities as others and thus morally, if not legally, denies them their civil rights (Gollnick & Chinn, 2006).

A learner's dialect is closely related to her or his cultural identity and overall self-esteem. School programs that are effective with students of culturally different backgrounds are sufficiently flexible to accommodate the range of dialects learners bring to school. While speaking a nonstandard dialect may have detrimental economic, social, and educational consequences for students, teachers should nonetheless accept, value, and appreciate a student's language.

Dialects also pose a challenging issue for educators, who can address them in several ways: (1) accommodate all dialects, based on the assumption that they are all equal, (2) insist on learners speaking only one dialect in school, and (3) accept dialects for certain uses but insist on standard English in other situations. Educators should allow dialects in social and recreational situations (i.e., other than formal classroom discourse) but should encourage students in school settings to use standard English, because it is the primary written and spoken language in the United States. Such a compromise allows students to use dialects as it recognizes the social and economic implications of being able to function in standard English.

Language and Culture: Inseparable Relationships

English as a second language (ESL) and multicultural education are two closely related concepts. Learners acquire language through socialization, and, in turn, language shapes perception of the physical and social worlds in which they live. It is not possible to effectively address linguistic differences without acknowledging and respecting cultural differences. Likewise, it is not possible to respect cultural differences without acknowledging and respecting the importance of a person's language.

Learners think about and understand the world in their native tongue, which is intricately tied to their identity. Ignoring or devaluing learners' native language denies an important part of the rich past and present cultural experiences learners bring to school. Thus, it is critical for classroom teachers to acknowledge and respect children's home language, whether it is a completely different language or an English dialect.

Multicultural Programs Emphasizing Language Diversity

Perceptive educators at all school levels understand how respect for language diversity is a prerequisite to effective multicultural programs. They support language diversity by doing the following:

1. Ensuring that linguistically different learners have teachers trained to work with second-language learners
2. Understanding that a student might have sufficient ability in English to socialize in the hallways yet may need support to comprehend academic language usage
3. Relating learning to students' life experiences, prior knowledge, and cultural perspectives
4. Validating, respecting, and building, whenever possible, on students' native language abilities
5. Recognizing, not eliminating, and in fact valuing dialects

Effective Strategies for Linguistically Different Learners

Several important general lessons emerge when one considers the specific culturally responsive instructional programs and practices. When instructional processes are consistent with the cultural orientations, experiences, and learning styles of African, Hispanic, Arab, and Asian American and American Indian students, their school achievement improves significantly. This success is most evident when students learn culturally relevant curricular content, teacher attitudes and expectations, and instructional actions strategies. Students come to school having already mastered many cultural skills and ways of knowing. To the extent that teaching builds on these capabilities, academic success will result.

Academic performance is maximized when multiple areas of learning (e.g., academic, cultural, personal) are facilitated at once and difference teaching techniques are used, all within the cultural contexts of various cultural groups. Culturally responsive practices unveil some solutions to the seemingly unsolvable mystery of the perpetual underachievement of students who are diverse. They are not being taught in school the way they learn in their cultural communities. This discontinuity interrupts their mental schemata and makes academic learning harder to achieve.

Teachers can help by doing these things:

1. Directing activities (a strategy that research suggests is highly effective in teaching English), during which students listen and respond to effective role models

2. Providing classroom situations in which students follow distinct patterns every day and have the time and environment to concentrate on language and educational content

3. Allowing students to help students—they may be more likely to ask for language clarification from another student than from the teacher, or they may be better able to communicate with another student with similar language skills

4. Asking for volunteers, then asking for group responses, and establishing a pattern of taking turns that requires all students to participate orally

5. Taking special care to speak clearly and to use concrete references, repetitions, rephrasings, gestures, visual aids, and demonstrations

6. Providing curricular materials on an appropriate cognitive level; for example, a teacher should not give a book written for a kindergarten student to a sixth-grader

7. Using whole-language activities whenever possible, so students will have opportunities for rich, meaningful interactions with both written and oral language

8. Providing opportunities for recounts (essentially extended versions of known information and answer exchanges), accounts (narratives the teller generates to provide new information), event casts (ongoing narratives interesting to both teller and listener), and stories (the telling of a narrative) in which learners practice second-language skills, both chronologically and thematically

9. Encouraging students to work in cooperative groups so maximum language interaction can occur; primary language speakers can assist second-language learners and provide role models

10. Reading appropriate books aloud (actually an excellent idea for all learners), so linguistically different learners can hear pronunciations and words in context

11. Allowing students to read books and then give oral book reports to small groups; second-language learners can have role models and can practice English skills

12. Allowing learners to write messages, letters, cards, and notes and read them in English

Bilingual Education and English as a Second Language

The language diversity in the United States extends into the schools, and in large urban and metropolitan school districts, nearly a hundred different languages may be spoken. Whereas some students are bilingual in English and their native language, others either do not speak English at all or have limited English-speaking skills. Indications are that the number of students with limited English-speaking skills will continue to increase (Gollnick & Chinn, 2006).

Some learners are competent in English; others, however, may speak only Spanish, the second most common language in the United States; one of the many Asian languages; or a less common language such as Arabic or Tongian. This section looks at efforts such as bilingual education and English as a second language (ESL) programs (or the teaching of English to speakers of other languages), which attempt to address the needs of learners of culturally different backgrounds.

Some confusion exists concerning bilingual education and ESL programs, which many often assume to be synonymous. In the United States, the teaching of English is an integral aspect of bilingual programs, but the teaching of English in and by itself (ESL) does not constitute a bilingual program. Both programs promote English proficiency for students whose English is limited.

Bilingual education is generally defined as "the use of two languages as media of instruction" (Baca & Cervantes, 1989, p. 24). Bilingual education has received federal funds as a provision of the Bilingual Education Act of 1968, which Congress reauthorized in 1974, 1978, and 1984 (Gollnick & Chinn, 2006).

Bilingual education reinforces the student's home language and culture and simultaneously teaches the ability to function in another language. Instruction in both skills and content is usually in the student's home language and in English. The most important legal action related to bilingual education was the

1974 *Lau v. Nichols* decision, which pointed to the need for some type of special instructional program for students with limited English-speaking ability.

ESL programs rely exclusively on English for teaching and learning. Educators use ESL programs extensively in the United States as the primary means of assimilating limited-English-speaking students into the linguistic mainstream as quickly as possible. The main feature of the program is that educators place less emphasis on the maintenance of home language and culture than on English-language acquisition (Hernandez, 1989).

The emphasis of an ESL program is concentrated in three major areas (TESOL, 1976):

1. *Culture:* Integrating students' cultural experiences and background into meaningful language learning
2. *Language development:* Teaching structures and vocabulary relevant to students' learning experiences
3. *Content-area instruction:* Applying techniques from second-language learning to subject learning and to subject matter presented in English

Table 11.1 provides an overview of ESL programs.

Celebrating and Responding to Cultural Diversity

Recognizing the Effects of Cultural Diversity

Educators usually do not question the premise that culture plays a major role in a learner's overall achievement and attitudes toward school. The ultimate challenge, however, is to recognize cultural diversity as a strength on which to build a solid education. The first step is to respond to diversity with a sense of positiveness, rather than view it as a hurdle to be overcome.

One example of diversity among groups is the variety of formal and informal rules governing interaction between individuals. When classroom interactional patterns are not consistent or compatible with those that children and adolescents experience in their homes and community, such variations may cause problems. For example, variations in how and when the teacher says something (although perhaps unintentional) as well as what is said may interfere with learning and damage attitudes toward school (Gollnick & Chinn, 2006). Some differences are easily recognized, but educators sometimes overlook the less

table 11.1

Questions and Answers about English as a Second Language (ESL)

What Is English as a Second Language?

English as a second language (ESL) is intensive English-language instruction by teachers trained in recognizing and working with language differences. The ESL program is required by state laws in school districts with students who have limited English-language skills.

What Is an ESL Program?

- An ESL program is structured language instruction designed to teach English to students whose English-language skills are limited.
- ESL instruction considers the student's learning experiences and cultural backgrounds.
- ESL is taught through second-language methods that are applied to the teaching of mathematics, science, and social studies.

What Is the Purpose of an ESL Program?

- An ESL program develops competence in English.
- English-language skills are taught through listening, speaking, reading, writing, and grammar.
- A student's instructional program is modified to make learning English easier.

Who Should Be Enrolled in an ESL Program?

- Students in prekindergarten through grade 12 who speak or hear a language other than English in their home and who have difficulty in English are eligible.

Who Is Responsible for Teaching an ESL Program?

- Teachers who are specially trained, tested, and certified to teach ESL programs.

visible aspects of the culture associated with everyday etiquette and interaction, as well as with the expression of rights, obligations, values, and aspirations.

An excellent example of how cultural backgrounds affect learning is the manner in which teaching and learning environments are structured according to rules that the students and their community do not share. Several differences may surface: how students and teachers interact, how teachers control and monitor behavior, what kinds of behaviors people use to intervene, what kinds of organizational patterns exist, and whether teachers expect learners to participate by interrupting another speaker for a chance to voice an opinion. American Indian learners, for example, might perceive instructional demands as strange or contradictory to cultural expectations. American Indian learners who should respond competitively might feel that such instructional expectations violate their desire for cooperation and group efforts.

Children have many diversities such as family types, ethnicities, cultures, and abilities. The challenge facing educators is to implement educational programs that address differences and create an atmosphere in which harmony and diversity reign. Each child should be understood as an individual, and individually appropriate learning should be planned. Other directions include creating an atmosphere of acceptance, addressing personal biases, promoting attitudes of acceptance, encouraging open communication, building the competence of children, and incorporating instructional technology.

An equitable response to differences among learners includes the following:

1. Encouraging students to build and maintain self-esteem
2. Using the ethnic backgrounds of students to teach effectively
3. Helping students overcome their prejudices
4. Expanding the knowledge and appreciation of the historical, economic, political, and social experiences of ethnic and national groups
5. Assisting students in understanding that the world's knowledge and culture have been, and continue to be, created from the contributions of all cultural groups and nations

A response should also include the provision of environments in which students can learn to participate in the dominant society while maintaining distinct cultural differences. Educators can work toward such responses by demonstrating respect and support for differences, by reflecting diversity in the curriculum, and by using positive differences to teach and interact with learners.

Building Cultural Identities

An individual's cultural identity is based on a number of traits and values that are related to national or ethnic origin, family, religion, gender, age, occupation, socioeconomic level, language, geographic region, and exceptionality (Gollnick & Chinn, 2006). The interaction of these factors and the degree to which individuals identify with different subcultures or cultural groups that share political and social institutions and other distinctive cultural elements determine the identity to a large degree. Rather than allow "different is wrong" perceptions to prevail and to lower learners' opinions of cultural identities, perceptive educators recognize learners' cultural identities and assist learners in developing positive, healthy, cultural identities.

Educators who celebrate the richness that cultural diversity brings to the classroom readily recognize the need to build or enhance learners' cultural identity. Family and cultural ties are so important to every learner that teachers should give these aspects prime consideration in teaching and learning experiences.

Learners' earliest experiences are of home and family, and language is an important part of this background. Teachers should remember the importance of respecting learners' cultural backgrounds, and at all times they should avoid abusing or dishonoring them. A first step in building a learner's cultural identity is for educators to understand that learner's heritage, values and traditions, and language. While efforts to ensure self-esteem and positive cultural identities should be an ongoing process, educators should also work toward helping learners have positive attitudes toward school.

Case Study

The Dangers of Labeling

Dr. Strobecker, principal of Cedarwood Elementary School, was looking through students' permanent records when several labels caught her eye: "behaviorally maladjusted," "slow learner," "retarded," "below average," "gifted," "troublemaker," "unmotivated," "emotionally disturbed," and other labels that educators can imagine. Upon seeing these labels, she realized the dangers of labeling: Teachers sometimes expect too little, sometimes too much; learners are often in the wrong group; and the labels assigned to learners in elementary school may affect them their entire lives. Further, such labeling may be both unprofessional and unethical. She admitted to herself that, although labeling learners has the potential for helping, the practice should be limited only to those cases in which that will be the clear outcome.

Dr. Strobecker knows that, as a principal, she has the professional responsibility for addressing the situation. There are several things she might do. First, she should make teachers aware of the dangers of labeling; second, she should encourage teachers to read professional articles that deal with labeling and alternatives; third, she should encourage teachers to diagnose learners by using the most objective and reliable means; and fourth, teachers should assign labels only when the diagnosis is accurate and in the learner's best interest.

Questions for Discussion:

1. It is easy to label someone as "slow learner," "gifted," or something else. Sometimes, people think labeling is in the best interest of the learner. Discuss how

educators can make objective decisions and provide the best educational experiences without labeling.

2. Has anyone in your group ever been labeled with some term—perhaps "lazy," "unmotivated," "gifted," or "high achiever"? How did that label make her or him feel? If it was a negative label, did it motivate her or him?

3. Dr. Strobecker has the professional responsibility for addressing the situation, but how might she go about doing this? Can she demand that teachers not label students, or does she need to try to get them to understand the dangers of labeling? How can she evaluate her success in working with the teachers?

Summing Up

Educators who base educational experiences on the individual and cultural characteristics of children and adolescents should:

1. Recognize the various models and orientations of diversity and adopt the culturally different model as the basis for instruction and personal interaction.

2. Recognize that the learning styles and cognitive processes of learners from different cultural backgrounds may differ from those of the dominant population.

3. Provide carefully planned experiences for children and adolescents with exceptionalities.

4. Recognize the importance of developing positive cultural identities.

5. Plan activities that teach learners from both culturally different and the majority population the importance of cultural diversity and the many contributions of people from different cultures.

6. Plan special experiences for learners from language-minority backgrounds, and recognize the differences between bilingual education and ESL programs

7. Understand that attitudes, values, and beliefs of culturally different children and adolescents differ from those of the majority culture, and do not expect minority learners to forsake their cultural identities to achieve school success.

8. Recognize gender as a variable that affects children and adolescents, and recognize the complex relationship between gender and culture.

Suggested Learning Activities

1. Visit several schools to determine how or on what basis they group learners or place them in special classes. Does it appear that racial segregation occurs as a result of grouping or placement? To what extent are students labeled? What efforts are being made to reduce the negative effects of labeling?

2. Respond to the language dilemma many learners face: Many cannot speak English well enough to understand educators or to cope in a predominantly English-speaking society. What are the roles of administrators, classroom teachers, speech correctionists, and language specialists? What suggestions can you offer for helping learners with limited English-speaking skills?

3. Consider the following Implementing Research, which looks at how teachers must recognize students' sense of personal identity, an important condition for them to be receptive to learning.

Implementing Research

Affirming Diversity

Teachers can tell when students are tired, hungry, or bored, but their less obvious needs should also be addressed. Hoerr (2007) writes about how teachers need to affirm diversity to promote students' strong sense of personal identity, which underlies their learning. Children need to feel valued for who they are, both as individuals and as members of a particular group. Whether a student's group identity stems from race, ethnicity, socioeconomic status, gender, or sexual orientation, it must be affirmed. Hoerr calls for developing an affirming formal curriculum and informal curriculum, involving enrichment activities and accomplishments that the school spotlights.

Hoerr also maintains that engaging in dialogue with minority groups is more powerful than the curriculum in showing each student how the group is valued. How do we define minorities in our school? and How should we define them? are questions that should be raised at a faculty meeting. One way to begin with such groups is to look at those who are not in the mainstream.

Implementing the Research

1. Hoerr makes some excellent points. Educators and administrators need to consider how minority groups might perceive their personal identities. Do they see themselves as Hispanic, poor, or lesbian or gay? Make a plan for determining what identities a student has.

2. To what aspects of the informal curriculum is Hoerr referring? Consider the hidden curriculum. Discuss how a school can be accepting but in reality have a hidden curriculum that says something else. Plan an evaluation scale to determine the hidden curriculum.

3. Plan an agenda for engaging with minority groups; also determine topics that should be discussed. Determine whether your group will focus on culture, social class, or some other difference.

Source: Hoerr, T. R. (2007). Affirming diversity. *Educational Leadership, 64*(6), 87–88.

Suggestions for Collaborative Efforts

Form groups of three or four that, if possible, represent U.S. cultural and gender diversity. Working collaboratively, focus your group's attention toward the following efforts.

1. Survey several programs designed to address the needs of gifted learners from different cultural backgrounds. What instruments or techniques determine eligibility? To what extent do the instruments measure the unique abilities and talents of learners from different backgrounds? Do the programs expect learners to change to meet the demands of the program, or do programs reflect knowledge of cultural diversity?

2. Make a list of commonly held stereotypical beliefs about boys and girls (e.g., boys should not cry, girls have a tendency to giggle a lot). Observe the girls and boys in your class to test the validity of your list. Next, have the boys and girls make a list, and have a discussion of the differences between girls and boys. How might an educator's expectation of girls or boys affect teaching situations? How do members of your group feel these stereotypical beliefs affected them when they were in elementary or secondary school?

Expanding Your Horizons

Additional Journals, Books, and Internet Sites

Christensen, L. M. (2007). Children and social change in Alabama: 1965–2005. *Social Studies and the Young Learner, 20*(1), 22–24.

> As the title implies, this author looks at children's living conditions over a forty-year time period.

Crotteau, M. (2007). Honoring dialect and culture: Pathways to student success on high-stakes writing assessments. *English Journal, 96*(4), 27–31.

> This author looks at an important diversity topic—honoring students' home dialects when preparing them to take state writing tests.

Garcia, E. E. (2005). *Teaching and learning in two languages: Bilingualism and schooling in the United States.* New York: Teachers College Press.

> Garcia provides an interesting book on how some students are challenged with learning in two languages.

King, N. J. (2007). Exit strategies: Cultural implications for graduation tests. *Principal Leadership, 8*(1), 42–47.

> King looks at assessment and cultural differences in this informative article.

Kraft, M. (2007). Toward a school-wide model of teaching for social justice: An examination of the best practices of two small schools. *Equity and Excellence in Education, 40*(1), 77–86.

> Kraft studies how a commitment to socially just pedagogies influences the core practices and policies of a school—mainly, social justice regardless of diversity.

Verdugo, R. R. (2007). English-language learners: Key issues. *Education and Urban Society, 39*(2), 167–193.

> The writer discusses the presence of English-language learners (ELLs) in American public schools and related educational issues.

Wade, R. C. (2007). Service learning for social justice in the elementary classroom: Can we get there from here? *Equity and Excellence in Education, 40*(2), 156–165.

> This article focuses on forty elementary school teachers' efforts to involve diverse students in social justice service-learning experiences, along with supporting strategies.

School District of Palm Beach County. www.palmbeach.k12.fl.us/Multicultural/ MulticulturalNew/MultiCurric.htm

> The multicultural curriculum focus is on the development and implementation of a range of multicultural curriculum topics/units, as well the delivery of training and resources for educators, students, and the community. The multicultural curriculum includes Hispanic/Latino studies, Haitian and Haitian American studies, Holocaust studies, women's studies, and multicultural studies.

ERIC Digests. www.ericdigests.org/pre-9218/secondary.htm

> This ERIC Digests provide an introduction to multicultural activities that has been motivated by at least four intentions: (1) to remedy ethnocentrism in the traditional curriculum; (2) to build understanding among racial/cultural groups and appreciation of different cultures; (3) to reduce intergroup tensions and conflicts; and (4) to make the curricula relevant to the experiences, cultural traditions, and historical contributions of the nation's diverse population.

King George County Public Schools. www.kgcs.k12.va.us/cult

> King George County (VA) Public Schools has a Division-Wide Multicultural Education Advisory Committee with representatives from all four schools. These individuals meet several times throughout the school year to research the concept of multicultural education and curriculum and study how the concepts are being implemented in other schools and institutions throughout the United States and the world.

New Horizons for Learning. www.newhorizons.org/strategies/multicultural/hanley .htm

> This author looks at the scope of multicultural education and suggests components of effective programs.

Education Resources Information Center (ERIC). www.eric.ed.gov/ERICWebPortal/ custom/portlets/recordDetails/detailmini.jsp?_nfpb=true&_&ERICExtSearch_Search Value_0=ED354231&ERICExtSearch_SearchType_0=eric_accno&accno=ED354231

> This study was conducted to determine whether formal instruction in multicultural education would produce changes in pre-service teachers' beliefs about basic concepts related to the topic.

Parents, Families, and Caregivers of Culturally Diverse Backgrounds

Understanding the material and activities in this chapter will help the reader to:

◆ Understand that the traditional view of parents and families has changed to a more contemporary perspective of parents, families, foster parents, guardians, one-parent families, two-parent lesbian or gay families, and caregivers.

◆ State several reasons for including parents, families, and caregivers of culturally diverse backgrounds in parent-involvement programs in elementary and secondary schools.

◆ Understand that both immediate and extended families should be included in schools, especially because African, Arab, Asian, European, and Hispanic American as well as American Indians place considerable value on the extended-family concept.

◆ State at least five reasons that parents, families, and caregivers of culturally different backgrounds resist teachers' efforts.

◆ Understand that considerable diversity (including intracultural, generational, and socioeconomic differences) results in difficulty as teachers plan for typical or prototype families.

◆ List the essential elements of effective parent-involvement programs.

◆ Explain procedures and factors that parents and teachers should consider during conferences.

◆ Explain the essential aspects and considerations of forming a parent advisory committee designed to address the needs and concerns of families from culturally different backgrounds.

◆ Understand the importance of parent and family education, and explain how such programs can assist families from culturally diverse backgrounds.

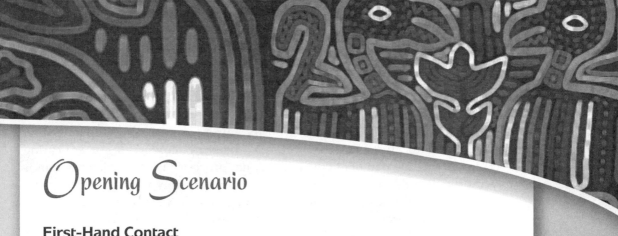

$\mathcal{O}$pening $\mathcal{S}$cenario

First-Hand Contact

Mr. Johnson, principal at Central Middle School, encourages teachers in his school to have first-hand contact with people of various cultures. He praises teachers who take courses focusing on cultural diversity, attend seminars and conferences, and read professional books and journals. These are all excellent sources, he thinks, but he still wants teachers to have first-hand contact, which is imperative if genuine knowledge and respect are to develop.

Mr. Johnson encourages first-hand contact in several ways. First, he expects and encourages teachers to be integral members of the community and to participate in as many social and cultural activities as possible. Second, he encourages parents and families from culturally different backgrounds to visit the school any time, not just for parent conferences. During these impromptu visits, Mr. Johnson urges teachers to meet parents and families and to discuss items of interest. Third, he encourages home visits, which are scheduled at times convenient for the parents. These visits provide a means for teachers to get to know family members on a more personal basis. Although the principal requires the teachers to record their observations and perceptions, the purpose of the visits is neither to judge nor to condemn. He believes that knowledge of cultural diversity contributes to improving attitudes toward people with differences, regardless of degree or type. ◆

Overview

For years, educators have recognized the importance of involving parents in children's education. Whether through involving, conferring, or educating, efforts to include parents in the educational process have paid rich dividends. Until the past decade or so, however, educators mainly worked with middle- and upper-class European Americans and ignored other races, cultures, and ethnic groups, probably because educators lacked knowledge of unique backgrounds and special needs of culturally diverse parents and families. As schools increasingly reflect the cultural diversity that characterizes the nation, educators will be challenged to involve, educate, and confer with all parents and families. This chapter focuses attention on parent involvement and conferences and suggests that educators should implement parent-education programs designed to acquaint families of culturally different backgrounds with U.S. school systems.

Involving and Educating Parents, Families, and Caregivers

That parent involvement has a positive effect on student achievement and overall school progress is undeniable. An even more compelling reason to seek the involvement and participation of parents is to have them understand the U.S. school system, its expectations, and its predominantly middle-class white educators. Families from diverse cultures may feel uncomfortable conversing with educators and participating in school-sponsored events. The educator's challenge is to involve parents of all cultural, ethnic, racial, and social class groups, rather than only middle- and upper-class European American parents.

Defining the Issue

The issue for educators, however, is more complex than simply convincing parents to visit the school. It includes making conscientious efforts in several areas: explaining the school's function, making parents feel welcome and valued, educating parents about their children and adolescents, and involving parents in their children's and adolescents' education whenever possible. Only with the involvement and participation of all parents can schools genuinely reflect multiculturalism and address the needs and concerns of learners and parents from culturally different backgrounds.

Behavioral consultation is defined as a systematic form of service delivery in which two or more persons work together to identify, analyze, remediate, and evaluate an individual's needs. It is characterized by a problem-solving process, adherence to behavioral assessment techniques, reliance on behavioral intervention strategies, and evaluation of outcomes.

Sheridan (2000) explains conjoint behavioral consultation, an extension of behavioral consultation that combines the resources of the home and school to effect positive change in children. It is an indirect model of service delivery in which parents, teachers, and a consultant work together to address the academic, social, and behavioral needs of a child. Problems are identified, defined, analyzed, and treated through mutual and collaborative interactions between parents and teachers with the guidance and assistance of a school psychologist. The model promotes a partnership model that allows opportunities for families and schools to work together for the common interest of children and build on and promote capabilities of family members and school personnel.

An advantage is that conjoint behavioral consultation emphasizes the need to consider factors that might be counterproductive to relations with people from diverse backgrounds. For example, people from backgrounds other than European American might hold different orientations toward values such as social relationships, achievement, activity, and time.

The Advantages of Parent Involvement and Education

The reasons for and advantages of parents and teachers working as partners and for teachers providing appropriate educational experiences for parents have been well documented. A strong positive correlation exists between parent involvement and pupil school achievement, increased student attendance, positive parent–child communication, improved student attitudes and behavior, and more parent–community support of the schools.

Children of all backgrounds deserve the full consideration of teachers and parents; for children and parents of culturally different backgrounds, the need may be even greater. Many parents and families of culturally different backgrounds do not understand school expectations. Some expect high achievement in all areas from their children and adolescents. Many have difficulties communicating with the school. Much can be gained, in terms of improved overall school achievement and improved cultural and interpersonal relationships between parents, teachers, and students, when educators actively seek parent and family involvement.

Changing Perspectives of Parents, Families, and Caregivers

The twenty-first century has seen a dramatic change in what we consider parents and families. In the past, most (certainly not all) families consisted of two-parent families—one woman and one man. Currently, a much broader perspective of parents and families is accepted. *Parents* can be immediate parents, members of extended families, foster parents, guardians, one-parent families, two-parent lesbian or gay families, and caregivers. Perceptive educators realize they should avoid sending letters and school information to "Mr. & Mrs." What if the home situation is one parent? Or a lesbian or gay family? So many combinations exist that few, if any, assumptions can be made about what constitutes parents and families.

Understanding Both Immediate and Extended Families

Another important reason for educators to promote parent involvement is to recognize the differences between European American and other families' beliefs toward the family. Whereas European Americans focus more on the immediate family, families of most other cultures include extended-family members, such as grandparents, aunts, uncles, and cousins.

The implications of extended families are readily apparent for educators. Rather than conferring with, educating, or involving only the mother and father, educators should make conscientious attempts to recognize immediate and extended families.

Reasons for Parents' Resisting Teachers' Efforts

Some parents resist teachers' efforts to involve them in the educational process, whether these efforts include conferences, involvement activities, or serving on committees. Why might parents and extended-family members from minority cultures resist teachers' efforts? First, some cultures may harbor distrust and negative feelings toward professionals of other cultural backgrounds. Parents and children who harbor such attitudes have difficulty believing that professionals of differing cultural backgrounds understand them and want what is best for them. Parents with such powerful feelings of distrust will, in all likelihood, shun a teacher's efforts to build a working relationship between school and family.

Second, family members often fear disclosing personal problems or familial matters that might reflect negatively on themselves, the family, or the father's ability to manage home affairs. To reveal difficulties in the family may arouse feelings of shame in some cultures and the perception of having failed the family.

Parents often do not understand the U.S. school system and its expectations. For example, major differences exist between U.S. teachers and Indochinese teachers: Indochinese teachers are accorded higher levels of respect than are teachers in the United States; they are often awarded honorific titles; they expect students to bow, avoid eye contact, and not ask questions. Because Indochinese parents in their native lands do not take active roles in schools, they have difficulty understanding PTA and other parent-involvement programs. They view the teacher as the expert and feel that making suggestions to teachers about the education of children is inappropriate. Likewise, immigrant parents are often baffled by group activities, independent projects, and library research, because in their cultures, the lecture method is considered the most effective means of teaching (West, 1983).

Points to Ponder 12.1

Addressing Language Barriers

Consult with the communication disorders specialist or ESL specialist in a school and the social service agencies in the community to learn how to work with and assist parents and family members whose language poses a barrier to effective communication. Make a list of publications, resource people, and special programs that help parents and families from culturally diverse backgrounds.

Asians' great respect for teachers and the learning process can actually pose a potential barrier. These parents are often reluctant to challenge the teacher's authority, and they sometimes feel that communicating with teachers may be perceived as disrespectful. Although these parents are usually attentive listeners, they seldom initiate contact with teachers and administrators, rarely ask questions, and seldom offer comments.

Cultural conflicts over child-rearing expectations and differing value systems also disturb many Asian families. As they arrive at the need to make child-rearing decisions on such issues as diet preference, sex education, dating patterns, and obedience to parents, these families are often torn between Eastern and Western manners, expectations, moral standards, and traditions.

In Gender Perspectives 12.1, Smith (2007) discusses the sometimes complex transition from middle school to high school. He looks at the transition in terms of parents, gender, and racial concerns.

Understanding Cultural Diversity

Educators can readily see the reasons for understanding cultural diversity among families. However, they might have more difficulty reducing the myths, stereotypes, and other "baggage" that educators (and other professionals in U.S. society) have about parents and families from differing cultural backgrounds.

Gender Perspectives **12.1**

THE TRANSITION TO HIGH SCHOOL

Smith (2007) focuses on parents' and students' perceptions of the transition to the ninth grade. His survey measured students' feelings about academic, social, and organizational aspects of high school.

Parents and students were generally looking forward to increased academic and social opportunities in high school. In particular, students would have some freedom to choose courses and participate in extracurricular activities. Parents had considerable concern about social issues, such as students fitting in, being bullied, and experiencing peer pressure; the students exhibited lower levels of concern with these issues and felt positive about interacting with more and older students in high school.

Smith also reports some interesting gender differences in how boys and girls viewed the transition. Girls had lower expectations about social opportunities in the eighth grade, but their social experiences ended up being more positive than boys in high school. There were not any significant differences in boys' and girls' perceptions of academic issues in the ninth grade. Both groups reported significantly lower levels of support when they reflected back to their eighth-grade teachers and parents.

A few significant differences existed between black and white students. For example, black students had slightly lower expectations in their academic, social, and organizational perceptions of the transition during eighth grade. They also felt less support than their white peers.

We recommend this worthwhile article to both principals and teachers. School transitions can be difficult for students and their parents. Planned and methodical preparation can reduce much of the perceived difficulty with transitions.

Source: Smith, J. S. (2007). The transition to high school: Perceptions and reality. *Principal, 87*(1), 74–75.

When reaching decisions about families, we cannot overemphasize the need for objectivity. Educators cannot reach objective decisions concerning whether and to what extent to involve parents and families when they believe such statements as "These parents just don't care," "The father is an alcoholic," "The father never lets his wife speak," or "Neither the mother nor the father has any ambition; they are satisfied to live off welfare." Educators who stereotype parents will probably do little to get to know and involve parents and families in their individual classrooms and certainly not in the overall school program.

An educator should not think he or she knows the prototypical "American Indian family," "African American family," or any other "family." For example, African American families are so diverse that some believe that there is no such thing as a typical African American family.

Socioeconomic differences play a significant role in determining how a person acts, lives, thinks, and relates to others. Low wages; unemployment or underemployment; lack of property, savings, and food reserves; and having to meet the most basic needs on a day-to-day basis easily lead to feelings of helplessness, dependence, and inferiority. Differences in values, attitudes, behaviors, and beliefs among the various socioeconomic groups warrant the professional's consideration, especially because some minority groups' members come from the lower socioeconomic classes.

Regrettably, a person's socioeconomic status is sometimes thought to indicate his or her ambitions or motivation to achieve. It is a serious mistake to stereotype people according to social class—to assume, for example, that the lower classes lack ambition, do not want to work, or do not want to improve their education status. It is not unreasonable to suggest that people of the lower socioeconomic levels—whether African, Arab, Asian, European, Hispanic American, or American Indian—want to improve their social status in life but that they meet with considerable frustration when faced with low education, high unemployment, conditions associated with poverty, and the racism and discrimination still prevalent in U.S. society.

Generational differences are another reason that an educator must not assume homogeneity within a culture. Older generations may be more prone to retain Old World values and traditions, because they tend to live in close proximity to people of similar language, traditions, and customs, whereas young people are likely to move anywhere in the United States.

One generational difference involves facility with the English language. While older generations may have lived in cultural enclaves with others who speak their native languages or who speak English at similar levels of fluency, younger generations who can communicate effectively in English are better able to cope in a predominantly English-speaking society.

Use this list of questions to examine your own perceptions:

1. Are my opinions of parents and families based on myths and stereotypes or on accurate and objective perceptions?
2. Have my experiences included positive first-hand contact with people from culturally different backgrounds?

3. What means have I employed to learn about the customs, traditions, values, and beliefs of all people?
4. Do I understand the extended-family concept, or do I only think "too many people live in the same house because of poverty conditions"?
5. Am I prejudiced, or do I have genuine feelings of acceptance for all people, regardless of culture, ethnicity, race, and socioeconomic background?
6. Do I hold the perceptions that American Indians are alcoholics, that African American families are headed by single females, that Asian Americans are the model minority and have achieved what represents the American Dream, or that Hispanic Americans have large families and live on welfare?
7. Can I perceive that aunts, uncles, and grandparents are as important as more immediate-family members (that is, the mother and father)?
8. Do I understand the rich cultural backgrounds of families, and am I willing to base educational experiences on this diversity?
9. Do I know appropriate sources of information to learn more about parents and families from culturally diverse backgrounds?
10. Do I have the motivation, skills, and attitudes to develop close interrelationships with parents and families from culturally different backgrounds?

Trumbull, Rothstein-Fisch, and Greenfield (2001) maintain that differences in culture often block communication between teachers and parents. Teachers who teach children who are diverse know that the challenges extend beyond language. Even as educators try to help children of diverse backgrounds deal with the U.S. education system, their own teaching methods and most routine classroom expectations can result in perplexing conflicts with the children's cultural ways of knowing and behaving. The authors explain that a student may resist offering a right answer after another student has answered incorrectly, in order not to embarrass that person in front of the group. It is not only immigrant children who challenge teachers: U.S.-born students—American Indians, African Americans, and Hispanic Americans whose families have lived here for generations—may also feel alienated by common classroom practices.

Trumbull, Rothstein-Fisch, and Greenfield (2001) explain the Bridging Cultures project, which sought to improve cross-cultural communication in the classroom. The cultural framework is a tool for understanding how the expectations for a student at school may conflict with the values of the students' family. For example, European American parents often stress making their children socially and economically independent. This emphasis on self-reliance affects nearly all European American family decisions. In contrast, collectivist societies are quite hierarchical and point their children in a different direction. They encourage the children to be contributing members of a family unit. Children are expected to understand and act on a strong sense of responsibility to the group, the family, and the community. Again, in contrast, children in individualistic societies are expected to make educational and occupational decisions that develop their own potential, usually without regard for how their success may benefit their families.

Effective Parent, Family, and Caregiver Involvement

Elements of Effective Programs

Effective parent-, family-, and caregiver-involvement programs should reflect the needs of the specific culture. Factors should be considered such as length of time in the United States, socioeconomic status, sexual orientation, and the culture's gender expectations for girls and boys. We do not believe educators should purchase a "one-size-fits-all" program, because either the teacher will have to revise its components or the program will not reflect the needs of the specific cultures. Just as Mr. Johnson in the Opening Scenario wanted first-hand contact with people of diversity, people of specific cultures deserve knowing and understanding to make parent-involvement programs responsive to their needs.

We emphasize the need for individuality in involvement programs, but we also think effective programs share these qualities:

1. Written policies demonstrate to volunteers that the school is taking the effort seriously and provide some context for the actual program.
2. Administrative support is evident in all aspects of the program. Teachers and volunteers know administrators will provide financial support, current instructional materials, and assistance for teachers.
3. Training programs (e.g., removing barriers, overcoming language problems, and providing cultural sensitivity training) are provided for teachers and others working with the program.
4. Training programs emphasize a partnership approach among teachers and parents, families, and caregivers, rather than an approach whereby the teacher simply lectures.
5. There is clear and effective communication between the home and school. Such communication is two sided rather than one sided.
6. A network system is used to identify additional resources and information.
7. There is planned assessment of all phases of the program.

Most programs designed to work with families have served mainly English-speaking families who know how to benefit from parent–teacher programs. Educators need to consider cross-cultural perspectives when working with families. To lessen the problems associated with communication, both written and oral, the educators in the parent-involvement program at Emerson School in Rosemead, California, sent letters in four languages to parents and conducted meetings in six languages. The program encourages parents to offer, in their native languages, their input and opinions about school services. The school then translates their responses and reports back in the parents' native languages.

Parents, Families, and Caregivers of Culturally Different Backgrounds

A prerequisite to understanding culturally diverse parents and families is gaining accurate and objective knowledge about expectations, needs, and challenges facing people with differing cultural backgrounds. Without doubt, educators can improve their understanding by reading books and journals, taking courses, and attending professional conferences. Although these means can provide considerable insight into cultural diversity and should be an integral part of the educator's learning agenda, first-hand contact with individuals continues to be one of the most effective means of gaining an accurate perspective of cultural diversity.

First-hand contact has an advantage that other means cannot always provide: learning directly about people and their individual attitudes, values, and beliefs. With understanding and knowledge, the potential exists for genuine feelings of caring and empathy to develop between people of differing races, cultures, and ethnic backgrounds.

Although there is probably no adequate substitute for first-hand contact with parents and families, it is possible to gain information through a parent survey. The most effective means would be to use a parent survey in addition to first-hand contact. It is important for the educators who design the survey to remember that some questions may be culturally sensitive; for example, questions that might not be offensive to European American populations might be construed as an invasion of privacy by many parents and families from culturally different backgrounds. Examples of culturally sensitive questions are those on child-rearing techniques, sex education, dating patterns, and parental authority.

Parette and Petch-Hogan (2000) suggest that communication with families is increasingly important in schools today. Parents of culturally/linguistically diverse students should be involved in sharing of culture, participating as assistants on field trips, assisting in arts and crafts, assisting with music and recreational activities, and participating actively in the special-education planning process. Such involvement causes a problem for some diverse families, especially those with language differences, different cultural expectations, and mistrust of or lack of experience with U.S. education systems. The authors focus on communication and contacts with families; location of meetings and supports; providing information training; understanding family priorities, needs, and resources; family lifespan issues; family functions; and family communication styles.

Educators may decide to develop the survey in the parents' native language, rather than risk that the survey will not be completed or that problems will result from poor communication. Generally speaking, parent surveys should be clear and short, require only a brief amount of time to complete, and avoid conveying middle-class European American perspectives.

Parents, families, or caregivers often went to schools where their culture was the majority, and many associate with people mainly from their own cultures. Parents in these situations have little experience with people who are different. Having little knowledge of the culture, or worse yet, harboring cultural stereotypes and prejudicial views can lead to conflicts and confusion about the role of teachers as well as the responsibility of the school. The following eleven questions may serve as a beginning point to understand parents', families', and caregivers' concerns.

1. Do you feel that educators in your child's or adolescent's school understand and meet the overall needs and concerns of learners from different cultural backgrounds?
2. Do you feel that school policies recognize that children and adolescents of culturally different backgrounds differ from the European American population?
3. Does the media center (children's and adolescents' books, films, other visual material) reflect the cultural diversity of the school?
4. How well has the school succeeded in employing a faculty and staff (administrators, teachers, library media specialists, special personnel, speech therapists, guidance counselors, psychologists, school nurses) that reflects the cultural diversity of the student body?
5. Do you feel that school expectations (competition, motivation, achievements, aspirations) reflect the values and expectations of learners of culturally diverse backgrounds?
6. Do you feel that extracurricular activities in the school reflect the needs and interests of children and adolescents of culturally diverse backgrounds?

7. Do teaching methods and strategies (lecture format, small group, coopera-tive learning, ability grouping) reflect a concern for the educational well-being of all learners?

8. Has the school provided opportunities to offer opinions, input, advice, and suggestions concerning improvement of the school program or changing an aspect you would like to see changed?

9. Is your child progressing toward or succeeding at goals that you feel are important?

10. Do you feel the school provides information and assistance concerning social service organizations?

11. What comments or suggestions do you want to offer concerning your child or adolescent in school?

Home Visits

Home visits may be one of the most effective ways for teachers to get to know learners, their immediate and extended families, and their home environment and culture. Families from different cultural backgrounds often perceive fam-ily roles differently, have differing expectations of the schools, and expect older family members to play significantly greater child-rearing roles. The only way to understand such differences is to get to know the families personally.

Home visits can provide valuable informa-tion about learners and their homes, but perhaps an even greater benefit is that learners and their families see that educators care and are interested in all children and adolescents. Parents from cul-turally different backgrounds may also feel more at ease in their own surroundings than they would in the (perhaps) strange and sterile school environment.

Before the home visit, educators should call or send a note to the parents and establish a time that is convenient for both the teacher and the parents. At the beginning of the visit, the teacher should talk informally with the parents and the child for a few minutes to establish a friendly tone and to reduce the parents' anxiety. At all times, teach-ers should remember that they are visitors and should avoid judging situations and conditions in

Points to Ponder 12.2

Visiting in the Home

Visiting in the homes of children and adolescents can raise sensitive issues, especially with parents and families of culturally different backgrounds. Perceiv-ing family life and parenting practices from different cultural perspectives can result in misunderstanding. For example, a middle-class African American educator might fail to understand a Hispanic or Asian American family. Make a list of "do's and don'ts"—those behaviors you should demonstrate and should not demonstrate in an effort to show understanding and respect for the parents' cultural heritage.

the home. Parents will have greater confidence in the teacher if they think the discussion will be held in confidence.

Communication

Educators in multicultural situations must recognize that some communication behaviors are to be understood rather than expected. Listening behaviors that are typical and expected of middle-class white parents might be far different from those that people of other cultural backgrounds exhibit. For example, maintaining eye contact might be considered rude in some cultures. Likewise, body postures are also culturally based. Educators should not assess parents' and families' interest and commitment to children's education by using middle-class European American standards and expectations.

Humans communicate at several levels simultaneously: through verbal expression, or what they say; through body language or nonverbal expression, or how they behave; and through emotional responses, or how they show what they feel. The more congruent these levels of expression are, the more meaningful or understanding the communication becomes to others. One can easily recognize the importance of understanding the various types of communication with families of differing cultural backgrounds.

Whether communicating through speaking directly, telephoning, or writing to parents, educators are responsible for not allowing language or communication differences, verbal or nonverbal, to interfere with overall communication. Several factors warrant consideration. First, the parents' English skills might not allow effective communication. Second, nonverbal communication might pose a problem; for example, the European American who looks an American Indian directly in the eye while communicating might be considered rude, and the educator might think an American Indian's glancing away indicates disinterest or irritation.

Another example of problems that can result from nonverbal communication occurs with Asian American parents and families, who are especially sensitive to nonverbal messages and who may construe a teacher's folded arms or other casual gestures as indicative of an indifferent attitude. Educators should avoid jargon with which parents might be unfamiliar: *PET, assertive discipline, critical thinking, cooperative learning, mastery learning, percentiles,* and terms associated with computers or technology, for example.

Telephoning represents another means of communicating with parents and demonstrates the teacher's personal interest in both the learner and the parents. Positive telephone contacts can significantly affect a child's school performance;

conversely, negative calls can have a negative effect. As with other forms of communication, teachers must exercise caution when using the telephone to communicate with parents.

Telephoning is a great way to encourage parents to attend meetings, conferences, and other school events. It can be extremely threatening, however, to parents and families of culturally different backgrounds, because they have come to expect bad news whenever a representative of the school calls. Guidelines for minimizing parent and teacher misunderstanding include these:

1. Address parents as Mr. or Mrs., because parents from different backgrounds often do not receive the same respect and courtesy as other people.
2. Use a tone of voice that expresses respect and courtesy, because a call from school often raises anxiety levels.
3. Discuss the child's or adolescent's positive points before discussing the problem to be solved.
4. Use language the parent understands and a tone that does not sound condescending.
5. Respond with empathy if the parent has difficulty understanding unfamiliar educational concepts.

Educators can also write notes and letters to keep parents informed of children's progress and of administrative and record-keeping problems and concerns, schedule changes, special events, holidays, workshops, field trips, and other items of interest. Effective notes are clear, concise, and positive and may speak to parents and family members in their primary language. Unless used systematically, however, notes and letters have limited value in reinforcing the child's academic performance or social and emotional behavior and are best used as one component of the overall parent and teacher communication.

Volunteers

Parent volunteers can contribute significantly to the quality of the services offered to learners in the school. Here are four important reasons for using volunteers:

1. Relieving the professional staff of nonteaching duties
2. Providing needed services to individual children to supplement the work of the classroom teacher
3. Enriching the experiences of children beyond those normally available in school

4. Building a better understanding among citizens of school problems and stimulating widespread citizen support for public education

Although parents are the most frequent volunteers, siblings, relatives, older elementary and secondary students, college students, senior citizens, business and professional groups, and other members of the community can volunteer to participate in school activities.

Parents and extended-family members from all cultures have numerous talents and skills to share with children and adolescents. People from differing cultural backgrounds, however, often consider educators and schools as both authoritarian and worthy of honor and praise. Therefore, some people might be hesitant to "interfere" with school routines or may feel that their talents are not worthy to be shared with the school. The administrator's and teacher's role in this situation is to encourage and convince people that schools are open to new ideas and that their talents are worth sharing. To accomplish such a goal, educators should send home, at the beginning of the school year, a parent-involvement questionnaire designed to determine skills, talents, and areas of interest.

Serving on committees is another way parents and extended-family members can become involved in classrooms and school. Through committee work, parents contribute to the classroom and school and learn about program development, operation, staffing, and evaluation. Parents also develop an appreciation for staffing concerns, curriculum development, fiscal exigencies, materials and equipment needs, and other demands of the instructional program.

As with other forms of involvement, these parents and families might not understand the purpose of committees and how they function. Educators must work toward making the composition of the committee representative of the diversity of the student body. Guidelines for parents working on school committees include the following:

1. Remember the committee's purpose and objectives.
2. Be confident of the committee's ability to accomplish the assigned task.
3. Begin small, and take one step at a time.
4. Function within the school, and become an integral part of the classroom or school.
5. Seek financial, administrative, informational, and other assistance when necessary.

Parent involvement is an important factor in promoting the successful transition of youth with disabilities into adulthood. Geenen, Powers, and

Lopez-Vasquez (2001) surveyed American Indian, African American, Hispanic American, and European American parents to assess their level of participation in their child's transitioning activities. They found that culturally and linguistically diverse groups report higher levels of participation than European American parents. Parent participation might be particularly important for culturally and linguistically diverse youth, as a strong relationship between parents and the school can promote cultural understanding and responsiveness in transition planning. Ethnically diverse groups often emphasize norm-related behaviors and define adult roles differently, and parents can be a valuable resource in helping educators understand, identify, and support transition outcomes that are valued in a child's culture.

Parents of all ethnic groups are likely to encounter barriers to school participation, including parental fatigue, lack of parental knowledge regarding their rights and school procedures, logistical constraints (e.g., lack of child care), rigid or limited options for parental involvement in educational planning, and language. However, for culturally and linguistically diverse parents and families, the problems are made more formidable by racism, discrimination, insensitivity, and cultural unresponsiveness.

Parent–Teacher Conferences

The parent–teacher conference presents an opportunity for parents and teachers to exchange information about the child's school and home activities. It also provides an occasion to involve parents in planning and implementing their child's educational program. When teachers contact parents to schedule progress report conferences, they should explain the purpose of the conference.

To lessen the parents' anxiety about the conference, teachers might provide parents with a written agenda. Educators should also remember that the purpose of the conference is the child and school progress, not the teacher's or parents' personal, social, emotional, or marital problems. Although these issues may affect the learner's overall school progress, educators should direct the focus of the conference toward areas of school function.

The agenda for the parent–teacher conference might include discussion of the learner's test scores or assessment results. Although most parents, regardless of cultural background, might benefit from an explanation of the terms normally associated with measurement and evaluation, parents might need even more detailed information. Test results are often a concern for parents and children, and parents may react strongly to results that indicate their child or adolescent is functioning at a lower level than most learn-ers. Educators should ask parents from differing cultural backgrounds to state their understanding of the information and make sure parents under-stand the results and conclusions. Teachers should make a sincere effort to alleviate any anxiety that parents express over possible misuse of test results.

Parent–teacher conferences have the poten-tial to be beneficial for all involved but can result in hard feelings, frustration, and a breaking off of communication completely. Here are several suggestions for having positive conferences, but please remember that there is no special formula for success:

Points to Ponder 12.3

Determining Concerns during Parent–Teacher Conferences

Make a list of possible concerns and barriers that might interfere with the success of the parent–teacher conference. How will you motivate parents and families (who might feel that speaking forthrightly to the teacher is disrespectful) to speak, voice concerns, and make suggestions?

1. Begin to work toward positive relationships with parents, families, and caregivers before the first conference or informal meeting.
2. Have an ongoing dialogue with parents, families, and caregivers. For instance, notify them of positive achievements and accomplishments, special dates, and the details of the reporting system.
3. Occasionally ask students to participate in the conference, so they will know what is being said. Such an effort to avoid distrust and suspicion often pays rich dividends.
4. Make the conference as comfortable as possible. Provide a comfortable seating area for the teacher with the parents, families, or caregivers (rather than have the teacher sit behind the desk).
5. Make it clear how parents, families, and caregivers can help the child, and conclude the conference with at least one positive comment.
6. Avoid educational jargon that might confuse the participants, but explain terms in detail when the slightest suspicion or doubt arises.

Parent Advisory Councils

A parent advisory council can be an excellent means of providing parents and families of culturally diverse backgrounds opportunities to voice opinions and generally influence the overall operation of the school. By having a council com-position that reflects the cultural diversity of the student body, council repre-sentatives (or parents who make suggestions and comments through selected representatives) can offer specific suggestions for devising the school curriculum and making the teaching and learning environment more multicultural in nature. Council members might want to discuss the cultural diversity of the administrative and teaching staff, how the curriculum and teaching and learning process reflect diversity, policies that groups of differing cultural backgrounds might not understand, methods of making the school more multicultural in nature, or any topic that might seem relevant at the time.

An advisory council can serve as a liaison between school and classroom and between home and community, and it can function as a permanent parent-to-parent communications committee to announce meetings, special events, personnel changes, and other notices of interest. The advisory committee can also assume responsibility for organizing and directing ad hoc or temporary committees.

Orientation sessions might be in order, especially for parents and families who may not understand the purpose of the council, may feel that parents would be meddling in schools' business, or may not understand procedures by which meetings work. An orientation meeting can help council members feel better prepared and feel more comfortable about future meetings. Suggested topics for an orientation session include council role and authority, purpose, district organization, value and functions of committees, decision-making procedures (perhaps including a brief session on Robert's Rules of Order), how to disagree and the value of expressing a different view, and expectations of members.

Parent, Family, and Caregiver Education

The concept of parent education dates back to the 1800s and carries differing definitions and perceptions that have resulted in a variety of forms and emphases. A wide array of activities continue to be appropriate for parent-education programs. These range from family and cultural transmission of child-rearing values, skills, and techniques to more specific parenting behaviors. Specifically, however, we define the term *parent education* as planned activities that are designed to educate parents about their children and adolescents, goals of U.S. school systems, and ways they can help their child or adolescent experience success, both academically and behaviorally, in school.

Although schools should develop parent-education programs specifically for individual learners and their parents, some programs help parents with special needs, enhance knowledge of family life, teach techniques for changing attitudes and behaviors, help parents change their own negative behaviors, provide health and sex education information, and teach parents how to help with the education process.

The need for parent education has been documented: Parents become more involved and develop more positive attitudes toward school activities; parents often dread the changes in their child's or adolescent's development; parents sometimes absolve themselves of responsibility; and parents often need assistance in understanding curricular areas. The need results from the heightened concern about pressures related to more working mothers, the effects of geographic mobility, divorce rates, and economic uncertainties as well as from parents needing relevant information for children's social, physical, emotional, and intellectual development.

The realities, however, pose a dilemma that demands educators' understanding. Although parent-education programs have become routine aspects of many early childhood programs, evidence indicates that many middle and secondary school educators have not developed parent-education programs. Early childhood education appears to have made substantial progress in planning and implementing parent-education programs and has provided the framework in both theory and practice for schools or other levels.

Rationale for Involvement Programs

Two reasons speak to the importance of parent education: understanding the various developmental periods and responding appropriately to children's and adolescents' behavior. Although we address each reason separately, close and intricate relationships between the two areas warrant parental recognition and understanding.

Effective parent-education programs provide experiences that show a developmental basis for children's and adolescents' behavior. Rather than allow parents to assume that they have failed in parenting roles or to absolve themselves of responsibility for behavior, programs can help parents understand the developmental changes and the contemporary world of children and adolescents.

Specifically, parents need to understand the cause-and-effect relationship between development and behavior. The cause of certain behavior may result from children's and adolescents' quest for independence and from peer pressure to experiment with alcohol, drugs, sex, and other challenges to authority.

Basically, educators should provide programs that convince parents that their children are not necessarily "going bad" or "turning into hoodlums" and that, although understanding changes in behavioral patterns may be difficult for parents, children and adolescents need to feel accepted and understood. Parents need to understand that feeling guilty or absolving themselves of responsibility may result in even worse attention-getting or even delinquent behaviors. Parents need to understand the effects of one-parent homes on development and behavior. At the same time, educators should emphasize that not all behavior results from family disruption.

Special Needs of Parents, Families, and Caregivers

Planning parent-education programs for parents and families from differing cultural backgrounds requires that educators look at issues, topics, and formats from the perspective of these parents and families. Prepackaged programs or programs that European Americans in middle- or upper-class suburban schools use might not be adequate for culturally diverse parents and families, whatever their social class.

Although special needs vary with culture, social class, and geographic area, what specific needs might parents and families have? After an objective and accurate needs assessment, educators might find that parents of diverse cultural backgrounds require educational assistance in understanding such areas as school expectations, parents' roles in the school, tests and assessment scores, children's and adolescents' development, appropriate social services agencies and organizations that can provide assistance, homework and how to get help, school committees and parent advisory councils, and other involvement activities. This list provides only a few examples, but it suffices to show that parent-education programs should be designed for a specific cultural group and not rely on a program that parents may not understand or feel is not culturally relevant.

Methods and activities selected for the parent-education program determine the success of the effort. Programs for minority parents should not rely too heavily on reading material (unless participants are clearly proficient in English), should not expect parents to take active vocal roles in the beginning stages, and should not expect or require parents to reveal situations or information that may be personal or a negative reflection on the family or the home.

Formats of Parent-Education Programs

Teachers must reach a decision about whether to employ a prepackaged parenting program that may lead to a loosely organized discussion group or to develop a program that addresses parental needs for a particular school. Prepackaged programs have several advantages (e.g., they require less preparatory time and little revision), but they may not be applicable to a diverse range of cultures.

Developing a parent-education program based on specific family and community needs might prove effective, and parents might receive it more enthusiastically. The format of the program can take several directions and should reflect the needs and interests of individual schools and parents.

Before scheduling planning sessions, educators should conduct an assessment or needs inventory to determine preferred methods and content. Parent-education modes may include lectures, discussion groups, CD-ROMs, computer programs, videotapes, cassettes, and PowerPoint presentations. Parents may schedule appointments with available parent educators to discuss confidential and personal matters concerning their children and adolescents that they do not want revealed in large-group settings.

Parent-education sessions will undoubtedly stimulate questions, comments, and other discussion. Rather than relying on a lecture format with a large group, the leader of the session should allow time for parents to speak or meet in small groups. Sometimes, one of the leader's most effective approaches may be to let parents know that other parents experience similar problems.

In all likelihood, it will be difficult to purchase a prepackaged parent-education program that meets the needs of parents from a number of cultural backgrounds. For example, African American parents might not experience the same challenges as American Indians. Likewise, first-generation Asian Americans probably do not experience the same problems as third-generation Asian Americans. We think it might be more feasible to design programs with individual cultural groups in mind.

Helping Parents Understand School Expectations and Parents' Roles

A major role of parent-education programs should be to help parents of differing cultural groups understand the school's expectations and the parents' role in the teaching and learning process. Designing such a program requires educators to assess the needs and concerns of the specific culture. For example, although American Indian and Asian American parents might have similarities, they have substantial differences that necessitate culture-specific programs.

First, educators need to recognize that some parents and families, especially of more recent generations, might not understand U.S. school expectations and perspectives, which place emphasis on individual achievement, competition, and responsibility for one's own possessions. Parents and families of differing cultural backgrounds should not encourage their children and adolescents to adopt middle- or upper-class white perspectives. Instead, educators can explain to parents the differing cultural expectations (e.g., group versus individual achievement, competition versus working together, sharing versus ownership) of various cultural groups. Educators should also explain the school's expectations in other areas, such as curricular matters, instructional strategies, classroom management and discipline, homework and extracurricular activities, and other aspects of the school that parents and families may need assistance in understanding.

Second, educators should make clear the parents' roles and responsibilities in their children's or adolescents' education. Sometimes, people from different cultural backgrounds may think they do not know enough about U.S. school systems to make a contribution, or they may perceive the school as an authoritarian institution that does not appreciate input and suggestions. The educator's role is to change misconceptions of the schools and to show that learners' academic achievement and overall school progress can be enhanced when parents take an active role in the school. In meeting this goal, educators need to show all parents and families the following:

1. They are responsible for encouraging and helping their children and adolescents in all phases of the teaching and learning process.
2. They are encouraged to visit the school and voice their input, recommendations, and suggestions.
3. They are encouraged to participate in conferences, involvement activities, parent-education sessions, and parent advisory councils.

Case Study

Parent Advisory Councils

Dr. Suarez, principal at Westview High School, carefully planned his parent advisory council. The composition of the council was all important this academic year, for several reasons: The state department of education had mandated increasingly stringent academic rules that could threaten the academic standing of low-achieving students; the number of students from diverse cultural backgrounds was increasing; several acts of racism had occurred the previous school year; and his faculty was almost all white and middle class. Dr. Suarez thought parents could play a significant role this year, especially if he could convince leaders of the various diverse communities to participate.

He wondered what issues he might raise as the council progressed with its work. His list grew: grades, racism, evaluation, his district's inability (or lack of initiative, he thought) to employ faculty and staff members from culturally diverse backgrounds, language programs, school policies, curricular materials, instructional practices—the list seemed endless. "This will certainly be a challenging year," Dr. Suarez thought. He wanted to create a council with cultural diversity proportional to that of the student body.

What problems might this diversity of the council bring? Again, his list grew: differing expectations of schools and teachers, misunderstandings about U.S. schools, language and communication problems, reluctance to take an active role, and not understanding the role of the council. For the members from different cultural backgrounds, Dr. Suarez planned an additional meeting to provide opportunities to answer questions, resolve concerns, and become better acquainted.

Even with the pressing issues and challenges involving all members, regardless of culture, on the council, Dr. Suarez perceived this as a positive time—a time when his school's role in helping learners from different backgrounds could be defined more accurately and a time of enhanced acceptance and understanding.

Questions for Discussion:

1. Dr. Suarez faces an array of challenges to bring to the parent advisory council. How should he proceed? Place them all on the agenda at one time? Start with one or two and then expand? Try to prioritize the challenges? If you were Dr. Suarez, what would be your first step? Why?
2. How would you begin to form the parent advisory council? Would it be representative of the student body? How often would you meet? Would you chair the committee or ask a parent to chair?
3. What can Dr. Suarez do about his concern that more stringent academic rules could threaten the academic standing of some students? Educators have a professional responsibility to obey the mandates of the state and school district, but standards should not be reduced to accomplish these goals. Formulate a plan that Dr. Suarez could use to abide by the mandates and also maintain standards.

Summing Up

Educators who want to involve parents and families from culturally different backgrounds should:

1. Understand the extended-family concept, and plan educational experiences for both immediate and extended-family members.
2. Understand that parents and families may resist teachers' efforts to involve them in school activities.

3. Understand parents as individuals with intracultural, socioeconomic, and generational differences.

4. Learn as much as possible about parents and families through first-hand contact, parent surveys, and any other means that provide accurate and objective information.

5. Visit the homes of students to gain a better understanding of family backgrounds, values, customs, and traditions.

6. Ensure that communication between the school and family reflects a genuine understanding of the problems that might result from language and communication differences, both verbal and nonverbal.

7. Plan and conduct parent–teacher conferences so that parents will understand the purposes and procedures of the conference process.

8. Ensure that parent advisory councils have a composition that represents the cultural, ethnic, and racial composition of the student body, and ensure that the councils address the specific needs and concerns of parents and families from differing cultural backgrounds.

9. Understand that parent-education programs are especially important for parents who might not understand the school's roles and expectations and who may need assistance with their child or adolescent in a predominantly European American school and society.

Suggested Learning Activities

1. Prepare a parent survey designed to obtain information from parents and families of different cultural backgrounds. List questions that will provide specific information about what parents and families expect from schools, how teachers can help children and adolescents, and how parents and families can contribute to the educational process. In preparing this survey, what are some precautions you might want to consider?

2. Design procedures for an effective parent advisory committee with the purpose of involving parents and families. Your design should consider what means you will use to engage participants of all cultural backgrounds, the overall goals of the committee, how the committee will report to the general school population, a sample agenda (for an individual meeting and for the school year), how you will accommodate participants who are not proficient in English, and any special factors that educators should consider when dealing with minority populations.

3. Read the following Implementing Research, which looks at an article called "What Families Want." Then consider ways that educators can better meet students' and teachers' needs.

Implementing Research

What Families Want

Although Americans of all backgrounds believe education is the key to the good life, many people do not think schools are delivering on the promise for black and Hispanic students. It appears that blacks, Hispanics, and whites have common aspirations for their children to have successful school experiences and to prepare them for future educational experiences. However, Wadsworth and Remaley (2007) think U.S. schools have made only a half-hearted effort to provide equal education opportunities for all. Stark differences exist between the education of whites and that of blacks and Hispanics. Dropout rates are dismal for both of these demographic minority groups.

According to Wadsworth and Remaley's interpretation of public opinion surveys done by Public Agenda, families give schools low marks on standards as well as classroom atmosphere. Black parents and students are more likely to be satisfied with their local school's performance. They share similar concerns about the lack of funding for schools. While the standards issue is worrisome, blacks and Hispanics give worse marks to classroom atmosphere. Dropout rates, truancy, fighting, and drug use are all problems that need to be addressed. Lastly, black and Hispanic parents are twice as likely as whites to think the superintendent has not done a good job.

Interestingly, a significant number of teachers confirmed the parents' and students' opinions.

Implementing the Research

1. Educators need to make a plan to improve one or two aspects of their schools per year. Addressing all the problems at one time would be overwhelming, but setting realistic priorities each year would have the potential for improving the schools.

2. Educators need to work to improve the *perceptions* of schools. While we agree with many of Wadsworth and Remaley's interpretations, we do not believe U.S. schools are this bad. Educators need to work on improving what people think about schools.

3. We all need to focus attention on what we can do to help black and Hispanic students. We need to determine the causes of their school problems and then form a concerted plan to address the problems.

Source: Wadsworth, D., & Remaley, M. H. (2007). What families want. *Educational Leadership, 64*(6), 23–27.

Suggestions for Collaborative Efforts

Form groups of three or four that, if possible, represent our nation's cultural and gender diversity. Working collaboratively, focus your group's attention toward the following efforts:

1. With the help of your group, prepare a survey to determine the reasons that parents might resist educators' efforts. Using the results, write a plan in which your goal is to obtain the family's participation and involvement.

2. Arrange an opportunity for each member of your group to meet with a parent or extended family member to learn what problems they experience with U.S. schools. Have as many cultural groups represented as possible. As a group, decide on a list of questions that might provide the information you want. Then, as a group, share your responses to determine whether you can establish a plan or agenda for addressing parents' and families' concerns. Caution: Remember that some cultures hold schools and educators in high regard and therefore might not want to share concerns and problems. In such cases, you should respect their privacy.

3. Design a program to involve parents, families, and caregivers from culturally diverse backgrounds. Plan how you will invite and obtain their participation, help them understand that elementary and secondary schools need their participation, and teach them appropriate activities or utilize their individual expertise. List several points that educators should consider (and propose an appropriate response), such as parents' language difficulties, lack of understanding of U.S. schools, and the immense respect that some parents, families, and caregivers have for educators.

 ## Expanding Your Horizons

Additional Journals, Books, and Internet Sites

Chiu, M. M. (2007). Families, economies, cultures, and science achievement in 41 countries: Country, school, and student level analyses. *Journal of Family Psychology, 21*(3), 510–519.

> Chiu looks at several factors regarding science achievement and promotes family involvement.

Congress, E. P., & Gonzalez, M. J. (2005). *Multicultural perspectives in working with families.* New York: Spring.

> These authors offer considerable insights and suggestions for working with families in multicultural situations.

Duke, C. (2007). Conceptualizing special education services in small learning communities. *Urban Education, 42*(5), 412–431.

> Duke explains how special education and small learning communities can be connected to be better for the students.

Scott, P. (2007). Successfully bringing parents into the classroom. *Principal, 87*(1), 64–65.

Scott looks at the importance of involving parents and offers suggestions for success.

Seda, C. (2007). Parental involvement unlocks children's educational potential. *Essays in Education, 19*(2), 150–159.

Seda looks at ways parental involvement can promote students' interest and academic achievement.

Sprunger, K. A. (2007). A dynamic partnership. *Kappa Delta Pi Record, 43*(2), 92–93.

Sprunger maintains that partnerships between teachers and parents are essential for student learning.

Wherry, J. H. (2007). Back to school: A fresh start for parent involvement. *Principal, 87*(1), 8.

Wherry explains the importance of parental involvement and renewing parental involvement.

Educational Resources Information Center (ERIC). www.eric.ed.gov/ERICWebPortal/custom/portlets/recordDetails/detailmini.jsp?_nfpb=true&_&ERICExtSearch_SearchValue_0=EJ621433&ERICExtSearch SearchType_0=eric_accno&accno=EJ621433

These authors report on a survey of 308 African American, Hispanic American, American Indian, and European American parents that found that culturally and linguistically diverse parents are active in transition-planning activities and that, in some instances, the level of reported participation by minority-group parents surpassed that of European American parents.

Find Articles. http://findarticles.com/p/articles/mi_m0JSD/is_1_62/ai_n9484153

This site is a useful tool to help readers find appropriate articles on multiculturalism and parent involvement.

Goliath. http://goliath.ecnext.com/coms2/gi_0199-3330032/Multicultural-literacy-starts-at-home.html

This article maintains that multicultural literacy starts at home by supporting parental involvement in multicultural education. It offers a parent resource kit, parent plan for Title 1, and parent-involvement research.

National Center for Culturally Responsive Educational Systems. http://nccrest.edreform.net/subject/parentparticipation

This site provides a wealth of information on parent involvement in elementary and secondary schools.

Tufts University. www.cfw.tufts.edu/topic/3/66.htm

Tufts University has a wide-ranging Internet site with many helpful topics, including multiculturalism and parent involvement.

Administrators and
Special School Personnel

Understanding the material and activities
in this chapter will help the reader to:

◆ Explain why the cultural diversity of administrators, faculty, and staff should reflect that of the student population.

◆ List several roles of administrators, special educators, librarians/media specialists, counselors, and communications disorders specialists in a school that promotes multiculturalism at all levels.

◆ List several ways administrators can lead school personnel in efforts to promote multiculturalism.

◆ Explain the unique challenges that face special-education teachers in diagnosing and remediating learners from culturally different backgrounds.

◆ Explain how the librarian/media specialist can select appropriate print and nonprint materials that accurately portray children and adolescents from all cultural backgrounds.

◆ Explain how the school counselor can understand culturally different children and adolescents and select culturally appropriate counseling techniques and testing instruments.

◆ Explain how the communications disorders specialist can accurately distinguish between communications disorders and communications variations.

◆ Explain, from the teacher's perspective, how the various professionals can work together and how the teacher can most effectively utilize the various areas of expertise for the benefit of learners of all cultural backgrounds.

Opening Scenario

Culturally Relevant Educational Experiences

Mrs. Miller, a seventh-grade teacher at Evergreen Middle School, has twenty-eight students in her class: twelve European Americans, eleven African Americans, two Hispanic Americans, and two Asian Americans. Mrs. Miller recognizes that the school, its policies, and its teaching and learning practices are predominantly white and middle class in perspective. Many students have to obey rules they do not understand, work toward meeting expectations and levels of motivation that are compatible with white perspectives, and learn to use cognitive styles similar to those of middle-class white learners. Mrs. Miller understands the need for change but also realizes she has limited time, resources, and expertise. For her students' welfare, she has decided to seek the principal's assistance.

Mrs. Johnson, the principal, listens attentively to Mrs. Miller's concerns. She agrees not only that the sixteen students of culturally different backgrounds need culturally relevant educational experiences but also that the twelve European American students need to acquire a better understanding of the other learners (and vice versa). Mrs. Johnson and Mrs. Miller decide to form a committee to address the learners' needs. The committee consists of Mrs. Johnson, Mrs. Miller, another seventh-grade teacher, one European American parent who has expressed interest, and three parents from other cultural groups (one from each group represented).

Mrs. Johnson has made a list of her and the committee's recommendations:

1. The task calls for the commitment of administrators, faculty, and parents; it is not something Mrs. Miller should tackle alone.
2. All parents—majority culture and minority cultures—should be notified (and their advice sought) of the effort to meet learners' needs and to provide multi-cultural experiences for all learners.
3. Textbooks and other curricular materials should be examined for bias, stereotypes, and cultural relevance.
4. Teaching and learning practices and the school environment should be examined from an administrative perspective.

Mrs. Johnson thinks these steps will serve as a good starting point and that, from an administrative perspective, this is a manageable agenda. Viewing this agenda as only a first phase, Mrs. Johnson starts to consider how the efforts can become a total-school effort. ◆

Overview

Genuine multicultural education efforts include more than lofty goals and school philosophies. The school's effort to recognize and celebrate cultural diversity should demonstrate total-school involvement by including the efforts of all school personnel. A commitment to multicultural education also includes an administration, faculty, and staff that reflect the cultural diversity of the student body. Employing school personnel of all cultural backgrounds at all levels shows respect for diversity; however, educators still need to work together, within their individual areas of expertise, to provide learners with educational experiences that address both individual and cultural needs. This chapter shows, from the classroom teacher's perspective, how administrators and special school personnel can contribute to the overall multicultural education program.

Administrators, Faculty, and Staff: Toward a Total-School Effort

Multicultural education programs and curricula may have lofty goal statements, but perhaps the best measure of a school's commitment to cultural diversity is the actual cultural, ethnic, sexual orientation, gender, and racial composition of the administration, faculty, and staff. Specifically, do school personnel reflect the cultural diversity of the student population? If school personnel are predominantly from one background, one might justifiably ask whether the school administration is striving for the goals of the multicultural education program. Learners of various cultural backgrounds who hear the rhetoric of multiculturalism but see members of their cultural group represented only in custodial positions might question the school's commitment to equal opportunity.

Defending the goal of employing school personnel of varying cultural backgrounds is not difficult. First, having diverse school personnel shows students a commitment to include all people, regardless of cultural, ethnic, and racial backgrounds; second, such a policy shows a respect for the legal mandates that ensure equal opportunity for people of all cultures. Having the school staff reflect the diversity of the student body is undoubtedly a fundamental goal and a prerequisite to showing respect for cultural diversity and for equal opportunity under the law. Deliberate recruitment programs aimed at professionals of differing cultural backgrounds can contribute to employing faculty and staff more representative of our nation's diversity.

Responsive multicultural education programs include a commitment by professionals at all levels to multiculturalism and an acceptance of all learners regardless of diversity. While classroom teachers might have the most influence because of their proximity to many learners, administrators have a major responsibility for ensuring the implementation of multicultural procedures. Similarly, special educators and communication disorders specialists must project equal dedication, enthusiasm, and commitment to the overall school goals of acceptance and respect. The following sections examine the roles of administrators and special school personnel, show how classroom educators can work most effectively with these professionals for the benefit of learners, suggest a means of evaluating professional efforts, and suggest how all educators can encourage service learning.

The demographic shifts and often negative social relations in schools and communities have resulted in some educators considering the research and literature on practices in multiculturalism to promote cross-cultural understandings among students, faculty, and staff. Leistyna (2001) suggests that multicultural professional development can improve cultural relations and educational opportunities. Professional development should be a major component in any multicultural education effort, because some educators can have a negative impact on students' self-image, academic achievement, and overall school relations. One example of multicultural professional development is sensitivity training that sensitizes teachers to other cultures and also affirms diversity.

For multicultural professional development to be most successful, facilitators and participants must move beyond internationalizing multiculturalism and reducing issues of diversity to immigration, especially since the families of some of the most disenfranchised children have been in the United States for generations. Such a professional development effort should include the development of deeper understandings of what defines culture in order to be able to move beyond discussions of values, beliefs, group ethos, language, and practices and to understand how these elements are produced within the context of abuses of power (Leistyna, 2001).

Administrators

Roles in Multicultural Education

The administrator's primary responsibilities include ensuring that multicultural education programs are carefully and methodically planned and that procedures are implemented to meet specific goals and objectives. Administrators require the ability and motivation to challenge and to lead school personnel toward responsive efforts. Although their participation might not include extensive first-hand efforts with youngsters of differing cultural backgrounds, their commitment and leadership remain crucial to the success of the overall school program and to generating other professionals' enthusiasm toward multicultural efforts. Administrators' efforts and the zeal they bring to this task undoubtedly determine the degree of success of the multicultural education program.

A major role of administrators is to provide learners with faculty and staff that reflect the cultural diversity of the student body and the community. The recent push for increased teacher certification standards might challenge principals who seek teachers from as many cultural backgrounds as possible. Most states have initiated minimum competency tests for all beginning teachers. Some claim that these tests measure teaching effectiveness, but an unintended result is that the number of minority teachers is rapidly declining.

A second challenge to administrators is to provide appropriate leadership efforts for an all-school approach to multicultural education. Teachers often base their dedication or enthusiasm for educational programs on the administrator's apparent commitment. Administrators should demonstrate leadership toward specific objectives, convey a genuine respect for cultural diversity, and demonstrate a willingness to be involved. These efforts may be among the most important, because the administrator is a major influence in the overall effectiveness of the programs and can lead faculty and staff members toward excellence in all professional endeavors.

A third challenge for principals is to deal affirmatively with the racial attitudes of their staffs. For many teachers and other staff members, joining the school ranks is their first sustained contact with members of another culture, and they may enter the situations not only lacking knowledge but fearful of confronting the issue of race. Such feelings can lead to an uneasiness that not only hurts work performance but can also do further harm to racial relations.

Another role in which administrators can offer significant contributions is communicating with and involving parents and community leaders. The administrator is in a position to assume the role of communicating the purposes of the multicultural education program to all parents.

Parents and other community members may erroneously view the multicultural education program as a "frill" or as a program that takes much-needed resources away from the curriculum or other school activities. Parents may be skeptical of programs that were not integral parts of their own educational experience and of which they might have little knowledge. Programs that are misunderstood will likely receive little support from the general public. Such a situation requires a skilled and competent administrator who is able to garner the support of parents and other community members.

Principals who work in effective schools demonstrate confidence in students' ability to learn, a commitment to ensure students' success, and an understanding of students and their communities. Principals should do these things:

1. Believe that all their students can learn and reflect this belief in their goals.
2. Be concerned with the least successful students in their schools, rather than be satisfied that some students are doing above-average work.
3. Broaden the base of recognized achievement by acknowledging nontraditional accomplishments, particularly with minority students.
4. Acknowledge students who have exceptionally good attendance or punctuality records.

Principals must believe that all students can learn, have confidence in their students, involve parents in their children's education, reflect on the impact of the reform movement, and push for appropriate role models for all learners.

Gender Perspectives 13.1 looks at the gender differences in principals' approaches to planning.

From the Perspective of Classroom Teachers: Working with Administrators

Classroom educators need administrators' attention and support. Teachers and administrators must not work in isolation and risk the possibility that they will move toward different goals. Administrative support of teachers is imperative.

What, then, can educators do as they work with, and seek assistance from, administrators? Classroom educators who have direct contact with learners of various cultural backgrounds are in the best position to determine learner needs and convey these needs to administrators.

Educators, keeping in mind the many demands placed on administrators, must make their concerns known and insist on changes. Presenting the problem or concern is the first step. Working with the principal (suggesting, providing input, and offering recommendations) is the second step. Classroom educators, who have a better perspective on problems than administrators,

Points to Ponder 13.1

Seeking Information from Principals

Ask one or more principals or assistant principals to describe their multicultural education programs and their specific roles in the program. Specifically, seek information on how they have led school efforts to ensure that their school effectively reflects U.S. diversity. Ask also about school philosophy, library materials, efforts to celebrate cultural diversity, programs for students whose English proficiency is limited, and cultural diversity among their faculty and staffs.

Gender Perspectives 13.1

PRINCIPALS' APPROACHES TO PLANNING

Howley, Howley, and Larson (2007) investigated principals' preferred approaches to planning. Planning is a necessary or at least unavoidable process for linking organizational ends (e.g., goals, targets, anticipated outcomes) with organizational means (e.g., resources and technical processes). Recent attention to school-based management has shifted the burden to planning, especially for instructional improvements, to the principal. In fact, planning may be the only effective means for principals to address change and provide direction for their schools, whereas failing to plan might place their schools in jeopardy. These authors concluded that female principals are more attentive than males "to the human side of enterprise" (p. 32).

The authors' findings provide the basis for several tentative conclusions: (1) Female principals seem to be attentive to the types of planning that current reform initiatives call for; (2) female principals' planning seems to focus on the technical core of schooling; and (3) principals who have been in the role for a large proportion of their career seem either circumspect or cynical about the usefulness of planning.

Interestingly, the authors found that the percentage of years spent in administration was a negative predictor of planning.

Source: Howley, A., Howley, C. B., & Larson, W. (2007). Principals approach planning: The influence of gender and experience. *Educational Planning, 16*(1), 31–47.

must take responsibility for explaining the problems in accurate and objective terms. Once a problem has been explained and classified, the classroom educator's responsibility is to follow through on appropriate plans and strategies.

Evaluation of Administrators' Efforts and Commitment

Administrators' effort and commitment to multicultural education should be evaluated, just as educators' teaching effectiveness and learners' academic achievement are evaluated. The Evaluation Checklist provides examples of items to assess in determining administrators' effectiveness.

Evaluation Checklist

1. The principal demonstrates and models respect for all forms of diversity among students and their parents and families.
2. The principal seeks to employ faculty and staff of as many different cultures as possible.

3. The principal seeks to provide financial resources and other less tangible forms of support for the multicultural education program.
4. The principal works cooperatively with the school faculty and staff to provide effective multicultural educational experiences.
5. The principal supports a total-school program (curriculum, instruction, and environment), rather than the occasional teaching-unit approach.
6. The principal accepts responsibility for acting as a catalyst and for providing significant leadership for the multicultural education program.
7. The principal arranges for convenient sessions for parents and families of differing cultural backgrounds to voice concerns and suggestions.
8. The principal recognizes cultural differences among people as traits to be valued rather than to be eliminated or remediated.
9. The principal evaluates the efforts of faculty and staff and offers constructive criticism and positive suggestions in areas needing improvement.
10. The principal coordinates efforts of faculty and staff members toward a common goal of recognizing and building on cultural differences.

Special Educators

Roles in Multicultural Education

Special-education personnel can play significant roles in the multicultural education program. Tasks confronting them include the cultural considerations surrounding testing and assessment, the legal aspects of educating children with disabilities, the psychosocial variables affecting the teaching and learning process, and the effective coordination of efforts between special-education and regular classroom teachers.

Students of culturally different backgrounds are overrepresented in special-education classes. In the past, children who came from poor families or from homes where English was the second language or not spoken at all often ended up in special-needs classes. The role of special-education teachers includes responding to the increasing cultural diversity among learners by using culturally appropriate assessment devices and making placement decisions that reflect an understanding of cultural differences.

Testing and Assessment

Special-education teachers, like all educators, should exercise extreme caution when labeling learners of different cultural backgrounds. They must carefully distinguish between *disability* and *difference*. They must not make placement decisions based on faulty evidence or culturally biased assessment instruments.

Teachers should not consider learners intellectually inferior because of poor performance on standardized tests. Scores on standardized tests too often influence teachers' expectations of learners' academic performance in the classroom. Teachers must maintain high expectations for all learners, regardless of cultural background. A standardized test score can provide an indication of a student's degree of assimilation but provide little evidence of an individual's intelligence (Gollnick & Chinn, 2006).

In developing tests and in using the results of standardized tests, special-education teachers and all educators should recognize the inherent cultural bias that favors students of the majority culture. In fact, few tests have been developed from the perspective of a culturally diverse group. One such test is the Black Test of Bicultural Homogeneity (BITCH), which is based on urban African American culture and includes language and terms familiar to this culture. Although African Americans consistently score higher on this test than do members of the majority culture, it is rarely used to determine intelligence of individuals or groups (Gollnick & Chinn, 2006).

Special-education teachers should be constantly aware of the cultural biases among tests and remind themselves not to rely on test scores as the only indication of students' intelligence. Like all educators, special-education teachers should employ a number of culturally appropriate assessments and other sources of information to avoid basing placement decisions and judgments of intelligence on faulty data.

Legal Perspectives

Special-education teachers must understand the increasingly prominent role of the federal government in special education. The government has done more in recent years to promote the education rights of learners with disabilities than in the entire history of the nation. During this period, legislation has been notable for an affirmation of the education rights of students with disabilities. It addresses the problems of students who have disabilities as well as those who have limited proficiency in English. It also has provisions for nondiscriminatory assessment, parental involvement, and expanded instructional services.

From the teacher's perspective, the Education for All Handicapped Students Act of 1975 (PL 94-142) was a landmark law for students with disabilities in general and for culturally and linguistically different populations in particular. Among the most important provisions of PL 94-142 are those addressing the right to due process, protection against discriminatory testing during assessment, placement in the least restrictive education environment, and individualized education programs. In essence, PL 94-142 addresses the basic rights and equal protection issues with respect to the evaluation, identification, and placement of learners with disabilities. Under this law, assessment should serve to identify learners with disabilities and to guide instructional planning based on established educational goals.

Litigation, as well as PL 94-142, has also dramatically affected the educational system. Court cases have examined the legality of assessment, classification, and placement of low-achieving children and the right of learners who are severely disabled to a free and public education. These cases and other similar litigation have led to the establishment of the following legal standards:

1. Assessment of intellectual capabilities using measures in English is inappropriate for students with limited English proficiency.
2. Identification of children as mildly mentally retarded requires consideration of factors such as adaptive behavior, sociocultural group, and motivational systems, in addition to measures of intelligence.
3. The degree to which culturally different groups have been overrepresented in special-education classes for the educably mentally retarded (EMR) is sufficient to constitute bias. Causes of the overrepresentation have included (a) failure to consider linguistic and cultural factors; (b) failure to identify appropriately and to determine the eligibility of disabled students, and failure to provide proper procedures and special services; and (c) excessive reliance on IQ test results as placement criteria.
4. Factors such as item bias on measure of IQ and discriminatory instruments alone do not suffice to account for misplacements and disproportionate representation of learners from culturally different groups in special-education classes.

In summary, from a classroom educator's perspective, the placement procedures that special-education teachers employ must be in accordance with PL 94-142 and the litigation addressing the rights of the disabled. Classroom teachers are responsible for helping special educators understand all learners and the role of psychocultural factors in learning and assessment.

From the Perspective of Classroom Teachers: Working with Special Educators

From the perspective of the classroom educator, the special-education teacher should be considered a major instructional resource. Although teacher accreditation requirements mandate that all teachers have at least a basic knowledge of disabilities, most regular classroom teachers lack expertise in the techniques of working with children who have disabilities, especially those from culturally diverse backgrounds. When student needs can be addressed in the regular classroom,

classroom educators should seek help from special-education teachers. Similarly, regular educators should rely on qualified special-education teachers to handle students who, by law, cannot benefit from education in a regular classroom setting.

Special-education teachers must respond to the classroom educator's request to assess students in need and provide culturally appropriate testing and assessment. They work with regular classroom teachers to provide appropriate educational experiences for all students with disabilities (regardless of cultural background). They must understand the effects of cultural factors on the teaching and learning process. The classroom teacher should perceive special-education personnel as valuable resources whose training and expertise can contribute to the education of nearly any exceptional (or so-called normal) learner.

Classroom educators must follow appropriate procedures for referring students to special-education teachers. They must help special-education teachers understand learners' cultural diversity and provide follow-up as the special-education teacher recommends. It is important that regular classroom teachers view special-education teachers as partners and not as people on whom to "dump" unwanted students. Special-education teachers can provide educational assistance to learners who have disabilities as well as those who do not. In many cases, the organization of the school and the legalities of the referral process require regular classroom teachers to take the initial steps.

Evaluation of Special Educators' Efforts and Commitment

The following checklist provides special educators with a means of self-evaluation to determine strengths, weaknesses, and overall commitment to promoting cultural diversity. Ask yourself each question and answer it in terms of your responsibilities as a special-education teacher.

Self-Evaluation Checklist for Special Educators

1. Do I value and respect cultural diversity in all forms and degrees?
2. Do I recognize differences between disabilities and cultural diversity, or do I perceive differences as liabilities or deficiencies in need of remediation?
3. Do I coordinate the efforts of administrators, faculty, and staff to provide the least restrictive environment for all disabled learners?
4. Do I support a racially and culturally diverse faculty and staff for all youngsters with disabilities?
5. Do I insist that screening and placement procedures recognize cultural diversity and that such procedures follow legal mandates and guidelines for special education?

6. Do I work with parents and families on a regular basis, help them understand programs for learners with disabilities, and make referrals to appropriate social service agencies?

7. Do I use testing and assessment instruments with the least racial, cultural, and social-class bias?

8. Do I provide opportunities for youngsters with disabilities to be mainstreamed or integrated with nondisabled learners of all cultural backgrounds whenever possible?

9. Do I plan learning experiences that recognize differences in language and dialect?

10. Do I support community recognition and efforts to provide appropriate educational experiences for learners with disabilities from both majority and minority cultural backgrounds?

Librarians/Media Specialists

Roles in Multicultural Education

The librarian/media specialist in a multicultural setting must understand the cultural diversity of his or her school and build a library and media collection that shows positive portrayals of all cultural groups. Librarians and media specialists also work with classroom educators in positive, constructive ways that demonstrate a respect for and commitment to providing appropriate multicultural education experiences.

Selecting Culturally Appropriate Print and Nonprint Media

School librarians and media specialists, like all educators, are challenged to meet the needs of an increasingly diverse student population. Chapter 9 emphasized the importance of positive portrayals of children and adolescents from varying cultural backgrounds and the necessity of addressing problems of sexism, racism, stereotyping, and outright omissions. Libraries are responsible for ensuring that books, magazines, audiovisual materials, computer software, and all library and media materials positively and realistically represent characters of many cultural backgrounds with whom learners can relate.

One of the better and more pragmatic solutions to librarians' and media specialists' and teachers' problems has been offered by the Council on Interracial Books for Children, which regularly evaluates children's materials, trade books, textbooks, and other educational resources. This text (especially the appendix) provides examples of accurate literary descriptions of children and adolescents from various cultural backgrounds. Librarians/media specialists can refer to Table 9.1, a checklist for determining racism and sexism in children's books.

Coordinating Efforts with Classroom Teachers

Like other professionals working in elementary and secondary schools, librarians and media specialists and classroom educators must work together for the welfare of children and adolescents. Librarians/media specialists can be a valuable resource for regular classroom teachers. They can supplement learning experiences or provide a children's literature–based approach to instruction. Some classroom teachers received their education training before accrediting associations required experiences in multicultural education. For these teachers especially, librarians and media specialists can suggest culturally appropriate books for all children.

From the Perspective of Classroom Teachers: Working with Librarians/Media Specialists

The professional paths of classroom educators and school librarians/media specialists should probably cross more than they do. Teachers bring or allow learners to visit the library during a specified time, during which the librarian/media specialist might or might not have an activity planned. Teachers sometimes remain with students during the library period and make suggestions or encourage students' interest in books and reading. In other situations, teachers leave the students and work elsewhere.

From the perspective of classroom educators, the librarian/media specialist should be considered a prime resource professional. He or she can teach learners about the library and about books and magazines that provide positive cultural images. Teachers and librarians/media specialists must work together.

Librarians' and media specialists' roles in supporting the multicultural education program include stocking the library and media center with books, magazines, and other materials that accurately portray children and adolescents from various cultural groups; assisting classroom educators to choose and use these books; ensuring that library collections have works by nonwhite authors and illustrators; ensuring that library holdings and materials are accessible to all students, regardless of social class and cultural background; and assisting students as they search for reading materials.

The classroom educator's responsibilities include working with the librarian/media specialist (suggesting acquisitions and completing book request forms) to secure a multicultural library; encouraging students of all cultures to read books that provide accurate portrayals of learners from different cultural backgrounds; encouraging learners to read books by qualified authors; and working with the librarian/media specialist to plan activities that feature well-written reading materials.

Evaluation of Librarians'/Media Specialists' Efforts and Commitment

The following checklist provides self-evaluation questions librarians and media specialists can use to rate their own effectiveness.

Self-Evaluation for Librarians/Media Specialists

1. Do I acquire a collection of print and nonprint media that provides positive and accurate examples of children and adolescents from various cultural groups?
2. Do I have an overall library program that contributes to the school's multicultural education program?
3. Do I work with teachers and other educators to plan appropriate multicultural experiences for all learners?
4. Do I have a system that makes library materials accessible to all learners, regardless of cultural or socioeconomic background?
5. Do I plan developmentally and culturally appropriate teaching and learning activities for learners of all cultural groups?
6. Does the library have multicultural materials that are appropriate for varying reading, interest, and developmental levels?
7. Have I established and approved criteria for evaluating the appropriateness (cultural, gender, socioeconomic, etc.) of print and nonprint media?
8. Do I seek input and suggestions for library purchases from teachers, organizations promoting cultural diversity, and interested parents?
9. Have I acquired a professional library of print and nonprint materials for educators who want to improve their professional knowledge of cultural diversity?

Counselors

Roles in Multicultural Education

The role of school counselors includes understanding culturally different children and adolescents, providing culturally responsive counseling, understanding testing and assessment issues, and working with classroom teachers for the welfare of all learners.

Understanding and Counseling

Cultural, intracultural, ethnic, and racial differences are important considerations in the counseling of children and adolescents in multicultural situations. Learners are not a homogeneous population. They differ widely as individuals and particularly as pertains to culture, gender, generation, and socioeconomic status.

Children are basically now oriented and view their world, their cultures, their peers, their language, and their morality from a child's perspective. Adolescents function developmentally in a stage between childhood and adulthood and are developing self-concepts and cultural identities that will affect their entire adult lives.

American Indians

The dismal situations of many American Indian children suggests that guidance and counseling are the best vehicles for helping these children. Herring's (1989) suggestions include the following:

1. Counseling intervention should be highly individualized.
2. Assessment should have minimal socioeconomic or cultural bias.
3. Counselors should recognize learning styles and life purposes.
4. The child's culture must not be devalued.
5. Methodologies should place high value on self-worth.
6. The school counselor should help the school staff become sensitive to the needs of American Indians.

African Americans

School counselors should consider African American learners' individual heritages and special needs, rather than assume too much cultural homogeneity. Specifically, school counselors can organize self-awareness groups that emphasize self-appreciation through cultural heritage; explore the nature and importance of positive interpersonal relationships; conduct social behavior guidance groups; and offer motivation sessions and guidance workshops in areas such as academic planning, study skills, and time management.

Arab Americans

Counseling Arab Americans might be a little more intimidating, since more has been written on counseling other cultural groups. Still, counselors can look at the challenges these students face and implement counseling strategies that are culturally appropriate for the Arab culture. Suggestions for counselors include these:

1. Realize that Arab culture has been basically ignored in the school system, and it deserves to have culturally appropriate counseling strategies.
2. Develop a genuine awareness of the Arab culture and acknowledge, rather than devalue, the student's culture.
3. Remember that children's and adolescents' perceptions of situations and events might differ from the perspectives of youths of other cultures.
4. Avoid making assumptions about religious beliefs—if in doubt, ask the student about his or her religious beliefs, traditions, and customs.
5. Recognize the importance of the family, both immediate and extended, and respect it being patriarchal and hierarchal with regard to age and sex.
6. Provide counseling strategies that promote self-esteem and cultural identities.
7. Consider the students' generational status and the accompanying acculturation that might have occurred and how these might affect counseling intervention.

Asian Americans

Suggestions for counseling Asian Americans include the following:

1. Determine individual strengths and weaknesses, and assess cultural backgrounds.
2. Understand each learner's degree of acculturation.
3. Understand Asian Americans' difficulty in exhibiting openness. In a culture that regards restraint as a sign of emotional maturity, admitting problems is thought to reflect badly on the entire family.
4. Understand that overly confrontational, emotional, and tense approaches may cause additional problems and turmoil for Asian American learners.
5. Learn about individuals and their respective cultures; ask about the culture, accept the learner's world, develop cultural and ethnic sensitivity and consciousness, and avoid stereotyping.

Hispanic Americans

For the most effective multicultural intervention, counseling suggestions include these:

1. Use active counseling approaches that are concrete, specific, and focus on the student's behalf.
2. Develop an awareness of the individual's culture.
3. Use approaches that take the client's frame of reference as a vehicle for growth.
4. Examine prejudices and attitudes toward Hispanic Americans.

5. Make home visits if possible, and make reference to the family during sessions.

6. Call students by their correct names. In Puerto Rico and elsewhere, people have two last names: The first is that of the family, and the second is that of the mother's family. Using the wrong name is an insult and may raise identity questions.

7. Accept the role of expert, but work to relinquish the role of authority. Clients must accept responsibility for their own lives.

European Americans

Counselors working with European Americans should consider the tremendous diversity among individuals as well as individual cultures. European Americans come from many different geographic regions and cultural backgrounds. For example, children and adolescents with Hungarian backgrounds differ significantly from those with Greek backgrounds. Likewise, Polish people differ from Italians. Counselors should use extreme caution when forming decisions about cultural backgrounds, religious beliefs, and other personal characteristics. Suggestions for counseling European Americans include the following:

1. Understand some cultures' (such as that of Italians) allegiance and commitment to family members and to the overall welfare of the family.

2. Understand the language problems of some children and adolescents and how these problems affect school work, interpersonal relationships, and willingness to become active participants in U.S. society.

3. Understand cultural traditions that, in some cases, have been taught and emphasized for many generations, and understand how these cultural traditions might conflict with U.S. values and expectations.

4. Understand that considerable effort might be necessary to build trust in the counseling relationship.

5. Understand such differences as social class and generational status (e.g., the differences in perspectives of a first- and a third-generation child or adolescent) and the effects of these differences on counseling sessions.

Testing and Assessment

The counselor's goal in assessment is to minimize ethnocentrism and to maximize culturally appropriate information. Assessment in counseling and psychotherapy includes interviewing, observing, and testing, as well as analyzing documents. To what extent does cultural diversity affect assessment? Will a characteristic indigenous to a specific culture be mistakenly perceived and assessed using European American middle-class standards?

Two important issues in multicultural assessment include whether psychological constructs or concepts are universally valid and how to counter the effects of diagnosing and placing false labels. Other questions related to multicultural assessment are as follow:

1. What level and type of assessment are indicated?
2. Which tests are most useful and why?
3. What are the ethical and legal responsibilities associated with multicultural assessment?

Are multicultural groups being assessed with instruments actually designed for middle-class white clients? Without appropriate assessment strategies, counseling professionals are unable to diagnose problems, to develop appropriate goals, and to assess the outcomes of intervention. Specific assessment issues include initial client assessment, clinical judgment, standardized and nonstandardized assessment, and the outcome of counseling evaluation.

From the Perspective of Classroom Teachers: Working with Counselors

Counselors may work with individuals, small groups, and large classes. The classroom educator may initiate the first contact between a school counselor and a troubled student.

Classroom teachers, who have daily contact with learners, may be the first professionals to detect a potential problem. Individual teachers are in a prime position either to ask the counselor for direct assistance or to refer students with problems to the counselor. It is wise for teachers and counselors to determine the best means of referring students, of coordinating and scheduling large-group counseling, and of determining the correct needs of learners from diverse cultural backgrounds.

Counselors may provide several forms of assistance to classroom teachers and their students. Considering the many demands on the counselor's time and expertise, however, the teacher may have to initiate contact or inform the counselor of special areas of concern. Generally speaking, counselors can do these things:

1. Determine and facilitate joint efforts of administrators and other educators to improve an adolescent's self-concept and cultural identity.
2. Provide assistance in suggesting culturally appropriate instruments and in interpreting test scores of learners of culturally different backgrounds.
3. Work with families of all cultural backgrounds (both immediate and extended) in parent-education endeavors.

4. Offer parents meaningful roles in school governance, and offer families opportunities to support the teaching and learning process at home and at school.
5. Provide individual and small-group counseling in areas of concern to all learners, such as peer acceptance and approval.
6. Provide large-group counseling sessions in areas such as involvement meetings, rules meetings, and values-clarification meetings.
7. Suggest culturally relevant materials to help all children and adolescents better understand each other's cultures.
8. Work with older students in career planning, and suggest appropriate subjects needed to pursue career plans.
9. Help learners deal with concern over body development, the desire for social acceptance, and the conflicts between adult expectations and peer expectations of culturally appropriate behaviors.
10. Design special programs for at-risk learners who are from culturally different backgrounds.

Classroom educators should view their roles and those of counselors as complementary. Because classroom educators have the most daily contact with learners from various cultural backgrounds, they are usually in the best position to detect learners with problems, make referrals, and to follow up on counselors' efforts. Likewise, the classroom teacher and the counselor should always know each other's purposes and strategies and, whenever possible, provide joint efforts for the benefit of the learners.

Evaluation of Counselors' Efforts and Commitment

As with all professionals, the counselor's efforts and commitment to promoting cultural diversity and to working with classroom educators should be evaluated periodically. The following checklist can serve as a means of self-evaluation.

Self-Evaluation for Counselors

1. Do I recognize that all children and adolescents differ in their cultural background, perspectives, traditions, and worldviews?
2. Do I plan culturally appropriate counseling strategies that reflect learners' cultural backgrounds?
3. Do I recognize that traditional tests and assessment devices may not measure the abilities and talents of all learners because of their differing cultural backgrounds?
4. Do I recognize that families differ according to cultural backgrounds (e.g., in sex roles, expectations, and child-rearing techniques)?

5. Do I work with classroom educators for the overall welfare of learners from all cultural backgrounds?
6. Do I suggest special service agencies and resources that respond to the needs of learners and their families in all cultures?
7. Do I recognize the dangers of racial bias and cultural stereotypes and work to overcome these limitations?
8. Do I recognize the richness that cultural diversity adds to both elementary and secondary schools?
9. Do I recognize the need for all students to experience appropriate multicultural education experiences?
10. Do I recognize the need to use resources (e.g., films and other materials) that portray positive images of children's and adolescents' cultural backgrounds?

Communications Disorders Specialists

Several titles designate the professional working with speech-disabled learners, including *speech-language clinician, speech correctionist, speech clinician,* and *speech therapist,* but we prefer *communications disorders specialist* because the term is sufficiently broad in nature to include communication problems of children and adolescents from various cultural groups. The communications disorders specialist who works in multicultural settings has a broad knowledge of communication and understands unique communication situations, such as dialects, bilingualism, and teaching of English as a second language (TOESL), as well as the various assessment challenges and the differences between home and school language.

Roles in Multicultural Education

Because communication is such a vital human aspect to learners of all cultural and ethnic backgrounds, communications disorders specialists play an important role in helping educators distinguish between disorders and differences. They can also help learners who are experiencing differences with communication for any reason. All communications disorders specialists need to become sensitive to cultural diversity and to develop cross-cultural communication competencies as they work with children classified as non-English proficient (NEP) and as having limited English proficiency (LEP).

A primary role of the communications disorders specialist is to distinguish between communications disorders and communication variations and to convey to classroom educators the differences between the two. Communications disorders include speech disorders (impairment of voice, articulation, or fluency) and language disorders (the impairment or deviant development of comprehension of a spoken or written symbol system).

Communications disorders specialists in multicultural situations must distinguish between *disorders* and *variations.* Learners who use a particular dialect or regional accent should not be labeled as having a disorder in need of elimination.

A second, closely related role of the communications disorders specialist is to understand and to help classroom educators to understand the difference between school language and home language. A learner may appear so quiet and withdrawn that the educator wonders if the child or adolescent has physical or emotional problems. The same child or adolescent at home and in the community shows considerable verbal proficiency.

When substantial differences exist between conversational language use in the home and official use in the classroom, children and adolescents often appear to have low verbal ability. Despite being verbal in nonschool settings, these learners may talk very little in the classroom and, even then, use only simple words and sentences. In such a situation, the communications disorders specialist might have to convince the classroom educator that the child or adolescent is not speech disabled and is not in need of remediation or therapy.

Another goal of the communications disorders specialist is to understand dialect differences—among learners from differing cultural backgrounds as well as learners of the majority culture. Understanding and responding appropriately to the dialect of the learner within a classroom can be a complex and sensitive issue.

First, the specialist and teacher should recognize that dialects are not communicative disorders and should not treat them as such. The teacher should note, however, that a dialect and a communications disorder can coexist. If, for example, a learner with a Spanish or African American dialect also has defective articulation or stutters, the classroom educator should refer the learner to the communications disorders specialist.

Teachers and communications disorders specialists should learn to distinguish accurately between linguistic diversity and disorders. Dialects should not be considered less than but merely different from that which is recognized as standard English. A teacher is in a strategic position to promote understanding and acceptance of a child who has a dialectal difference.

From the Perspective of Classroom Teachers: Working with Communications Disorders Specialists

The classroom educator should view the communications disorders specialist as a valuable resource person with a wide range of expertise. Working in a complementary fashion for the welfare of learners, the communications disorders specialist and the classroom educator can determine whether communication problems exist that need to be remediated or whether students are simply manifesting variations that should be accepted and appreciated.

Considerable interaction should occur between classroom educators and communications disorders specialists. First, the communications disorders specialist and the teacher need to consult with each other about their goals for a learner and how they expect to accomplish these goals. They should evaluate what success they achieve. Such interaction can be formal or informal, or the communications disorders specialist can provide the teacher with copies of written therapy progress reports sent home to parents.

Second, the classroom teacher has more contact with parents and spends more school hours with learners, who may talk about their feelings, wants, and life at home. Some information that a teacher receives from learners or their parents may be important to the communications disorders specialist, and the teacher should pass it on.

Third, the teacher is in an ideal position to provide the communications disorders specialist with information about a learner's speech and language function in the classroom and in informal situations, such as in the hallway or lunchroom or on the playground. The teacher may also be able to provide reminders to the child during the habit-forming stages of therapy, when the child can best produce the targeted speech behaviors but still must make them a habit in all communicative situations. Fourth, the communications disorders specialist requires the teacher's input on referrals and in establishing whether there is an adverse effect on education because of a communicative problem.

The communications disorders specialist's responsibilities include appropriate assessment, therapy, scheduling, and consultation with teachers and parents. Other responsibilities in multicultural situations include understanding the communication problems of children and adolescents, conveying to teachers an assessment of disorders and variations, and providing a climate of understanding and acceptance for all learners.

The classroom teacher plays a major role in the lives of learners by serving as an important role model and a major force in shaping ideas and has an influence on emotional development. The classroom educator's responsibilities include being a good speech model; creating a classroom atmosphere conducive to communication; accepting learners, and encouraging classmates to accept learners with communications problems; consulting with the communications disorders specialist; detecting possible communications disorders and making referrals; reinforcing the goals of the communications disorders specialist; and helping the learner catch up on what he or she missed while at therapy. Another responsibility is fully participating when a decision has been made to place the child in a limited- or non-English-proficient program.

Evaluation of Communications Disorders Specialists' Efforts and Commitment

The following self-evaluation checklist enables communications disorders specialists to evaluate their efforts and commitment to multicultural education.

Self-Evaluation Checklist for Communications Disorders Specialists

1. Do I recognize and accept all learners, regardless of cultural, ethnic, or social class backgrounds?
2. Do I recognize how the increasing cultural diversity in U.S. school systems affects the roles and responsibilities of the speech professional?
3. Do I distinguish between communicative disorders and communicative variations?
4. Do I understand dialects as differences and not as disorders?
5. Do I plan appropriate communication for NEP or LEP students and seek the appropriate professionals to help these students?
6. Do I work with professionals responsible for bilingual students and assist as needed?
7. Do I work with classroom teachers and other school personnel in joint efforts to help children and adolescents of differing cultural backgrounds with communications disorders?
8. Do I understand the various speech and language disorders, and am I able to assist learners from differing cultural backgrounds who are having communications problems?

Service Learning

Administrators, special school personnel, and classroom teachers should encourage students to become involved with multicultural communities, whether in direct learning or service opportunities. Not only does service learning address children's and adolescents' feelings of altruism and idealism, but it also reinforces the content that they learn in school and helps them develop the skills to be productive citizens in a multicultural society. In essence, students become involved in activities related to the needs of the community while they are advancing academic goals and acquiring essential skills in real-life contexts (Hope, 1999).

The idea behind service learning is not just to involve students in multicultural communities (which in and of itself is also a worthwhile idea) but also to *reinforce* or *refine* actual learning objectives from the classroom. Students can tutor younger children or adults, organize a clean-up effort for environmental protection, or help preserve an endangered-wildlife area. Rather than having a one-size-fits-all program, each school needs to consider its own individual student population and community to see how community learning projects can be tied into instructional objectives and the multicultural education program.

*C*ase *S*tudy

Seeking the Special Educator's Help

Mrs. Heath, a tenth-grade social studies teacher, has noticed that four of the five American Indian students in her class seem uninterested. She wonders whether the students are really unmotivated, whether they have reading problems or attention deficits, or whether the topics being studied simply are uninteresting to them. Fully realizing the consequences of making judgments based on erroneous beliefs, Mrs. Heath takes her concern to the special-education teacher in the school.

Mrs. Blackmon listens carefully to Mrs. Heath's concerns. Mrs. Blackmon first decides to test the students' reading abilities to determine their reading vocabulary and comprehension skills. Second, she explains to Mrs. Heath that American Indians often listen without looking a person in the eye and that looking interested might be more of a white perspective, one that might not cross cultural boundaries.

Mrs. Blackmon feels that although the students' reading abilities are below grade level, they basically can read. She offers several suggestions to help Mrs. Heath and the students. First, she will work with the students two or three times a week to improve their reading comprehension. Second, she will help Mrs. Heath to provide some culturally relevant materials. Third, she will help Mrs. Heath to develop a better understanding of American Indian learners.

Without labeling or making unjustified placements, both teachers realize the importance of working as a team to help the American Indian learners. Each recognizes that working separately will not result in the most effective educational experiences for the learners. A coordinated effort, with each teacher reinforcing and building on the efforts of the other, will best address the needs of the American Indian learners.

*Q*uestions for *D*iscussion:

1. In your school experiences, have you noticed that some students seem uninterested or unmotivated? What specific characteristics or behaviors led you to believe they were uninterested? Could these have been attributed to cultural differences? Assuming they were interested (but did not show it), how would

their behaviors or characteristics affect *your* teaching behaviors or attitudes toward their learning?

2. While these two teachers seemed to have an effective collaboration, how else could they have worked together to benefit all learners and, in this case, American Indians?

3. What culturally relevant materials (see the Appendix) or teaching methods can you suggest that might be appropriate for American Indians?

Summing Up

Educators who are working toward the involvement of the entire school professional staff in the multicultural education program should:

1. Encourage all administrators and special school personnel to offer whole-hearted commitment and support to the multicultural education program. They should not perceive the effort as someone else's responsibility.

2. Convey to administrators, special-education teachers, counselors, librarians/media specialists, and the communications disorders specialist the importance of a total-school effort in the multicultural education program.

3. Emphasize the necessity for cultural diversity among the administration, faculty, and special school personnel that reflects the composition of the school and community.

4. Encourage administrators, special-education teachers, librarians/media specialists, counselors, and communications disorders specialists to recognize and respond appropriately to their unique roles in the multicultural education program.

5. Encourage administrators and special school personnel to work with regular classroom educators.

6. Convey the importance of evaluating all professionals (by self, peer, or administrator) for the purpose of learning ways to contribute to the overall multicultural program.

Suggested Learning Activities

1. Visit an elementary or secondary school to learn how administrators and special school personnel contribute to the multicultural education program. Are roles clearly defined, or are they assumed, whereby professionals simply do whatever appears to benefit the learner? How might administrators and special school personnel better address the needs of learners of differing cultural backgrounds?

2. Some professionals and the general public feel that learners of minority cultures are overrepresented in special-education classes. Meet with a special-education teacher to discuss the concern of overrepresentation. What legal mandates and

placement procedures protect minorities from being placed in special-education classes simply for being different from mainstream learners?

3. Consider the following Implementing Research, which looks at collaboration among school counselors and school psychologists.

Implementing Research

Collaboration among School Counselors and Psychologists

School counselors and school psychologists have a prime opportunity to collaborate to help children and adolescents. A culturally competent school is one that is successful in both meeting the challenges and seizing the opportunities associated with multiculturalism and diversity.

Simcox, Nuijens, and Lee (2006) propose a four-stage model of collaboration for school counselors and school psychologists. This model will contribute to providing culturally competent schools:

- *Level I: Student-Centered Interventions*—This level focuses on school counselors' and school psychologists' facilitating student development to ensure optimal academic development. It includes individual interventions as well as social development in needed areas.
- *Level II: Family Empowerment*—Educators have long recognized the importance of the family in educational pursuits, but sometimes the family is perceived as having a negative influence on academic achievement. Still, collaboration between families and schools can be productive in terms of academic achievement and psychosocial development.
- *Level III: Collegian Collaboration*—The school counselor and school psychologists can organize and facilitate professional development workshops for educators on ways to effectively develop a culturally competent school.
- *Level IV: Brokering Community Resources*—These professionals should partner to form alliances with key business, religious, civic, and political stakeholders from diverse community backgrounds.

Implementing the Research:

1. With regard to Level I, Student-Centered Interventions, educators and counselors can facilitate student development by promoting self-esteem, working toward social justice among students, working on motivation (remembering cultural concerns about motivation), promoting social development (e.g., the ability to get along with others), and working cooperatively with students of differing backgrounds.

2. In an effort to promote positive influences, teachers and other educational professionals can explain the goals of the school and individual classrooms and the need to promote social justice for all students. Teachers can also provide

experiences that reflect learners' cultural and socioeconomic backgrounds. It is important to remember objectivity, professionalism, and the need to avoid confrontations that might result from cultural misunderstandings.

3. Professional development workshops on ways to contribute to schools becoming culturally competent include topics such as diversity and its effects on student learning and achievement; cultural characteristics, especially those that are often misunderstood (avoiding stereotypical generalizations); parent involvement and education programs; and providing culturally relevant curricula, learning environment, and assessment experiences.

Source: Simcox, A. G., Nuijens, K. L., & Lee, C. C. (2006). School counselors and school psychologists: Collaborative partnerships in promoting culturally competent counselors. *Professional School Counseling, 9*(4), 272–277.

Suggestions for Collaborative Efforts

Form groups of three or four that, if possible, represent our nation's cultural and gender diversity. Working collaboratively, focus your group's attention toward the following efforts:

1. Prepare an evaluation scale that determines how print and nonprint media portray culturally different children and adolescents. Pinpoint such factors as objectivity, accuracy, stereotyping, gender values, and actual people from the various cultural groups (and what they are doing) and their contributions to an increasingly multicultural world. With the help of a librarian/media specialist, prepare a list of print and nonprint materials that provide an honest portrayal of all people, regardless of cultural background.

2. Brainstorm in your group to list special ways that administrators and special school personnel can contribute to multicultural education programs. How does your group think these professionals can contribute to or complement classroom teachers' efforts? What books or other materials can your group suggest to help each of these professionals?

3. How might educators and librarians/media specialists coordinate efforts to most effectively serve children and adolescents of various cultural backgrounds? Consider books, poems, speakers, films, plays, skits, computer software, and occasions to celebrate diversity.

Expanding Your Horizons

Additional Journals, Books, and Internet Sites

Andrews, M. L., & Ridenhour, C. S. (2006). Gender in schools: A qualitative study of students in educational administration. *Journal of Educational Research, 100*(1), 35–43.

These authors maintain that prospective principals must be prepared to lead schools committed to serving girls and boys equitably.

Howley, A., Howley, C. B., & Larson, W. (2007). Principals approach planning: The influence of gender and experience. *Educational Planning, 16*(1), 31–47.

These authors looked at principals' approach to planning and found gender differences.

Mitra, D. L. (2007). The role of administrators in enabling youth–adult partnerships in schools. *NASSP Bulletin, 91*(3), 237–256.

Mitra calls for administrators to take a role in youth–adult partnerships and offers suggestions for successful participation.

Richardson, J. (2007). Leaders can ensure that all students have access to quality teaching. *Journal of Staff Development, 28*(1), 61–62.

Richardson asserts that students can have quality teaching when educators have the proper staff development.

Tatum, B. D. (2007). *Can we talk about race? And other conversations in an era of school resegregation.* Boston: Beacon Press.

Educators at all ranks need to have a candid discussion of race at a time when some schools seem to be resegregating.

Education World. www.education-world.com/a_admin

This site looks at lesson planning, professional development, administrators, and technology integration. Specific pages address Nature of the Work, Working Conditions, Training, Other Qualifications, and Advancement, Employment, Job Outlook, and Earnings.

ERIC Digests. www.cricdigests.org/pre-9220/exceptional.htm

This ERIC Digest article focuses on multicultural education for exceptional children. After remaining level through most of the 1980s, the child population of the United States is on the rise. The number of persons under the age of eighteen will increase from 64 million in 1990 to 67 million in the year 2000. The number of babies born in 1988—3.9 million—was the greatest since 1964.

George Mason University. http://classweb.gmu.edu/cip/r/rs/rs-special.htm

This site provides special-education and culture resources for general instructional purposes, along with special-education and culture links for specific grade levels.

Rethinking Schools Online. www.rethinkingschools.org/special_reports/bilingual/Himu151.shtml

This site looks at the origins of multiculturalism, noting mainly that multicultural education can be traced historically to the civil rights movement. African American scholars and educators, working in conjunction with civil rights movement leaders, provided much of the leadership of multicultural education.

Issues for the Twenty-First Century

Understanding the material and activities in this chapter will help the reader to:

◆ Explain how racism continues to affect the United States, although conditions are better than they used to be.

◆ Explain why people often blame victims for the conditions affecting their lives, instead of seeking more plausible causes.

◆ List the arguments, pro and con, of standardized testing, and explain how culture affects testing.

◆ Describe how the issue of language and communication affects individuals and social institutions.

◆ List the responsibilities of professional educators to teach and promote social justice.

Opening Scenario

Recognizing Problems

Mrs. Smith, a tenth-grade English teacher, said despairingly, "I do not know what to do! Why don't these students try to work harder and improve their grades? They just sit there all day and do nothing. They didn't know today what I taught them yesterday. How do they expect to make something of their lives? I will never understand these people."

The assistant principal, Mr. Allen, overheard this classic blaming-the-victim statement and noted that it failed to recognize the real problem. All too often, people—especially those from culturally diverse groups—are blamed for being uneducated, slow learners, poor, and unable to find employment.

Mr. Allen thought of the consequences of such thinking and of considering all people from a middle-class, European American perspective. He knew that a serious effort was needed to look for more valid social, economic, and educational causes. The implications of blaming the victim can be widespread and influence educational decisions such as grouping, questioning, curricular trends, and teaching and learning activities. Yet the problem extends even further: Students are being blamed for not wanting to learn when they really do want to learn, and they are considered too unmotivated to change when, actually, change is extremely difficult. ◆

*O*verview

Multicultural education has progressed considerably as a means of explaining diversity and teaching acceptance of all people, but several issues remain unresolved. Educators should do whatever they can at least to reduce the impact of each issue; they cannot, however, solve them all. A societal response is necessary to combat racism and discrimination, the tendency to blame victims for their plights, and the issue of testing and assessing learners of culturally different backgrounds. This chapter examines some of the issues, not to make educators feel guilty or negligent but to describe obstacles to the progress of multicultural education and to show where present and future challenges lie.

 # Racism, Discrimination, and Social Injustice

Progress

Without doubt, people today are more aware of racism, discrimination, and social injustice. Even during times of racist acts, evidence suggests that there has been notable progress: More people from diverse cultures are joining the workforce in positions that require more than manual labor or custodianship. Opportunities in housing (although admittedly not equal) have improved, doors to higher education are open to the culturally diverse, and federal legislation guarantees equal rights for all people.

Examples of progress and the improved relationships between majority cultures and people of culturally diverse backgrounds can be looked on with pride, but educators must be careful not to assume that "all is well." There is room for improvement in reducing racism and discrimination and in providing a just and equal society for all people.

Lingering Racism, Discrimination, and Social Injustice

Although there has been progress toward reducing racism and discrimination, most would also agree that the U.S. society as a whole still has hurdles to overcome. More than fifty years after *Brown v. Board of Education* and more than forty years after the Civil Rights Act of 1964, racism and discrimination continue to impede the progress of many people. Increasingly, we see acts of violence toward people of all races and cultures and the increasing number of skinheads or neo-Nazi groups. Racial slurs, threats, slogans, physical assaults, and conflicts occur in schools across the nation. While *Brown v. Board of Education* ruled against legal segregation, de facto segregation (or segregation by the fact) continues to exist. Similarly, even with the Civil Rights Act, notable gaps in income and level of position continue to exist among racial groups, and in some cases, the differences are becoming more acute.

Institutional racism affects many children in the United States. Although people have voiced such issues as equal opportunity, desegregation, and inequities in educational achievement in recent years, few schools have developed deliberate and systematic programs to address these problems. Some believe that society has eliminated racism through legislative and special pro-

Points to Ponder **14.1**

Keeping a Constant Vigil against Racism

As stated previously, it is unlikely that racism will ever be completely eliminated. Still, racism affects and hurts all cultures and deserves to be addressed. Concerned educators and others should keep a constant lookout for racism—racist remarks, racist jokes, and racist actions. Name four or five specific steps educators can take to address racism.

grams, but overt racism and institutional racism continue to occur. Whereas many educators are on guard against racism of all forms, institutional racism, which is less blatant and therefore more dangerous, continues to hurt the aspirations and talents of many learners.

Racism or perceived racism can lead to stress for Asian Americans, just as it can for people of all cultures. In Gender Perspectives 14.1, Liang, Alvarez, Juang, and Liang (2007) examine coping, racism, and gender differences.

 # Blaming the Victim

Responsibility of Being a Victim

An issue facing some learners and their educators is where to place the blame for the minority person's plight. In essence, should the victim or the society be held accountable? For example, should lower-class African Americans blame themselves for their high unemployment rate and poverty, or should they blame a racist society that allows discrimination? Must American Indians blame themselves for their high school dropout rate and high level of alcoholism? Should Hispanic and Asian learners get the blame for their poor English skills? Responsive educators recognize that such questions are examples of the "blaming-the-victim" issue. They realize that children and adolescents are often victims of racism and discrimination and that all too often they cannot change the conditions surrounding their lives.

There are two orientations toward victims. First, people who hold a person-centered orientation emphasize the individual's motivation, values,

Gender Perspectives 14.1

COPING, RACISM, AND GENDER

Although most of the research on racism has focused on African Americans, new research is focusing increasingly on Asian Americans. Liang, Alvarez, Juang, and Liang (2007) examined stress and coping theory as a mediator of the relationship between perceptions of racism and racism-related stress among Asian Americans. Their results indicated that coping mediated the relationship between racism and racism-related stress differentially by gender.

These authors also identified an association between experiences with racism and lower levels of self-concept among Japanese Americans and Chinese American adolescents. Racism also predicted lower self-esteem and greater depression for Asian American youth. Among Chinese American adults, racism contributed to higher levels of psychological distress. The more men perceived racism, the more likely they were to use support-seeking strategies. The more women perceived racism, the more likely they were to use active coping strategies. Women were more likely than men to use emotional support as well as to vent their emotions. Men were more likely than women to resort to alcohol.

Liang, Alvarez, Juang, and Liang (2007) completed a comprehensive study on racism and stress, but the topic needs additional study. We think educators and counselors have long known (or expected) that racism leads to stress, but now we need to know how to work with both genders to reduce this stress. We also have a responsibility to reduce racism whenever possible.

Source: Liang, C., Alvarez, A. N., Juang, L. P., & Liang, M. (2007). The role of coping in the relationship between perceived racism and racism-related stress for Asian Americans: Gender differences. *Journal of Counseling Psychology, 54*(2), 132–141.

feelings, and goals. A person's success or failure is attributed to individual skills or inadequacies, and many people correlate ability and effort with success in society. Second, the system-blame view holds that success or failure is generally dependent on the social and economic system rather than on personal attributes.

It is easier for some people to blame victims for their condition than to look for more specific societal and economic causes. The consequences of blaming the victim, however, often extend further than just thinking that people deserve blame for their shortcomings. Blaming learners for their conditions is a practice that excuses or justifies many unjust actions: poor-quality educational programs in areas with victims, outdated and worn-out textbooks and curricular materials; teachers who give victims less wait time during questioning sessions, belief that poor or minority students cannot learn, and a plethora of other reactions.

More Humanistic Perspectives

Educators should offer a personal and professional commitment to victims of discrimination. Teachers must understand how children and adolescents become victims and the difficulty victims have in changing their lives. On a larger scale, educators should do their part in working to reduce the racism, poverty, despair, injustice, and discrimination that contribute to the victimization of people.

Points to Ponder 14.2

Avoiding Blaming the Victim

People sometimes find it convenient to blame the victim for such problems as language difficulties, being poor or homeless, and even for being culturally different. Working in groups of three or four, name several examples of blaming the victim. Think of an exercise that will show middle and secondary school students the problems associated with blaming the victim.

Testing and Assessment

History of Standardized Testing

Standardized testing dates back to the mid-1800s, and in fact, the problems associated with standardized testing have been similar over the years. The first documented use of standardized tests dates back to the period 1840–1875, when U.S. educators changed their focus from educating the elite to educating the masses. The earliest tests were intended for individual evaluation, but test results were used inappropriately to compare students and schools.

As millions of immigrants came to the United States in the nineteenth century, standardized tests became a way to ensure that all children were receiving the same standard of education. At the turn of the century, the focus of testing shifted from achievement testing to ability testing for the purpose of classifying students. Schools wanted to weed out students who were not going to succeed academically. Consequently, many ethnic groups faced new discrimination.

Educators have long known that standardized testing instruments are prepared from white, middle-class perspectives; however, they still test children and adolescents from culturally diverse backgrounds with these instruments that do not satisfactorily measure intelligence. One issue is why educators and testing specialists administer these assessment devices, especially when they have concluded that learning styles and cognitive strategies differ among cultures.

Valid and Invalid Uses of Tests and Test Scores

Valid uses of test scores include using standardized tests to provide a national ranking, predict future achievement, provide a means of curriculum evaluation, assist with policy decisions, and serve as a device to identify weak areas of the curriculum. Invalid uses of test scores include providing financial incentives for teachers with high student test scores, graduation or certification testing, a means of evaluating teaching, and a method of evaluating and comparing schools and school districts.

Several recommendations include the following: (1) Test score interpretation must be valid; test scores measure only a sample of a large domain of knowledge, and they should not be considered a means of evaluating the school curriculum or instructional emphasis. (2) Test score uses must be valid and educators need to examine and evaluate the consequences of standardized testing—for example, reporting test scores by racial or ethnic categories rarely serves useful purposes.

Zehr (1999) maintains that Hispanic students are not being tested properly, nor are their scores on standardized tests being used for the right purposes. Calls are being made for better tests for assessing Hispanic students, particularly those with limited proficiency in English. Nearly half of the nation's Hispanic students are considered to be have limited proficiency in English, and about 75 percent of students who fall under that category are in high-poverty-area schools. In addition, test scores should be used to hold schools accountable for providing an adequate education to Hispanic students.

Until that time, some question whether Hispanic's test scores should be used to keep them from being promoted or from graduating (Zehr, 1999). States are increasingly using statewide assessments to ensure that standards and learning benchmarks are being met. Plus, educators need to know if children are learning what is supposedly being taught. With this responsibility in mind, it is imperative that educators ensure the validity and reliability of assessment devices (Pappamihiel, 2002).

One major issue related to standardized testing and limited-English-proficient (LEP) students is the fact that many times these assessments are indirect tests of English proficiency rather than content mastery. In other words, LEP students cannot accurately demonstrate their knowledge of content and skills without relatively high fluency in English. They may know the content in their native language but not be able to express it because they lack sufficient knowledge of English.

Accommodations for these students are controversial. The most common accommodations for LEP students include flexible settings, flexible times, flexible scheduling, and the use of a translation dictionary. Still, some think these accommodations are rarely effective and can give the impression that LEP students are being given an advantage when they are not. Also, some think LEP students lack opportunities to learn in the classroom. LEP students often face serious hurdles due to their language limitations and also when schools test information that was inappropriately taught or cannot be expressed.

Language and Communication

Language and communication have been sensitive and controversial issues with far-reaching implications for learners and educators. Whereas some argue that English should be the primary language for all, others feel that a person's native language is a personal and precious aspect of his or her cultural heritage. The issue extends further, however. Should students be allowed to learn in their native language? What should educators do about dialects? Should learners actually become bilingual? This section focuses on dialects, bilingual education, English as a second language, and nonverbal communication.

Dialects

Although English is the primary language of the United States, numerous English dialects are spoken throughout the country. *Dialects* are variations of a language that groups of speakers share. The language variation typically corresponds to other differences among groups, such as ethnicity, religion, culture, geographic location, and social class (Gollnick & Chinn, 2006). It is important to emphasize that all people speak in a dialect of their native language.

Dialect is a popular term that carries a negative connotation. It sometimes refers to a particular variety of English that may have a social or geographic basis and that differs from what is usually considered standard English. Dialects may include such variations as black English, Hawaiian Pidgin English, and rural Appalachian English (Gollnick & Chinn, 2006).

What should multicultural educators do about dialects? One group has suggested that students be allowed to learn in their own dialects and that to do otherwise only further disables learners. Others have argued that schools have the responsibility for teaching each student standard English to better cope with the demands of society. There is little doubt that the inability to speak standard English can be a decided disadvantage to an individual in certain situations, such as seeking employment (Gollnick & Chinn, 2006).

There are several alternatives for handling dialects in the educational setting: The first is the accommodation of all dialects, based on the assumption that they are all equal. The second is the insistence that only a standard dialect be allowed in the schools; this alternative allows for the position that functional ability in such a dialect is necessary for success in personal as well as vocational pursuits. A third alternative is a position between the two extremes, and it is the alternative educators most often choose. They accept native dialects for certain uses but encourage and insist on standard English in other circumstances. Students in such a school setting may read and write in standard English, because this is the primary written language they will encounter in this nation. They are not required to eliminate their natural dialect. Such a compromise allows the student to use two or more dialects in the school. This compromise acknowledges the legitimacy of all dialects, while it recognizes the social and vocational implications of being able to function using standard English (Gollnick & Chinn, 2006).

Bilingual Education

According to the National Center for Education Statistics, 58 percent of all LEP students were born in the United States and 74 percent are Spanish speakers. The next largest language group is the Vietnamese, with 3.9 percent. Although bilingual programs for non-Spanish-languages groups can be found, few actually teach children to read and write in their native languages before teaching them these skills in English. These programs are bilingual only in the sense that they contain some measure of native-language support.

The theory behind bilingual education is that children must first fully develop their native language before they can achieve academic proficiency in a second language—a process that takes five to seven years, according to its proponents. In practical terms, children must be taught to read and write in their native language before they are taught those skills in English.

In a review of the research on bilingual education programs, Porter (1997) summarizes the findings of a General Accounting Office report that looked at five school districts. She thinks these findings are representative of all public schools with LEP students:

- Immigrant students are almost 100 percent non-English-speaking on arriving in the United States.
- LEP students arrive at different times of the school year, which causes upheavals in classrooms and educational programs.
- Some high school students have not been schooled in their native lands and lack literacy in any language.

◆ There is a high level of family poverty and transiency and a low level of parental involvement in students' education.

◆ There is an acute shortage of bilingual teachers and of textbooks and assessment devices in the native languages.

According to Porter (1997), the efforts being made and the money being invested in special programs to help immigrant, migrant, and refugee schoolchildren who do not speak English when they enter schools are largely misguided. The politically righteous assumption is that these groups cannot learn English quickly and must be taught all their subjects in their native languages for three to seven years while English is introduced gradually.

Porter (1997) does not think such policy is beneficial for most LEP students. In fact, her experience and a growing body of research show no benefits from native-language teaching, either in better learning English or better learning school subjects. Further explaining the issue, Porter also discusses the difficulty of voicing criticism of bilingual education programs "without being pilloried as a hater of foreigners and foreign languages and of contributing to the anti-immigrant climate" (1997, p. 31).

Proponents of bilingual education have recommended that children learn their native language prior to introduction of English. They believe that competencies in the native language provide an important literacy foundation for second-language acquisitions as well as for academic learning. Opponents recommend introduction of the English curriculum from the very beginning of the student's schooling experience, with only a minimal use of the native language. This approach is typically combined with an English as a second language (ESL) component.

English as a Second Language

English as a second language (ESL) programs are often confused with bilingual education. In the United States, the learning of English is an integral part of bilingual programs. However, the teaching of ESL, in and by itself, does not constitute a bilingual program. Both bilingual education and ESL programs promote English proficiency for limited-English-proficient (LEP) students.

The approach to instruction distinguishes the two programs. Bilingual education accepts and develops native language and culture in the instructional process. Bilingual education may use both the native language and English as the medium of instruction. ESL instruction, however, relies exclusively on English as the medium to assimilate LEP children into the linguistic mainstream as quickly as possible. Hence, some educators place less emphasis on the maintenance of home language and culture than on English-language acquisition, and they view ESL programs as viable means of achieving these goals (Gollnick & Chinn, 2006).

Beginning during the times of increased immigration from southern and eastern Europe at the turn of the century, there has been a concern in the United States about immigrants' ability to understand and embrace the principles of democracy. Language was seen as a part of the Americanization process. In recent years, English has become a central topic surrounding the education of immigrant students. Part of the difficulty is that most policy makers and members of the public have little information about what actually happens in schools. Still, far-reaching decisions are often made about immigrant children and how they should be taught English.

Educators of all curricular areas need to develop an understanding of ESL students—their problems, strengths, challenges, and individual characteristics. They can also gain an understanding of the language dilemma: Immigrant students must learn, yet considerable confusion exists in the public's mind about how students can best acquire the academic English necessary to succeed in school. Policy makers need to understand the challenges that immigrant students face and realize the far-reaching consequences of their decisions. Children and adolescents need instruction in English for success (social, personal, and economic); however, it might also be necessary to provide educational experiences in their native language, at least until students develop proficiency in English.

Nonverbal Communication

The issue of nonverbal differences and misunderstandings can be frustrating for both students and educators. To reduce the difficulty often associated with this form of communication, educators must analyze particular nonverbal behaviors when students do not respond as educators expect. Miscommunication may result from several nonverbal behaviors: A student may appear inattentive even when he or she is listening, a student may look away from the teacher when called on or addressed, or a student may interrupt at times that appear inappropriate to educators.

It is easy to jump to the conclusion that a student is not showing respect, when actually she or he is simply not following the unwritten rules of the classroom. In most school settings, educators expect learners from culturally different backgrounds to become bicultural and to adopt the nonverbal communication of the majority culture of the school. The ill effects of the issue lessen when educators also learn to operate biculturally in the classroom (Goll-nick & Chinn, 2006).

 ## Accepting the Responsibility to Be Professionally Qualified and Committed

First and foremost, educators must accept responsibility for being trained to work with students of differing cultural backgrounds. Regardless of the multicultural education program and its goals, efforts will succeed only when educators are trained in cultural diversity, understand the effects of culture on learning, and are able to convey genuine feelings of acceptance and respect for all people. Professional education for all teachers, not just those planning to teach in multicultural areas, should include content methodologies courses that show the relationship between culture and learning and how to address this relationship in teaching situations; first-hand practica and clinical experiences in working with learners from diverse cultural backgrounds and socioeconomic classes; and appropriate experiences in interpersonal skills.

We reemphasize that professional responsibilities include broad expertise in content, instructional techniques, and the ability to work with learners from differing cultural backgrounds. Responsibilities extend even further, however. Having knowledge of people, but holding on to racist attitudes and the belief that "different is wrong" will not provide responsive multicultural education. Knowing that a relationship exists between cultures and education is a prerequisite to effective teaching, but continuing to teach with styles and strategies appropriate only for one culture fails to meet the needs of children and adolescents of other cultures.

Ensuring Cultural Diversity in All Curricular Materials

A major responsibility that educators must accept is the commitment to ensure cultural diversity in all curricular materials. Educators play a significant role as they scrutinize all print and nonprint materials for bias and racism. This issue includes omissions as well as distortions. Educators are responsible for being on the lookout for material that shows people's culture in a derogatory light or in demeaning situations or that shows minorities in stereotypical images. Only two decades ago, families were portrayed as two-parent, white, and living in white houses with picket fences. Educators in most situations can readily perceive that most learners would be unable to understand or relate to such images in stories. While there has been considerable progress, educators continue to be responsible for insisting on materials and adopting textbooks that include culturally diverse characters and their families only in positive, fulfilling roles.

Ensuring That the Multicultural Emphasis Permeates All Curricular Areas and the School Environment

Another major responsibility of educators is working toward multicultural-ism in all areas of the curriculum and school environment. A basic assumption of this text is that multicultural education should be a broad-based effort that has the full cooperation and support of all school personnel, rather than a half-hearted effort.

Because schools are representative of our culturally pluralistic society, they must plan appropriate learning experiences for different children: Ameri-can Indian, African, Arab, Asian, Hispanic, and European American, as well as children and adolescents from differing economic, social, and religious back-grounds. Educators must answer many questions: Which (or perhaps whose) religious holidays will be observed? How will cultural differences affect testing and assessment? What special problems will learners from diverse cultures bring to school? How will learning styles differ?

These and other questions raise the overall question of what, specifically, should educators do. A one-time multicultural week or single unit featuring Afri-can American history, tacos, and oriental dresses and customs will not suffice. Such approaches have not worked and will not work, because mere awareness of diversity does not necessarily result in acceptance and respect for individu-als within the cultural group. The curriculum, learning environment, and the mindset of learners and faculty and staff must become multicultural in nature and must reflect the cultural diversity of the school.

Well-meaning multicultural education programs may serve only cosmetic purposes if students and school personnel harbor long-held cultural biases and stereotypes. Schools must not presuppose learners' abilities and behaviors based on stereotypes and myth: The school curriculum must genuinely respect cultural diversity and regard all learners objectively.

Involving Parents, Families, and the Community

Educators' recognition of the role of parents, the family, and the community in the multicultural education effort is an absolute prerequisite to the multicultural education program's success. Actually, two aspects are at stake, and both play a significant role in determining the success of the multicultural education program.

First, including both immediate and extended families and community members demonstrates concretely that educators are serious about accepting and promoting multiculturalism outside the school boundaries. When educators show that their efforts do not stop at the schoolhouse gate, such a commitment adds credence to the multicultural education program's efforts.

Second, parents, families, and community members can play significant roles when they come to visit schools and offer their participation. Educators may have to deal with parents' language differences, misunderstandings associated with U.S. school systems, and the reluctance of some parents to share strengths. Although overcoming these challenges requires both time and energy, the benefits outweigh the efforts expended.

Our devoting an entire chapter (Chapter 12) to including parents, families, and caregivers from differing cultural backgrounds shows how important we believe their role in education to be. The main issue is the extent to which educators genuinely want to effect multiculturalism. Children and adolescents who see only white parents in schools could easily conclude that cultural diversity is not as valuable as educators suggest. Although educators usually find it is easier to gain the attention of middle- and upper-class white parents, perceptive educators recognize the need to involve parents and families of many different cultures.

Points to Ponder 14.3

Promoting School Involvement

Many parents, families, and caregivers are regularly involved in school activities during the elementary school years. However, around the middle school years, involvement begins to wane, and in some cases, it all but disappears during the secondary school years. What can educators do to maintain the involvement of parents, families, and caregivers, especially minorities?

Case Study

Turning Ideals into Realities

Dr. McDonald, a high school principal, looked objectively at her school's lofty goals, objectives, and philosophical statements about multiculturalism, which spoke eloquently of valuing, recognizing, accepting, and respecting all people, regardless of differences. Then she compared these statements with what was actually happening in the schools. Surely the students could see that much of what was occurring was only rhetoric with no substance.

Without being overly pessimistic or cynical, Dr. McDonald asked herself several questions about the extent to which educators respect and address diversity:

- Do school policies reflect a concern for social justice and an understanding of the many different types of diversity?
- Do instructional practices reflect the diverse ways students receive and organize knowledge?
- Is there an understanding of motivation and competition in relation to learners from diverse cultural heritages and socioeconomic levels?
- Are efforts made to promote acceptance and social interaction between learners of all cultures?
- Is there a genuine respect for all people—their socioeconomic status, culture, gender, and sexual orientation?
- Do educators understand testing and assessment as they relate to the various diverse groups?
- Are the educators professionally trained and competent to work with students of diversity?

Dr. McDonald decided that creating a methodical plan was necessary to address these and other issues and concerns. Such an effort would take a large-scale approach and would include discussion groups, committees, in-service programs and activities, speakers, and an improved professional library.

Questions for Discussion:

1. Should Dr. McDonald take a large-scale approach (eight to ten goals per year) or should she take a smaller approach (one to three goals per year)? There are advantages and disadvantages of both ways. What approach do you think will provide the best results for teachers and students?
2. Generally speaking, do you think multicultural efforts are "only rhetoric with no substance"? If rhetoric, how might we make multiculturalism a genuine effort? In addition to diversity in curricula and teaching methods, how can schools create acceptance of others and their differences? Include honest respect, social justice, and different ways of thinking—one that perceives all cultures in equal perspectives.
3. How can Dr. McDonald address sexual orientation? While this a form of diversity that deserves recognition, not all people agree that the topic should be mentioned in schools. What programs or workshops might Dr. McDonald provide for teachers to help them understand sexual orientation as a type of diversity? What programs should educators provide for students? Remember to consider grade level and developmental level of learners.

Summing Up

Educators who understand the issues facing multicultural education and the challenges that such programs will face in the future should:

1. Understand that several issues affect the social and educational progress of children and adolescents from different cultural backgrounds and contribute to the degree of support the multicultural education program receives.
2. Understand the futility of blaming the victim for life conditions, develop more enlightened perspectives of the reasons people become victims, and recognize the difficulty in overcoming victim status.
3. Understand that a relationship exists between culture and testing and that learners' cultural backgrounds can significantly affect standardized test scores.
4. Remember that the language issue includes dialectal differences, bilingual education, and teaching of English as a second language and that all educators need to address learners' language differences and needs.
5. Remember that the ultimate success of any multicultural education program depends on every teacher's commitment to the program and to the acceptance of and respect for all people, regardless of differences or backgrounds.

Suggested Learning Activities

1. Discuss with several educators ways in which teachers may, knowingly or unknowingly, blame the victim for learning problems, socioeconomic conditions, or language problems. List several consequences of blaming the victim. Rather than blame victims for particular conditions, how can educators gain a better or more objective perspective of learners' conditions?
2. Write *your* definition of *multicultural education*. In your opinion, what differences should multicultural education include? Should it be only cultural, or should it include social class, gender, and religion? For example, do you think there is a culture of religion or a culture of social class? Does your definition include only knowledge of differences, or is appreciation of differences acknowledged or implied? Why are individual definitions of multicultural education important?
3. Consider the following Implementing Research, which looks at discarding the cultural deficit theory, a point we have tried to emphasize in the book.

Implementing Research

Discarding the Cultural Deficit Theory

Harry and Klingner (2007) explain that minorities are placed disproportionately in special-education classes. The categories with the highest minority-group placement are also those in which placement criteria are based on clinical judgment:

educable mental retardation, emotional/behavioral disorders, and learning disabilities. African American students are represented in the category of educable mental retardation at twice the rate of white peers; in the category of emotional/behavioral disorders, they are represented at one and one-half times the rate of white peers. In some states, American Indians and Hispanic Americans are overrepresented in the learning disabilities group. The root of this problem is intertwined in U.S. history.

Harry and Klingner (2007) look at the cultural deficit theory—the belief that some cultures or races are inferior or deficient in learning skills or ability to behave. The authors maintain that certain environment experiences could be exclusionary—poverty, detrimental home and community involvement, or lack of opportunity to learn. However, poverty itself does not cause learning difficulties.

When the tendency for intrinsic deficits is combined with the tendency to interpret cultural and racial differences as deficits, the result is often discrimination against minority students. Harry and Klingner (2007), who are opposed to the cultural deficit theory, argue that creating disability categories has become a way for schools to dodge their responsibility to provide high-quality general education. The deficit model is based on the normative development of students whose homes and communities have prepared them for schooling long before they enter school.

Implementing the Research

1. As we have proposed in this text, educators should stop thinking in terms of the cultural deficit theory, especially when students' placements and educational decisions are being made.

2. Educators should take advantage of recent revisions in the Individuals with Disabilities Act (IDEA) that allow for tiered interventions.

3. Professional educators will understand the history of racism and discrimination (perhaps unintentional in some cases) that has held back some minority groups.

Source: Harry, B., & Klingner, J. (2007). Discarding the deficit model. *Educational Leadership, 64*(5), 16–21.

 # Suggestions for Collaborative Efforts

Form groups of three or four that, if possible, represent U.S. cultural and gender diversity. Working collaboratively, focus your group's attention toward the following efforts:

1. Make a list of assessment instruments (and the addresses of publishers) that claim to reduce cultural bias in their test items. Provide two or three examples

of culturally biased test items. How might educators determine cultural bias in assessment instruments?

2. Survey a number of schools in an urban area with a significant percentage of students from culturally different backgrounds. What programs do these schools have to address language differences? Do language-minority youngsters receive equal opportunities, or are learners sometimes expected to learn and deal with language problems simultaneously? Looking at your survey, what language programs or approaches appear more likely to meet the needs of language-minority learners?

3. Educators often create their own professional development plans for improving multicultural competencies—for example, understanding diversity and the effects of culture on learning and providing culturally appropriate educational experiences for all students. In your collaborative groups, suggest a goal for a development plan, such as gaining first-hand experiences, completing college coursework, reading professional journals, and having in-service training.

 # Expanding Your Horizons

Additional Journals, Books, and Internet Sites

Amobi, F. A. (2007). The message or the messenger: Reflection on the volatility of evolving novice teachers' courageous conversations on race. *Multicultural Education, 14*(3), 2–7.

> Amobi maintains that audiences sometimes oppose the messenger more than the message in discussion of race.

Berriz, B. R. (2006). Unz got your tongue—What have we lost with the English-only mandates? *Radical Teacher, 75,* 10–15.

> Berriz, a fifth-grade teacher, thinks both educators and students have lost with English-only mandates.

Bonilla-Silva, E. (2006). *Racism without racists.* New York: Rowman & Littlefield.

> In this book, Bonilla-Silva explores with systematic data the nature and components of post–civil rights ideology.

Clark, C. (2006). What do we really mean when we say "Bilingual/Bicultural." *Multicultural Education, 14*(1), 56–58.

> Clark is uncomfortable with the terms *bilingual* and *bicultural* because they seem to refer to Latino people.

Harry, B., & Klingner, J. (2007). Discarding the deficit model. *Educational Leadership, 64*(5), 16–21.

> Harry and Klingner recommend doing away with the cultural deficit model.

Kraft, M. (2007). Toward a school-wide model of teaching for social justice: An examination of the best practices of two small public schools. *Equity and Excellence in Education, 40*(1), 77–86.

> This author investigated how a commitment to a socially just pedagogy influences the core and practices of schools.

Verdugo, R. R. (2007). English-language learners: Key issues. *Education and Urban Society, 39*(2), 167–193.

> As the title suggests, Verdugo looks at key issues in English-language learning.

America Online. http://members.aol.com/lacillo/multicultural.html

> This site is devoted almost entirely to multicultural issues.

American Speech–Language–Hearing Association (ASHA). www.asha.org/about/leadership-projects/multicultural

> The Office of Multicultural Affairs (OMA) of ASHA addresses cultural and linguistic diversity issues related to professionals and persons with communication disorders and differences.

Conflict 911. http://conflict911.com/resources/Diversity_and_Multicultural_Issues

> This site explores resolving conflict within a multicultural environment, noting the need to understand and appreciate innate diversities. You can increase your understanding by reading the articles in this category. Tips are offered on resolving conflict in a diverse workplace. The site also explores the relationship between culture and conflict.

Virginia Youth Violence Project. http://youthviolence.edschool.virginia.edu/juvenile-violence/multicultural-issues.html

> This site looks at multicultural issues as they relate to youth violence.

www.asha.org/about/leadership-projects/multicultural/readings

> ASHA's Multicultural Issues Board has assembled six fact sheets and twenty-six lists of suggested readings and related materials for individuals interested in obtaining a more in-depth understanding of multicultural issues.

Appendix

Literature for Children and Adolescents

African American

Applegate, Katherine. *Home of the Brave*. Feiwel & Friends, 2007. Ages 10–14

Booth, Coe. *Tyrell*. Scholastic, 2006. Ages 14–17

Cooney, Caroline B. *Diamonds in the Shadow*. Random House Children's Books, 2007. Ages 12–17

Draper, Sharon M. *Copper Sun*. Simon & Schuster Children's Publishing, 2006. Ages 14–17

Draper, Sharon M. *Fire from the Rock*. Penguin Group, 2007. Ages 12–17

Houston, Julian. *New Boy*. Houghton Mifflin Company, 2005. Ages 12–15

Johnson, Angela. *A Sweet Smell of Roses*. Simon & Schuster Children's Publishing, 2005. Ages 5–8

Myers, Walter Dean. *Street Love*. HarperCollins Publishers, 2006. Ages 13–18

Myers, Walter Dean. *What They Found: Love on 145th Street*. Random House Children's Books, 2007. Ages 14–18

Sachar, Louis. *Small Steps*. Random House Children's Books, 2006. Ages 10–13

Smith, Sherri L. *Sparrow*. Random House Children's Books, 2006. Ages 12–15

Stroud, Bettye. *The Patchwork Path. A Quilt Map to Freedom*. Candlewick Press, 2005. Ages 5–9

Vaught, Susan. *Stormwitch*. Bloomsbury Publishing, 2005. Ages 11–15

Weatherford, Carole Boston. *Freedom on the Menu: The Greensboro Sit-Ins*. Penguin Group, 2005. Ages 5–9

American Indian

Alexie, Sherman. *The Absolutely True Diary of a Part-Time Indian*. Little, Brown Books for Young Readers, 2007. Ages 12–17

Bruchac, Joseph. *Bearwalker*. HarperCollins Publishers, 2007. Ages 10–13

Bruchac, Joseph. *Wabi: A Hero's Tale*. Penguin Group, 2006. Ages 12–17

Erdrich, Louise. *The Game of Silence*. HarperCollins Publishers, 2007. Ages 9–12

Garcia, Emmett Shkeme. *Coyote and the Sky: How the Sun, Moon, and Stars Began*. University of New Mexico Press, 2006. Ages 11–17

Lerangis, Peter. *Smiler's Bones*. Scholastic, 2005. Ages 10–15

Marsden, Carolyn. *Bird Springs*. Penguin Group, 2007. Ages 8–11

Moonshower, Candie. *The Legend of Zoey*. Random House Children's Books, 2006. Ages 9–12

Orona-Ramirez, Kristy. *Kiki's Journey*. Children's Book Press, 2006. Ages 7–10

Pearsall, Shelley. *Crooked River*. Random House Children's Books, 2005. Ages 10–14

Taylor, C. J. *All the Stars in the Sky: Native Stories from the Heavens*. Tundra Books, 2006. Ages 8–12

Tingle, Tim. *When Turtle Grew Feathers: A Folktale from the Choctaw Nation*. August House Publishers, 2007. Ages 3–7

Wallace, Bill. *The Legend of Thunderfoot*. Simon & Schuster Children's Publishing, 2006. Ages 8–12

Wise, Bill. *Louis Sockalexis: Native American Baseball Pioneer*. Lee & Low Books, 2007. Ages 7–10

Arab American

Egypt

Bower, Tamara. *How the Amazon Queen Fought the Prince of Egypt*. Atheneum Books for Young Readers, 2005. Ages 8–11

Platt, Richard. *Egyptian Diary: The Journal of Nakht*. Candlewick Press, 2005. Ages 8–11

Iraq

Khedari, Betool. *A Sky So Close*. Haymarket Books, 2001. Ages 14–18

Winter, Jeanette. *Librarian of Basra: A True Story from Iraq*. Harcourt, 2005. Ages 5–9

Libya

Stolz, Joelle. *The Shadows of Ghadames*. Delacorte, 2004. Ages 8–12

Palestine

Baraket, Ibtisam. *Tasting the Sky: A Palestinian Childhood*. Farrar, Straus, & Giroux, 2007. Ages 11–16

Carmi, Daniella, & Lotan, Yael. *Samir and Yonatan*. Arthur A. Levine Books, 2000. Ages 8–12

Da Costa, Deborah. *Snow in Jerusalem*. A. Whitman, 2001. Ages 5–9

Ellis, Deborah. *Three Wishes: Palestinian and Israeli Children Speak*. Groundwood Books, 2004. Ages 11–16

Muhawi, Ibrahim, & Kananah, Sharif. *Tunjur! Tunjur! Tunjur! A Palestinian Folktale*. Marshall Cavendish Corporation, 2006. Ages 3–8

Tunisia

Gioanni, Alain. *Arafat: A Child of Tunisia*. Blackbirch Press, 2005. Ages 5–9

General Arab Countries

Demi. *Muhammad*. Margaret K. McElderry Books, 2003. Ages 8–12

Discovering World Cultures: The Middle East. Greenwood, 2004. Ages 11–14

Fernea, Elizabeth Warnock. *Remembering Childhood in the Middle East: Memoirs from a Century of Change*. University of Texas Press, 2003. Ages 15–18

Ganeri, Anita. *Muslim Festivals throughout the Year*. Smart Apple Media, 2004. Ages 8–12

Harik, Ramsay M., & Marston, Elsa. *Women in the Middle East: Tradition and Change*. Franklin Watts, 2003. Ages 11–17

Hartman, Sarah. *Middle Eastern Crafts Kids Can Do!* Enslow, 2006. Ages 5–9

Johnson-Davies, Denys. *Goha the Wise Fool*. Philomel Books, 2005. Ages 5–9

Mahdi, Ali Akbar. *Teen Life in the Middle East*. Greenwood, 2003. Ages 14–18

Marston, Elsa. *Figs and Fate: Stories about Growing Up in the Arab World Today*. George Brazillier, 2005. Ages 10–14

Nye, Naomi Shihab. *Flag of Childhood: Poems from the Middle East*. Aladdin Paperbacks, 2002. Ages 8–12

Nye, Naomi Shihab. *Nineteen Varieties of Gazelles: Poems of the Middle East*. Greenwillow Books, 2002. Ages 12–17

Asian American

Choi, Yangsook. *Behind the Mask*. Farrar, Straus, & Giroux, 2006. Ages 5–8

Cummings, Mary. *Three Names of Me*. Albert Witman & Company, 2006. Ages 8–13

Headley, Justina Chen. *Nothing but the Truth (And a Few White Lies)*. Little, Brown & Company, 2006. Ages 14–18

Kadohata, Cynthia. *Kira-Kira*. Atheneum Books for Young Readers/Simon & Schuster, 2004. Ages 10–14

Kadohata, Cynthia. *Weedflower*. Simon & Schuster Children's Publishing, 2006. Ages 10–13

Lee-Tai, Amy. *A Place Where Sunflowers Grow*. Children's Book Press, 2006. Ages 6–9

Lewis, Rose A. *Every Year on Your Birthday*. Little, Brown & Company, 2007. Ages 4–8

Lin, Grace. *The Year of the Dog*. Little, Brown & Company, 2006. Ages 8–11

Look, Lenore. *Ruby Lu, Empress of Everything*. Simon & Schuster Children's Publishing, 2006. Ages 6–9

Namioka, Lensey. *Mismatch*. Random House Children's Books, 2005. Ages 10–14

Park, Linda Sue. *Project Mulberry*. Random House Children's Books, 2005. Ages 9–12

Recorvits, Helen. *Yoon and the Christmas Mitten*. Farrar, Straus, & Giroux, 2006. Ages 3–7

Salisbury, Graham. *House of the Red Fish*. Random House Children's Books, 2006. Ages 10–14

Wong, Joyce Lee. *Seeing Emily*. Harry N. Abrams, 2005. Ages 14–18

Yang, Gene Luen. *American Born Chinese*. First Second, 2006. Ages 13–18

European American List

Sweden

Lindgren, Astrid. *The Red Bird*. Scholastic, 2005. Ages 7–9

Sandin, Joan. *At Home in a New Land*. HarperCollins, 2007. Ages 6–9

Wahl, Mats. *The Invisible*. Farrar, Straus, & Giroux, 2007. Ages 12–17

Spain

Aska, Warabe. *Tapicero Tap Tap*. Tundra Books, 2006. Ages 4–7

Grandbois, Peter. *The Gravedigger*. Chronicle Books, 2006. Ages 12–15

Hoffman, Alice. *Incantation*. Little, Brown Books for Young Readers, 2006. Ages 14–18

Jellen, Michelle. *Spain or Shine*. Penguin Group, 2006. Ages 11–14

United Kingdom

Cooper, Susan. *Victory*. Simon & Schuster, 2006. Ages 9–13

King, Donna. *Kick Off*. Houghton Mifflin Company, 2007. Ages 8–12

France

Hartnett, Sonya. *The Silver Donkey*. Walker Books, 2006. Ages 9–13

McCaughrean, Geraldine. *Cyrano*. Oxford University Press, 2006. Ages 14–18

Ireland

Dowd, Siobhan. *A Swift Pure Cry*. Random House Children's Books, 2006. Ages 14–18

Melling, O. R. *The Summer King*. Harry N. Abrams, 2006. Ages 13–17

Italy

Hamilton, Martha, & Weiss, Mitch. *Priceless Gifts: A Folktale from Italy*. August House, 2007. Ages 5–8

Lasky, Kathryn. *The Last Girls of Pompeii*. Penguin Group, 2007. Ages 10–13

Germany

Schmemann, Serge. *When the Wall Came Down: The Berlin Wall and the Fall of Soviet Communism*. Houghton Mifflin Company, 2006. Ages 11–17

Zusak, Marcus. *The Book Thief*. Random House, 2006. Ages 14–18

General Europe

Byers, Ann. *The History of U.S. Immigration: Coming to America*. Enslow, 2006. Ages 10–13

Morpurgo, Michael. *I Believe in Unicorns*. Walker Books, 2006. Ages 7–11

Peacock, Louise. *At Ellis Island: A History of Many Voices*. Simon & Schuster, 2007. Ages 7–10

Tan, Shaun. *The Arrival: Brothers*. Penguin Group, 2006. Ages 7–11

Hispanic American

Bernier-Grand, Carmen T. *César: Si, Se Puede! Yes, We Can!* Marshall Cavendish Corporation, 2004. Ages 8–12

Brown, Monica. *My Name Is Celia: The Life of Celia Cruz*. Northland Publishing, 2004. Ages 5–9

Canales, Viola. *The Tequila Worm*. Random House Children's Books, 2005. Ages 12–17

Carlson, Lori Marie. *Red Hot Salsa: Bilingual Poems on Being Young and Latino in the United States*. Henry Holt & Company, 2005. Ages 13–18

Charlton-Trujillo, E. E. *Prizefighter en Mi Casa*. Random House Children's Books, 2006. Ages 10–13

Hobbs, Will. *Crossing the Wire*. HarperCollins Publishers, 2006. Ages 12–16

Lopez, Jack. *In the Break*. Little, Brown & Company, 2006. Ages 14–18

Manzano, Sonia. *A Box Full of Kittens*. Simon & Schuster Children's Publishing, 2006. Ages 3–7

Mora, Pat. *Doña Flor: A Tall Tale about a Giant Lady with a Great Big Heart*. Random House Children's Books, 2005. Ages 4–8

Muñoz Ryan, Pam. *Becoming Naomi León*. Scholastic, 2004. Ages 8–12

Saenz, Benjamin Alire. *Sammy and Juliana in Hollywood*. HarperCollins Publishers, 2004. Ages 14–18

Sanchez, Alex. *Getting It*. Simon & Schuster Children's Publishing, 2006. Ages 12–16

Sanna, Ellyn. *Latino Folklore and Culture: Stories of Family, Traditions of Pride*. Mason Crest Publishers, 2006. Ages 12–15

Soto, Gary. *Accidental Love*. Harcourt Children's Books, 2006. Ages 11–15

Soto, Gary. *Help Wanted: Stories*. Harcourt Children's Books, 2005. Ages 11–14

References and Additional Readings

100 Questions and answers about Arab Americans: A journalist's guide. *Detroit Free Press* www.freep.com/jobspage/arabs.

Abrams, R. D. (1993). Meeting the educational and cultural needs of Soviet newcomers. *Religious Education, 88*(2), 315–323.

Abalos, D. T. (2007). *Latinos in the United States: The sacred and the political.* Notre Dame, IN: University of Notre Dame Press.

Aberle, J. M., Krafchick, J. L., & Zimmerman, T. S. (2005). FAIR: A diversity and social justice curriculum for school. *Guidance and Counseling, 21*(1), 47–56.

Abrams, L. S., & Gibson, P. (2007). Reframing multicultural education: Teaching white privilege in the social work curriculum. *Journal of Social Work Education, 43*(1), 147–160.

Abudabbeh, N. (1996). Arab families. In M. McGoldrick, J. Girodano, & J. K. Pearce (Eds.), *Ethnicity and family therapy* (2nd ed.) (pp. 333–346). New York: Guilford.

Ajrouch, K. J. (2004). Gender, race, and symbolic boundaries: Contested spaces of identity among Arab American adolescents. *Sociological Perspectives, 47*(4), 371–392.

Alba, R. D. (1985). *Italian Americans into the twilight of ethnicity.* Englewood Cliffs, NJ: Prentice-Hall.

Al-Hazza, T., & Lucking, R. (2005). The minority of suspicion: Arab Americans. *MultiCultural Review, 14*(3), 32–38.

Allen, J., & Labbo, L. (2001). Giving it a second thought: Making culturally engaged teaching culturally engaging. *Language Arts, 79*(1), 40–52.

Altshuler, S. J., & Schmautz, T. (2006). No Hispanic student left behind: The consequences of "high stakes" testing. *Children & Schools, 28*(1), 5–14.

Alvarez, A. N., Juang, L., & Liang, C. T. H. (2006). Asian Americans and racism: When bad things happen to "model minorities." *Cultural Diversity and Ethnic Minority Psychology, 12*(3), 477–492.

American Psychological Association, Task Force on Socioeconomic Status. (2007). *Report of the APA Task Force on Socioeconomic Status.* Washington, DC: American Psychological Association.

Andrews, M. L., & Ridenhour, C. S. (2006). Gender in schools: A qualitative study of students in educational administration. *The Journal of Educational Research, 100*(1), 35–43.

Anokye, A. D. (1997). A case for orality in the classroom. *The Clearing House, 70*(5), 229–231.

Ariza, E. N. (2000). Actions speak louder than words—Or do they? Debunking the myth of apathetic immigrant parents in education. *Contemporary Education, 71*(3), 36–38.

Armitage, J. S., & Dugan, R. E. (2006). Marginalized experiences of Hispanic females in youth-based religious groups. *Journal for the Scientific Study of Religion, 45*(2), 217–231.

Asher, N. (2007). Made in the (multicultural) U.S.A.: Unpacking tensions of race, culture, gender, and sexuality in education. *Educational Researcher, 36*(2), 65–73.

August, D., Goldenberg, C., & Rueda, R. (2006). Native American children and youth: Culture, language, and literacy. *Journal of American Education, 45*(3), 24–37.

Axelson, J. A. (1999). *Counseling and development in a multicultural society* (2nd ed.). Monterey, CA: Brooks/Cole.

Baca, L. M., & Cervantes, H. T. (1989). *The bilingual special education interface.* Columbus, OH: Merrill.

Banks, J. A. (1988). *Multiethnic education: Theory and practice.* Boston: Allyn & Bacon.

Barack, L. (2006). HS gender gap studied. *School Library Journal, 52*(6), 22.

Barnett, R. C., & Rivers, C. (2007). Gender myths and the education of boys. *Independent School, 66*(2), 96, 98.

Barrera, R. M. (2001). Bringing home to school. *Scholastic Early Childhood Today, 16*(3), 44–56.

Baunach, D. M. (2001). Gender inequality in childhood: Toward a life course perspective. *Gender Issues, 19*(3), 61–86.

Bell-Scott, P., & McKenry, P. C. (1986). Black adolescents and their families. In G. K. Leigh & G. W. Peterson (Eds.), *Adolescents in families* (pp. 410–432). Cincinnati, OH: Southwestern.

Berriz, B. R. (2006). Unz got your tongue: What we have lost with the English-only mandates. *Radical Teacher, 75*, 10–15.

Bigelow, B. (2007). Rethinking the line between us. *Educational Leadership, 64*(6), 47–51.

Binder, A. J. (2000). Why do some curricular challenges work while others do not? The case of three Afrocentric challenges. *Sociology of Education, 73*, 69–91.

Birenbaum, M., Nassar, F., & Tatsuoka, C. Y. (2007). Effects of gender and ethnicity on fourth graders' knowledge states in mathematics. *International Journal of Mathematical Education in Science and Technology, 38*(3), 301–309.

Birkel, L. F. (2000). Multicultural education: It is education first of all. *Teacher Educator, 36*(1), 23–28.

Black, S., Wright, T., & Erickson, L. (2001). Polynesian folklore: An alternative to plastic toys. *Children's Literature in Education, 32*(2), 125–137.

Blanchett, W. J. (2006). Disproportionate representation of African American students in special education: Acknowledging the role of white privilege and racism. *Educational Researcher, 35*(6), 24–28.

Bolgatz, J. (2005). *Talking race in the classroom.* New York: Teachers College Press.

Bonner, F. A., & Jennings, M. (2007). Never too young to lead: Gifted African American males in elementary school. *Gifted Child Today, 30*(2), 30–36.

Boyle-Baise, M., Epler, B., McCoy, W., Paulk, G., Clark, J., Slough, N., & Truelock, C. (2001). Shared control: Community voices in multicultural learning. *The Educational Forum, 65*, 344–353.

Brown, P. L., & Abell, S. K. (2007). Cultural diversity in the science classroom. *Science and Children, 44*(9), 60–61.

Butler, D. A., & Manning, M. L. (1998). *Gender differences in young adolescents.* Olney, MD: Association for Childhood Education International.

Campano, G. (2007). *Immigrant students and literacy: Reading, writing, and remembering.* New York: Teachers College Press.

CampbellJones, B., & CampbellJones, F. (2002). Educating African American children: Credibility at the crossroads. *Educational Horizons 80*(3), 133–139.

Carpenter, S., Zarate, M. A., & Garcia, A. A. (2007). Cultural pluralism and prejudice reduction. *Cultural Diversity and Ethnic Minority Psychology, 13*(2), 83–93.

Carroll, M. (2001). Dim sum, bagels, and grits: A sourcebook for multicultural families. *Booklist, 97*(12), 1096.

Castleman, B., & Littky, D. (2007). Learning to love learning. *Educational Leadership, 64*(8), 58–61.

Chan, E. (2007). Student experiences of a culturally-sensitive curriculum: Ethnic identity development and conflicting stories to live by. *Journal of Curriculum Studies, 39*(2), 177–194.

Chang, M. T. (2001). Is it more than about getting along? The broader educational relevance of reducing students' racial biases. *Journal of College Student Development, 42*(2), 93–105.

Chavkin, N. F., & Gonzalez, J. (2000). Mexican immigrant youth and resiliency: Research and promising programs. Charleston, WV: ERIC Clearinghouse on Rural Education and Small Schools. (ERIC Document Reproduction Service No. ED 447990)

Chiang, L. H. (2000). Teaching Asian American students. *Teacher Educator, 36*(1), 58–69.

Chiu, M. M. (2007). Families, economies, cultures, and science achievement in 41 countries: Country, school, and student level analyses. *Journal of Family Psychology, 21*(3), 510–519.

Chong, D., & Kim, D. (2006). The experiences and effects of economic status among racial and ethnic minorities. *American Political Science Review, 100*(3), 335–351.

Christensen, L. M. (2007). Children and social change in Alabama: 1965–2005. *Social Studies and the Young Learner, 20*(1), 22–24.

Clark, A. A., & Dorris, A. (2006). Welcoming Latino parents as partners. *Principal Leadership, 7*(3), 22–25.

Cohall, A. T., Cohall, R., Dye, B., Dini, S., Vaughn, R. D., & Coots, S. (2007). Overheard in the halls: What adolescents are saying, and what teachers are hearing. *The Journal of School Health, 77*(7), 344–350.

Congress, E. P., & Gonzalez, M. J. (2005). *Multicultural perspectives in working with families.* New York: Spring.

Connor, C. M., & Craig, H. K. (2006). African American preschoolers' language, emergent literacy skills, and use of African American English: A complex relation. *Journal of Speech, Language, and Hearing Research, 49*(4), 771–792.

Consedine, N. S., Sabag-Cohen, S., & Krivoshekova, Y. S. (2007). Ethnic, gender, and socioeconomic differences in young adults' self-disclosure: Who discloses what and to whom? *Cultural Diversity and Ethnic Minority Psychology, 13*(3), 254–263.

Constantine, M. G., & Blackmon, S. M. (2002). Black adolescents' racial socialization experiences: Their relations to home, school, and peer self-esteem. *Journal of Black Studies, 32*(3), 322–335.

Crawford, J. (2007, June 6). A diminished vision of civil rights. *Education Week, 26*(39), 30–31.

Crotteau, M. (2007). Honoring dialect and culture: Pathways to student success on high-stakes writing assessments. *English Journal, 96*(4), 27–31.

Datnow, A. (2006). *Integrating educational systems for successful reform in diverse contexts.* England: Cambridge University Press.

Demmert, W. G., Grissmer, D., & Towner, J. (2006). A review and analysis of the research on Native American students. *Journal of American Education, 45*(3), 5–23.

Demmert, W. G., McCardle, P., Mele-McCarthy, J., & Leos, K. (2006). Preparing Native American children for academic success: A blueprint for research. *Journal of American Education, 45*(3), 92–106.

Dils, A. K. (2002). Service learning can narrow the potential mismatch between future teachers and their students. *ACEI Focus on Teacher Education, 3*(1), 1–3.

Doan, K. (2006). A sociocultural perspective on at-risk Asian American students. *Teacher Education and Special Education, 29*(3), 157–167.

Duffy, J. (2007). *Writing from these roots: Literacy in a Hmong-American community.* Honolulu: University of Hawaii Press.

Duke, C. (2007). Conceptualizing special education services in small learning communities. *Urban Education, 42*(5), 412–431.

Education and gender. (1994, June 3). *Congressional Quarterly Researcher, 4*(21), 482–503.

Eisner, E. (2006). The satisfactions of teaching. *Educational Leadership, 63*(6), 44–46.

Erkut, S., Szalacha, L. A., Coll, C. G., & Alarcon, O. (2000). Puerto Rican early adolescents' self-esteem patterns. *Journal of Research on Adolescence, 10*(3), 339–364.

Espinosa, G. (2007). Today we act, tomorrow we vote: Latino religions, politics, and activism in contemporary U.S. civil society. *Annals of the American Academy of Political and Social Science, 612*(1), 152–172.

Farver, J. M., Yiyuan, X., Bakhtawar, R., Narang, B. S., & Lieber, E. (2007). Ethnic identity, acculturation, parenting beliefs, and adolescent adjustment. *Merrill-Palmer Quarterly, 53*(2), 184–215.

Feng, J. (1994, June). Asian-American children: What teachers should know. *ERIC Digest,* 1–2.

Ferdman, B. M. (2000). "Why am I who I am?" Constructing the cultural self in multicultural perspective. *Human Development, 43*, 19–23.

Fish, L. S. (2000). Hierarchical relationship development: Parents and children. *Journal of Marital and Family Therapy, 26*(4), 501–510.

Fitzpatrick, K. M., Dulin, A. J., & Piko, B. F. (2007). Not just pushing and shoving: School bullying among African American learners. *The Journal of School Health, 77*(1), 16–22.

Flanagan, C. A., Gill, S., Cumsille, P., & Gallay, L. S. (2007). School and community climates and civic commitments: Patterns for ethnic minority and majority students. *Journal of Educational Psychology, 99*(2), 421–433.

Fleming, W. C. (2007). Getting past our myths and stereotypes about Native Americans. *Education Digest, 72*(7), 51–57.

Ford, D. Y., & Harmon, D. A. (2001). Equity and excellence: Providing access to gifted education for culturally diverse students. *The Journal of Secondary Gifted Education, 12*(3), 141–147.

Fryer, R. G. (2006). Acting white. *Education Next, 6*(1), 52–59.

Galen, J. (2007). Late to class: Social class and schooling in the new economy. *Educational Horizons, 85*(3), 156–167.

Gallavan, N. P. (2000). Multicultural education at the academy: Teacher educators' challenges, conflicts, and coping skills. *Equity and Excellence in Education, 33*(3), 5–12.

García, E. E. (2005). *Teaching and learning in two languages: Bilingualism and schooling in the United States.* New York: Teachers College Press.

Geenen, S., Powers, L. E., & Lopez-Vasquez, A. (2001). Multicultural aspects of parent involvement in transitional planning. *Exceptional Children, 67*(1), 265–275.

Gerber, D. A. (2001). Forming a transnational narrative: New perspectives on European migrations to the United States. *History Teacher, 35*(1), 61–77.

Gollnick, D. M., & Chinn, P. C. (2006). *Multicultural education in a pluralistic society* (7th ed.). Upper Saddle River, NJ: Merrill.

Gorski, P. C. (2006). Beyond propaganda: Resources from Arab film distribution. *Multicultural Education, 13*(3), 56–57.

Grattet, Y. (2000). Hate crimes: Better data or increasing frequency? *Population Today, 28*(5), 1, 4.

Haboush, K. L. (2007). Working with Arab American families: Culturally competent practice for school psychologists. *Psychology in the Schools, 44*(2), 183–198.

Hackman, H. (2006). I exist: Voices from the Middle Eastern lesbian and gay community. *Multicultural Education, 13*(3), 56–57.

Hale-Benson, J. E. (1986). *Black children: Their roots and their culture* (rev. ed.). Baltimore, MD: Johns Hopkins University.

Hamilton, K., & Krashen, S. (2006). Bilingual or immersion? *Diverse Issues in Higher Education, 23*(5), 23–26.

Hays, D. G., & Chang, C. Y. (2003). White privilege, oppression, and racial identity development: Implications for supervision. *Counselor Education and Supervision, 43,* 134–145.

Hays, D. G., Chang, C. Y., & Dean, J. K. (2004). White counselors' conceptualization of privilege and oppression: Implications for counselor training. *Counselor Education and Supervision, 43,* 242–257.

Henry, B., & Klingner, J. (2007). Discarding the deficit model. *Educational Leadership, 64*(5), 16–21.

Hernandez, H. (1989). *Multicultural education: A teacher's guide to content and process.* Columbus, OH: Merrill.

Herring, R. D. (1989). Counseling Native American children: Implications for elementary school counselors. *Elementary School Guidance and Counseling, 23,* 272–281.

Hodgkinson, H. (1998). The demographics of diversity. *Principal 78*(1), 26–32.

Hoerr, T. R. (2007). Affirming diversity. *Educational Leadership, 64*(6), 87–88.

Hope, W. C. (1999). Service learning: A reform initiative for middle school curriculum. *The Clearing House, 72*(4), 236–238.

House, N. G. (2005). Reclaiming children left behind. *School Administrator, 62*(1), 10–15.

Howard, A. S., & Solberg, S. H. (2006). School-based social justice: The achieving success identity pathways program. *Professional School Counseling, 9*(4), 278–287.

Howard, G. R. (2007). As diversity grows, so must we. *Educational Leadership, 64*(6), 16–22.

Howard, T. C. (2001). Telling their side of the story: African American students' perceptions of culturally relevant teaching. *Urban Review, 33*(2), 131–149.

Howard-Hamilton, M. F. (2000). Creating a culturally responsive learning environment for African American students. *New Directions for Teaching and Learning, 82,* 45–53.

Howley, A., Howley, C. B., & Larson, W. (2007). Principals approach planning: The influence of gender and experience. *Educational Planning, 16*(1), 31–47.

Huber, L. K. (2000). Promoting multicultural awareness through dramatic play centers. *Early Childhood Education Journal, 27*(4), 235–238.

Huguet, P., & Regner, I. (2007). Stereotype threat among schoolgirls in quasi-ordinary classroom circumstances. *Journal of Educational Psychology, 99*(3), 545–560.

Ingalls, L., Hammond, H., Dupoux, E., & Baeza, R. (2006). Teachers' cultural knowledge and understanding of American Indian students and their families: Impact on a child's learning. *Rural Special Education Quarterly, 25*(1), 16–24.

Iseke-Barnes, J. M. (2000). Ethnomathematics and language in decolonizing mathematics. *Race, Gender, & Class, 7*(3), 133–149.

Iyer, A., Leach, C. W., & Crosby, C. J. (2003). White guilt and racial compensation: The benefits of self-focus. *Personality and Social Psychology Bulletin, 29*(1), 117–129.

Jackson, R. L. (1999). White space, white privilege: Mapping discursive inquiry into the self. *Quarterly Journal of Speech, 85,* 38–54.

Jeffries, R., Nix, M., & Singer, C. (2002). Urban American Indians "dropping out" of traditional high schools: Barriers & bridges to success. *High School Journal, 85*(3), 38–46.

Jenks, C., Lee, J. O., & Kanpol, B. (2001). Approaches to multicultural education in preservice teacher education: Philosophical frameworks and models for teaching. *The Urban Review, 33*(2), 87–105.

Johnson, L., & Joshee, R. (2007). *Multicultural education policies in Canada and the United States.* Vancouver, Canada: University of British Columbia Press.

Jones, K., & Ongtooguk, P. (2002). Equity for Alaska Natives: Can high-stakes testing bridge the chasm between ideals and realities? *Phi Delta Kappan, 83*(7), 499–503, 550.

Joshua, M. B. (2002). Inside picture books: Where are the children of color? *Educational Horizons, 80*(3), 125–132.

Juang, L. P., & Liang, M. X. (2007). The role of coping in the relationship between perceived racism and racism-related stress for Asian Americans: Gender differences. *Journal of Counseling Psychology, 54*(2), 132–141.

Kaiser Family Foundation. (2007). *Key facts: Race, ethnicity & medical care.* Menlo Park, CA: The Henry J. Kaiser Family Foundation.

Kao, C., & Hebert, T. P. (2006). Gifted Asian American males: Portraits of cultural dilemmas. *Journal of the Education of the Gifted, 30*(1), 88–117.

Keats, D. M. (2000). Cross-cultural studies in child development in Asian cultures. *Cross-Cultural Research, 34*(3), 339–350.

Kellough, R. D., & Kellough, N. G. (2008). *Teaching young adolescents: A guide to methods and resources for middle school teaching.* Upper Saddle River, NJ: Pearson Prentice-Hall.

Kelly, N. J., & Kelly, J. M. (2005). Religion and Latino partisanship in the United States. *Political Research Quarterly, 58*(1), 87–95.

Ketter, J., & Lewis, C. (2001). Already reading texts and contexts: Multicultural literature in a predominantly white rural community. *Theory into Practice, 40*(3),175–183.

Kettler, T., Shiu, A., & Johnsen, S. R. (2006). AP as an intervention for middle school Hispanic students. *Gifted Child Today, 29*(1), 39–46.

Killen, M., & Stangor, C. (2001). Children's social reasoning about inclusion and exclusion in gender and race peer group contexts. *Child Development, 72*(1), 174–186.

King, N. J. (2007). Exit strategies: Cultural implications for graduation tests. *Principal Leadership, 8*(1), 42–47.

Kitano, M. K., & Perkins, C. O. (2000). Gifted European American women. *Journal of the Education of the Gifted, 23*(3), 287–313.

Klecker, B. M. (2006). The gender gap in NAEP fourth-, eighth-, and twelfth-grade reading scores across years. *Reading Improvement, 43*(1), 50–56.

Koppelman, K. L., & Goodhart, R. L. (2005). *Understanding human differences: Multicultural education for a diverse America.* Boston: Allyn & Bacon.

Kraft, M. (2007). Toward a school-wide model of teaching for social justice: An examination of the best practices of two small schools. *Equity & Excellence in Education, 40*(1), 77–86.

Krezmien, M. R., Leone, P. E., & Achilles, G. M. (2006). Suspension, race, and disability: Analysis of statewide practices and reporting. *Journal of Emotional and Behavioral Disorders, 14*(4), 217–226.

Kulczycki, A., & Lobo, A. P. (2002). Patterns, determinants, and implications of intermarriage among Arab Americans. *Journal of Marriage and Family, 64,* 202–210.

Lalas, J. (2007). Teaching for social justice in multicultural urban schools: Conceptualization and classroom implication. *Multicultural Education, 14*(3), 17–21.

Latinos in school: Some facts and findings. (2001). *ERIC Digest No. 162.* (ERIC Clearinghouse on Urban Education No. ED 449288)

Lee, G. L., & Johnson, W. (2000). The need for interracial storybooks in effective multicultural classrooms. *Multicultural Education, 8*(2), 28–30.

Lee, G. L., & Manning, M. L. (2001). Working with Asian parents and families. *Multicultural Education, 9,* 23–25.

Lee, J. (2002). Racial and ethnic achievement gap trends: Reversing the progress toward equity? *Educational Researcher, 31*(1), 3–12.

Lefkowitz, E. S., Romo, L. P., & Corona, R. (2002). How Latino American and European American adolescents discuss conflicts, sexuality, and AIDS with their mothers. *Developmental Psychology, 36*(3), 315–325.

Leiding, D. (2007). Planning multicultural lessons. *Principal Leadership, 8*(1), 48–51.

Leistyna, P. (2001). Extending the possibilities of multicultural professional development in public schools. *Journal of Curriculum and Supervision, 16*(4), 282–304.

Lems, K. (1999). The Arab world and Arab Americans. *Book Links, 9*(2), 1–13.

Lewis, A. (2006). Student health. *Education Digest, 72*(2), 72–73.

Liang, C. T. H., Alvarez, A. N., Juang, L. P., & Liang, M. X. (2007). The role of coping in the relationship between perceived racism and racism-related stress for Asian Americans: Gender differences. *Journal of Counseling Psychology, 54*(2), 132–141.

Lie, Gwat-Yong. (2000). Multicultural perspectives in working with families. *Families in Society: Journal of Contemporary Human Services, 81*(5), 544.

Lundeberg, M. A., Fox, P. W., & Puncochar, J. (1994). Highly confident but wrong: Gender differences and similarities in confidence judgments. *Journal of Educational Psychology, 86,* 114–121.

Lutz, T., & Kuhlman, W. D. (2000). Learning about culture through dance in kindergarten classrooms. *Early Childhood Education Journal, 28*(1), 35–40.

MacGillivray, I. K., & Kozik-Rosabal, G. (2000). Introduction. *Education and Urban Society, 32*(3), 287–302.

Mahoney, A. S. (n.d.) The gifted identity formation model. www.counselingthegifted.com/articles/insearchofID.html

Manglitz, E. (2003). Challenging white privilege in adult education. *Adult Education Quarterly, 53*(2), 119–134.

Mathews, R. (2000). Cultural patterns of South Asian and Southeast Asian Americans. *Intervention in School and Clinic, 36*(2), 101–104.

Maxwell, L. A. (2007). The "other gap." *Education Week, 26*(23), 26–29.

McAllister, G., & Irvine, J. J. (2000). Cultural competency and multicultural teacher education. *Review of Educational Research, 70*(1), 3–24.

McCollough, S. (2000). Teaching African American students. *The Clearing House, 74*(1), 5–6.

McFalls, E. L., & Cobb-Roberts, D. (2001). Reducing resistance to diversity through cognitive dissonance instruction: Implications for teacher education. *Journal of Teacher Education, 52*(2), 164–172.

Menchaca, V. D. (2001). Providing a culturally relevant curriculum for Hispanic children. *Multicultural Education, 8*(3), 18–20.

Mendoza, J., & Reese, D. (2001). Examining multicultural picture books for the early childhood classroom: Possibilities and pitfalls. *Early Childhood Research and Practice, 3*(2), 1–30.

Midobuche, E. (2001). Building cultural bridges between home and the mathematics classroom. *Teaching Children Mathematics, 7*(9), 500–502.

Miller, L. (2007, July 30). American dreamers. *Newsweek,* 24–33.

Mitchell, K., Bush, E. C., & Bush, L. (2002). Standing in the gap: A model for establishing African American male intervention programs with public schools. *Educational Horizons 80*(3), 140–146.

Mitra, D. L. (2007). The role of administrators in enabling youth–adult partnerships in schools. *NASSP Bulletin, 91*(3), 237–256.

Mohatt, G. V., Trimble, J., & Dickson, R. A. (2006). Psychosocial foundations of American performance in culture-based education programs for American Indians and Alaska Native youth: Reflections on a multidisciplinary perspective. *Journal of American Education, 45*(3), 45–59.

Monroe, C. R. (2006). African American boys and the discipline gap: Balancing educators' uneven hand. *Educational Horizons, 84*(2), 102–111.

Montgomery, D. (2001). Increasing Native American Indian involvement in gifted programs in rural schools. *Psychology in the Schools, 38,* 467–475.

Moon, T. R., & Callahan, C. M. (2001). Curricular modifications, family outreach, and a mentoring program: Impacts on achievement and gifted identification in high-risk primary students. *Journal of Education of the Gifted, 24*(4), 305–321.

Morris, R., Pae, H. K., Arrington, C., & Sevcik, R. (2006). The assessment challenge of Native American educational researchers. *Journal of American Indian Education, 45*(3), 77–91.

Mueller, M. P., & Bentley, M. L. (2007). Beyond the "Decorated Landscape" of educational reform: Toward landscapes of pluralism in science education. *Science Education, 91*(2), 321–338.

Muffoletto, R., & Horton, J. (2007). *Multicultural education, the Internet, and the new media.* Cressville, NJ: Hampton Press.

Mulvihill, T. M. (2000). Women and gender studies and multicultural education? Building the agenda for 2000 and beyond. *Teacher Educator, 36*(1), 49–57.

Myers, J. P. (2003). *Dominant-minority relations in America: Linking personal history with the convergence in the New World.* Boston: Allyn & Bacon.

Naber, N. (2000). Ambiguous insiders: An investigation of Arab American invisibility. *Ethnic and Racial Studies, 23,* 37–61.

National Assessment of Adult Literacy. (2007). Washington DC: National Center for Educational Statistics.

National Research Council. (1989). *Everybody counts: A report to the nation on the future of mathematics education.* Washington, DC: National Academy Press.

National Urban League. (2007). *The state of black America: Portrait of the black male.* New York: Author.

Nel, J. (1994). Preventing school failure: The Native American child. *The Clearing House, 67,* 169–174.

Newman, C., & Ralston, K. (2006). *Profiles of participants in the national school lunch program.* Washington, DC: U.S. Department of Agriculture.

Nieto, S. (2008). *Affirming diversity: The sociopolitical context of multicultural education.* Boston: Allyn & Bacon.

Olney, M. F., & Kennedy, J. (2002). Racial disparities in VR use and job placement rates for adults with disabilities. *Rehabilitation Counseling Bulletin, 45*(3), 177–185.

Opitz, M. F., & Harding-DeKam, J. L. (2007). Understanding and teaching English language learners. *Reading Teacher, 60*(6), 590–602.

Pappamihiel, N. E. (2001). Moving from the ESL classroom into the mainstream: An investigation of English language anxiety in Mexican girls. *Bilingual Research Journal, 25*(1 & 2), 1–8.

Parameswaran, G. (2007). Enhancing diversity education. *Multicultural Education, 14*(3), 51–55.

Parette, H. P., & Petch-Hogan, B. (2000). Approaching families. *Teaching Exceptional Children, 33*(2), 4–10.

Payne, C. R., & Welsh, B. H. (2000). The progressive development of multicultural education before and after the 1960s: A theoretical framework. *Teacher Educator, 36*(1), 29–48.

Perez, S. A. (2002). Using Ebonics or black English as a bridge to teaching standard English. *Contemporary Education, 71*(4), 34–37.

Perkins-Gough, D. (2007). Focus on adolescent English language learners. *Educational Leadership, 64*(6), 90–91.

Peterson, K. M., Cross, L. F., Johnson, E. J., & Howell, G. L. (2000). Diversity education for preservice teachers: Strategies and attitude outcomes. *Action in Teacher Education, 22*(2), 33–38.

Phillion, J., & He, M. F. (2005). *Narrative and experience in multicultural education.* London, England: Sage Publications.

Phinney, J. S. (2000). Identity formation across cultures: The interaction of personal, societal, and historical change. *Human Development, 43,* 27–31.

Porter, R. O. (1997). The politics of bilingual education. *Society, 34*(6), 31–39.

Portman, T. A. A., & Herring, R. (2001). Debunking the Pocahontas paradox: The need for a humanistic perspective. *Journal of Humanistic Counseling, Education and Development, 40,* 185–199.

Powers, K. (2005). Promoting school achievement among American Indian students throughout the school years. *Childhood Education, 81*(6), 338–342.

Quinn, A. E. (2001). Moving marginalized students inside the lines: Cultural differences in classrooms. *English Journal, 90*(4), 44–50.

Quiocho, A. M. L., & Daoud, A. M. (2006). Dispelling myths about Latino parent participation in schools. *The Educational Forum, 70,* 255–267.

Ramos, I., & Lambating, J. (1996). Risk taking: Gender differences and educational opportunity. *School Science and Mathematics, 96*(2), 94–98.

Richards, H. V., Brown, A. E., & Forde, T. B. (2007). Addressing diversity in schools: Culturally responsive pedagogy. *Teaching Exceptional Children, 39*(3), 64–68.

Richardson, J. (2007). Leaders can ensure that all students have access to quality teaching. *Journal of Staff Development, 28*(1), 61–62.

Rodriguez, A. P. (2000). Adjusting the multicultural lens. *Race, Gender, and Class, 7*(3), 150–177.

Rosselli, H. C., & Irvin, J. L. (2001). Differing perspectives, common ground: The middle school and gifted education relationship. *Middle School Journal, 32*(3), 57–62.

Ruiz, S. Y., Roosa, M. W., & Gonzales, N. A. (2002). Predictors of self-esteem for Mexican American and European American youths: A reexamination of the influence of parenting. *Journal of Family Psychology, 16*(1), 70–80.

Russell, N. M. (2007). Teaching more than English: Connecting ESL students to their community through service learning. *Phi Delta Kappan, 88*(1), 770–771.

Sandefur, S. J., Watson, S. W., & Johnston, L. B. (2007). Literacy development: Science curriculum, and the adolescent English-only classroom. *Multicultural Education, 14*(3), 41–50.

Sanders, G. L., & Kroll, I. T. (2000). Generating stories of resilience: Helping gay and lesbian youth and their families. *Journal of Marital and Family Therapy, 26*(4), 433–442.

Sapon-Shevin, M. (2000/2001). Schools fit for all. *Educational Leadership, 58*(4), 34–39.

Sarroub, L. K. (2005). *All American Yemeni girls: Being Muslim in a public school.* Phildelphia: University of Pennsylvania Press.

School practices to promote the achievement of Hispanic students. (2000). ERIC Digest No. 153. (ERIC Document No. ED 439186)

Schwartz, W. (2000). *New trends in language education for Hispanic students.* New York: ERIC Clearinghouse on Urban Education. (ERIC Documentation Reproduction Service No. 442913)

Schwartz, W. (2001). *Strategies for improving the educational outcomes for Latinas.* New York: ERIC Clearinghouse on Urban Education. (ERIC Document Reproduction Service No. ED 458344)

Scott, P. (2007). Successfully bringing parents into the classroom. *Principal, 87*(1), 64–65.

Scourby, A. (1984). *The Greek Americans.* Boston: Twayne.

Scribner, A. P., & Scribner, J. D. (2001). *High-performing schools serving Mexican American students: What they can teach us.* Charleston, WV: ERIC Clearinghouse on Rural and Small Schools. (ERIC Document No. 459048)

Seda, C. (2007). Parental involvement unlocks children's educational potential. *Essays in Education, 19*(2), 150–159.

Shafer, G. (2001). Standard English and the migrant community. *English Journal, 90*(4), 37–43.

Shealey, M. W., & Collins, T. (2007). Creating culturally responsive literacy programs in inclusive classrooms. *Intervention in School and Clinic, 42*(4), 195–197.

Sheridan, S. M. (2000). Considerations of multiculturalism and diversity in behavioral consultation with parents and teachers. *The School Psychology Review, 29*(3), 344–353.

Shin, R., Daly, B., & Vera, E. (2007). The relationships of peer norms, ethnic identity, and peer support to school engagement in urban youth. *Professional School Counseling, 10*(4), 379–388.

Simcox, A. G., Nuijens, K. L., & Lee, C. C. (2006). School counselors and school psychologists: Collaborative partnerships in promoting culturally competent counselors. *Professional School Counseling, 9*(4), 272–277.

Slavin, R. E. (1983). *An introduction to cooperative learning.* New York: Longman.

Slavin, R. E. (1996). Cooperative learning and middle and secondary schools. *The Clearing House, 69*(4), 200–204.

Sleeter, C. E. (2000). Creating an empowering multicultural curriculum. *Race, Gender, and Class, 7*(3), 178–196.

Sleeter, C. E., & Grant, C. A. (2007). *Making choices for multicultural education: Five approaches to race, culture, and gender* (5th ed.). Hoboken, NJ: John Wiley & Sons.

Smith, J. S. (2007). The transition to high school: Perceptions and reality. *Principal, 87*(1), 74–75.

Sprunger, K. A. (2007). A dynamic partnership. *Kappa Delta Pi Record, 43*(2), 92–93.

Starnes, B. A. (2006). What we don't know can hurt them: White teachers, Indian children. *Phi Delta Kappan, 87*(5), 384–392.

Stoesz, D. (2007). Letter to the editor. *Journal of Social Work Education, 43*(2), 347–349.

Stormont, M., Stebbins, M. S., & Holliday, G. (2001). Characteristics and educational support needs of underrepresented gifted adolescents. *Psychology in the Schools, 38*(5), 413–423.

Tamura, E. H. (2001). Asian Americans in the history of education: An historical essay. *History of Education Quarterly, 41*(1), 58–71.

Tatum, B. D. (2007). *Can we talk about race? And other conversations in an era of school resegregation.* Boston: Beacon Press.

Taylor, S. V. (2000). Multicultural is who we are: Literature as a reflection of ourselves. *Teaching Exceptional Children, 32*(3), 24–29.

Ten quick ways to analyze children's books for racism and sexism. (1974, November 3). *Interracial Books for Children, 5*(3), 6–7.

TESOL (Teachers of English to Speakers of Other Languages). (1976). Position paper on the role of English as a second language in bilingual education. Washington, DC: Author.

Texeira, M. T., & Christian, P. M. (2002). And still they rise: Practical advice for increasing African American enrollments in higher education. *Educational Horizons, 80*(3), 117–124.

Thompson, G. L. (2000). What students say about bilingual education. *Journal of At-Risk Issues, 6*(2), 24–32.

Thornton, B., Collins, M., & Daugherty, R. (2006). A study of resiliency of American Indian high school students. *Journal of American Indian Education, 45*(1), 4–16.

Tiedt, P. L., & Tiedt, I. M. (1999). *Multicultural teaching: A handbook of activities, information, and resources* (2nd ed.). Boston: Allyn & Bacon.

Trafzer, C. E., & Keller, J. A. (2006). *Boarding school blues: Revisiting American Indian educational experiences.* Lincoln: University of Nebraska Press.

Trevino, A., & Mayes, C. (2006). Creating a bridge from high school to college for Hispanic students. *Multicultural Education, 14*(2), 74–77.

Trumbull, E., Rothstein-Fisch, C., & Greenfield, P. M. (2001). Ours and mine. *Journal of Staff Development, 22*(2), 10–14.

Tsai, J. L., Mortensen, H., & Wong, Y. (2002). What does "being American" mean? A comparison of Asian American and European American young adults. *Cultural Diversity and Ethnic Minority Psychology, 8*(3), 257–273.

U.S. Bureau of the Census. (1993a, September). *We the American . . . Asians.* Washington, DC: Author.

U.S. Bureau of the Census. (2007). *Statistical abstracts of the United States.* Washington, DC: Author.

Van Galen, J. (2007). Late to class: Social class and schooling in a new economy. *Educational Horizons, 85*(3), 156–167.

Verdugo, R. R. (2007). English-language learners: Key issues. *Education and Urban Society, 39*(2), 167–193.

Viadero, D. (2000, March 22). Lags in minority achievement defy traditional expectations. *Education Week,* www.edweek.net/ew/ew_print story.cfm?slug=28causes.h19

Viadero, D., & Johnston, R. C. (2000). Lifting minority achievement: Complex answers. *Education Week, 19*(30), 1, 14–16.

Villegas, A. M., & Lucas, T. (2007). The culturally responsive teacher. *Educational Leadership, 64*(6) 28–33.

Wade, R. C. (2000). Service learning for multicultural teaching competency: Insights from the literature for teacher educators. *Equity and Excellence in Education, 33*(1), 21–29.

Wade, R. C. (2007). Service learning for social justice in the elementary classroom: Can we get there from here? *Equity & Excellence in Education, 40*(2), 156–165.

Wadsworth, D., & Remaley, M. H. (2007). What families want. *Educational Leadership, 64*(6), 23–27.

Walker, J. (2006). Principals and counselors working toward social justice: A complementary leadership team. *Guidance and Counseling, 21*(2), 114–124.

Wallace, B. C. (2000). A call for change in multicultural training at graduate schools of education: Educating to end oppression and for social justice. *Teachers College Record, 102*(6), 1086–1111.

Warren, S. R. (2002). Stories from the classrooms: How expectations and efficacy of diverse teachers affect the academic performance of children in poor urban schools. *Educational Horizons, 80*(3), 109–116.

Wassermann, S. (2007). Dare to be different. *Phi Delta Kappan, 88*(5), 384–390.

Weaver, H. N. (2000). Culture and professional education: The experiences of Native American social workers. *Journal of Social Work Education, 36*(3), 415–428.

Weeber, J. E. (2000). What could I know of racism? *Journal of Counseling and Development, 77,* 20–23.

Weiner, M. F. (2006). Talking race in the classroom— A review of Jane Bolgatz's Talking race in the classroom. *Teachers College Record, 108*(1), 29–32.

Wertsman, V. F. (2001). A comparative and critical analysis of leading reference sources. *Multicultural Review, 10*(2), 42–47.

West, B. E. (1983). The new arrivals from Southeast Asia. *Childhood Education, 60,* 84–89.

Wherry, J. H. (2007). Back to school: A fresh start for parent involvement. *Principal, 87*(1), 8.

Wiest, L. R. (2001). Teaching mathematics from a multicultural perspective. *Equity and Excellence in Education, 34*(1), 16–25.

Wilder, L. K., Jackson, A. P., & Smith, T. B. (2001). Secondary transition of multicultural learners: Lessons from the Navajo Native American experience. *Preventing School Failure, 45*(3), 119–124.

Williams, E. R. (2007). Unnecessary and unjustified: African American parental perceptions of special education. *The Educational Forum, 71*(3), 250–261.

Williams, S. (2001). *Trends among Hispanic children, youth, and families*. Washington, DC: Child Care Trends. (ERIC Documention No. ED 453313)

Willis, A. I., & Lewis, K. C. (1999). Our known everydayness: Beyond a response to white privilege. *Urban Education, 43*(2), 245–262.

Willis, S. (1994). Teaching language-minority students. *ASCD Update, 36*(5), 1–5.

Winawer-Steiner, H., & Wetzel, N. A. (1996). German families. In M. McGoldrick, J. K. Pearce, & J. Giordano (Eds.), *Ethnicity and family therapy* (2nd ed.). (pp. 496–516). New York: Guilford Press.

Wingfield, M. (2006). Arab Americans: Into the multicultural mainstream. *Equity and Excellence in Education, 39*(3), 253–266.

Wingfield, M., & Karaman, B. (1995). Arab stereotypes and American educators. *Social Studies and Young Learners, 7*(4), 7–10.

Witkow, E. R., & Fuligini, A. J. (2007). Achievement goals and daily school experiences among Asians, Latino, and European American backgrounds. *Journal of Educational Psychology, 99*(3), 584–506.

Wolfe, M. M., Tang, P. H., & Wong, E. C. (2001). Design and development of the European American values scale for Asian Americans. *Cultural Diversity and Ethnic Minority Psychology, 7*(3), 274–283.

Wolfsberg, J. S. (2007). Successful prevention of underage drinking and other drug use: An integrated approach. *Independent School, 66*(2), 104–107.

Wong, F., & Halgin, R. (2006). The "model minority": Bane or blessing for Asian Americans. *Journal of Multicultural Counseling and Development, 34*(1), 38–49.

Yager, T. J., & Rotheram-Borus, M. J. (2000). Social expectations among African American, Hispanic, and European American adolescents. *Cross-Cultural Research, 34*(3), 283–305.

Yurkovich, E. E. (2001). Working with American Indians toward educational success. *Journal of Nursing Education, 40*(6), 259–269.

Zehr, M. A. (1999, September 22). Hispanic students "left out" by high stakes tests, panel concludes. *Education Week, 19*(3), 5.

Zehr, M. A. (2000, November 8). Un dia nuevo for schools: Overview. *Education Week, 20*(10), 1.

Name Index

Subject Index